CUSTEROLOGY

CUSTEROLOGY

THE ENDURING LEGACY OF THE INDIAN WARS
AND GEORGE ARMSTRONG CUSTER

MICHAEL A. ELLIOTT

THE UNIVERSITY OF CHICAGO PRESS
CHICAGO AND LONDON

Michael A. Elliott is associate professor of English at Emory University.

The University of Chicago Press, Chicago 60637
The University of Chicago Press, Ltd., London
© 2007 by The University of Chicago
All rights reserved. Published 2007
Paperback edition 2008
Printed in the United States of America
17 16 15 14 13 12 11 10   4 5 6 7
ISBN-13: 978-0-226-20146-7 (cloth)
ISBN-13: 978-0-226-20147-4 (paper)
ISBN-10: 0-226-20146-5 (cloth)
ISBN-10: 0-226-20147-3 (paper)

Library of Congress Cataloging-in-Publication Data

Elliott, Michael A.
    Custerology : the enduring legacy of the Indian wars and George Armstrong
Custer / Michael A. Elliott.
        p. cm.
    Includes bibliographical references and index.
    ISBN-13: 978-0-226-20146-7 (cloth : alk. paper)
    ISBN-10: 0-226-20146-5 (cloth : alk. paper)
    1. Little Bighorn, Battle of the, Mont., 1876. 2. Custer, George
Armstrong, 1839–1876. I. Title.
    E83.876.C983E55 2007
    973.8'2092—dc22

                                                        2007010880

♾ The paper used in this publication meets the minimum requirements
of the American National Standard for Information Sciences—
Permanence of Paper for Printed Library Materials,
ANSI Z39.48-1992.

CONTENTS

ILLUSTRATIONS

INTRODUCTION

WES ANDERSON'S 2001 FILM *THE ROYAL TENENBAUMS* BEGINS WITH ELI CASH describing the novel that has made him a literary celebrity, *Old Custer*. "Everyone knows Custer died at Little Bighorn," Owen Wilson, who plays Cash, deadpans. "What this book presupposes is, *maybe he didn't*."[1] It is a throwaway line to introduce the shallow intelligence of Cash, who parades for the literati in a fringed buckskin jacket and cowboy hat. We get the point: Cash is a one-trick pony who has been able to captivate the reading public by taking a simple fact of history and turning it on its head. He is right, after all, about one thing. Everyone does know Custer, and what everyone knows about Custer is that he died—famously, or maybe infamously, overwhelmed by a massive force of Indians at the Battle of the Little Bighorn. For most Americans, as for Eli Cash, Custer's death has come to be regarded as something less than a historical event and something more like the punch line of a joke, and not even a very funny joke at that.

This book tells a different story about Custer—a story that takes note of humorous allusions such as Eli Cash's but that also tries to make sense of the locations in the contemporary life of the United States where Custer continues to be taken quite seriously. Indeed, Eli Cash may come closer to the truth than he thinks, for in a sense, Custer continues to live. Each year, on the anniversary of the June Sunday on which Custer led more than two hundred cavalrymen to their demise at the hands of Lakota Sioux, Cheyenne, and Arapaho Indians, enthusiasts converge on the land where the battle occurred to commemorate, debate, and reenact what took place.

There are two separate amateur historical societies devoted to Custer and the Battle of the Little Bighorn that hold annual symposiums and publish their research, there are groups of Native Americans who come to the recently constructed Indian Memorial at the Little Bighorn battlefield each year to recall the Indian victory there, and there are individuals who travel to Montana each year to dress in nineteenth-century uniforms so that they can ride into battle and die with Custer. University presses and smaller private ones devoted to Western Americana produce a steady stream of new books on Custer, the Little Bighorn, and the Seventh Cavalry; conventional wisdom—unproven, as far as I can tell—holds that among the battles fought in North America, only Gettysburg is the subject of as much ink as the Little Bighorn.

I refer to this arena of historical interpretation and commemoration as "Custerology." Custer enthusiasts have their own term, "Custeriana," to refer to the books, photographs, paintings, films, and other material objects related to the subject of their interest. I have chosen Custerology, however, to emphasize that my focus is on the continuing production of knowledge of Custer and the nineteenth-century Indian Wars in which he fought. Custerology therefore includes not only those who seek to honor the memory of Custer and his Seventh Cavalry but also those who celebrate the indigenous resistance that defeated him—and believe that by doing so they are providing historical redress for the injustices suffered by American Indians, particularly Plains Indians, at the hands of the United States. What I hope to explain in this book is how Custer and the Little Bighorn can be publicly commemorated for such contradictory purposes, for indeed these very contradictions are what keeps Old Custer so vibrantly alive in the historical imagination of Americans at the turn of the twenty-first century.

One of my premises is that from the late nineteenth century to the present, the historical commemoration of Custer and the Battle of the Little Bighorn has been as a medium through which the United States expresses its collective ambivalence about its relationship with the indigenous peoples who have lived within its borders. One way to explain this ambivalence would be to conclude that there are two competing interpretations of the Indian Wars currently in the United States: one that sees the United States' military conquest of the Indians of North America as a glorious triumph and another that sees it as ruthless exploitation. But the picture of a two-sided debate with clear-cut, opposing sides oversimplifies the way that history is actually written, spoken about, and memorialized in the United States today. To begin, the public commemoration of the Indian Wars suggests that these positions are not always mutually exclusive, that the celebration of U.S. Manifest Destiny can be layered with expressions of sincere remorse about its costs. This kind of emotional matrix may seem to be the special province of white Americans concerned about the guilt of their historical forebears, but the relationship of contemporary American Indians to the nineteenth-century Indian Wars has its own complexities. After all, Custer commanded a multiracial force at the Little Bighorn that included contingents of Crow, Arikara, and Santee Sioux scouts. Because the Crow reservation surrounds what is now called Little Bighorn Battlefield (as opposed to *Custer* Battlefield) National Monument, Crows have played a particularly crucial role in the commemoration of this battle, including the reenactments discussed in the final chapter of this book.

Indeed, the Native American intellectual and artistic resurgence of recent decades has done as much to keep the figure of Custer in circulation as the work of non-Indian historians. Vine Deloria Jr. (Standing Rock Sioux) titled his political manifesto *Custer Died for Your Sins;* the novelist James Welch (Blackfeetts/Gros Ventre) wrote a book of history titled *Killing Custer;* the novel *Green Grass, Running Water* by Thomas King (Cherokee) includes a dreamy, buckskin-wearing character from Michigan named George Morningstar (a reference to one of Custer's Indian nicknames); William S. Penn (Nez Percé) published a collection of his essays under the title *Feathering Custer.* Sherman Alexie (Spokane/Coeur d'Alene) has brought Custer and the Little Bighorn into his fiction, poetry, and also the screenplay for the 1998 film *Smoke Signals,* directed by Chris Eyre (Cheyenne and Arapaho). In the film, young Spokane Indian men kneel on the floor of a basketball gymnasium, one of them dribbling the ball to produce the beat of the missing drum that the others pretend to play. They sing:

> Oh, I took the ball to the hoop and what did I see?
> Oh, I took the ball to the hoop and what did I see?
> General George Armstrong Custer was a-guarding me, a-guarding me!

It is another joke, once again only peripheral to the narrative action of the film. But as the scene progresses, with the young men jesting about which nineteenth-century Indian warriors would have played the best basketball, the significance of the song emerges. These Indian youths are the same age as those who fought—and fought with—Custer, but they are uncertain as to how they should incorporate that nineteenth-century legacy into their late-twentieth-century lives. Fortunately, their resources include both an historical consciousness and a sense of humor. "Some days, it's a good day to die," one of them quips later in the scene. "Some days, it's a good day to play basketball."[2]

Custerology includes the official monuments at the Little Bighorn battlefield and the meetings of the amateur historians devoted to the lives of General Custer and his men, but it also includes films like *Smoke Signals* and other acts that register the historical presence of the Indian Wars for a larger public. The question that drives my inquiry is why Custerology continues to flourish at a historical moment that professes aversion to the military conquest of American Indians that Custer himself epitomized. Part of the answer rests in the nature of Custer's defeat at the Little Bighorn, which has allowed non-Indian Americans to commemorate the defeat of the Seventh Cavalry as a glorious sacrifice for more than a century while at the same time giving Plains Indians the opportunity to extol a brave history of anticolonial resistance. Indeed, as I will have other occasions to observe, it is impossible to imagine that the iconic status of Custer and the Little Bighorn would have been achieved if the Seventh Cavalry had been victorious there. What we all know, as Eli Cash reminds us, is that Custer *died*.

Defeat, though, is only one piece of the puzzle of Custerology at the turn of the twenty-first century. Although frequently maligned, multiculturalism has stood as one of the dominant cultural ethics of the last quarter-century in the United States. Indeed, multiculturalism so thoroughly saturates the public life of the United States that its conceptual geography can be difficult to map. As David Hollinger has pointed out, the rubric of multiculturalism arose in the late twentieth century in defense of and as a supplement to affirmative action policies in hiring and admission practices.[3] Unlike cultural pluralist movements earlier in the century, multiculturalism emphasizes the inclusion of people of color. Most significantly, it not only encourages the tolerance of cultural and racial difference but valorizes diversity as a positive good in and of itself. In fact, one of the flashpoints of the "culture wars" of the 1990s—one that continues to smolder today—is the question of whether and how the recognition of cultural difference should be reconciled with the model of the United States as a single, unified national culture driven by a shared consensus. To some skeptics, multiculturalism is a pathway to a splintering cultural separatism; to others, it is simply a softer, more palatable version of an enforced national unity.

One focus of multiculturalism has been the necessity of recovering and articulating histories that reflect the kind of diversity of experience that it seeks to recognize in the present. In some instances, that movement has dovetailed with the "social history" of the late twentieth century that sought to detail lives of more common people than the generals and presidents who dominate textbooks and monuments. At the same time, it has also focused on the ways that past Americans have experienced regimes of power such as slavery, territorial dispossession, and segregation. The legacy of Vietnam has contributed to the ways in which Americans commemorate violence and suffering in their history, for Americans of the 1960s and 1970s struggled with how to recognize a defeated army whose soldiers were casualties of a conflict that many believed to be unjust and unnecessary. Those soldiers who perished in Vietnam came to be regarded as "a blood payment for the *sins* of the nation—a stunning inversion of the traditional interpretation, which claims blood sacrifice as the key to the *life* of the nation," Edward Tabor Linenthal writes (emphases in original).[4] Three sites constructed in the U.S. capital after the Vietnam War—the black granite of the Vietnam Veterans Memorial (1982), the United States Holocaust Museum (1993), and the National Museum of the American Indian (2004)—all have been shaped by an age that seeks to memorialize the victims of violence, especially state-sponsored violence, and, in the last case, to celebrate the experiences of those groups who have been marginalized by the nation.

The commemoration of Custer would seem to be a poor fit for the multicultural age. The Battle of the Little Bighorn has long been regarded as one of the closing acts in the drama of Manifest Destiny—and Custer as a final star of the show in his willingness to sacrifice his own life for the progress of the United States over the last holdouts of renegades. In what still stands as the most compelling explication of the Custer myth to date, Richard Slotkin argued in *The Fatal Environment* (1985) that Custer's Last Stand vaulted into the iconography of American history because it served as an "ideological object" that distilled a global conflict between the forces of "civilization" and "savagery." The Indians who defeated the Seventh Cavalry, he demonstrates, were understood in the late nineteenth century as counterparts of the freed blacks in the South who threatened to rise against their former masters, laborers in the north whose anarchic strikes could disrupt the economic machinery of the nation, and even non-Christian foreigners like the Turks who dared to resist the Great Powers of Europe. Custer and the Last Stand, Slotkin shows, embodied a frontier ideology that taught certain Americans how to believe in the righteousness of their own cause and how to regard those who opposed them. Custer was the perfect figure for his own time and for the decades that followed—particularly as the United States began its imperial ventures overseas—

and Slotkin draws a line from the frontier myth of the nineteenth century to the Vietnam War of the twentieth.[5]

If Slotkin's argument suggests why Americans might want to eschew Custer as a figure who had been made to serve agendas of white racism and U.S. imperialism, his description of the frontier as the central myth of the culture of the United States suggests why it has been impossible for them to do so. Multicultural revisionism has not led Americans— non-Indians or Indians—away from Custer and the Indian Wars but back to them. Between 1984 and 1996, *four* major biographies of Custer were published, the first and most popular of which—Evan S. Connell's novelistic *Son of the Morning Star* (1984)—inspired a television miniseries.[6] During that same period, annual reenactments of the Battle of the Little Bighorn were revived by whites and Crows who live in the vicinity of the Little Bighorn, federal legislation changed the name of the battlefield itself, a new Indian memorial at the battlefield was authorized by the U.S. Congress, and a series of books were published that exponentially increased the availability of testimony of American Indians who participated in or witnessed the conflict. Perhaps the best example of how the multicultural appeal of indigenous cultures could generate interest in the nineteenth-century frontier army during this period is a film that has nothing directly to do with Custer at all: *Dances with Wolves* (1990). While the film ostensibly sympathizes with the plight of the Lakotas in the face of the encroaching federal army, the real hero of the film is the white Lieutenant Dunbar, played by Kevin Costner.[7] The film updates the Westerns of the early twentieth century by having Costner desert his army post to live with Indians, but "going native" and fighting Indians are never too far apart in the white American imagination. Small wonder that the next book by Michael Blake, who wrote the novel on which Costner's film was based, would be a novel of Custer's final days, told from Custer's point of view.[8]

As multiculturalism has been in ascendance in the arenas of mass media, public history, and education, indigenous peoples in the United States have entered a new historical phase in their relationship with the U.S. government. Sometimes referred as the era of self-determination, the last few decades have seen increased recognition on the part of the U.S. federal government of the desirability of, as Richard Nixon stated in a 1970 presidential message on Indian policy, "an Indian future . . . determined by Indian acts and Indian decisions."[9] American Indians (or Native Americans; I will use both terms in this book) have claimed a nation-to-nation relationship with the U.S. federal government since the United States negotiated its first treaty with Indian nations in the aftermath of the Revolutionary War. What has shifted has been the recognition of those claims by non-Indians, though that recognition has seldom been as straightforward or as total as most American Indian leaders and intellectuals would like. Rather, the struggle of recent decades has been for Native American tribal governments to win both political and juridical autonomy from local and state jurisdictions, as well as to achieve greater economic self-sufficiency on behalf of tribal constituents.

American Indian political leaders and intellectuals frequently use the term *sovereignty* to describe these goals. Tribal sovereignty, they contend, is an exercise of power inherent to tribal peoples that predates contact with European peoples. While the sovereignty of tribal nations has been *recognized* on a limited basis by the United States—notably via the Commerce Clause of the U.S. Constitution and the treaty-making process—tribal nationalists contend that recognition docs not in fact *confer* sovereignty, which they believe is inherent to indigenous nations. Because tribal sovereignty is rooted in a vision of indigenous peoples as distinct and self-governing entities, American Indians today claim a unique political status as citizens of both their tribal nation and the United States. (They are also citizens of the individual state in which they live, a third kind of citizenship.) While differences exist among Native American intellectuals about the precise contours of tribal sovereignty, and especially about its limits, a crucial point of agreement is that sovereignty defines what it means to be Indian primarily through political relationships, rather than through definitions of race or culture. David E. Wilkins and K. Tsianina Lomawaima conclude their book on the subject by noting, "American Indian people are not merely another 'minority,' defined as an ethnic group or an economic class, because tribes possess a nation-to-nation political relationship with the federal government. That unique political relationship is founded on the principle of tribal sovereignty, on the facts of treaty negotiation and ratification, and on the contractual and voluntary federal assumption of a trust responsibility and relationship to tribes." [10]

While tribal sovereignty extends back prior to the arrival of Europeans in the Americas, the use of the English word *sovereignty* to denote the right of American Indians to organize as semiautonomous nations has a much more recent history. Vine Deloria Jr., one of the central figures in recent Native American intellectual history, wrote that when he began his work as an activist in the 1960s, the favored term was *self-determination. Sovereignty,* he explained, was first used in conjunction with the "fish-ins" that took place in the Pacific Northwest during the end of that decade, when tribes claimed that the treaties they negotiated with the United States in the nineteenth century had preserved for them specific fishing rights that were distinct from what the current regulations of the state allowed.[11] In the decades that followed, *sovereignty* became a way for tribal peoples to assert that they possessed rights, powers, and autonomy beyond what the state and even federal governments had recently recognized. Sovereignty—which always involves an insistence that American Indian tribes did not negotiate away all of their inherent power in their treaties with the United States *and* that they continue exist in a nation-to-nation relationship with the United States—has formed the legal underpinning of the American Indian gaming boom of recent decades. Equally substantial, though less publicized, land recovery efforts have been initiated by tribes. Since the mid-1960s, tribes in the continental United States have added a total of 7.5 million acres to their land base, an increase of 15 percent.[12]

Sovereignty, crucially, turns on the organization of American Indian tribes as political entities. When the Red Power movement emerged in the late 1960s, it had fostered a pantribal consciousness born out of the common experiences of colonialism endured by Indians across the United States. The island of Alcatraz was seized on Thanksgiving Day 1969 by a group calling itself "Indians of All Tribes." The American Indian Movement (AIM) had its roots in urban settings where Indians (often living away from reservations because of the federal relocation programs of previous decades) formed intertribal communities.[13] Sovereignty, however, emanates from each individual tribe and its claim to a form of autonomy; it claims political power for the tribes as discrete entities. Therefore, the political discourse of sovereignty among American Indians that began in the 1970s—and continues to this day—has emphasized that indigenous identity is formed through the relationship of an individual to his or her tribe and its constituent parts, such as clans. Indians are not only "Indians," but Cheyennes and Crows and Navajos and Hopis and Choctaws and Creeks and so on. Even those tribes living in geographical proximity to one another, as this book will show, can have distinct stories.

While this book does not discuss tribal sovereignty in great detail or present an argument on its behalf, I have been influenced by the contention that the relationship between the United States and American Indian tribes should be considered primarily in political terms. The Indian Wars of the nineteenth century have been understood as both racial conflicts between white and nonwhite peoples and cultural conflicts between groups who preferred radically different and incompatible manners of living. To think of these conflicts as political, on the other hand, emphasizes the decisions that were made on all sides regarding the negotiation of agreements and the strategic use of violence as both the United States and the tribes of the North American Plains sought to produce a secure future for their nations. While the logic of racism surely did play a role in the violence of the frontier, and while distinct conceptions of land use, economy, and society shaped the struggles between the United States and Plains Indians at every turn, the nineteenth-century Indian Wars were driven by the political questions of territorial governance—who would get to live on what land and how they would be governed. For the United States, these battles were fights to incorporate the territory that the Indians claimed and, as a kind of afterthought, perhaps some of the Indians who once lived on that land; for those Plains Indians who chose military resistance (and not all did), the fighting was part of their long struggle against that colonial incorporation and for a degree of political autonomy.

The manner in which I take political claims of tribal sovereignty as a compass point for discussing the public history of Custer and the Battle of the Little Bighorn is one way that this work departs from Slotkin in *The Fatal Environment* and his later *Gunfighter Nation*. Unlike Slotkin, who might be best described as a cultural historian, I am a thorough presentist—someone whose interest in history is focused on how that history, including prior acts of historical commemoration, is experienced in our current age. While I discuss the history of Custer, the Little Bighorn, and the Indian Wars in this book, readers who are seeking original historical insights—particularly on military matters—are likely to be disappointed. Though this book offers historical background and discussion, its primary focus is on the ways in which the commemoration of U.S.-Indian violence occurs in the contemporary United States, how Indians and non-Indians alike continue to tell stories in public places about the struggles that took place on this continent over a century ago. Those stories continue, I argue, because the matters that motivated those struggles, the questions about the place of indigenous peoples and their nations within the United States, remain unresolved. To put it another way, Indians and non-Indians alike need to keep returning to the Little Bighorn for some of the same reasons that George Armstrong Custer was ordered there in 1876.

One way to approach this topic would have been to chart a narrative chronology of Custerology from the moment of Custer's famous Last Stand demise to the present, with each chapter taking on a different generation. The first chapter provides an overview of this chronology, but the book as a whole follows a spatial organization: each chapter focuses on a particular site of public history within the topography of Custerology. Some of these locations—the battlefields where Custer engaged in his best-known Indian battles—are quite specific. Others are broader: the Michigan town that Custer adopted as his own; the Black Hills in South Dakota, where he led a significant military expedition. I have also allowed myself one abstraction in this schema, "the library," which refers not so much to a particular library as to the collection of books that any historical enthusiast could assemble. In all of these chapters, I describe the commemorative activities that occur there, how those activities have come into being, and, when appropriate, the nineteenth-century history behind them. My aim has been to reveal in each location the layers of historical commemoration that inform, revise, and sometimes even ignore one another. What interests me is the cumulative effect that these histories generate, the way that traveling through the historical landscape can be like trying to decipher generations of handwriting scribbled over one another on the same page—all devoted to the same subject but each having its own perspective. A historian's task might be to imagine how the page looked when it was first clean and easily legible; my goal has been to describe what it is like to stand at a variety of physical locations in our contemporary moment and read all of the writing simultaneously—both the faded letters and the new ones, the bold type and the tiny scrawl. If I have not traveled everywhere, it has been because there has been so much to see.

The book begins and ends with the Battle of the Little Bighorn itself. Chapter 1 includes a brief description of the battle as well as a short history of the enterprise of Custerology. The focus of the chapter, however, is on the part of the battlefield that was designated in 1946 as Custer Battlefield National Monument and then renamed Little Bighorn Battlefield National Monument in the early 1990s. In 2003, the Indian Memorial was dedicated there, and I describe those dedication ceremonies and the varieties of patriotism on display there as a way of introducing modes of historical feeling that will reappear throughout the chapters that follow.

Chapters 2, 3, and 4 follow the arc of Custer's career from the small Michigan city that he adopted as his home while he rose to prominence as a Civil War hero, to the southern Plains where he made his name as an Indian fighter, to the Black Hills of the Dakota Territory where he led an expedition that touched off a gold rush. Chapter 2, "Being Custer," focuses on the person of Custer himself and his relentless self-fashioning, and then it turns to one of the foremost interpreters of that personality today, the "living historian" Steve Alexander, who lives with his wife in the same house that Custer once shared with *his* wife. Chapter 3, "Lives on the Plains," considers the logic and rhetoric of Indian fighting in Custer's time by explicating his most successful fight against American Indians, his attack on a Cheyenne and Arapaho village on the Washita River in 1868. The chapter asks why this conflict remains so much less known than the Battle of the Little Bighorn and discusses recent efforts to memorialize the violence at the Washita by incorporating the Washita Battlefield National Historic Site into the National Park Service. Both this chapter and the following one attempt to provide a historical context for the violence of the nineteenth-century Indian Wars by discussing the treaties that failed to prevent it.

Chapter 4, "Into the Black Hills," pairs Custer's 1874 Black Hills expedition with an account of a recent expedition of a different kind to that region: the 2005 annual meeting of the Little Big Horn Associates (LBHA) in Rapid City, South Dakota. The LBHA is one of the two major amateur historical societies devoted to Custer and to the Little Bighorn—retaining the three-word spelling of the battle ("Little Big Horn") instead of the two-word spelling ("Little Bighorn") that most historians currently use— and I could have just as easily written a similar chapter about the other major national organization, the Custer Battlefield and Museum Historical Association (CBHMA). This chapter explores the texture of the historical enthusiasm in the LBHA by providing a detailed account of one of the conferences that the organization (like the CBHMA) holds each year. By showing what does—and does not—interest the members of the LBHA in the Black Hills, I hope to show how the specialized endeavor of Custerology represents something larger in terms of the way that contemporary American culture regards the place of Native Americans in the United States. This question also figures in the following chapter, "Testimony in Translation," which is the most textually oriented chapter in the book and the only one not concerned with an actual physical location. In the chapter, I trace the ways that Custerology has relied upon Indian testimony about the Battle of the Little Bighorn and note that Custerologists have produced a stunning body of Indian accounts of the battle. In fact, the Battle of the Little Bighorn appears to be the event in United States history for which we have the greatest number of Indian accounts in print.

In the final chapter, "Little Bighorn Forever," the book returns to the land where the Battle of the Little Bighorn occurred and provides accounts of the rival reenactments that occur there each June on the battle's anniversary. The first, sponsored by the town of Hardin, Montana, is a revival of an earlier reenactment that was staged there from the late 1960s to the early 1970s. The second is sponsored by the Real Bird family and takes place on Crow Indian land adjacent to the National Monument. In both cases, I am interested in how these reenactments have flourished in the post–*Dances with Wolves* era. I contend that their appeal comes from the way that they both foreground their connections with Native American participants—even though they allow white audience members to engage in a nostalgic replay of the Westerns of Manifest Destiny so popular in the mid-twentieth century.

My conclusions about Custerology have been shaped by both my research methods and my relationship to other scholarship on historical commemoration. What remains of this introduction discusses these matters and concludes with an autobiographical indulgence. Those who cannot wait for Last Stand Hill may wish to skip to chapter 1.

———⇒•◦•⇐———

The approach to Custerology that I take in this book participates in the "scholarly fascination with things memorable" that, as Kerwin Lee Klein has observed, has emerged in tandem with shifts in public commemoration of history during the post-Vietnam era.[14] In other words, as the American public has been more involved than ever in acts of historical commemoration during recent decades, scholars have followed suit by trying to explain what these activities reveal about contemporary society. The shared premise of this scholarship is that the social remembrance of the past constitutes a form of collective self-fashioning. "Commemoration makes society conscious of itself as it affirms its members' mutual affinity and identity," Barry Schwartz writes in his study of the national memory of Abraham Lincoln.[15] I seek to understand the kinds of self-consciousness and mutual affinities that the commemoration of the Indian Wars produces, as well as to document how those acts of commemoration may also be means of articulating affinities that distinguish groups from each other. In other words, acts of commemoration can be points of consensus *and* dissension, often simultaneously.

One of the earliest theorists of this subject, the sociologist Maurice Halbwachs, wrote of "the localization of memory" to explain how "frameworks of collective memories" bind individuals together to form distinct groups.[16] Halbwachs had in mind social units such as the family, the religious group, or the socioeconomic class, but the terms of his discussion could also apply to the historical enthusiasts, both non-Indian and Indian, who approach the history of conflicts like the Little Bighorn with distinct beliefs about their significance.

Much of the recent scholarship that seeks to understand the processes that Halbwachs outlines does so by employing the term *memory* as a counterpoint to *history*. Memory, in such formulations, often represents the collective mass, the popular, and particularly traditions of those ethnic or racial groups that are believed to have been excluded from the traditions of an elitist history. Here memory is fragmented, oral, and dynamic, in contrast to written histories that attempt to produce unified narratives of cause and effect.[17] While the strict opposition between memory and history along these lines can be exaggerated and facile, this set of terms has also offered a starting point for considering the problems of the historical recovery of the history of mass suffering, particularly the experiences of European Jews under the Holocaust but also the experiences of African Americans under New World slavery and the experiences of indigenous peoples under colonialism.

This emphasis on collective memory has refocused historical studies on the activities of remembrance and commemoration that take place in the present. The French historian Jacques Le Goff, for instance, has called for a "history of the present" that would presuppose "that history is no longer concerned only with the past, that 'a history' based on a sharp break between the present and past is over." Le Goff contends that the historian must focus on the way that the historical is produced in the contemporary world, by a public "obsessed by the fear of losing its memory in a kind of collective amnesia."[18] An even more influential formulation of this argument has been put forward by Le Goff's compatriot and collaborator Pierre Nora, who has written about the necessity of attending to *lieux de mémoire*—literally, "sites of memory"—that are constituted out of what he and Le Goff considered to be a shared anxiety at the turn of the twenty-first century over losing touch with the historical past. Nora emphasizes, though, that contemporary sites of memory that have been created out of this fear do not preserve the actual past but rather produce the illusion of historical experience by referring to other acts of historical memory.[19] While I believe that Nora overstates his case—probably as a result of his nostalgia for an earlier moment in historiography—his emphasis on the self-referentiality of sites of memory has indeed been useful to me, and it is a point to which I will return in the chapters that follow, especially chapter 6. The acts of memorialization that take place in the landscape of Custerology have as much to do with earlier acts of memorialization as with the history of what actually occurred in the 1860s and 1870s.

Though I have been influenced by the scholarship on collective memory, I prefer to think of Custerology as a study of *public history*. That term not only makes more sense to me because it suggests that popular memorialization is in fact an act of history but also more accurately describes my own emphasis in the chapters that follow. I am interested in the way that public places, gatherings, and works of commemoration—including books—render the historical conflicts between American Indians and the United States. Unlike a historian, I do not generally consider the ways that Indians or soldiers may have remembered that violence in order to discover new evidence about the past, even though I examine the collection of such remembrances in chapter 5. As a student of public history, I give particular weight to physical locations that have been sanctioned by groups—especially the U.S. government in the form of the National Park Service—and attempt to describe the ways audiences or visitors experience those commemorative sites. Though I occasionally refer to ways that Custer, the Little Bighorn, or the Indian Wars appear in mass media (as this introduction shows), film and television figure only marginally in this book. I would not want to deny the power of those electronic images, but in the case of these subjects, I have found that mass media rarely capture the emotional or intellectual complexity produced by the experience of place—the journey through the historical landscape—that I have endeavored to describe.

To pursue this goal, I have employed a research methodology that participates in both historiography and ethnography—an elaborate way of saying that I have both read things on the page and talked to people. (The scholarly works that have influenced me most include those by historians like Edward Tabor Linenthal, who has written books about both U.S. battlefields and the commemoration of the Oklahoma City bombing, and anthropologists like Richard Handler and Eric Gable, who have written a masterful study of Colonial Williamsburg.)[20] On the one hand, Custerology has produced a thick textual archive—hundreds of books, newspaper and magazine articles, newsletters, novels—and to comprehend the way that Custer and the Little Bighorn have been commemorated requires a working knowledge of this archive and its development. On the other, the historical landscape of Custerology is composed of physical terrain— monuments and museums, for instance—that requires firsthand observation, especially of the way in which they are interpreted for and by their public constituents. My own disciplinary training, finally, is in the field of literary criticism, which means that I have a particular interest in the way that language is used to convey experience. For that reason, I tend to privilege the written statements of those active in the world of Custerology, but I have found that the written record is frequently insufficient as a map of this commemorative terrain. Indeed, one of the pleasures of this research has been the opportunity to speak with many individuals who, in spite of their different interpretations of and investments in the history of the Indian Wars, share a common sense of its great significance.

In the late twentieth century, it became a common observation that ethnography (the term used for the description of cultures and cultural practices by anthropologists) must always be suspect: the social scientist's presence alters the social scene that he or she is trying to record, and his or her biases, often unrecognized, shape the entire process of information gathering and documentation. A tribal storyteller, to use a simple example, might not be willing to share certain tales with an outsider, might choose certain stories over others based on what she believes the social scientist wants to hear, or might speak in a way that is difficult for the social scientist to record. Therefore, because an observer can never record a perfect, completely objective account of a social setting, the reader of an ethnography should always be wary when the writer tries to pass off the account as a complete and unadulterated "inside" account of another culture. I am quite familiar with this line of thinking because my last book studied the production of ethnography in the late-nineteenth- and early-twentieth-century United States—and now this critical insight applies to my own research as well. I have seen repeatedly how a notebook or a tape recorder can change a conversation, and I have no doubt that someone responds differently to questions posed over the telephone or e-mail from a distant academic than they might to questions asked by a close acquaintance.

There is no way to entirely compensate for the distortion that a recording observer can bring to any social activity. Moreover, the precise nature of that distortion can depend on the identity of the observer. I have witnessed, for instance, how acutely self-conscious historical reenactors become when a television or documentary video camera is turned on. More important for this book, I have no doubt that my travels in the world of Custerology have been affected by the fact that I am not an American Indian, nor does my appearance suggest American Indian heritage. To point this out is not to say that Custerologists—even the most enthusiastic Custerphiles—harbor a closet racism that would have led them to reject an Indian interlocutor. (Custer aficionados, in my experience, are eager to talk to *any* willing listener about their historical passions.) However, it is a common assumption in the world of Custerology—among both white aficionados and Indian tribalists—that non-Indians and Indians have different stakes in the history of the Indian Wars. Given this premise, it is hardly surprising that a white enthusiast might speak in a different manner, even while trying to convey the same information, to a blond academic who teaches American literature than to, say, a tribally affiliated scholar with an appointment in Native American studies. By the same token, it seems likely that a tribal activist might feel more comfortable speaking with the latter, who, upon receiving different information, might write a very different account of the world of Custerology from the one that you hold in your hands.

In attempting to provide a kind of deep map of the historical landscape of Custerology, I have tried to approach my subjects with a sense of fairness, to get down on the page their own logic for engaging with Custerology in the way that they do—even when I do not wholly agree with that logic myself. This requires a substantial amount of description of the acts of historical commemoration and the people who have engaged in them. While I have tried to articulate my own conclusions about Custerology and its significance, I have also tried to write the book in a manner that allows my readers to reach their own.

⊰·◦·⊱

During the time that I have been researching and writing this book, the most frequent inquiry I have received—from both my academic colleagues and those whom I have interviewed—is how I became interested in this topic. It is a legitimate question, particularly since I have asked a version of it to dozens of others, but I have still often found myself stumbling over the answer. Though I risk crossing into the realm of narcissism, it seems appropriate to offer here a more articulate response to the question.

The origin of my interest in Custerology is an afternoon in 1999 when I was supposed to be working on the revisions of another manuscript. As a diversion, I began to read reviews of novels by authors I admire that had been posted on the Web site of an Internet bookseller. Like most professors of literature, I have firm opinions about what constitutes literary quality and significance—and I am by turns amused and appalled when nonprofessional readers disagree with my taste. By chance, I came across a page of comments responding to *Killing Custer,* a history of the Battle of the Little Bighorn that I had not yet read but that was written by an author, James Welch, whose novels I regularly include in my courses. What surprised me at first was the depth of emotion that Welch's writing about the Little Bighorn and the Indian Wars produced, particularly the negative reaction of readers who were obviously deeply knowledgeable about the Indian Wars but were not professional historians.

As I thought about this, I became aware of something that seemed equally significant to me: my own ignorance about Custer, the Battle of the Little Bighorn, and the Centennial Campaign of which it was a part. Like

Eli Cash in *The Royal Tenenbaums*, I knew that Custer died in a famous "last stand," but I could not have said much more about the conflicts that brought the Seventh Cavalry to Montana or their aftermath. What made my lack of familiarity particularly troublesome was that I was certified as a scholar of late-nineteenth-century U.S. literature and culture and had a particular interest in literary productions by and portrayals of Native Americans. My post-Vietnam education had eschewed military topics and instead focused on social movements, favoring "culture" over war, diversity over violence. To put it another way, I knew all about the arguments put forward by Vine Deloria Jr. in *Custer Died for Your Sins* but nothing about the figure named in the title.

In the period that followed, I read Welch's book—as well as Brian Dippie's study of Custer in popular culture, Paul A. Hutton's eclectic *Custer Reader*, W. A. Graham's even more eclectic *Custer Myth*, and Custer's own memoir, *My Life on the Plains, or Personal Experiences with Indians*—and began to learn about the extensive network of amateur enthusiasts engaged with this history. I paid my first visit to the battlefield and to the reenactments in 2002, and in 2003 I traveled to Monroe, Michigan, to interview Steve and Sandy Alexander, attended my first annual convention of the Little Big Horn Associates, and went to see the Washita Battlefield National Historic Site for the first time. By then, I knew that I wanted to try to understand the power of these places and to tell their stories.

This chronology means that I have conducted most of my research, both in the library and in "the field," in the years following the 2001 attacks on the World Trade Center and the Pentagon. The effects that those attacks had on the public culture of the United States—the increase in overt displays of national patriotism, the military actions in Afghanistan and Iraq, the increased awareness of the legacy of mass violence—figure in the first and final chapters of this book in explicit ways, but that context has undoubtedly played a role in my entire project. In the epilogue, I offer some tentative conclusions about how this contemporary climate continues to shape Custerology and what lessons Custerology may have for the twenty-first century. Since the United States began its most recent war in Iraq, Americans have once again recognized that their nation constitutes an imperial power and have again become divided over the correctness, the costs, and the ultimate purpose of American military power exercised overseas. These debates will continue, and I believe that Custerology— which turns our attention back to the imperial relationship of the United States to the tribes of American Indians—will also continue to flourish as a reservoir of historical knowledge for all sides. Custerology has taught me the necessity of being more cognizant of the histories of military violence, of realizing that the commemoration of military violence has both political roots and political effects, and of understanding that we cannot avoid further military action by ignoring the presence of militarism in our historical landscape. It strikes me that all those who participate in the commemoration of the Indian Wars, regardless of their identity or investment in that history, would agree on these last points. Therefore, they can serve as an appropriate prelude to the next chapter, which describes the dedication of a war memorial under the theme "Peace through Unity."

1

GHOST DANCING ON
LAST STAND HILL

Crow Agency, Montana

I WILL BEGIN THIS CHAPTER WITH TWO STORIES ABOUT THE WAY THAT THE Battle of the Little Bighorn has been remembered in the twenty-first century. The first is a work of short fiction by Sherman Alexie, a Spokane / Coeur d'Alene author who is among the best-known American Indian writers working today. Alexie's story, first published in 2002, is titled "Ghost Dance."[1] The title references a religious movement that circulated among American Indian tribes in the western United States—including those who had fought at the Little Bighorn—starting in the late 1880s. Widespread adherence to the Ghost Dance, many believed, could bring back the buffalo, restore the land, and return the tribes to the patrimony that had been denied them. The U.S. government, fearing that the movement would lead to an armed uprising, ordered a termination of the dancing and deployed the U.S. army in 1890 to bring in those Ghost Dance adherents who had left their designated reservation agencies. The best-known incident from this suppression is the one that is often used to conclude histories of U.S.-Indian military conflicts, the Wounded Knee massacre. At Wounded Knee Creek, the Seventh Cavalry was in the process of disarming a band of Lakotas before marching them to Pine Ridge Agency. When an older Lakota resisted giving up his weapon and accidentally discharged it, the soldiers opened fire. Somewhere between 150 and 300 Lakotas, including many women and children, were killed in the ensuing bloodshed; 25 U.S. soldiers were killed as well, many by friendly fire.

Alexie's story, though, does not depict the events surrounding the historical Ghost Dance or Wounded Knee. Written for a compilation of "thrilling tales" designed to evoke the lurid genre fiction of the mid-twentieth century, "Ghost Dance" is a gruesome work that begins with white police officers bringing two Indian hitchhikers to the cemetery at the Little Bighorn Battlefield for a midnight execution on the anniversary of the battle. For the police, Little Bighorn is the place "where it all went to shit," where the "damn Indians" ruined the course of U.S. history by killing Brevet Major General George Armstrong Custer and more than two hundred of his Seventh Cavalry in 1876. When the racist whites kill the Indian men, however, the blood spilled in vengeance awakens the rotting corpses of the Seventh Cavalry soldiers buried at the battlefield; hundreds of zombies rise from their graves, devour the cops, and proceed to wreak havoc on the surrounding population, regardless of racial or cultural identity. At the end of "Ghost Dance," the Seventh Cavalry zombies are still terrorizing the countryside, though an FBI agent, apparently non-Indian, seems to have developed the supernatural ability to receive visions of the zombies' violence as they perpetrate it. It is a bizarre story.

The second story may be less literary, but it is perhaps equally strange and certainly more germane to this chapter. On June 25, 2003—the 127th anniversary of the battle—thousands of Indians and non-Indians gathered at the Little Bighorn Battlefield National Monument to witness the celebration of a new feature of the commemorative landscape there, a memorial dedicated to the Indians present at the battle, both those who fought against the Seventh Cavalry and those Crow and Arikara Indians who fought as scouts with it. At an amphitheater located at the base of the hill on which the Indian Memorial stands, like the older monument marking the mass grave of the enlisted men who died with Custer, the official ceremony proceeded with appropriate pomp and circumstance.[2] Flags fluttered, songs were sung, and dignitaries—tribal chairs, a governor, a senator, and the secretary of the interior—sat in neat rows at the side of the podium. Early in the program, a moment of confusion left the space behind the microphone vacant; a man wearing a red windbreaker and a feathered headdress strode forward to seize the opportunity. "My name," he told the audience, "is Oyate Wacinyapi. My English name is Russell Means."

The applause that greeted Means, an Oglala Lakota and Ihanktonwan Sioux, suggested that his audience already knew who he was. The former spokesperson for the American Indian Movement (AIM) and occasional actor had not been included in the official program, but no one was surprised that he found his way to the microphone. His unscripted speech of fifteen minutes recounted his own history of coming to the battlefield to protest the absence of visible commemoration for the Indians who fought there, thanked everyone from the staff of Senator Ben Nighthorse Campbell to the Libertarian Party of Montana for supporting the new memorial, and denigrated the monument erected in 1881 to honor George Armstrong Custer and his men as a "phallic symbol" and a "statement of patriarchal society's power."

But what made Means's speech notable was that he began by sounding less like a radical activist and more like a conservative pundit. He lamented to the crowd the increasing fragmentation of America into a nation of hyphens: Asian-Americans, Latino-Americans, Anglo-Americans, African-Americans. The moniker "American Indian," he said, demonstrates that the indigenous peoples of the United States understand the dangers of ethnic fragmentation. "*We* put 'American' *before* our ethnicity. . . . We know what it is to be an American, and that's why we are so proud to put it before our ethnicity. . . . By putting your ethnicity first, that's where your mind goes, and where your heart goes. . . . You have to put *American* first. [Applause.] And then, that's when we develop a culture together."

Even if his scene stealing were straight out of the provocateur handbook, Means's castigation of ethnic separatism was hardly what one might expect from someone so long involved in efforts to win tribal self-determination. A goal of AIM, after all, was the recognition of American Indian tribes as sovereign nations, self-governing political entities. While tribal sovereignty might seem to some to be compatible with a vision of the United States as a single national community, many (if not most) Americans would consider it to be a challenge to that vision. After his speech, an independent filmmaker, in the course of taping an interview, hinted that Means had left this activist agenda out of his speech. What about tribal self-determination? the interviewer asked. What does the Indian Memorial at the Little Bighorn battlefield have to do with sovereignty? Means squared to the camera and his eyes lit up. "It has *everything* to do with sovereignty," he said. "It tells us that our people—that we have the right to defend our land by any means necessary." [3]

This last point makes sense. The presence of the Indian Memorial, wholeheartedly welcomed by the U.S. National Park Service and financed by the federal government, indeed implicitly recognizes that the Lakota Sioux, Cheyennes, and Arapahos in the village at the Little Bighorn acted with legitimacy and justice. But recognition of that legitimacy also undermines Means's earlier suggestion that Indians "put American first." The Indians at the Little Bighorn in 1876 were fighting *against* a forced unity that they feared would mean their cultural and political obliteration; they fought *against* their incorporation into the United States on the terms that the United States had named. In other words, to say that the Indian Memorial has "everything" to do with tribal sovereignty and the right of tribal nations to defend themselves (with a nod to Malcolm X) "by any means necessary" redefined the memorial in opposition to the official theme of both the dedication ceremonies and the Indian Memorial itself, a theme that Means explicitly endorsed in his borrowed time at the speaker's podium: "Peace through Unity."

I dwell on the incongruities of Russell Means's words on that day neither to chide him for sloppy logic nor to laud him for his slippery rhetoric. The emotional and logical excesses of his speech that day suggest to me an echo of what drives Alexie's pulp-fiction zombies—a sense of the Little Bighorn as a place of unresolved and unresolvable energies that have yet to find a concrete form in the contemporary political expressions of either the United States or its tribal nations. One the one hand, the battlefield has been a place where Indians come to articulate an oppositional, even separatist stance toward the United States—their sense of themselves as distinct peoples. On the other, the Little Bighorn has also been a site for spectacles of patriotic allegiance to the United States, a nationalism that seeks to unify those people living within its boundaries. While these two forms of political emotion have been in conflict at the Little Bighorn battlefield for more than a century, they have more recently converged.

In this chapter, I will try to tell the story of this convergence, to explain how the commemoration of the Battle of the Little Bighorn could be the locus of such contradictory and complicated forms of historical and political feeling. Though the focus of this book is exclusively on Custer and the Little Bighorn, the kind of historical commemoration I discuss here is hardly unique. In fact, the construction of this new monument at the battlefield epitomizes the intersection of two significant trends: the vogue of commemoration that took hold in the final decades of the twentieth century and the related efforts to memorialize the lives of those who have previously been considered the "victims" or the "defeated" of historical processes that produced an unequal distribution of power and material benefit. However, like all acts of historical commemoration, the dedication of the Indian Memorial was enmeshed in a particular history of public representation—generations of books, films, television shows, monuments, and museums that constitute a kind of collective palimpsest of cultural memories. The Indian Memorial was the result of years of effort on the part of activists and employees of the National Park Service who were determined to change the physical landscape, and thus the symbolic landscape, of the battlefield. In doing so, they ushered in a new chapter in the history of Custerology, a history that begins with a relatively simple battle.

On the morning of June 25, 1876, an estimated six to eight thousand American Indians were camped in southern Montana along the banks of the Little Bighorn River, which many of them called the Greasy Grass. The majority were Lakota Sioux, whose five camp circles were arranged according to band: Brulé, Oglala, Sans Arc, Minneconjou, and Hunkpapa. There was a sixth circle, too, made up of Cheyenne Indians who had become allies of the Lakotas, as well as a few Arapaho Indians who were visiting the Cheyennes. The size of this encampment had nearly doubled during recent weeks, as the so-called summer roamers had left their agencies and reservations in the Dakota Territory to join with those who had braved the winter and a cold, cruel spring. The result was a village impressive in its size, and some of its leaders were doubtless already wondering how long the rolling hills surrounding the river could sustain this many people and their grazing horses.

For the time being, though, those living along the Little Bighorn had every reason to feel confident. Eight days earlier, while the village was relocating to this site, 750 Sioux and Cheyenne warriors, including Crazy Horse, had mounted an attack on federal troops marching north along the Rosebud River, to the east of the Little Bighorn. The warriors faced an opposing force almost double in size—nearly 1,300 fighting for the United States, including 250 Crow Indians, longtime enemies of the Sioux—yet were able to turn them back and away from the village. Now reunited, the village could field somewhere between 1,500 and 2,000 fighting men. The Indians knew that there were other federal troops on the march, trying to find them and drive them back to their assigned reservations, but they took the fight on the Rosebud as evidence that their numbers and determination would enable them to prevail.

That afternoon, their convictions were put to a new test. Mayhem erupted at the southern end of the village; blue-coated federal troops charged across the river, deployed into a skirmish line, and fired into the village. While children, women, and the elderly ran toward safety in the opposite direction, Indian warriors (mostly Lakota Sioux) prepared their weapons and mounted a swarming, decisive counterattack that quickly demoralized the soldiers. In less than an hour, the federal troops were retreating from the timber where they had hoped to make their stand; they recrossed the river and dashed up to a hilltop, where they would assume a defensive position and hope they could maintain it until some kind of relief arrived.

At about the same time that the Indian warriors began noticing the soldiers' retreat, they heard gunfire from a new direction—the northern, or downstream, end of the village. Warriors began leaving the first fight to meet a contingent of troops who had come to a ford in the river near the Hunkpapa camp and were moving back into the hills, trying to circle around that end of the village. The Lakotas and Cheyenne rode off—some to counter their movements directly and others to encircle them from their rear. [4] This second fight would be an even more decisive victory for the Indians and would sear this day into the consciousness of the nation that had opposed them. By nightfall, the 211 men who had attacked the village from downstream were all dead in the ravines and hills surrounding the Little Bighorn River. Among them was George Armstrong Custer.

On his final day, Custer was a thirty-six-year-old lieutenant colonel who was still, as was the custom, frequently addressed using the general's rank that he had earned in the Civil War—a practice that historians and biographers have continued after his death. [5] He was ambitious, which was hardly unusual for a career officer who had risen to glory at an early age. He almost certainly hoped that a major victory in the campaign against the Sioux and Cheyennes would lead to promotion, perhaps eventually putting him on the path toward regaining the general's star that he first wore in the Civil War at the improbably young age of twenty-three. If he was no longer as flamboyant in appearance as he had once been—the receding hairline perhaps sobered him a little—he was every bit as confident in his abilities as a leader of troops in combat. By all accounts, he was a bold, aggressive, and often inspiring field commander of cavalry. His trademark was not so much tactical brilliance as a combination of self-confidence, daring, and, at least until this day, luck.

Custer's Seventh Cavalry was one of three forces in the field as part of the U.S. army's campaign targeting those Lakota Sioux Indians, as well as Cheyennes with them, who had rejected their designated reservations in the Dakota Territory. The army had gauged roughly where these "hostile" Indians were camped, and the three columns of troops were converging in the hope that they would be unable to escape. Custer had no way of receiving news about the Rosebud fight, in which the Indians had succeeded in knocking one of the columns out of commission for the rest of the summer. Nor did he have an accurate estimate of the number of Indians who had banded together; all the documents that precede his last battle suggest that he had been led to expect a village no larger than half the size of what he found.

Custer's main concern was not being outnumbered but being eluded. Conventional army wisdom held that the principal asset of Plains Indians was their mobility, their ability to disperse instantly into smaller groups that could travel more quickly and easily than army columns burdened by clumsy supply trains and the difficulty of finding suitable forage for their horses. From the moment on June 22 when the Seventh Cavalry left its camp on the Yellowstone for Custer's final march—first south along the Rosebud and then west to the Little Bighorn—every decision that its leader made was driven by this fear of evasion.

Custer's contingent comprised nearly 650 men: 31 army officers, 566 enlisted men, an assortment of civilian quartermaster employees, a newspaper reporter, and his sixteen-year-old nephew, who, along with two of his brothers and a brother-in-law, would die with him.[6] Custer also traveled with thirty-five Indian scouts, mostly Arikara but including six Crows and a few Sioux. This was a large force, but it might have even been larger. Custer had refused additional infantry and two Gatling guns, both of which, he thought, would make the Seventh Cavalry less mobile and less able to take its opponents unaware. The final days of Custer's life were hot, dusty, arduous ones for his men, as he pushed them forward along the trail that the Indian village had left as it moved from the Rosebud River to the Little Bighorn. Early on the morning of June 25, the scouts had sighted the village from a gap in the Wolf Mountains known as the Crow's Nest; Custer joined them, but the morning haze prevented him from seeing the pony herds more than a dozen miles away that the scouts pointed out. Nevertheless, he planned for his troops to lie low for the rest of the day and then attack the next morning, when most of the Indians would still be sleeping.

This plan quickly unraveled as Custer heard reports that his forces had been discovered—both by Indians riding near the scouting party and by others who had found a box of hardtack that had accidentally dropped from one of the pack trains. Fearing that the main village would soon learn of the position of the Seventh Cavalry from these Indians—a fear that, it turns out, was unfounded—he ordered his officers to prepare their companies as quickly as possible to resume the march and attack. As they rode westward again, Custer split off two smaller groups: one company would travel behind with the mules and supplies; another, composed of three companies, would scout upstream, to the south. Then, he divided the bulk of the regiment—about five hundred men and officers—one last time.

Three companies would charge into the village at its southern end under Major Marcus Reno; the other four would ride with Custer to the north—and to their deaths.

Since that day, thousands of pages have been written to describe what happened to the federal troops at the Little Bighorn, but perhaps nothing has been as succinct as the assessment attributed years later to Iron Hawk, a Hunkpapa Lakota who fought in the battle. "These Wasichus," he said, using a Lakota word for whites, "wanted it, and they came to get it, and we gave it to them."[7]

—————➤◆◄—————

One reason that the Battle of the Little Bighorn has compelled generations of military historians and amateur enthusiasts to sift through the evidence of what occurred there is that little else beyond these bare facts can be established with absolute certainty. The unknown, and seemingly unknowable, facts of the Battle—its so-called mysteries—have been the subjects of passionate debate and bitter dispute. For instance, since the moment that newspaper reporters began conveying the story of Custer's demise, estimates of how many Indians were camped along the river when Custer attacked, or how many Indians took up arms against him, have varied widely. One lieutenant who survived on the hilltop upstream said there were nine thousand Indian warriors—a number that has seemed to historians to be too high—while his comrades said the Native American force was fewer than half that. The lower estimates were still notably larger than what several recent studies of the fight have suggested.[8] It has taken more than a hundred years to reach a loose consensus on the number of Indians fighting Custer and his men, and it could take at least a hundred more to reach an agreement on the tactics that they used. In fact, the exact movement of the forces during the fight, both the Native American warriors and the cavalry soldiers under Custer, remains one of the most contentious topics among the cadre of professional and amateur historians who study the Little Bighorn, groups to which we will return in chapters 4 and 5.

Unanswered questions about numbers, times, and locations, though, are really just echoes of the deeper conflicts that have persisted about the behavior of Custer, his officers, and his men—and about who should take responsibility for a defeat that quickly became more significant as a national mythic spectacle than as an actual military loss. From the moment that news of the battle reached the newspapers—more than a week after Custer's death—every comment on the feats and follies of the men who fought there has been tethered to the issue of culpability. It is a matter so enduring that mock courts-martial of a resurrected Custer are still staged regularly by a South Dakota group that assembles for this purpose. In 1998, the Indiana University School of Law even held its own Custer court-martial featuring Supreme Court Justice Ruth Bader Ginsburg as the presiding judge on the panel of three distinguished legal minds hearing the case. Dressed in nineteenth-century army blue, "Major General" Ginsburg pronounced the court's unanimous finding that Custer violated the United States' Articles of War "by failing to conduct appropriate reconnaissance and by dividing his force in the face of a numerically superior enemy."[9]

One hope among those seeking to extend and verify the historical record of the Battle of the Little Bighorn has been that testimony by Indian participants could provide the key—not only because Indians were the only ones who could provide eyewitness accounts of the final hours of Custer's battalion but also because it was presumed that Indians would be less interested in whether Custer or one of his officers were at fault. Yet that same testimony has put into circulation stories about the battle that historians have spent over a century trying to disprove: reports that at least some of Custer's men were drunk, that a group of them committed mass suicide, that Custer's own son (by a Cheyenne Indian woman) was present at the battle, that Custer hoped a great victory at the Little Bighorn would catapult him into the presidency of the United States, to name a few.[10]

The most lurid rumor of all, though, did not have an Indian origin. Rain in the Face, a Hunkpapa Lakota, had once been placed under arrest by Custer's brother Tom, and newspapers printed stories that at the Battle of the Little Bighorn, the warrior tore open Tom Custer's body and cut out his heart in revenge. The story had enough currency that Elizabeth Bacon Custer, George's widow, included it in the first of her memoirs.[11] Henry Wadsworth Longfellow made it the subject of a poem—though Longfellow cast Custer himself, not Tom, as the victim of Rain in the Face's sanguinary malice:

> Rain-in-the-Face, in his flight
>   Uplifted high in air
> As a ghastly trophy, bore
> The brave heart, that beat no more,
>   Of the White Chief with yellow hair.[12]

From the enlightened, free-verse perspective of most Americans today, pursuing the mysteries of the Battle of the Little Bighorn might seem as outdated as both the style and content of Longfellow's poetry. But these controversies surrounding Custer and his fate persist because the fight between the Seventh Cavalry and the village of Lakota Sioux, Cheyenne, and Arapaho was, as all military conflicts surely are, a political contest over competing visions of power. The Battle of the Little Bighorn resulted from and participated in a long struggle over questions of territorial governance and conflicting claims of sovereignty, as well as the implementation of solutions to these problems. For Custer and the Seventh Cavalry, the campaign had also become entangled with the divisive, never-ending battle between the political parties in the United States. As much as a military leader might want to divide the business of soldiering from the ugly world of partisan bickering, George Armstrong Custer could no more separate the two than his modern-day counterparts are able to do. Custer, in fact, nearly had lost the command of the Seventh Cavalry because of his participation in hearings aimed at exposing the corruption of the Ulysses S. Grant administration—a political blunder that infuriated the president to such a degree that he was ready to punish Custer by keeping him on the military sidelines.

Partisan politics, though, ended up serving Custer well, if only posthumously. Democrat newspaper editors—particularly James Gordon Bennett of the *New York Herald*—seized on his defeat at the Little Bighorn as a signal of the catastrophic failure of Republican policies and corruption among the government Indian agents who had been appointed by Grant's administration. Grant himself told the press that he regarded "Custer's massacre as a sacrifice of troops, brought on by Custer himself, that was wholly unnecessary."[13] The editorial page of the *Herald,* conversely, placed the blame squarely on the shoulders of the commander-in-chief: "The deplorable truth is that President Grant is chiefly responsible for the appalling miscarriages which have attended this disastrous campaign against the Sioux."[14] Bennett wasted no time in launching a campaign to raise funds for a Custer monument; for him and for other foes of Grant, transforming the slain general into a figure of glory made the president and his cronies appear as villainous blackguards.

The political wrangling of the 1870s played a part in transforming Custer from an historical footnote to a household name, but only a part. Like the 168 words that Abraham Lincoln spoke when dedicating the national cemetery at Gettysburg, Custer's defeat at the hands of the Sioux and Cheyenne would have been little remembered had it not resonated with America's body politic more deeply than anyone at first could recognize. In 1876, the nation was simultaneously commemorating its centennial and emerging from an economic depression; it had defeated secession, but the work of reconstruction and reunification still remained incomplete; the United States had spanned the continent yet still appeared to have only the loosest of grips over wide swaths of it. In other words, the United States in 1876 was a nation celebrating the achievement of its Manifest Destiny yet wondering whether that destiny had been achieved at all, and if so, at what price.

The Battle of the Little Bighorn gave a country at once confident and doubtful what it needed and would continue to need: a hero defeated in spectacular fashion—and defeated not just by anyone but by the American Indians considered to be the last holdout of savagery on a continent otherwise secured for civilization. While Americans today frequently regard the struggle over the enslavement, emancipation, and civil rights of African Americans as the central conflict of their country's history, the national imagination of the nineteenth century was configured differently. Even in the decades after the Civil War, the status of free blacks was still too divisive and unresolved a question—one that could mar the harmony of a newly reunited country—for most white Americans to consider emancipation to be the central act of their national drama. On the other hand, whites, particularly those living east of the Mississippi, could look at the conflicts taking place between the U.S. army and the Plains Indians through the ennobling lens of distance. What they saw had all the elements of a melodrama: on the one hand, a desperate people setting loose their most violent, treacherous impulses in order to resist the inevitable, and on the other, brave men performing the dangerous work of securing the frontier for a more enlightened order. More than any other, the victory of civilization over American Indians stood as the quintessential American narrative—a heroic, if somewhat tragic, story that distinguished, above all, the struggles and sacrifices of America's New World from Europe's old one. This is the same story mined so brilliantly by William Cody in the various manifestations of Buffalo Bill's Wild West show, a show that changed over time but that consistently drew upon the dramatic incorporation of the American West into the United States—and that avoided referring either to the Civil War or to slavery.[15]

Part of the power of this story in the American imagination—at least in the imagination of white Americans—emanated from the ambivalence that it generated. It has often been stated that white Americans of the nineteenth century thought of Indians in one of two ways: either as treacherous savages whose removal and perhaps even extermination were necessary to the safety of civilization or as noble savages whose decline and disappearance would be the price of progress.[16] In the 1870s, this emotional matrix did produce distinct and opposing stances among non-Indians toward what was called "the Indian Question," leading to conflicts between reformers (mostly living on the Eastern seaboard) who thought military action against Indians to be unjust and Western settlers who thought military action was long overdue. For many non-Indian Americans, though, these feelings of sympathy and disdain were not so sharply divided from one another; they were capable of holding both attitudes simultaneously—supporting the violent dispossession of American Indians throughout the continent while still lamenting the fate that they suffered. One could cheer for the blue-coated soldiers and still be saddened that each of the army's victories brought the day closer when Indians would no longer roam freely in the great open spaces of the American West.

Custer himself understood this ambivalence and even shared it. In *My Life on the Plains,* his memoir published two years before the Battle of the Little Bighorn, America's best-known Indian fighter declared, "If I were an Indian, I often think I would greatly prefer to cast my lot among those of my people adhered to the free open plains rather than submit to the confined limits of a reservation, there to be the recipient of the blessed benefits of civilization, with its vices thrown in without stint or measure."[17] We will return later to this passage, which has become a touchstone of Custerology. Here Custer neatly demonstrates the bind in which Americans of his time placed the indigenous peoples of the Plains. They could either submit to the confinement of the reservation—and be disdained for no longer being "free" Indians—or they could face the army that Custer so eagerly led into battle. This impossible set of choices was the product of the contradictory desires that Custer shared with many of his generation, desires that Indians both remain as they were on the "free open plains"—almost as aesthetic objects to be appreciated for their beauty and antiquity—and that they be removed as impediments to the civilization of railroads, mines, and farms.

For many Americans, the fate of Custer and his men at the Little Bighorn fed these same desires. Custer was not simply a victim of government corruption or poorly considered policies, in spite of what the *Herald* argued, but a martyr of the long march of civilization toward its ultimate dominion over the earth. If Custer had led his Seventh Cavalry to victory in Montana, he would now be as well remembered as his contemporaries Nelson Miles, George Crook, John Gibbon—hardly household names. Instead, the soldiers of Custer's Seventh Cavalry were treated as descendants of the Spartans at Thermopylae and of the Texans at the Alamo. The image of Custer and his men being overwhelmed by hordes of bloodthirsty

Indians reminded Americans that this was a genuine struggle with not only triumphs but also epic losses. Military victories over the Plains Indians seemed small and even sordid by comparison; the Battle of the Little Bighorn proved that the army had both a worthy foe and a worthy hero in the slain general. One need not feel guilty about the fate of the Indians if they were capable of this kind of carnage.

Those whose lives were distant enough from the battle not to be touched directly by its blood and dust could regard the Battle of the Little Bighorn as the grand closing chapter of a book that had been nearly forgotten by the modern age. Here were the risks, the sacrifices, the emotions that modernity had sorely neglected. A decade after the tremendous suffering of the Civil War, here was a heroism less complicated and more easily recognizable than anything that could be found in the murky work of national reconstruction. No less savvy a student of the paradoxes of the American body politic than Walt Whitman comprehended immediately the enduring power that Custer's death would hold over the nation. Within a day of reading about the Battle of the Little Bighorn, Whitman submitted "Death-Sonnet for Custer" to the *New York Tribune*.[18] In his poem, the self-appointed national bard employed the visual details—the "tawny hair flowing in battle . . . bearing a bright sword in thy hand"—that would become stock features of visual representations of Custer for decades to come, even if Custer's hair had actually been cropped close for this campaign and the Seventh Cavalry had left their sabers behind.[19] Whitman had an instinctive flair for employing the kind of imagery that would prove indelible over time.

However, Whitman's most insightful comments on the Custer phenomenon came five years later, when he recounted his experience of viewing John Mulvany's *Custer's Last Rally*, one of the many paintings that Whitman's "Death-Sonnet" seemed to prefigure. In describing the painting, the poet blurs the work of art and the historical event it represents:

There are no tricks; there is no throwing of shades in masses; it is all at first painfully real, overwhelming, needs good nerves to look at it. Forty or fifty figures, perhaps more, in full finish and detail, life-size, in the mid-ground, with three times that number, or more, through the rest—swarms upon swarms of savage Sioux, in their war-bonnets, frantic, mostly on ponies, driving through the background, through the smoke, like a hurricane of demons. A dozen of the figures are wonderful. Altogether a Western, autochthonic phase of America, the frontiers, culminating typical, deadly, heroic to the uttermost; nothing in the books like it, nothing in Homer, nothing in Shakespeare; more grim and sublime than either, all native, all our own and all a fact.[20]

The collision of short, descriptive phrases in Whitman's prose produces an almost lyrical disorder to his description of both the painting and the battle. The sheer volume of action distracts him. Yet as his description proceeds, the heroism of cavalry comes to the foreground; he goes on to extol Custer and the "muscular, tan-faced men" who die with him. The "swarms upon swarms of savage Sioux," by contrast, recede into the background of the writing—but it is hard to imagine Whitman's rapture without them. In his formulation, the conflict with indigenous enemies makes it possible for the United States to claim the battle as a unique and constitutive moment of its history not shared by any other nation. The ferocity of the defense of their land by the Lakota Sioux (and also the Cheyenne) was what made this moment "all our own," truly "autochthonic," and different from the European battles of Homer and Shakespeare. Whitman's manner of thinking continues as histories regularly treat the Battle of the Little Bighorn and the Plains Indian wars of the nineteenth century as conflicts wholly separate and distinct from the international military conflicts that would dominate the century that followed.

Custer's afterlife began with poems like Whitman's and paintings like Mulvany's; it continued because this kind of praise has generated an equal measure of skepticism since the moment news of the Little Bighorn reached the U.S. newspapers. For every person ready to proclaim Custer a hero, there has been another—like President Grant—ready to label him a fool. The debate over who should bear the blame for the Seventh Cavalry's debacle at Little Bighorn has driven generations of investigations into the mysteries of what actually occurred there. In the immediate aftermath of the battle, the two alternative scapegoats—Major Marcus Reno and Captain Frederick Benteen—were still alive, and discussions of the battle were often written by those who wished to either exonerate or criticize one of them. In fact, Reno, who led the initial charge toward the village from upstream, eventually requested that a court of inquiry be convened so that he could receive a fair hearing on the charges being leveled against him by Custer's hagiographic biographer, Frederick Whittaker. (The court found that Reno's conduct—particularly the hasty retreat he ordered—was far from exemplary but did not merit any type of formal censure.) Benteen, on the other hand, had nursed enmity against Custer long before 1876, but he reserved his harsh judgments of his late commander for private letters and other informal exchanges. Benteen's correspondence, in fact, put into circulation sordid rumors about Custer's personal life, including allegations of extramarital affairs, that would find their way into print decades later.[21]

Benteen and, to a lesser extent, Reno had their followers among those still fighting the Battle of the Little Bighorn, but Custer had one who could not be trumped: his widow, Elizabeth. Only thirty-four years of age at the time of her husband's death, Libbie Custer became a vigorous and staunch defender of her husband's reputation both behind the scenes, where she encouraged those writers and historians sympathetic to her husband, and in front of them, as a lecturer and the author of three of her own books. It became an oft-told story among Custer aficionados in the first half of the twentieth century that Elizabeth was so well regarded within the U.S. army, especially among those from the Seventh Cavalry who survived the Little Bighorn, that many who had evidence damning her husband refused to put it into print as long as she was alive. Theodore Goldin, a private who had charged the Indian village with Major Reno and waited on the hilltop with the other survivors for rescue, wrote as late as 1928 that "every man's heart bled" for the "loyal and loving" wife of General Custer. "This and this alone to-day is and will be as long as she lives, . . . responsible for the suppression of a lot of matters that may throw a clearer light on that campaign."[22] Regardless of whether there was a kind of informal gag order as long as Libbie Custer lived, she ended up outliving not just Benteen and Reno but nearly every other eyewitness to the battle. (Goldin survived her by two years, but his letters would not reach print until the 1950s.) Anyone waiting for her death to produce new testimony about the battle or General Custer would end up taking his story to the grave.

By the time Elizabeth did die in 1933, at the age of ninety, Custerology had solidified and organized itself around its competing interests. Not all were interested in vindicating or castigating George Armstrong Custer himself; just as many were dedicated to reconstructing his final movements. This military and historical puzzle has afforded generations of historical sleuths the endless pleasure of trying to solve a complex mystery while simultaneously searching for the missing clues that will reveal its secrets. To that end, some historians continued the work of collecting American Indian testimony, including the stories of several who did not participate in the battle themselves but learned about it through their family or tribe. Others combed through the printed record, searching archives and libraries for inconsistencies and clues that would yield new insight. Still others devoted themselves to gathering and printing the stories of enlisted men and scouts who had been overlooked. Relatively few Custerologists have

been professional historians. Many had spent all or part of their career in
the military; the rest came from other professional callings. Among the
most active of the twentieth century were an engineer, a newspaper editor,
a professor of physiology, and a podiatrist.[23]

Custerology has been the persistent endeavor of amateur historians for
more than a century, even though the reputation of Custer himself among
the larger public of the United States has fluctuated dramatically during that same period.[24] Poets such as Whitman and Longfellow may have
begun the elevation of Custer into the pantheon of American icons, but
it took Anheuser-Busch to complete the process. In 1895, the brewing
company commissioned Otto Becker to produce a lithograph of Cassily
Adams's painting *Custer's Last Fight* and then proceeded to distribute the
print to tens of thousands of barrooms across America as a decorative promotion (figure 1).[25] In the Becker lithograph, Custer stands, saber aloft,
surrounded by a landscape of corpses, ready to strike the Indian assailants
who besiege him. In the foreground, warriors prepare to scalp and muti-

Figure 1. Beginning in the 1890s, Anheuser-Busch distributed more than 150,000 copies of
Custer's Last Fight, a lithograph by Otto Becker. The brewing company was sending copies
to servicemen abroad, at the rate of two thousand per month, as late as 1942. (Reproduction
courtesy of the Bancroft Library, University of California–Berkeley.)

late fallen soldiers, and in the background, a mounted charge of Indians emerges from the dust of battle to spell Custer's doom. No performance of Buffalo Bill's Wild West Show—which incorporated "Custer's Last Rally" as its closing act for periods in the 1880s and 1890s[26]—or Hollywood production introduced so many Americans to Custer's gallant demise as Becker's lithograph did.

Hollywood did play an increasing role in shaping Custer's memory as the twentieth century proceeded, particularly as that memory began to suffer at the hands of writers seeking to debunk the story of his heroism as a mythic fallacy. The title of Frederick Van de Water's biography, *Glory-Hunter,* is a tip-off to the selfish, impulsive, foolish Custer portrayed inside its covers.[27] Van de Water published *Glory-Hunter* the year after Elizabeth Custer's death, and in it he furnished the model for the Custer who was portrayed in novels and histories unsympathetic to the general for years to come. But Van de Water could not compete with Errol Flynn, whose 1941 performance in *They Died with Their Boots On* would both inform a nation preparing for war about the need for martial sacrifice and inspire the next generation of Custer aficionados. Flynn's dashing, prancing Custer starts out as something of a flamboyant naïf, but his sense of honor and dedication to righteousness take center stage as the film comes to its conclusion at the Battle of the Little Bighorn. The film may be riddled with historical inaccuracies, but Flynn's performance has been venerated by Custerologists for generations. Moreover, *They Died with Their Boots On* comes much closer to the historical facts than does his 1940 film *Santa Fe Trail,* which features if not the worst, then surely the strangest, casting of a George Armstrong Custer on screen, with Ronald Reagan taking the role.[28]

Yet when Custerphiles rail against the damage that Hollywood has inflicted on their Cavalier in Buckskin, to use the title of a more recent biography, it is not Reagan they have in mind.[29] Instead, they direct their ire at Arthur Penn's 1970 adaptation of Thomas Berger's best-selling novel *Little Big Man,* which gives readers a Custer whose racism and megalomania crumble into insanity at the Little Bighorn. Such a portrait of Custer, they are quick to point out, is true neither to the novel (where Custer is pensive and melancholic as he approaches his final battle) nor to the man revealed in historical documentation. They argue that Penn sacrificed the ambiguity of Custer's character—his simultaneous wish to admire and to fight Indians—to a political statement that has less to do with the history of the American West than with the United States' involvement in Vietnam at the time the film was made. To make Custer the epitome of

U.S. imperialism—whether the nineteenth-century effort to conquer the Indian tribes of North America or the twentieth-century one to establish spheres of influence across the globe—strikes his advocates as both ahistorical and unfair.

These objections of the Custerphiles have some merit. Penn's film does have much more to say about twentieth-century Indochina than about the nineteenth-century Plains. But they have missed a larger matter. Even in the immediate aftermath of the Little Bighorn, the attention paid to Custer's last stand has always been part of Americans' long-standing, often fractious debate among themselves about the relationship of the United States to the rest of the world, about the history of its territorial expansion and the future of its global aspirations. Contemporary references to the figure of George Armstrong Custer often link, whether intentionally or not, the nineteenth-century project of continental expansion to its twentieth- and twenty-first century endeavors as a world power. Sherman Alexie's 1996 poem "Custer Speaks" ends with these lines:

> I was born again in Hiroshima.
> I was born again in Birmingham.
> I was born again in the Triangle Shirt Factory.
> I was born again in Chile.
> I was born again in Saigon.
> I was born again in Iraq.
> I was born again in Hollywood.[30]

Indeed, the Custer films of the early 1940s seem now to be directly tied to the run-up to the entrance of the United States into World War II, and Penn is not the only writer who used the figure of Custer to address the presence of American troops in Vietnam. In his book-length account of the 1965 Battle of Ia Drang, *We Were Soldiers Once . . . and Young,* Colonel Harold Moore recalls the pride he felt upon learning that his "airmobile" soldiers had been designated a unit of the Seventh Cavalry, making them the regimental heirs of Custer and his men.[31] Moore's troops even adopted the title of Custer's old regimental song, "Garryowen" (originally an Irish drinking tune), as their own slogan. In the film version, featuring Mel Gibson as Harold Moore, Custer not only serves as a reminder of the necessity of military heroism but also delivers a sense of foreboding. Gibson/Moore spends his last night before leaving for Vietnam staring at two pictures: a painting of Custer's last stand featuring Indians engaged in the gory work of scalping and mutilation, and an equally graphic black-and-white photograph of French soldiers killed at the hands of the Viet Cong.[32]

The most powerful site of Custer's reincarnation remains the place of his death, the rolling hills of the battlefield along the banks of the Little Bighorn River, now surrounded by the Crow Indian Reservation and the state of Montana. Three years after the Battle of the Little Bighorn, in 1879, the Secretary of War ordered the establishment of Custer Battlefield National Cemetery, and in 1881 a granite obelisk was erected on the hilltop where Custer made his last stand—colloquially called Custer Hill or Last Stand Hill—and where 220 of the U.S. soldiers who died in the battle were buried. (The bodies of officers had been exhumed and transported elsewhere for reburial in 1877; Custer's was buried at West Point.)[33] The cemetery at the foot of the hill became the resting place of casualties from other frontier fights, and the National Park Service assumed control of the site in the 1940s, the same decade it was renamed Custer Battlefield National Monument.[34]

Over time, anniversaries of the Battle of the Little Bighorn became occasions for the kinds of gathering common to major battlefields of the U.S. Civil War.[35] In 1886, on the tenth anniversary, a handful of Seventh Cavalry survivors (soldiers who had been in the battalion split off from Custer) met at the battlefield with Curly (also spelled Curley), a Crow man who had served the Seventh Cavalry as a scout, and Gall, a Hunkpapa Lakota who was among the best-known warriors of the Lakota resistance. The veterans and the newspaper reporters who covered the meeting, however, demonstrated only passing interest in professions of friendship between the former adversaries. They hoped Gall could tell them the precise story of Custer's defeat, the military mystery that remains at the heart of Custerology. Gall obliged them, first talking through an interpreter and then walking with them over the battlefield to illustrate the movements of cavalrymen and Indians.[36]

By the fortieth anniversary of the battle, in 1916, the celebration had assumed a different scale and tenor. Just three years after Union and Confederate veterans had met at the fiftieth anniversary of Gettysburg to honor each other's valor (without any reference to the problems that had impelled them to fight one another), spectators at the Little Bighorn battlefield witnessed a meeting between U.S. veterans of the battle and other U.S.-Indian conflicts with a contingent of Northern Cheyennes, including several who had fought there—all under the rubric of "Peace and Reconciliation."[37] The 1926 anniversary went even further. In front of a throng estimated in the tens of thousands, Edward S. Godfrey, who had been

a lieutenant in the Seventh Cavalry battalion that survived the Little Bighorn and later rose to the rank of brigadier general, rode at the head of a
mounted column of soldiers to Last Stand Hill and exchanged tokens of
friendship with White Bull, a Lakota Sioux chief who had led a column
of Sioux and Cheyenne Indians in their war regalia to the same spot. The
cavalrymen and the warriors rode off the field in pairs to emphasize their
reconciliation.[38] Two days later, General Godfrey participated in another
peacemaking drama—this time at the reburial of an unknown soldier
whose bones had recently been unearthed. As part of the interment ceremony, Godfrey and several Lakota veterans of the Little Bighorn, buried
an actual hatchet in what Godfrey called "a covenant of our common citizenship and everlasting peace" (figure 2).[39]

Participation in these symbolic activities could not entirely mask the
disjunction between the pieties of reconciliation and the claims of tribal
sovereignty that at least some of the Lakotas believed still valid. The record
suggests that both parties agreed on the need to proclaim an end to the
conflict between the United States and American Indians, but disagreed
on the question of which party was acting magnanimously in offering
reconciliation—and on what terms reconciliation should proceed. Standing before the tomb of the unknown soldier in 1926, the white veterans

Figure 2. The "burial of the hatchet"—interred with the remains of an unknown soldier—
took place during ceremonies commemorating the fiftieth anniversary of the Battle of the
Little Bighorn in 1926. The Indian on the left has been variously identified as Red Hawk, an
Oglala Lakota; White Bull, the Minneconjou nephew of Sitting Bull; and Red Tomahawk,
a Hunkpapa Lakota. He shakes hands with General Edward S. Godfrey. (Photograph by
Elsa Spear Byron; reproduction courtesy of the Museum of the Rockies.)

spoke of peace as an accomplishment that had been achieved by the conquest of the United States over a violent land. Luther Barker, the "commander" of the Kansas Indian War Veterans, described "the benefits derived from the Indian Wars on the frontier," including the possibility that "a young lady may mount her pony and ride all over this country in safety" —a freedom, Barker said, unavailable to her in 1876. Godfrey reached for grander themes and spoke of the Plains Indian Wars as part of "the struggle of the white civilization for supremacy, possession, development and culture, as against savagery and barbaric nature." He admitted that Indians had suffered "grievous wrongs" from the forces of expansion but emphasized that their "vengeance only hastened the doom that time awaited."[40]

On the other hand, Red Tomahawk, a Hunkpapa Sioux speaking through an interpreter, used this same occasion to speak about treaties. "I have honored and respected all the treaties that you ever signed with me," he said, "but time and again, you have broken those treaties with me, and time and again you have not kept your word with me. It makes my heart sad." Red Tomahawk, in fact, blamed the violence of the Battle of the Little Bighorn on the failure of the United States to honor provisions of the 1868 Treaty of Fort Laramie, which purportedly closed the Black Hills to white settlement. "That was the last treaty that was signed before the Custer Battle . . . and it was not very long after that the agreements were broken, and you see the results of unkept words on the top of the hill." Red Tomahawk went on to speak of his desire for "advancement and progress for my people" and said he placed his hope in "the rising generation of Indian children and the rising generation of white children," but he had made a significant point. Peace was not a victory won by the forces of modernity but something that American Indian tribes would grant in spite of their unresolved treaty claims.[41]

Nothing in the record of this event indicates that the dissonance between Red Tomahawk's speech and those of the U.S. veterans resonated in the ears of the latter. The 1920s was a decade in which the United States produced several official acts that registered sympathy with American Indians but kept their incorporation into the nation as the ultimate goal. The Indian Citizenship Act of 1924 finally extended full U.S. citizenship to all American Indians, and, even more important to the Lakota Sioux, in 1920 the U.S. Congress passed a jurisdictional act that allowed the Sioux to file claims in the U.S. courts emanating from the abrogation of the Fort Laramie Treaty of 1868. In 1923, three years before Red Tomahawk buried the hatchet with General Godfrey, the Sioux Nation had filed a claim for the Black Hills.[42] (As I discuss in chapter 4, the legal documents filed on behalf of the Sioux demanded monetary compensation for the unlawful taking of the Black Hills; some Lakota Sioux would later state that their lawyers had been mistaken, that the Sioux always intended to recover the land itself.)[43] The eagerness with which Godfrey and the other veterans greeted Red Tomahawk's actions suggests they misunderstood the complexities of his allegiance to the United States and his tribal nation as something much simpler and less threatening.

That kind of misunderstanding would become less possible in the final decades of the twentieth century, a shift dramatically illustrated and shaped in 1969 by the title of a single book: *Custer Died for Your Sins.* Written by Vine Deloria Jr., a Standing Rock Sioux who was raised on the Pine Ridge Reservation in South Dakota, *Custer Died for Your Sins* is subtitled *An American Indian Manifesto;* it is a sometimes angry, sometimes bitter, and sometimes humorous call for greater recognition of American Indian self-determination and a depiction of the ways that American Indians have been systematically marginalized by institutions of the contemporary United States. Custer hardly figures in the book at all, except in a chapter titled "Indian Humor." There, Deloria proclaims the general to be the "most popular and enduring subject of Indian humor" and explains that the source of the title of the book had been a bumper sticker labeling Custer "a blood sacrifice" for the failure of the United States to live up to its treaty obligations.[44] Like so many other political best sellers, Deloria's was more often cited than read, but the catchy title forged a link between the historical memory of Plains Indians Wars of the nineteenth century and late-twentieth-century American Indian activism. Moreover, Deloria's book resembled *Little Big Man*—particularly the film version that would appear not long after *Custer Died for Your Sins*—insofar as both called attention to Custer as the most recognizable figure in a national history portrayed as largely unjust.

In the wake of Deloria's book and the American Indian Movement that it supported, Indians who came to the battlefield in the 1970s and 1980s were much less willing to bury any hatchets, symbolic or otherwise. Nor would they allow themselves to be misunderstood. At first, the community of Custerologists was slow to react to the degree to which the politics of commemoration had shifted in a post-Vietnam era that increasingly interpreted U.S. national consolidation through the dark lens of global struggles against regimes of European colonialism. As the 1976 centennial of the battle approached, Custer enthusiasts presumed that the National Park Service would host elaborate commemorative ceremonies on a par with those that had occurred at the fortieth and fiftieth anniversaries of the battle. The Custer Centennial Committee prepared to handle a crowd of 100,000, and an affiliated group made plans for a reenactment of Custer's march to the Little Bighorn by hundreds in period uniform. But the Park Service feared the anniversary would generate sparks between the cavalry aficionados and American Indian activists, including AIM. The National Monument refused to allow reenactors on the official battlefield, and the threat of violence hung over a subdued, scaled-back centennial observance. Custerologists reacted with horror and chastised the Park Service for bowing—as they saw it—to a group of thugs intent on hijacking American history by force. When the prominent leader Russell Means, acting on behalf of AIM, arrived at the centennial ceremonies with a procession of one to two hundred Sioux and an upside-down American flag—and then demanded, and received, time on the speakers' platform—the Custer aficionados' fear that the Park Service would not preserve and protect the memory of their hero were confirmed. They fumed as a descendant of the general, retired Lieutenant Colonel George Armstrong Custer III, was neither officially recognized nor asked to speak.[45]

The decade that followed brought a series of similar controversies. No longer was the world of Custerology simply organized around debates of historical questions; it became, as well, a sphere in which questions of historical preservation and representation were passionately argued. From a distance, many of the matters of contention seem quite small—disputes over a quotation on the visitor center wall, about the books in the visitor center bookstore.[46] But in 1988, on the 112th anniversary of the battle, Means and AIM raised the stakes again. This time Means led a group that brought its own historical plaque of welded steel, planted it in the sod near the granite Custer monument, and set it in poured concrete. The plaque read:

> In honor of our Indian Patriots who fought and defeated the U.S. Calvary [sic]. In order to save our women and children from mass murder. In doing so, preserving rights to our Homelands, Treaties and Sovereignty. 6/25/1988

It was signed by George Magpie, the Northern Cheyenne man who made the plaque, but Means stepped forward as the mastermind behind the protest. "You remove our monument," he told the gathering crowd, "and we'll remove yours."[47]

In his influential study of American battlefields, Edward Tabor Linenthal characterizes the actions of Means and those with him in 1988 as "symbolic guerrilla warfare," language that reflects not only the confrontational style of protest over the lack of a monument to the Indians who fought at the Battle of the Little Bighorn but also the Manichean logic of the plaque. The claim of "Homelands, Treaties and Sovereignty" defended by "Indian Patriots" was grounded in an explicit separatism, an anti-Americanism that left little room for allegiance to the United States.[48] As the installation of the impromptu memorial proceeded, Means compared the 1881 obelisk dedicated to the memory of Custer and the Seventh Cavalry to a memorial to "Nazi officers erected in Jerusalem," a "Hitler national monument."[49] At this moment in 1988, he was a long way from asking anyone to "put American first" in order to "develop a culture together."

———=›•‹=———

Means's protest on behalf of "Indian Patriots" solidified the rhetoric of controversy surrounding what was then called Custer Battlefield National Monument. Those who believed that the Park Service's national monument should reflect the representational desires of American Indians, like Means, and those who argued that the sacrifice of Custer and his men for the project of national consolidation should remain the focus of the commemoration agreed on something crucial: this dispute over the symbolic space of the battlefield emanated from a historical period in which at least some tribal peoples on the Plains pronounced their political and military independence from the United States. That is, what has driven the conflicts over the commemoration of the Battle of the Little Bighorn is not only something that divides those who differently interpret the battle but also something that they share, namely, an understanding that the Indian Wars of the nineteenth century continue to matter to the political status of American Indian tribes today. What remained in contention was how exactly the kind of Indian patriotism represented by the plaque that Means and his supporters planted in Last Stand Hill should be registered in the commemorative landscape and how that patriotism should be situated in relationship to the U.S. patriotism that Custer and his Seventh Cavalry had represented for generations.

That question moved from the Little Bighorn itself to the halls of Congress in the aftermath of Means's protest. In 1990, U.S. Representative Ben Nighthorse Campbell, a member of the Northern Cheyenne tribe and at that time a Democrat from Colorado, and Ron Marlenee, a Republican from Montana, introduced a bill into Congress calling for the construction of a memorial at what was then called Custer Battlefield National Monument "to honor the Indian participants" in the Battle of the Little Bighorn.[50] The bill failed to make it out of Congress before the end of the session, and in the next year, 1991, Campbell reintroduced it. This time, however, he also introduced a second bill, seemingly prompted by comments made by the supporters of the first, to change the official name of the 765 acres administered by the federal government to Little Bighorn Battlefield National Monument.[51] The Indian Memorial had substantial support, much of it tacit but some of it active, within the community of historians and aficionados interested in the Little Bighorn battle; the name change, however, was a different matter. Campbell and his supporters argued that the label "Little Bighorn" would bring the battlefield into line with the naming practices of other units of the National Park Service, which are rarely named for a single individual, as well as with other battlefields, which are customarily named by victors rather than for the defeated. "It is a matter of writing history the way it should have been written in the first place," Campbell stated.[52]

Opponents of the name change used a term of then-recent coinage: "political correctness." Senator Malcolm Wallop, a Republican from Wyoming, argued that changing the name would do "considerable damage to the historical context" by detracting from the impact that Custer's death had on the United States. "Throughout history, the image of the Last Stand has far outweighed the actual military significance of the event," he pointed out, and went on to contend that preserving that image was not an attempt to "glorify" or "justify" the policies that brought the Seventh Cavalry to the Little Bighorn.[53] John Dingell, a House Democrat whose district included Custer's adopted hometown of Monroe, Michigan, went further. He claimed the proposed name change "demeans the American soldiers who died at Little Bighorn" by implying that the actions of Custer and his men were wrongs that, like the name of place where they died, needed to be corrected. "I say no wrong was committed there," he concluded. "I say no impropriety was committed by the American soldiers who died there." He then introduced into the record a resolution of the Monroe City Council: "Let the memory of 'Custer's Last Stand' live on."[54]

Most, though not all, Custer aficionados were equally indignant. Lowell Smith, then president of the Little Big Horn Associates, was quoted by the *New York Times* as calling the legislation "a bill of appeasement," and the newsletter of the LBHA filled with outraged letters.[55] Among the most irate were the surviving descendants of Custer himself, who regarded the name change as the product of—in the words of Brice C. Custer— a "National Guilt movement" that sought to expunge the Custer moniker as a way of making their ancestor a "sacrificial lion" (the title of Brice Custer's book) to appease its collective conscience.[56] After legislation changing the name of the battlefield passed through Congress and was signed by the president, Custerphiles continued to adopt this defensive position. In the decade that followed, they repeatedly charged that the park superintendents were friendlier to Indian viewpoints than to theirs— a charge that took on a new edge when two superintendents of Indian heritage—Barbara Booher (Cherokee and Northern Ute) and Gerard Baker (Mandan-Hidatsa)—were appointed in the 1990s.

In 1992, Russell Means returned to the renamed Little Bighorn National Monument, this time conducting a religious sun dance on non–Park Service land but near the road that connects the two noncontiguous portions of the Park Service battlefield. When Means claimed that the curiosity of tourists could disrupt the religious event, Booher acquiesced to his request to stop automobiles from driving to the more distant section of the battlefield (known as the Reno-Benteen hilltop).[57] Four years later, Baker allowed an "attack at dawn" ceremony to proceed, in which young Indian men proceeded to "count coup" (a warrior's action of striking the enemy to win honor) on the monument that marks the mass grave atop Last Stand Hill. The *Custer/Little Bighorn Battlefield Advocate,* a newsletter started in 1994 to respond to precisely these kinds of incidents, referred to the latter event as a "desecration" and called for an end to Baker's "racist regime."[58]

Though Custer aficionados have long considered Means their archnemesis, they have been more receptive to the proposal for a memorial to the Indians who fought in the Battle of the Little Bighorn. Unlike the name change, neither of the amateur historical societies devoted to Custer and the Little Bighorn (the LBHA and the Custer Battlefield Historical and Museum Association, or CBHMA) officially opposed the Indian Memorial, though the organizations' newsletters registered some objections ("What's next? Do we build a monument to the Japanese that died at Pearl Harbor and to the Mexicans that died at the Alamo?"),[59] and some members expressed concern that the new monument would be designed to overshadow the original obelisk honoring the Seventh Cavalry dead. The 1991 legislation authorizing the Indian Memorial (as well as the name change) created an advisory committee on its design and installation. However, the bill did not appropriate any money for this purpose, and fundraising efforts languished in the years that followed. Ten years later, the Park Service persuaded Congress to appropriate the necessary $2.3 million, and at least a few Custerphiles grumbled that federal tax dollars were being spent on a monument to those who were, at least in 1876, enemies of that same government.

The resulting memorial to those Native Americans who fought at Little

Figure 3. The obelisk marking the mass grave of Seventh Cavalry casualties was constructed at the top of Last Stand Hill in 1881. (Photograph by Michael A. Elliott.)

Bighorn seems almost deliberately designed to be the converse of the older one honoring Custer and those who fought with him. Like most monuments of its time, the 1881 marker (figure 3) rises from the highest prominence of land available; one walks around it to read the names of the dead and to see the land where they died. The Indian Memorial (figures 4 and 5) sits on the same ridge but at a slightly lower elevation. The main structure consists of circular earthworks that modestly rise from the landscape rather than standing at a right angle to it. Instead of walking up to or around the Indian Memorial, the visitor walks *into* it, where he or she is surrounded by panels of dark stone that memorialize the Indians who fought in the Battle of the Little Bighorn and their tribes: the Lakota Sioux, the Northern Cheyennes, and the Arapahos who battled the Seventh Cavalry, and the Arikaras and the Crows, whose members guided the cavalry. One can see the surrounding landscape, but only by looking through gaps in the circular structure of the memorial: in one direction, the visitor looks through a bronze wire sculpture portraying three mounted riders aided by a single woman on foot to see the valley adjacent to the battlefield, including the reservation town of Crow Agency. In the other direction, the visitor looks through a narrow "spirit gate" meant to let the

Figure 4. The approach paths to the Little Bighorn Indian Memorial, dedicated in 2003, lead inside an earthwork mound. The memorial opens up on one side so that visitors can see the surrounding landscape through a bronze wire sculpture. (Photograph by Michael A. Elliott.)

Figure 5. Inside the Indian Memorial, the visitor reads text and views images related to the Plains Indian tribes who fought at the Battle of the Little Bighorn. Through a "spirit gate," one can see the 1881 monument to the Seventh Cavalry dead. (Photograph by Michael A. Elliott.)

ghosts of the dead pass—which provides a striking view of Last Stand Hill and the 1881 monument on top of it.

One could easily use the contrast between the two monuments to draw facile conclusions about "Native" versus "Anglo" styles of memorialization—the first being rounded and harmonious with the land and the second angular and sitting in dominance on top of it. However, the differences between the two designs may have more to do with the aesthetic moments that produced them than with competing cultural idioms. The Last Stand memorial, like many others of the nineteenth century, shares the style of the Washington Monument, which was still under construction when the Battle of the Little Bighorn took place. The Indian Memorial more closely resembles a circular version of the Vietnam Wall, with brown stone instead of black. And like the Vietnam Wall, the Indian Memorial sparked controversies among the constituencies whom it was designed to serve. Some Indians from the tribes commemorated by the memorial complained that the Philadelphia design firm did not sufficiently represent Native interests; others were unhappy with the fact that the memorial honors those Indians who fought *with* the Seventh Cavalry as well as those who fought against them; and still others focused on particular elements of the design. The bronze *Spirit Warriors* sculpture designed by Lakota artist Colleen "Sister Wolf" Cutschall also drew attention because of the number of warriors (three, more significant in Christian traditions than in Indian ones) and because of supposed historical inaccuracies in the depiction of the warriors. In fact, a few tribal leaders publicly declared that they would not attend the dedication festivities.[60]

Those who did attend seemed less interested in the design of the memorial than in expressing their pleasure at the simple fact that so many tribal people had traveled to be together and that so many had a chance at a microphone, whether as part of the official program at the amphitheater behind the visitor center or at the open microphone inside the memorial itself. All of the Custer buffs with whom I spoke that day expressed pleasure as well, though their happiness had a different tenor. Many said they had feared that some or all of the Indians would charge Last Stand Hill to "count coup" on the older monument as had happened in the past, and they were relieved this history did not recur. Custer's advocates were not ready to see his opponents honored at the expense of those who had fought alongside him. Some also complained later that during the morning prayers and songs at the memorial, mounted Indians enforced a prohibition against photography with physical intimidation.[61] Yet these complaints faded as the day proceeded. Most of the non-Indian Little Bighorn enthusiasts with whom I spoke were plainly delighted that the battle they studied so carefully was receiving such lavish attention.

Like Means, speakers throughout the day repeatedly referenced the theme chosen for both the Indian Memorial and its dedication ceremonies: "Peace through Unity." Park Service materials, including signs placed near the memorial, emphasized that this slogan was chosen by two Indian elders, Austin Two Moons (Northern Cheyenne) and Enos Poor Bear Sr. (Oglala Lakota), both of whom had ancestors among the warriors at the Little Bighorn. As such mottoes usually are, "Peace through Unity" was uplifting enough to serve as a rallying point and general enough to prove inoffensive. In fact, if one were seeking to define the nature of the "unity" among those who attended the memorial dedication, one did not have to look hard, for everywhere one went, devotion to the contemporary United States—and particularly to the military defense of the nation—was on display. Scores of American Indian veterans, some in uniform, attended. An Oglala Lakota healer, George Amiotte, chanted morning prayers on the hilltop adjacent to the memorial wearing the four Purple Hearts and a Bronze Star that he earned in Vietnam pinned to traditional buckskins.[62] Soon after, Indian men and women from all branches of the service danced to a steady drumbeat among the throngs of horses and tourists. They wore their service uniforms and carried flags from veteran posts scattered throughout the reservations of the northern Plains.

These displays of allegiance to the United States military as part of the commemoration of those tribal peoples who engaged in military resistance *against* the United States were without irony. The dual patriotism of Indians—to their tribe and to the United States—who have fought in the U.S. military has been a crucial part of what it has meant to be an Indian in the twentieth, and now twenty-first, century.[63] For some, honoring veterans and valuing military service is a way of connecting contemporary tribal life to the practices of tribal warfare from an earlier time. Tribal leaders frequently point to the contributions of Indians to the U.S. forces in the two world wars, in Korea, and especially in Vietnam, as a way of demonstrating not only the bravery of their youth but also the sacrifices that they have made for the benefit of the United States as a whole. Only days before the dedication ceremony, I had heard a Crow man proudly state the exact number of young men and women from his reservation who were serving in Iraq and Afghanistan—a number that reflected a rate of military service much higher than in most American communities.[64] Seated among the honored guests at the formal memorial dedication ceremony was a living symbol of this patriotic tradition: the family of Private First Class Lori Piestewa, the Hopi Indian who had become, in Iraq, the first American Indian woman to die in combat while serving the U.S. armed forces. Under such circumstances, one could hardly be surprised that the Indian Memorial dedication ceremony opened with a Crow Indian woman singing a heartfelt rendition of Lee Greenwood's song "God Bless the U.S.A.," more colloquially known by its refrain: "I'm proud to be an American."

There was a time when such a demonstration of patriotic sentiment would itself have been a cause for celebration. From the late nineteenth to the early twentieth century, proponents of "Indian reform" believed that institutions such as boarding schools and missions could remake Indians from savage opponents to civilization into model citizens who were "Indian" in name only.[65] In the early twenty-first century, though, the old formulas of cultural assimilation no longer hold. For many at the Indian Memorial dedication, claiming allegiance to the United States was simply part of the way that they continued being Indian, even continued being people with tribal identities distinct from those of other Americans. At the same time, the songs, the flag waving, the proclamations of "Peace through Unity" kept generating an unanswered—and even unasked—question: peace from what? While the irony of proclaiming peace upon a historical battlefield is obvious enough to seem cliché, it is harder to explain why it should be necessary to declare "peace" at all on the hills of southern Montana in the first decade of the twenty-first century.

The desire for the kind of racial and historical reconciliation suggested by "Peace through Unity" has motivated an increase in the commemoration of the history of violence between whites and Native Americans, even if doing so, as Kenneth E. Foote points out, "flies in the face of an entrenched frontier mythology that celebrates the perseverance of white settlers in driving these cultures to extinction."[66] The construction of the Indian Memorial at the Little Bighorn is not an isolated example. As I will discuss in chapter 3, the U.S. Congress recently designated the Washita Battlefield—where Custer led the Seventh Cavalry in a winter attack against Black Kettle's Cheyenne and Arapaho village—a national historic site, and construction has begun on a new visitor center there. Even more dramatically, in 2000 Congress authorized the National Park Service to acquire land for a national historic site to preserve and interpret the 1864 Sand Creek Massacre perpetrated by Colorado militia against Cheyenne Indians (an encampment, like the one at Washita, under the leadership of Black Kettle). When the Sand Creek Massacre National Historic Site opened to the public in the summer of 2007, it became the only unit of the National Park Service to include the word *massacre* in its title.

Equally important, Washita and Sand Creek have been memorialized in order to articulate some measure of the losses suffered by American Indians during the nineteenth-century expansion of the United States.

The creation of these national historic sites has been aided by the post-Vietnam trend of memorializing defeat within the United States; the commemoration of the Vietnam War itself, and the soldiers who fought in it, is the most prominent example.[67] Indeed, in the case of both Washita and Sand Creek, the legislation authorizing the creation of the national historic sites makes particular provisions for the needs of contemporary descendants of the tribal peoples involved.[68] In other words, the United States has acknowledged and privileged those who were defeated in these armed conflicts. Of course, the practice of memorializing military loss is not new to the contemporary era. Most obviously, the "lost cause" of the South following the U.S. Civil War has inspired much commemoration since Reconstruction, and the Alamo was rehabilitated at the turn of the twentieth century as a way of articulating and solidifying a certain version of Texan identity, what Richard R. Flores calls "the Texas modern."[69]

In each of these instances, the public memory of defeat has served as a way of negotiating relationships among race, region, and nation. In particular, the memorialization of the Southern Confederacy and of the Texans' defeat at the Alamo has offered venues for the articulation of a white identity that claimed distinction from the larger United States, even as it considers itself to be a purer form of American patriotism. The 2004 film version of *The Alamo* produced by Disney's Touchstone Pictures registers this historical function of its subject by identifying the main characters as Texans and as U.S. citizens without acknowledging that the two forms of political affiliation were not precisely congruent in the historical moment being depicted. In the film, Sam Houston refuses to lead his troops into the field until his fellow white settlers "birth a nation" by drafting a constitution for the Republic of Texas, a constitution that creates a separate polity by declaring its independence from Mexico and simultaneously begins its incorporation into the United States. When Houston (played by Dennis Quaid) remarks that the defenders of the Alamo are fighting for the creation of "a government that can be legally recognized by all the nations of the world," the echoes of 1776 mean that the government in question seems to be both part of and independent from the United States.[70]

The multiple, competing forms of identification—racial, regional, national—that have been facilitated through sites of historical loss such as the Alamo suggest something of the symbolic power of defeat. As Wolfgang Schivelbusch has argued in *The Culture of Defeat,* the militarily vanquished can acquire an aura of moral authority that victors lack. "It is a short step from understanding defeat as an act of purification, humility, and sacrifice—a crucifixion of sorts—to laying claim to spiritual and moral leadership in world affairs," he writes.[71] Such claims are made possible by the malleable quality of defeat, which allows the defeated to imagine themselves through a set of contradictory but overlapping set of emotions: shame, incredulity, outrage, pride. Not only can the defeated eventually reinvent themselves as the future victors, Schivelbusch contends, but the victors can also appropriate the experience of the defeated as their own, as Northerners have often done in the United States. "The rest of the nation," he writes, offering examples from Ralph Waldo Emerson and Henry Adams, "was in fact capable of *indirectly* comprehending the experience of defeat through the metaphor of the South."[72]

Defeat has an even more elastic quality at the Little Bighorn. Indeed, the defeat of Custer at the Little Bighorn is the linchpin of the historical memory of the battle that has existed since 1876. If the Seventh Cavalry had been victorious over the combined forces of the Indian village—or even if the two sides had fought to a draw—it is unlikely that the Battle of the Little Bighorn would be regarded as anything more than one of many frontier clashes nearly forgotten by all except a handful of Western and military history specialists. Instead, Custer's spectacular defeat has enabled an uncritical veneration by generations of whites, for it has relieved them of the guilt that still accompanies memories of the colonization of American Indians. The power of Custer's defeat rests in its capacity to produce moral amelioration, to allow non-Indians and Indians alike to engage a military history whose moral, if not political, purpose has become suspect and discomfiting.

The articulation of defeat at the Little Bighorn has a second component as well, an almost reflexive judgment that has long been articulated by those who write and speak about the battle—that the Indians won this battle but lost the larger war. You can hear this pronouncement at the battlefield today from everyone from the Park Service interpretive staff to the narrators of the battle reenactments annually staged in the area to the historians who appear in television documentaries. Edward Godfrey knew the mantra in 1926: "The immediate result of that battle was a temporary victory of the red man's savagery; the ultimate result was . . . the triumph of the white man's civilization."[73] The speakers at the 2003 Indian Memorial dedication knew this formula as well. One tribal leader on the morning program even repeated it: "We won one battle but we lost the war."[74]

The Little Bighorn battlefield has become a place where the descendants of both sides can claim simultaneously the mantle of victory and the moral authority of defeat. The Lakotas, Cheyennes, and Arapahoes triumphed over Custer, but they also come to the battlefield to speak about the injustices of colonization; Custer enthusiasts and other non-Indians can celebrate the martial sacrifice of the Seventh Cavalry soldiers who died in the battle, and do so secure in the knowledge that the United States eventually prevailed in its efforts to consolidate its control over the northern Plains. The complexity and confusion that surround the claiming of victory (and defeat) at the Little Bighorn help to explain how Godfrey and Red Tomahawk could speak past one another in 1926, each of them from the high ground of victory. It also helps to explain how Russell Means could move from the inflexible position of the aggrieved in 1988 to the conciliatory posture he adopted in 2003, as well as other incongruent moments from the same ceremonies at the dedication of the Indian Memorial.

Consider, for instance, the historical anecdote offered by Secretary of the Interior Gale Norton during her remarks at the dedication ceremony. "Today's dedication," Norton told the crowd, "reminds me of a story that I've heard about Abraham Lincoln." After the conclusion of the Civil War, according to the story, Lincoln attended a celebration of jubilant Northerners where a military band played patriotic songs in triumph. Seeing Lincoln, the band leader asked the president to select a song. Norton finished the story: "The president paused for a few quiet moments. [Pause.] The crowd grew still. [Pause.] President Lincoln said, "Play 'Dixie.'" In those two words the president brought home the realization that we are one nation. . . . The battle we commemorate today was more recent; the conflict extended a far longer time. The wounds were immensely deep. This nation went for far too many years before anyone said the equivalent of President Lincoln's 'Play "Dixie."' Today's ceremony finally lets the healing songs begin at this place."

This historical incident is meant to exemplify the gracious victor's noble offer of the possibility of reconciliation to the beaten foe. What gets muddled in Norton's telling is the identity of the winners on the battlefield where she stood. As the defeated party at the Battle of the Little Bighorn, the United States (or its secretary of the interior) was not in the position to call for "healing songs" and order the band to play the Indian version of "Dixie," whatever that might be. By telling this story Norton had assumed the victor's prerogative of graciously extending a musical olive branch. Little Bighorn, by the logic of her story about Lincoln, is where Indians should be asking the bands to play the songs of the defeated party: "The Star-Spangled Banner," "America the Beautiful," "God Bless the U.S.A." That Natives did so during the dedication ceremony shows that they understood who had been triumphant on that battlefield.

Unless, of course, the application of the Lincoln anecdote is correct because the old formula, that the Indians were vanquished in a larger war of which the Little Bighorn was an isolated victory, holds as the governing rule of historical commemoration. To be sure, the formulation about the Indians' being defeated seems valid. Within a year of the battle, most of those Indians who had fought against the U.S. government were living on reservations—including Crazy Horse, who would be killed as he was being arrested in September 1877. By then, the sole holdouts on the northern Plains were in Canada, where Sitting Bull and his followers sought refuge. Sitting Bull returned to the United States in 1881 to surrender and made several trips to Midwestern and Eastern cities, most famously with Buffalo Bill's Wild West Show in 1885. However, he spent the better part of his final decade on the Standing Rock reservation, where he vied for prominence with other Sioux leaders and contested the authority of government agents.[75] Sitting Bull, too, would be slain in the course of an arrest; for him, death came at the hands of an Indian policeman in 1890, during the effort of the United States to suppress the practice of the Ghost Dance religion.

But the broader purpose of those Plains Indians battling the U.S. army at Little Bighorn and elsewhere in the 1870s was not simply to prevail militarily but to ensure a future for tribal communities. It is no exaggeration to say that in 1876 no white American—regardless of his or her position on the "Indian Question"—believed that American Indians would survive into the twenty-first century as American Indians, as people who continue to act in ways and act from convictions that they believe make them a part of a tribal community, make them Lakota or Cheyenne or Crow. Some whites thought that Indians would physically perish within the next generation. Others believed that assimilation held the possibility of physical survival and that future generations of Indians would biologically and culturally blend into the white American population until their Indian ancestry became nothing more than a curious relic.

Anyone at the Little Bighorn battlefield on the day of the dedication of the Indian Memorial would have realized that something different had occurred. Even Norton acknowledged in her speech that the United States "is a nation where today tribal sovereignty is recognized and respected"—a practically unthinkable sentiment for a U.S. official in Custer's time.[76] Up at the memorial itself, at the open microphone, speaker after speaker talked with optimism about the perseverance of tribal peoples and with hope about what the future might bring. They also talked about challenges of being Indian—the difficulties of maintaining cultural cohesion in the face of the problems that beset many reservation communities on the Plains, which remain some of the poorest communities in the United States. For them, the memorial was a testimony to their continued existence as tribal peoples and proof that their communities could become even stronger over time. Speaking at the Indian Memorial two years after its dedication, Ernest LaPointe, a descendant of Sitting Bull, expressed anger that a reporter covering the dedication ceremonies had compared the memorial to the Wailing Wall of Jerusalem (a term that, in fact, some Jews find derogatory as a name for the Western Wall). This was not a place for grief, he explained, but for pride.[77]

The complete outline of the variety of patriotism that has been articulated at the Little Bighorn battlefield includes the songs, symbols, and language of a consensus-driven U.S nationalism (putting "American first," as Means said), Norton's recognition of tribal sovereignty while simultaneously calling for "healing songs," and LaPointe's call for tribal peoples to further their existence as distinct nations. It is a patriotism rife with contradiction. With the strains of Manifest Destiny still lingering in the air, the Little Bighorn is a place where Indians have been cast as proto-Americans whose actions in that battle foreshadowed the kind of military service to the United States their descendants exhibited in the twentieth century. (Indeed, Indian men served the U.S. military in the nineteenth century, as the case of the scouts who rode with the Seventh Cavalry illustrates.) However, the Little Bighorn is also a place where Indians come to mark tribal nationalisms and to claim tribal self-determination and separation from the United States. The result is something more than a patriotism of dual citizenship that allows Indians to be loyal at once to the tribe and to the United States. Rather, I have come to think of the net sum of these possibilities as a kind of anti-national nationalism—or perhaps better called an anti-American Americanism—a patriotism that professes loyalty to the United States yet also remains deeply skeptical of the United States because of its history of colonization. This kind of patriotism allows Means to portray Indians as leading the charge into the melting pot and other tribal leaders to claim that Indians have led the charge into Iraq. But it also insists that Indian peoples have preserved the right to defend themselves as "Indian patriots"—and that this right will continue to be constitutive of their existence as tribal nations.

This kind of complex political sentiment is uncomfortable for most non-Indian observers, because it does not neatly fit into familiar categories. What was expressed during the dedication of the Indian Memorial was not a wholly anti-American separatism nor a patriotic allegiance to the United

States, but something in between. Moreover, this matrix of patriotic feeling does not include the kind of antistatist sentiment that has played a role in American nationalism since the colonists revolted against the British crown. Many of the American Indians who spoke during the Indian Memorial dedication were in fact official representatives of tribal governments whose presence and words called attention to the apparatus of tribal government; even those who were not called on tribal governments to do more, not less, to help their tribal communities.

These forms of thinking and feeling obviously emanate from the very specific histories of American Indian peoples who found themselves within the borders declared by the United States, histories in which Indians have been treated as both foreign and domestic subjects of the United States. At the same time, this configuration of conflicting patriotism—this anti-American Americanism—has also been influenced by two converging influences of the post-Vietnam era: first, the return of national patriotism as a response to the discordance of 1960s radicalism and to contemporary multiculturalism and, second, the critical reconsideration of the relationships among the United States and foreign peoples through colonization, empire, and even trade. In the case of the indigenous patriotism that I have been describing, a T-shirt that I have seen worn throughout Indian Country, including at the Little Bighorn battlefield, may best epitomize the complexity of this convergence. The shirt reproduces a nineteenth-century image of armed Apache warriors with the slogan "Homeland Security: Fighting Terrorism Since 1492." The combination of image and caption invokes the nineteenth-century anticolonial resistance to the United States as part of a long struggle to maintain tribal sovereignty while copying the wording and logic of the nationalist fervor that has gripped the United States since the 2001 attacks on the World Trade Center and the Pentagon. The creator of the original shirt, Matthew Tafoya (Navajo), reportedly designed it as an expression of unequivocal anti-Americanism; Indians who wave U.S. flags, he is quoted as saying, have been "brainwashed."[78] The language of the T-shirt, however, echoes expressions of post-9/11 U.S. patriotism so closely that it allows the wearer to participate in that national patriotism—to be outraged at the U.S. history of colonization while still supporting contemporary efforts to protect the United States from terrorism. The shirt echoes the contradictions of Means's calls for U.S. national unity and tribal sovereignty.

The Little Bighorn battlefield is the ideal place for a slogan such as this one, and not only because the conflict that was fought there was, indeed, a political one in which both sides believed that they were defending the "security" of their "homeland." Rather, this T-shirt suits the Little Bighorn battlefield so well because it is a place where the conflicting emotions generated by the history of the nineteenth-century Indian Wars have been nakedly on display since the battle was fought in 1876. The Indians who came to the dedication of the Indian Memorial in 2003, and who continue to come each year to the memorial on the battle's anniversary, extend a long tradition of coming back to the battlefield. Indians have returned to rearticulate the vision of military independence that the battle epitomizes, to recall the specific actions of the fighting that took place there, to consecrate friendship among the nations that fought there, to offer forgiveness to the men they fought against and their descendants, and to rededicate themselves to the hard struggle of cultivating their tribal communities. Many of those gestures are not consistent with one another, yet that inconsistency may be precisely why the battlefield remains so significant: it is a place where American Indians go to express the illogic of their histories, both personal and collective, of being colonial subjects in the United States.

The fraught connections between the nineteenth-century history of continental colonization and the twenty-first century practice of historical commemoration returns me to the horrific vision of Sherman Alexie's "Ghost Dance," where U.S. Cavalry zombies rise from the earth on the anniversary of the Battle of the Little Bighorn to continue the destruction that they wreaked in their own lifetime. Here, the continuation of the Indian Wars is by no means limited to the specific struggles of tribal nations for economic and political self-determination. Instead, the nineteenth-century pantribal Ghost Dance—which had at its core precisely that vision of tribal independence—is replaced by excessive, senseless carnage made comic through the idioms of pulp fiction and film. What I think Alexie's story renders correctly is the way that the history of the Indian Wars functions as a medium in the contemporary United States for something unmanageable, something that seems at first to be contained by our usual vocabulary of political sentiment—nationalism, racial chauvinism, nostalgia for imperialism—but that exceeds those terms, just as his own story begins in the generic mode of gothic horror and ends in a magical realist mode of enigmatic epiphany.

Yet Alexie's story also contains a critical misunderstanding of the Little Bighorn as a locus of these energies. With its cavalry rising from the graves at the taste of Indian blood, the story represents the ground of the battle as a site of repressed historical memory where the taboos of a violent past are contained only to come pouring out (or up) with the explosion of the dead from the earth. I would like to suggest that what makes Little Bighorn—both the physical battlefield and the battle itself as an event—such a compelling site of historical memory is that in fact this repression has never actually occurred. Rather, the confusion, confrontation, and struggle over the memory of the battle have always constituted an open, if evasive, conflict over the past, present, and future status of the United States as a colonial power and of American Indians as colonized peoples. The Little Bighorn is not where the ghosts of the past have been waiting to rise; it is where they travel above ground.

⟹⊷⊶⟸

Before returning to Custer himself, I will close this chapter with a final story from the dedication of the Indian Memorial. In the afternoon, I decided to take a break from the pomp and circumstance and walk up to the older monument, the granite memorial dedicated to the Seventh Cavalry on top of Last Stand Hill in 1881. By this point in the day, the crowds that had come for the dedication had begun to trickle away, and an increasing number of people at the battlefield were tourists who, as on any other summer day, had stopped for an hour or two on their way to Yellowstone, Mount Rushmore, or Glacier National Park; I was curious to see how they were faring. Unsurprisingly, the camera shutters were whirring by the monument, as tourists posed their families and looked down at the smaller markers placed on the slope of the hill to mark where the bodies of the soldiers had been recovered long ago. As I gazed with them, I overheard a conversation that had apparently been going on for some time between two men, one Indian and one white. The Indian had obviously participated in the morning ceremonies; his face was painted white except for a band of black that surrounded his eyes, like a mask, and he wore a long white blouse and leggings. The white man had a Southern drawl; he was from Little Rock, Arkansas, and wore a shirt indicating his membership in the Friends of the Little Bighorn, an organization that raises funds for battlefield preservation and volunteers to supplement the interpretive staff at the National Monument during the peak tourist season.

The Indian man, I later learned, was a thirty-three-year-old Oglala Lakota named Moses Brings Plenty, a descendant of the Brings Plenty who had fought on that same hill 127 years earlier. He was in the middle of a discussion of Custer's virtues and vices with the Friends volunteer—a debate, in fact, but a calm and reasonable one similar to those that have long passed back and forth between historians of the battle. (Moses Brings Plenty thought Custer himself was responsible for the bloodshed of Little

Bighorn; the volunteer thought the responsibility belonged to his superiors in the Grant administration.) Soon, though, their talk turned to the social and economic conditions facing American Indians today. What, the white volunteer wanted to know, was it like growing up on a reservation? How hard was it to find work? How did whites in the cities treat Indians? Brings Plenty was eager to talk about these things. In the same measured, patient tone that he had used to discuss the nineteenth century, he talked about his own difficulties in finding work, the racism he thought prevalent in the towns and cities near the Sioux reservations, and the anxieties he faced in raising his son. Soon he was not just talking to the single volunteer but to a small group of tourists—all, as far as I could tell, white—who were listening to the conversation and adding their own questions about Indian life. Brings Plenty often answered by connecting his own experiences to hopeful platitudes about the need for tolerance and harmony ("We are all climbing the mountain of life," he said at one point), and his audience was rapt.

Some combination of the occasion, his appearance, and the battlefield itself had licensed these tourists to put questions about Indian life to Brings Plenty that they either could not or would not have been able to ask in any other forum. Brings Plenty, I think, recognized this as an opportunity for real communication and even enjoyed the chance to speak his mind so forthrightly. For the moment, at least, Last Stand Hill became a place where the Indians talked and the whites listened.

A skeptic might ask whether a chance encounter at a tourist destination could really have a lasting effect on either party. But the fact remains that the Custer story has long been a medium through which non-Indians and Indians alike have expressed their conflicted feelings about the place of American Indians within the United States, both in its history and in its future. Brings Plenty and his interlocutors were simply extending that tradition further. Paradoxically, the place where Custer and his soldiers sought to make Indians disappear—by bringing them into the fold of the white mainstream or by killing those who resisted incorporation into the United States—became a place where Indians became visible to men and women who previously may not have had a straightforward conversation with a Native American person. For a time, the flesh and bones of living people, not only the ghosts of history, were dancing on Last Stand Hill.

2

BEING CUSTER

Monroe, Michigan

THE ICONOGRAPHY OF CUSTER AT THE BATTLE OF THE LITTLE BIGHORN derives from a collective desire on the part of white Americans to see their historical conquest of North America as a defensive, rather than offensive, history—a reaction to the threat of natural savagery compelled by the unstoppable machinery of progress instead of the result of calculated choices. How Custer's own death came to be fashioned as a mythic figuration of that process has been painstakingly analyzed by others, most notably by Richard Slotkin in *The Fatal Environment*.[1] The true emotional force of Custer's Last Stand, though, emanates from Custer's death and the afterlife of his image; the facts of his own biography seem almost superfluous to his posthumous fame. In a perverse way, the encounter of the Seventh Cavalry with the massive village on the Little Bighorn might be considered the final instance of the phenomenon that his biographers call "Custer's Luck": had Custer missed his chance at a glorious death in 1876, he would be regarded today simply one of the many colorful (and now obscure) military figures of his time. Given his success in the Civil War, he would probably receive slightly more historical interest than his peers in that last war against the Lakota Sioux—generals like George Crook, Nelson Miles, and Alfred Terry—but there would not be shelves groaning under the weight of Custer's name. Custer's demise, not the years that preceded it, is what gives his name its currency.

Yet the facts of Custer's life—his personality and his relentless self-fashioning—are significant to his posthumous status as an iconic figure in American history and to the creation of the Battle of the Little Bighorn as an ideological reservoir of American attitudes toward U.S.-Indian relations. The mere image of Custer surrounded by ferocious warriors on a dusty plain tells us little about the reasons that either side fought there. The historical Custer, on the other hand, can help us to understand why that image became so enduring. As the Nez Percé writer W. S. Penn explains in his essay "Feathering Custer," "It didn't take too long for him to be mythologized. But it was a real mythology in the sense that like the spherical accumulations of a pearl, at its center was the provocating grain of sand."[2] The difficulty of separating the pearl and the sand is especially acute in the case of Custer, who shared his nation's penchant for self-invention and who understood that the cultivation of personality could play a crucial role in a person's ability to lead. Custer loved the theater—his letters from New York and St. Louis brim with references to plays and actors—and he marked the various phases of his military career with new costumes that he thought fitting for the roles. Soldiering could be a grim profession, but he also treated it as a part to play. Small wonder that he should die in what would become a historical referent of one of the most important pastimes of the twentieth century—cowboys and Indians, a game played by children in backyards and adults on the silver screen.

Little evidence exists that Custer fantasized about participating in this game during his own childhood.[3] The son of a Midwestern farmer and blacksmith, he found in the profession of arms a chance to rise in a society that had its center in Eastern cities, not Western frontiers. The "metaphysics of Indian hating," to use Herman Melville's phrase, had nothing to do with his decision to pursue an appointment at West Point. Yet the significance of Custer's story—how a small-town military hero became the most famous Indian fighter in his nation's history—depends heavily on this absence of any kind of sustained animus toward Native peoples. Rather than a study in racial hatred, Custer provides an example of how a nation could simultaneously profess to love, even fantasize about, its indigenous peoples and refuse to believe that they would survive into the twentieth century. This chapter and the next revolve around those nineteenth-century fantasies and the ways they continue to shape the historical landscape of the twenty-first.

Custer rose to prominence in the Civil War by inhabiting a nineteenth-century version of manliness, a vision of military manhood that prized honor in a way recalling the aristocracy absent from American life. Later, he would adapt brilliantly to the frontier by embracing a different form of masculinity, one that emphasized the virility and potency of living on the frontier and having contact with indigenous peoples. The combination of these two models of nineteenth-century white manhood culminated spectacularly in the image of the Last Stand itself, in which Custer gallantly dies for the sake of his country at the hands of swarming Indians whose victory signifies the kind of primitive potency that he had once sought to draw upon. Even in death, being Custer was always a theatrical endeavor, and no one understood better than Custer how utterly serious a performance could be.

The film *They Died with Their Boots On*—still the best known cinematic portrayal of Custer's life—begins with Errol Flynn as plebe Custer, strutting into West Point in an outrageous costume. Wearing a dress uniform with gold braids and fur trim, a feather-festooned hat, and cavalier boots, Flynn's Custer is at first mistaken for a foreign general before the other cadets realize that he has grossly misunderstood his own importance.[4] Here, as in many other scenes, the film has strayed away from the historical record for dramatic effect. However, Flynn gets something essentially correct about the film's subject from the moment that he appears on the screen. As he prances and cavorts across the screen in tight-fitting trousers, tall boots, and carefully dressed locks, Flynn portrays a kind of masculinity that had long become antiquated by the time the film appeared in 1941. His dress and gestures capture Custer's excesses as he renders the mode of chivalric manliness to which Custer aspired. Flynn's Custer is as much dandy as cowboy, as much Merchant-Ivory as John Ford. As Custer grows into manhood over the course of the film, a thin, dapper mustache and trimmed, triangular goatee appear on Flynn's face. Both remain clipped and tidy through Flynn's heroic final moments at the Little Bighorn.

Flynn's buoyant, capering cavalier, idealistic and flamboyant, has a narrative ancestor in the first biography of Custer, Frederick Whittaker's *Complete Life of George Armstrong Custer* (1876). The London-born Whittaker served with distinction—rising from the rank of private to second lieutenant—in the Sixth New York Cavalry during the Civil War. The experience instilled in Whittaker a love for the cavalry and an admiration for Custer, who for a time had Whittaker's regiment under his command. After the war, Whittaker's writing career began in earnest; he would pen dozens of dime novels for the publishing house Beadle and Adams as well as a smaller number of novels with higher literary aspirations.[5] The Seventh Cavalry's demise at the Little Bighorn provided Whittaker with the opportunity to defend his beloved commander as well as to capitalize on the currency of Custer's death. The two-volume biography—643 pages in all—borrows heavily from Custer's own published memoirs and concludes with a testimonial from Lawrence Barrett, a popular actor whom Custer had befriended. After publishing the book, Whittaker continued to serve as Custer's posthumous advocate; he was a principal force behind the convening of a special court of inquiry in 1879 into the battlefield actions of Major Marcus Reno, whom Whittaker faulted for the Seventh Cavalry's defeat at Little Bighorn, as a way of shifting the blame away from the regiment's late commander.[6]

Whittaker's hagiographic *Complete Life* portrays a kind of rags-to-riches ascent from Custer's humble beginnings in the Midwest into his nation's pantheon of military heroes. The history of the Custer family, he writes in his first chapter, is the "record of a plain yeoman family, such as constitutes the bone and sinew of the country."[7] Though Whittaker's Custer does not come to West Point arrayed in Flynn's finery, he does possess a similar combination of courage and naiveté: "A tall, slender lad of seventeen, with frank, handsome face and fair hair, landed on the wharf at West Point, in the summer of 1857. A certain free, careless air told of the Western man, so different in his surroundings and bearing from the town-bred citizen of the East. It was our young hero, fresh from the independent merry life of the West, and plunged all alone into the peculiar life of West Point."[8] Custer's character, for Whittaker, starts with a kind of rural innocence that leaves his innate valor and idealism untainted by the trappings of the over-civilized city. In the *Complete Life*, Custer is a Westerner who first prevails over his peers, despite their advantages in education and social class, and then falls prey to the corrupt political machinations of the East. His real foes were never the Indians on the battlefield but the businessmen and politicians safely tucked away in their offices. *They Died with Their Boots On* amplifies this characterization further by fabricating a foil for Custer, Ned Sharp. Calculating and cowardly, Sharp rides on his father's coattails and ruthlessly pursues fortune, even to the point where he provokes the final war between the U.S. army and the Indians of the northern Plains. In this version, both soldiers and their Indian foes are the victims of a profit-driven society incapable of moral courage.

In its theme of the guileless (Mid-)Westerner taking on the sinister East, Whittaker's biography of Custer seems prescient. Custer is a kind of purer, less mysterious Gatsby. Even if Whittaker did not consciously anticipate the myths of self-making that would govern the twentieth century, he understood the appeal that Custer's biography would have for the generations that followed his. But the *Complete Life* also tells another kind of story about Custer's character, a story about a kind of masculinity that Whittaker deeply admires. As a boy, Whittaker writes, Custer displayed

a "strange compound of qualities": "He reminds us of one of Thackeray's schoolboys, full of vague poetical yearnings, tempered by the savage
freedom of overflowing physical strength and health, a boy all over, a boy
to the backbone, with the promise and potency of—who knows what? of
manhood. . . . Inside all the rough play of the champion wrestler of the
school, lay this hidden kernel of surpassing gentleness and love, that was
to make the foundation of the future knight."[9] This balance among physical toughness ("the rough play of the champion wrestler"), undisciplined
(or "savage") freedom, and civilizing, almost aristocratic virtue ("surpassing gentleness and love") is hardly unusual for the period in which Whittaker wrote. These were the qualities of a literary cavalier—from Sir Walter Scott and James Fenimore Cooper to the dime-novel vernacular that
Whittaker had already learned to speak. In such fiction, the unpolished
exterior of the male hero would be revealed by the narrative to be balanced
by an inner sense of refinement; in the case of Whittaker's characterization
of Custer, as the biography proceeds, the balance tips toward the latter.

Custer's "freedom," in other words, does not remain "savage" for very
long but becomes something else. Throughout the first half of the biography, Whittaker repeatedly remarks upon Custer's well-known sense of
style. At West Point, he writes, Custer's "bright locks gave him a girlish
appearance, which, coupled with the remarkable fact of his strictly tem-
perate habits [a debatable characterization of Custer's years as a cadet],
procured him the nickname of 'Fanny.'"[10] For a short time during the
Civil War, according to Whittaker, Custer neglected his grooming. "His
hair was beginning to grow long, and aided his careless dress to give him
a slouchy appearance, but even then there was something peculiar about
him that made people ask, 'Who is that young fellow?' It was not for more
than a year after that he came out as a dandy."[11] Finally, when Custer does
rise to the rank of general, Whittaker suggests that his appearance is in fact
a testament to his leadership abilities. "The boy general looked so pretty
and effeminate, so unlike the stern realities of war, that he was certain to
be quizzed and ridiculed unmercifully, unless he could compel the whole
army to respect him."[12]

One can draw a line from Whittaker's "pretty and effeminate" Custer
to the dashing attraction of Errol Flynn, but that is not my only point.
Rather, what interests me is the way that Custer's earliest mythologizer
emphasizes such genteel, almost explicitly feminine qualities—Custer's
careful attention to his appearance, his naiveté and innocence, his affectionate ties to others. Whittaker was not alone in describing Custer this
way. In an interview conducted shortly after the Battle of the Little Big-

horn, an officer who had served with him and with General Phil Sheridan in the Civil War described the latter as "always cool" while "Custer was always aflame." The officer continued: "He had a touch of romance about him, and when the war broke out he used to go about dressed like one of Byron's pirates in the Archipelago, with waving, shining locks, and a broad, flapping sombrero . . . but we all liked Custer and did not mind his little freaks . . . any more than we would have minded temper in a woman."[13]

Slotkin argues that such characterizations of Custer explain his emergence as a mythic figure because he embodied polar opposites, the masculine and the feminine.[14] I will suggest something slightly different. For someone such as Whittaker, the grooming, the prettiness, the gentleness did not make Custer "womanly" so much as identify him with a brand of manhood—the term *masculinity* would not become popular until after Custer's death—that was already becoming outdated in the 1870s.[15] In 1869, Thomas Bailey Aldrich had published *A Story of a Bad Boy,* a popular and influential novel that became the archetype for the "bad boy" books that flourished in the late nineteenth century. These books hit many of the same notes of Whittaker's Custer biography by emphasizing boyhood as a time of mischievous rebellion. Responding to concerns that American men were degenerating under the influence of sentimental women, the "bad boy" literature of postbellum America emphasized the reluctance of boys to be tamed by their mothers and teachers. "The Bad Boy writers," explains one scholar of the genre, "thus allow their male heroes to have limited contact with girls and women, but make clear that boys do not prefer such contact and will eventually escape feminine influence, even as they become men of culture."[16]

Consider how Mark Twain's *The Adventures of Tom Sawyer,* published the same year as the Battle of the Little Bighorn, reflects this emerging view of appropriate male comportment. While Twain's Tom Sawyer might share the love of "savage freedom" cherished by the young George Armstrong Custer, it seems impossible to imagine that the mischievous Tom—who spends the entire novel attempting to evade the disciplinary regime of his aunt Polly—would ever sport a "girlish appearance" or "c[o]me out as a dandy." (Twain would take this further in *The Adventures of Huckleberry Finn,* with an orphan protagonist who would rather "light out for the Territory" than submit to the influences of female-centered domesticity—implicitly choosing the company of Indians over the company of women.) By the early twentieth century, the dominant model for American manhood would be the rough-and-ready Teddy Roosevelt, not to mention the cowboy-aristocrat hero of Owen Wister's *Virginian*—both of whom would

later give way to the even rougher, more existential screen persona of John
Wayne.[17] Custer's sacrificial death at the Little Bighorn would play a role
after the fact in this history of American manhood during the turn of the
century, when figures like Roosevelt articulated how the military conquest
of nonwhite peoples could shore up white manhood. According to this
formulation, frontiersmen and their military descendants, like Custer's
cavalry, not only drew strength from the so-called primitive masculinity of
their foe but also secured the future of white civilization.[18]

Even though frontier heroes had been popular throughout the nineteenth century, this "rough rider" version of manhood, like Roosevelt's
actual Rough Riders, postdates Custer's life. Custer, instead, drew upon
a model of manliness that would become increasingly marginal after
his death, a model of the soldier as the courtly cavalier, the inheritor of
knightly virtue. It was a model that emphasized theatricality and performance as inherent to manly virtue and derived its cultural status from its
conscious evocation of the past. In a sense, it was deliberately anachronistic. From Whittaker's biography to Flynn's film and perhaps even to the
present, Custer evokes a way of being manly that is attractive because it
flaunts contemporary practice. Custer's masculinity was not only flamboyant but openly affectionate. Whittaker quotes, for instance, from Custer's
own writing about the departure of Southern cadets from West Point upon
the eve of the Civil War. "No school-girls," Custer wrote, "could have
been more demonstrative in their affectionate regard for each other than
were some of the cadets about to separate for the last time."[19] Custer, like
his contemporary Walt Whitman, viewed these relationships of male-male
camaraderie as both the products and the rewards of the mobilization of
tens of thousands of young men during the Civil War, which, despite its
terrible costs, offered a glimpse of a military society with its code of chivalry to a broad swath of Americans on both sides of the conflict.

A touchstone of Custerology, for instance, is Custer's battlefield rivalry
with Thomas L. Rosser. Custer and Rosser had been good friends at West
Point, and Rosser commanded Confederate cavalry as a general during
the Civil War. The two fought against one another several times during the
course of the war; at one point Custer rode to the front of his lines to salute
the distant Rosser. On another, Custer captured a wagon with a spare uniform belonging to Rosser; he then sent Rosser a letter asking him to direct
his tailor "to make the coat-tails of his uniform a little shorter"—so that
they might fit Custer better.[20] Years later, the two would meet again when
Rosser, as a civilian engineer, participated in an 1873 surveying expedition
along the Yellowstone River that Custer's Seventh Cavalry was assigned to

protect. Custer wrote to his wife that the two stayed up late into the night recounting their old battles. After the Battle of the Little Bighorn, Rosser wrote a letter to the *Chicago Tribune* praising his former foe and defending his actions during his final campaign.[21]

Custer's relationship with Rosser highlights much that Custer aficionados have found and still find attractive in him: his fierce loyalty to his friends, his sense of the military as a profession infused by male camaraderie, and his disinterest in the political ideologies that motivated the conflicts in which he participated. Indeed, the notion of the soldier as an apolitical professional seems crucial not only to the reception of Custer but also to military history writ large.[22] Custer's Civil War letters do not elaborate upon the justness of the Union's cause against the Confederacy. To the extent that Custer was concerned with wartime politics, the politics were the rising and falling fortunes of those generals whose fate might affect his own. Rather than celebrate the Union, his letters valorize the fighting itself. "Oh, could you but have seen some of the charges that were made!" he wrote to a female correspondent after a day of pitched battle. "While thinking of them I cannot but exclaim 'Glorious War!' "[23]

Custer's biographers, his contemporaries, and even Custer himself frequently used the phrase "Custer's Luck" in describing the circumstances of his rise from a second-lieutenant graduating in 1861 with the worst disciplinary and academic record in his West Point class to a decorated major general just four years later. Of course, any soldier who survived such a deadly conflict—especially one who put himself in harm's way as frequently and deliberately as Custer did—should be considered fortunate. But Custer's true fortune may have been in his being thrust into a time and place that called for his flair for the dramatic, for the extroverted gesture in the performance of duty. His early career is filled with feats of derring-do—manning a balloon on several occasions to spy on Confederate ranks, leading a charge across the Chickahominy River in May 1862 to conduct a dangerous daylight reconnaissance—that brought him to the attention of his superiors. In June 1863, General Alfred Pleasonton reorganized the Cavalry Corps and requested the appointment of three new brigadier generals, including George Armstrong Custer, who would command the Michigan Cavalry Brigade. The War Department confirmed his appointment on June 29; Custer was only twenty-three years old.

Custer's public career truly commenced at this moment. He was not, as he later bragged to his sister, "the youngest General in the U.S. army by over two years."[24] In fact, he was not, as is frequently claimed, the youngest person ever appointed to the general's rank.[25] Yet he acted the part of his new nickname, "the Boy General," and he sought to instill confidence in his troops. The Michigan Brigade was composed of four volunteer regiments, including the Fifth Michigan Cavalry, the regiment in which he had sought a colonelcy only weeks before. "At full strength," Gregory Urwin writes, "Custer's Michigan Cavalry Brigade was supposed to contain some 4,800 troopers, but there was probably not even half that number present and fit for duty" at the time that Custer assumed command.[26] Even with his brigade at half strength, Custer would be commanding thousands of men, many of who were older than he—and equally as or more seasoned by battle experience.

If Custer was daunted by this prospect, he refused to show it. Captain James Harvey Kidd later recalled his first meeting with his new general:

> Looking at him closely, this is what I saw: An officer superbly mounted who sat his charger as if to the manor born. Tall, lithe, active, muscular, straight as an Indian and as quick in his movements, he had the fair complexion of a school girl. He was clad in a suit of black velvet, elaborately trimmed with gold lace, which ran down the outer seams of his trousers, and almost covered the sleeves of his cavalry jacket. The wide collar of a blue navy shirt was turned down over the collar of his velvet jacket, and a necktie of brilliant crimson was tied in a graceful knot at the throat, the long ends falling carelessly in front. The double rows of buttons on his breast were arranged in groups of twos, indicating the rank of brigadier general. A soft, black hat with wide brim adorned with a gilt cord, and [a] rosette encircling a silver star, was worn turned down on one side giving him a rakish air. His golden hair fell in graceful luxuriance nearly or quite to his shoulders, and his upper lip was garnished with a blonde mustache. A sword and belt, gilt spurs and top boots completed his unique outfit.[27]

Much has been made of the uniform that Custer thought appropriate for leading the Michigan brigade. Whittaker thought he deliberately imitated the "splendor" of the Napoleonic cavalier Joachim Murat as a kind of "challenge to all the world to notice him."[28] In the 1934 *Glory-Hunter*, the unsympathetic Frederic Van DeWater noted that the "profusely embellished semi-brigand costume . . . could never be forgotten by a beholder" and called Custer "profusely asterisked and brass-bound."[29] The more recent Custer biographer Jeffry D. Wert—who reproduces the same passage from Kidd's memoir—wonders aloud at the history of this costume. How could Custer have procured it on such short notice? Did he have it ready and waiting? Regardless, Wert points out, Custer's dress testified to some long and serious consideration of how a commander should appear.[30] For at least some of Custer's contemporaries, the results were puzzling. One Union colonel pondered Custer in a letter to his family: "This officer is one of the funniest-looking beings you ever saw, and looks like a circus rider gone mad!"[31]

What made Custer's one-of-kind uniform truly remarkable, however, is that the reception it received—over time—was largely positive. Generals of his time could dress according to their own taste, and instead of being regard as a foppish, affected narcissism, Custer's self-presentation was regarded as admirable daring. It was as though Custer understood that his greatest asset as a leader was unbridled enthusiasm, and he decided to exaggerate this very feature to the point of excess. An older man—or one from a different background—could not have carried it off. "In the first place he was but a boy in years and feelings when the war commenced, and full of youthful extravagances," a Union officer would later write. "He had been brought up in a little Western country village and seen little or nothing of life until his graduation from the Military Academy simultaneously with the beginning of the war opened for him a career of wonderful brilliancy."[32] For those immersed in the Custer story, it can be easy to forget how foreign the idea of masculinity that he put forward seems from our contemporary vantage point. Our current notion of a military uniform, after all, is to make the individuals who wear it, well, uniform. Since the turn of the twentieth century, at least, it has been impossible to imagine an American general seeking to individuate himself by dressing à la Custer. (Douglas MacArthur, with his ivory cigarette holder clenched between his teeth, may have been the last to come close.) With Custer, bravery was reflected by a performed willingness to individuate oneself, to lead the ordinary by becoming an extraordinary man in every visible way. He aspired to be a kind of diva general.

By every account, Custer succeeded in inspiring his Michigan Brigade to match his own courage. At the Battle of Gettysburg, mere days after Custer assumed command, he led his troops in several charges that protected the flank of the Union forces from the attacks of J. E. B. Stuart's Confederate cavalry of "invincibles"—attacks that, had they succeeded, would have been disastrous to the Union cause. In each charge, Custer held his own saber aloft, pointed it at the enemy, and urged on his troops by invoking a mascot that had been adopted by Michiganders for decades: "Come on, you Wolverines!"[33] Custer's own report on the battle describes, for instance, the charge of one of the regiments he commanded advancing "to the attack of a force outnumbering them five to one." Custer continues describing the forces under his command:

Arriving within a few yards of the enemy's column, the charge was ordered, and with a yell that spread terror before them, the First Michigan cavalry, led by Colonel Town, rode upon the front rank of the enemy, sabring all who came within reach. For a moment, but only a moment, that long heavy column stood its ground; then, unable to withstand the impetuosity of our attack, it gave way in a disorderly rout, leaving vast numbers of dead and wounded in our possession. . . . I cannot find language to express my high appreciation of the gallantry and daring displayed by the officers and men of the First Michigan cavalry. They advanced to the charge of a vastly superior force with as much order and precision as if going upon parade; and I challenge the annals of warfare to produce a more brilliant or successful charge of cavalry than the one just recounted.[34]

"Impetuosity," "gallantry," "daring," "brilliant." This is the vision that Custer had for his cavalry. The bold, romantic language he uses in this report came from the same mindset that honed his personality at every turn.

If Custer's men doubted this hyperbolic assessment of their achievements, they never showed it. Not long after Gettysburg, the soldiers of the Michigan Brigade began wearing duplicates of Custer's scarlet necktie as a distinguishing symbol, "an emblem of bravado and challenge to combat," as a newspaper artist traveling with them put it.[35] James Harvey Kidd wrote to his parents less than a year after Custer had taken command: "For all that this Brigade has accomplished all praise is due to Gen Custer. So brave a man I never saw and as competent as brave. Under him a man is ashamed to be cowardly. Under him our men can achieve wonders."[36]

Custer and his men were among those who—fighting under Sheridan—gave the Union a cavalry equal to the Confederacy's. After Gettysburg, the Michigan Brigade engaged in a series of battles in upper Virginia and during the 1864 campaign gained renown as one of the most effective forces in the war. At Yellow Tavern, in May 1864, one of the brigade killed Stuart himself; a month later at Trevilian Station, an engagement Sheridan called "brilliant," Custer and his men found themselves surrounded by Rebels—only to manage to escape. As the brigade piled success upon success, Custer's picturesque dress and bold tactics made him a favorite of the Northern press. An illustration of him leading a cavalry charge graced the front page of *Harper's Weekly* (figure 6); the *New York Times* said he "displayed judgment worthy of Napoleon."[37] When Lincoln met the recently married Elizabeth Custer at the White House, he recognized her name immediately. "So," he said, taking her hand, "this is the young woman whose husband goes into a charge with a whoop and shout."[38]

HARPER'S WEEKLY.

JOURNAL OF CIVILIZATION

VOL. VIII.—No. 377.]   NEW YORK, SATURDAY, MARCH 19, 1864.   [$4.00 FOR FOUR MONTHS. $3.00 PER YEAR IN ADVANCE.

Entered according to Act of Congress, in the Year 1864 by Harper & Brothers, in the Clerk's Office of the District Court for the Southern District of New York.

BRIGADIER-GENERAL GEORGE A. CUSTER.—PHOTOGRAPHED BY BRADY.—[SEE PAGE 187.]

Figure 6. Custer leads the charge on the cover of *Harper's Weekly* in 1864.
(Reproduction courtesy of the Manuscript, Archives, and Rare
Book Library, Emory University.)

Custer's charges took their toll. Urwin, in his account of Custer's Civil War service, cites a statistic frequently mentioned by Custer aficionados: "Custer's Michigan Brigade sustained more casualties proportionately than any other comparable body of Union cavalry to do service in the Civil War."[39] The firsthand accounts give some of the details behind this claim. One of Kidd's official reports states that in the first ten minutes of fighting, "out of [the] 140 men I had engaged, 33 were killed or wounded; 12 were killed instantly, and 4 died before morning. The ground where the regiment fought was covered with rebel dead and wounded. The trees were riddled." For Kidd and his contemporaries, the carnage inflicted by and in Custer's Civil War cavalry was a point of regimental honor. "It is not boasting to say," the report continues, "that the gallantry displayed by the men of the Michigan brigade in this fight was extraordinary, unexampled."[40] One anonymous soldier, possibly from a Connecticut regiment who served alongside the Michiganders, even composed a poem to the "heroes of the Custer tie": "When the fierce charge the trumpets tell, / Their eyes flash fire, their bosoms swell. / With rifle cocked, and gleaming sword, / Like river through its cut bank poured, / Rush Custer's lads with deafening yell."[41] Of course, one does not have to look too hard in the history of the Civil War to find these kinds of glorifications of battlefield violence or even this kind of regimental pride. But the loyalty that Custer instilled in his men was unusual in tenor, particularly considering his age and lack of leadership experience prior to the war. In the Civil War battlefield, he had found an arena uniquely suited to what the nineteenth century would have called his "character." He was promoted in 1864 to command the entire Third Cavalry Division.

On April 8, 1865, after a long day of marching, Custer's division arrived at Appomattox Station, where three trains of supplies for Lee's Confederate army were waiting. As Custer's forces seized the trains, Lee's artillery began to open fire from their position a half-mile away. Rather than wait for reinforcements, Custer relied on his courage to carry the day and charged the Confederate positions. Albert Barnitz, an officer in the Second Ohio Cavalry at that time—and later an officer in Custer's Seventh Cavalry—would recall: "At this juncture, Custer came riding at full speed from the front and approaching the Second Ohio while he swung his drab-colored campaign sombrero, 'Here is the regiment I want. I want you to take that battery.'"[42] Another witness inspired to lyricism, Barnitz decided that what happened next was worthy of poetry; his "With Custer at Appomattox" runs more than eighty stanzas. Here are two:

Custer led!—with his flag unfurled!—
　　His breeze-blown standard of scarlet and blue,
Far-seen at the front when the fight waxed hot,
　　And the shells crashed loud, and the bullets flew!

Blithely he rode, and with dauntless air,
　　Girl-like, but resolute, into the fray,
With a luster of gold on his wind-tossed hair,
　　And jacket resplendent with bullion gay![43]

"Girl-like, but resolute," Custer captured two dozen cannons, two hundred wagons, and about one thousand prisoners.[44] The next morning, as he was preparing to attack once more, Custer received a white towel on a stick from the Confederate staff officer Major Robert Sims.

By that afternoon, Grant and Lee were signing terms of surrender in the farmhouse of Wilmer McLean. Sheridan paid McLean twenty dollars in gold for the table on which the documents were written and later presented it to Custer as a gift for his wife. "Permit me to say," Sheridan wrote in an accompanying note, "that there is scarcely an individual in our service who has contributed more to bring about this desirable result than your gallant husband."[45] By the night of April 9, the reconciliation of the North and South had begun. Custer later boasted that he invited seven Confederate officers, including several West Point friends, to spend that night with him in his tent.[46]

The Civil War was the crucible of Custer's age, and Custer participated in the entirety of its dramatic history, from the first Battle of Bull Run, where he arrived fresh from West Point, to the surrender at Appomattox. The narrative of the war itself, like his uniform, might have been custom-tailored to fit Custer. In the weeks after Appomattox, his rise from Midwestern cadet would become complete when he received the rank of major general of U.S. Volunteers; later, he would be awarded a "brevet"—or honorary—rank of major general in the regular army. Even before the conclusion of the Civil War, the *New York Tribune* took note of how the life of Custer seemed to cross over from reality to fantasy. "Future writers of fiction," it stated, "will find in Brig. Gen. Custer most of the qualities which go to make up a first-class hero[,] and stories of his daring will be told around many a hearth stone long after the old flag again kisses the breeze from Maine to the Gulf."[47] With his flamboyant dress and dramatic cavalry charges, Custer's Civil War career served as a living reminder of the military myths that could have easily disintegrated in the gross carnage of modern warfare; he represented a tradition of warfare in which the brave and honorable could rally their troops around the force of a personality and induce them to make the ultimate sacrifice for the sake of something as nebulous as "honor" or "glory." Custer's mode of chivalry, with his emphasis on camaraderie and his love of the West Point brotherhood, also had future utility: this set of values would provide a foundation for "the romance of reunion," with Union and Confederate veterans in the decades to come celebrating the valor and sacrifice of the Civil War by participating in historical amnesia about its divisive political matters, especially slavery.[48]

Custer's Civil War drama, though, would not be complete without a final curtain call. On May 23, 1865, he led his troops in the Grand Review of the Union army that marched through the nation's capital. Nearly forty years later, Helen Palmes Moss would write to Elizabeth Custer to tell her that she could not forget seeing on that day General Custer's "long, beautiful, flowing locks floating from beneath a broad brimmed sombrero, his commanding figure a sight to climax all that had gone before in my girlish imagination."[49] There would be more to remember. Perhaps startled by the onslaught of tossed bouquets or pained by the thorny rosebuds in an evergreen wreath—or perhaps urged by the general himself—Custer's horse reared and bounded wildly forward while his troops were marching. Before he could regain control of the horse, Custer crossed alone, as though he were a division of one, in front of the reviewing stand where President Andrew Johnson and General Ulysses S. Grant were seated. Bareheaded, his long hair blown back by the wind, the horse rearing high in the air, Custer drew his saber and saluted—becoming what the *Detroit Evening News* would call "a momentary vision," a fleeting, living memorial to his own fantastic story.[50] Truly, Errol Flynn could not have done any better.

<hr />

About two miles from the small, tidy town of Tecumseh, Michigan, a six-by-four-foot boulder sits between a two-story farmhouse and the low corrugated metal building of a sand and gravel contractor. There are no signs to direct a visitor here from the state highway that runs east and west through Tecumseh, and the town itself—less than an hour's drive southwest of Detroit—does not seem to be on any major thoroughfare. On the spring morning when I visited, two tiny American flags had been planted at the base of the rock. There was no sign of who had planted them, nor of who had affixed the small metallic plaque at the boulder's center, which bears a pair of crossed swords and the following text:

DON JUAN

THOROUGHBRED
1853–1866
DON JUAN WAS THE MOUNT OF OWNER

GEN. GEO. A. CUSTER

IN THE MAY 1865
WASHINGTON
GRAND REVIEW

The grave of Custer's horse may be only a minor feature in the historical landscape of Custerology, but the story of Custer's ride on Don Juan in the Civil War Grand Review is the kind of incident that has divided Custerphiles and Custerphobes for over a hundred years. For the former, the incident shows not only Custer's grace under pressure but also his understanding of how a dramatic gesture is occasionally the appropriate one in military life. Even some of his supporters think that in spite of his insistence that it was accidental, Custer deliberately staged the incident. How else could a master horseman riding a favorite mount have lost control? For Custer's detractors, Don Juan's dash represents the kind of reckless egotism that would lead him to make a series of foolhardy decisions eleven years later at the Little Bighorn. "The whole man with his flaws and his flairs is epitomized in that dash," declares the most scathing Custer biography. "He has been, he will be, prone to spectacular outbursts against ordered regularity; insurgent in his hunt for Glory. That runaway is at once his biography and his epitaph."[51]

Such "spectacular outbursts" are what have made Custer's anecdote-studded biography so appealing to the American imagination. In particular, this incident encapsulates the version of Custer that the people in this corner of southeastern Michigan like to remember: not Custer the Indian fighter eventually defeated in the hinterlands of the West but Custer the precocious, sometimes brilliant Civil War general leading Michigan's young men to victory—the Custer who chose, at some level, to be rooted in Michigan by marrying one of its young women, Elizabeth Bacon. The Civil War Custer evokes a kind of martial fantasy of flamboyant gallantry, of loyalty and camaraderie, and of recognition for personal courage. The seduction of the fantasy is in the promise of reward and honor for apolitical virtue; the attraction of the story emanates from a nostalgic desire for honor as an aristocratic value represented by Custer's particular dress — the oxymoronic nonuniform uniform—and treats military actions as separate from their political goals. In the post-Vietnam United States, where Americans regularly distinguish between the act of supporting U.S. troops in combat and the act of passing judgment on the policies that led them there, this version of military heroism remains compelling.

The Civil War career of George Armstrong Custer—a career that acted out this kind of heroism—seems less morally complicated than his later warfare against the Plains Indians, so much so that it would be easy to separate them entirely. Yet Indians never completely disappear from the cultural landscape of Custer's America, even Custer's Civil War America. After paying homage to Don Juan's grave, I turned back onto the state highway and stopped at a busy McDonald's for coffee and directions. The interior of the fast-food restaurant was decorated with large, bright oil canvases painted by a local artist, depicting the life of the Shawnee Indian for whom the town is named. In the early nineteenth century, Tecumseh— together with his brother, a man named Tenskwatawa but more often simply called the Prophet—organized a widespread alliance among Indians living in the Ohio River valley and near the Great Lakes. A combination of organized political resistance and spiritual revival, this alliance openly opposed the expanding presence of white Americans in the region to the point that Tecumseh and many of his followers fought on the side of the British in the War of 1812. Custer, of course, was not around to fight with those Americans who battled Tecumseh or any of the Indian allies of the British, but he did actively seek to honor the memories of those who fought for the United States in that war. For instance, he performed the highly ceremonial task of reading the roll of names at a "grand reunion" of the war's veterans in 1872.[52] There is some small oddity in the burial of one of Custer's mounts in a town named for a leader who fiercely fought against the same nation for which Custer so vigorously campaigned. Anyone traveling through Custer country, though, becomes quickly accustomed to this kind of ironic juxtaposition; it is as easy to ignore as Don Juan's grave itself, sitting back from the road among the trees, unobtrusively waiting for the next devotee of history to pay a visit.

Thirty miles east, and slightly south, of Tecumseh stands the city of Monroe, the home of La-Z-Boy, 1988 Miss America winner Kay Lani Rafko, and—for a portion of his life—George Armstrong Custer. Custer first came to Monroe at the age of ten to live with his married half-sister, Lydia Reed, and to attend a school better than those that could be found near his birthplace of New Rumley, Ohio. Throughout his adolescence,

Custer would shuttle between New Rumley and Monroe, and Monroe truly became his adopted hometown during the Civil War, when he used his leaves of absence to return there and became a recognizable fixture in Monroe society. More specifically, he used his leaves of absence to become a fixture in the life of Elizabeth Bacon, a Monroe native whose father, a probate judge and successful businessman, was one of its leading citizens. George and Elizabeth—known to friends and family as Autie (for Armstrong) and Libbie—were married in Monroe in February 1864, after Custer had won his general's star but before his portrait had been splashed across the pages of *Harper's Weekly*. The Custers lived in Monroe for the next twelve years during those periods when George was not posted to active duty; for George, Monroe was as much of a permanent home as an officer in the frontier military could have.[53]

Today, Monroe, the county seat of Monroe County, has a population of about twenty-two thousand. While the city flag proudly proclaims it to be "Michigan's only Port on Lake Erie," one sees little evidence in the town itself of the shipping that was once the center of its economic activities. The county chamber of commerce names Visteon (an automotive supplier that was once part of Ford) and North Star Steel as being among the top employers. Edward Knabusch and Edwin Shoemaker created their famous upholstered recliner here, and although its furniture is now manufactured elsewhere, La-Z-Boy still maintains its corporate headquarters in Monroe. Monroe Auto Parts, now part of a larger company named Tenneco, has also continued some of its operations in the county. While no community in the region was untouched by the rust belt exodus of the 1970s and 1980s, Monroe and the surrounding area seems to have been spared the wholesale devastation suffered by many Midwestern towns of its size. Two-story homes with porches from the early twentieth—or even the nineteenth—century evidence a long history of caretaking, but on a modest scale. Except for a few of the grander Italianate and Greek revival houses on Elm Street, near the river that bisects the town, there is little by way of visible opulence, either ascending or declining. Monroe is not a boom-or-bust town. The county offices downtown generate a steady stream of traffic and a steady base of customers for the small restaurants; the new marquee on the converted movie theater that hosted the premiere of *They Died with Their Boots On* announces its transformation into an "arts centre"; and the town has taken pains to develop the parkland near the lazy, winding River Raisin—first named River aux Raisin by French fur traders for the dried grapes they found growing along it—into a riverfront area attractive enough to draw about seventy-five hundred people to a summer jazz festival.

Near the riverfront rides Custer himself, memorialized in a bronze statue that faces those crossing the main bridge into downtown Monroe like a sentinel poised to meet an invasion. The statue, *Sighting the Enemy*, depicts the Boy General at Gettysburg, mounted and readying for the charge. Unveiled in 1910 by Elizabeth Custer, President Taft, and a host of other luminaries, the 34-foot-high, 7,500-pound statue has its own history of conflict. In the immediate aftermath of the Battle of Little Bighorn, the Democratic *New York Herald*—which proclaimed Custer a martyr to the failings of Grant's Republican administration—raised money for a Custer statue to be placed at West Point. Because the fundraising drive quickly lost momentum, the final product was not ready for installation until 1879. However, the statue committee had made a crucial error by failing to consult Elizabeth Custer throughout the process of selecting a sculptor, a model, and a pose. She was furious and refused to attend the unveiling. Though she never saw this first statue in person, the complaints of others about its likeness and its pose—"no soldier every held a sword and pistol in that way"—added to her initial sense of indignation. Soon after, she heard of a congressman's proposal to duplicate the West Point statue in Washington, D.C., and her outrage returned: "My blood boils at the thought of that wretched statue being repeated," she wrote in a letter. "Years of life in public and efforts at suppression have failed to quell my temperament and I get frantic at the very thought of this act." This time, Libbie Custer won the day, and the bill authorizing funds for the statue's reproduction failed.[34]

With the help of General Sherman, who advised her to demand the "*sole* and *exclusive* right to mark the grave of your husband," Libbie also succeeded in having the West Point statue removed.[35] When, more than twenty years later, groups in Michigan began to lobby the state legislature for funds for a Custer statue to honor his leadership of the Michigan Cavalry Brigade, they took pains to involve the widow Custer at every step. Her preference for Monroe over the state capital, Lansing, was enough to ensure that it would be located in her hometown, and she approved the winning proposal for the equestrian statue. During the festivities that accompanied the unveiling, Libbie reveled in the adulation paid to her late husband and nearly exhausted herself receiving the well wishes of Monroe citizens and veterans who had come to honor a soldier of their army. Her success, though, would not be permanent. When Libbie Custer unveiled the statue, it stood in Loranger Square, a central location shared by the county courthouse and First Presbyterian Church, where she and George were married. By 1923, the rise of automobile traffic led many in Monroe to judge the statue improperly placed. A drunken driver collided with it—and then told others that he saw a man on horseback riding into the car's path. Elizabeth wrote to her hometown to protest any relocation of the statue, but this time she would not prevail, and it was moved to an inconspicuous, almost hidden location in a rarely visited park. Local Custer aficionados like to relate how Libbie kept her vow not to return to Monroe once the town had flagrantly ignored her wishes.[56]

Enter Lawrence A. Frost. Born in 1907, Frost moved to Monroe in 1929 to start his career as a podiatrist. Soon he became friends with the remaining Custer family living in Monroe, especially Brice C. W. Custer, George Armstrong's great-grandnephew. Frost collected unusual footwear, and in 1939 Brice Custer gave him a pair of the general's boots—a pair, in fact, with a bullet hole from Custer's only Civil War wound, inflicted at the Culpepper Court House, Virginia, in 1863. Those boots started Frost's infatuation with Custerphilia, which would last until his death in 1990. He amassed thousands of Custer-related books and articles and, through his relationship with the Custer family, a collection of original telegrams, letters, military orders, and even photo albums that had belonged to George and Libbie. In 1950, he donated a small part of his collection to establish a Custer collection at the county library, and in 1967 he played a crucial role in founding the Little Big Horn Associates. By the time of his death, he had written twelve books on his hero, ranging from general treatments—*The Custer Album* (1964) and *General Custer's Libbie* (1976)—to studies of more obscure subjects, such as *General Custer's Thoroughbreds* (1985) and *General Custer's Photographers* (1986).[57]

By the final decades of his life, Frost had become a sainted figure in the community of amateur and even professional historians sharing his interest in Custer, a community to which we will return in chapter 4. The stories of Frost's generosity with his time—regularly giving tours of Custer-related sights to Monroe visitors—and his collection of Custeriana are legion, and they cast Frost as a kind of Custer prophet eagerly receiving new disciples into the fold. In fact, such stories trace a line of devotional descent from Elizabeth Custer and the Custer family to Frost and into the present. In a collection of remembrances published on the occasion of Frost's death, Thomas E. Bookwalter observed that Frost's efforts as a Custer defender "have taken Mrs. Custer's work even further than she had and have 'institutionalized' the preservation of the Custer story. . . . He completed the work Mrs. Custer began."[58]

That work included honoring Elizabeth Bacon Custer's original vision for the statue of her husband. While the statue could not be returned to

Loranger Square, Frost spearheaded an effort in the 1950s to relocate the statue to its present, highly visible location adjacent to the main bridge leading into the central business district. Custer's two living grandnephews attended the 1955 rededication and voiced their pleasure at seeing their ancestor restored to public prominence. According to Frost's own account, Charles Custer, then a colonel in the U.S. army, told the assembled crowd, "The City of Monroe today keeps faith with the devoted wife and widow of General Custer."[59] The "faith" seems to be still largely intact. Signs marking the city limits proclaim Monroe to be "Home of Gen. Custer," the city holds a Custer Days celebration each fall—recently expanded to an entire Custer Week—and the offices of the Monroe County Tourism Bureau even sell "Custer bars" of chocolate. The once-neglected statue has been kept clean, aided, perhaps, by the thorny hedges planted around it to discourage local youths from spray-painting the horse's genitals — a ritual prank at one time.[60]

The difficulty of having Custer as a kind of town historical mascot, of course, is his close association with the effort of the United States to use military force to dispossess Plains Indians of the lands they claimed. The very history that has made Custer so well known, in other words, has made him a suspect symbol in our postcolonial age. Monroe has responded to this dilemma by emphasizing Custer's Civil War career and his ties to the town through Elizabeth. In Monroe, Custer is not an Indian fighter as much as a victor on the fields of both battle and romance. *Sighting the Enemy*, after all, represents Custer at Gettysburg, not on the Plains, and when the statue was originally installed it was positioned to face south, not west.

Untangling the memory of George Armstrong Custer from the larger conflict between American Indians and Europeans is an endeavor fraught with difficulty, not only because Custer remains best known to the American public as an Indian fighter but also because it is impossible to ignore the presence of American Indians in the history of nearly any location in the United States. Monroe could hardly be considered a place that is known for its indigenous presence; in the 2000 census only 405 of the 145,945 residents of Monroe county identified themselves as belonging to the "American Indian or Alaska Native" category.[61] But American Indians do figure in Monroe's local-historical narratives—the stories the place tells about its own history. In its current location, the Custer statue *Sighting the Enemy* no longer faces south but north, directly toward a corner occupied by another historical marker, a sign explaining that the corner that Custer faces was the site of a U.S. fortification destroyed by the British and their

Indian allies in the War of 1812. Such a marker is hardly a major symbol of Native American presence; rather, it is one of the small ways that the human geography of the town, what one might call the cultural landscape of Monroe, registers that presence, and even registers a history of active Indian resistance to European colonialism.

Monroe's involvement with the military conflict between the United States and the Indians of North American is memorialized more overtly only a few miles from the Custer statue, at the River Raisin battlefield. In January 1813, about six hundred warriors from several Indian tribes, led by a Wyondot war chief named Roundhead, joined by British soldiers, attacked U.S. troops (mostly Kentuckians) at the Battle of the River Raisin. The British commander, Colonel Henry Procter, persuaded the Americans to surrender by promising that they would be treated as prisoners of war. Procter immediately took those Americans who could travel north to Detroit and left between thirty and sixty Americans under a guard of Indians that included Potawatomis. The night after Procter left, a group of the Indian guards slaughtered their prisoners in revenge for the battle deaths of their compatriots. The episode quickly became known throughout the frontier as the "River Raisin massacre," and "Remember the Raisin" became a rallying cry of American soldiers throughout the remainder of the war.[62] Monroe County continues to preserve the land where the violence occurred and administers a small battlefield museum.

Even in Monroe, far from Custer's dramatic achievements and failures, the image of Custer is necessarily juxtaposed to the memorialization of a conflict between colonial powers in which indigenous peoples fought against the United States. My point is not that Custer's actions in the American West were the result of his being surrounded by the history of earlier battles—although this history would have been palpable in his Ohio birthplace as well—but that it is impossible even in this small Midwestern city to participate in historical remembrance without somehow engaging the lives of American Indians. As much as a place like Monroe might wish to forget the controversies of Custer's Indian fighting, it cannot help recalling the larger history of North American colonialism, of which Custer's actions on the Plains were a part. To put it another way: In Monroe, like so many other places in the United States, Indians seem to be both nowhere and everywhere. The town would prefer to remember conflicts in which the United States emerges as a consolidated nation—the War of 1812, the Civil War—without preserving the memory of the dispossession of Native peoples that took place throughout what is now the United States. Indians, though, keep resurfacing. In fact, this became literally (if morbidly) true in the early 1990s, when the construction of a fountain in the town square, the same square where the Custer statue originally stood, unearthed American Indian bones. What happened next illustrates how even the most circumspect treatment of Native American history can also render that history invisible. The county halted construction, consulted the state commission on Indian affairs, and reburied the human remains in strict adherence to the tribal customs of the Potawatomi Indians.[63] Several Monroe citizens have told me this story, and each expressed pride in the way the episode demonstrates a careful regard and respect for Indians on the part of the Monroe community. However, the town square has no marker or sign to commemorate the remains that were once buried there or the Native settlement that the remains may indicate. The excavation of the bones inadvertently unearthed a history of Indians in the site of the town's center, but that history has been safely returned to the ground— buried, literally and figuratively.

Such episodes illustrate how American communities can simultaneously claim as forebears the Native Americans who occupied their land while distancing themselves from the history of often-violent dispossession that took place throughout North America. In Monroe, these contradictory implications may be most visible in the County Historical Museum, a place that, according to its former director Matthew Switlick, has become a kind of "pilgrimage" site for Custer aficionados.[64] Even the property on which the museum is located has historical ties to Custer. The home of Elizabeth Bacon, her father, and then her new husband stood on this land until it was moved to another location in the early twentieth century. As a young girl, Libbie could look onto the city's main thoroughfare, and a romantic, probably apocryphal story has the seven-year-old girl yelling out from the yard to the passing ten-year-old George, "Hello, you Custer boy!"—and then running back into the house, thrilled and mortified by her own audacity.[65] A more likely story has Libbie and her father some thirteen years later witnessing Custer, during a leave from the Civil War, weaving his way up the street under the effects of his last drunken spree. The next morning, Custer's sister Lydia begged him to take the temperance pledge, and not even his most virulent detractors have suggested that he ever broke it. But Libbie would remember what she saw when she was formally introduced to him a year later, and George had to overcome her recollection—as well as her father's worries about marriage to a military man—before his courtship was successful.[66]

A post office building replaced the Bacon home in the early twentieth century, and it was renovated in the early 1970s to house the museum. A

Custer exhibit, advertised on signs throughout town, takes up nearly a third of the display space and is clearly the museum's biggest draw. But Switlick understands that Custer can provoke a passionate negative response, and suggests that the museum has tried to defuse any anger in the way that it approaches Monroe's best-known resident. "We try to portray Custer as a Midwestern phenomenon," he says, explaining that the museum emphasizes the life of Elizabeth Bacon Custer as well as the military service of Custer's descendants. After all, he points out, both Elizabeth and the twentieth-century Custers spent more time in Monroe than George ever did. Moreover, Switlick says, the museum has made a conscious decision to treat Custer's career as an Indian fighter with circumspection. "We are a local museum," he states. "We don't have the resources to debate all of Western history." [67]

Despite Switlick's modesty, the museum's collection of material objects from the lives of Libbie and, especially, George Custer is impressive. Museum patrons can see mementos of the couple's early youth (the gown he wore as a baby and the doll cradle she rocked as a child), a guidon carried by the Michigan Brigade, and relics from Lee's surrender at Appomattox, including a swatch from the red tie that Custer wore there. The museum has several personal items (a lock of golden hair sent to Libbie, for instance) and even products of the general's interest in hunting and taxidermy, such as an elk's head believed to have been stuffed and mounted by Custer himself. It has reproduced Custer's office at Fort Lincoln, his last post, complete with more stuffed heads mounted over the desk and books from his library on top of it. When the National Park Service replaced the marble markers on Last Stand Hill at the Little Bighorn, the museum was able to acquire those that marked the places where the bodies of the Custers fell—George, his brothers Thomas and Boston, his nephew Autie Reed, his brother-in-law James Calhoun—and they are placed in the exhibit in front of a painting depicting the battlefield.

No matter how little knowledge one brings to this exhibit, one can walk away with a solid grasp of the outlines of Custer's life: Midwestern youth to West Point to Civil War to marriage to the Plains to Little Bighorn and to death. Furthermore, the exhibit continues beyond the marble memorials to give the patron a glimpse into his posthumous reputation. A large case is devoted to Libbie's long widowhood and her dedication of the Monroe statue. (The museum tactfully omits any reference to the West Point statue she despised.) And the final display of the exhibit takes Custer's legacy even further by documenting the military service of two of his grandnephews, Charles A. Custer and Brice C. W. Custer, both of whom retired as colonels from the U.S. army after having accumulated distinguished records of service in World War II and, in the case of Brice, Korea.

Approaching Custer "as a Midwestern phenomenon," as Switlick puts it, though, also means leaving some things out. I looked at the exhibits placed between the reproduction of Custer's Fort Lincoln desk and the memorial stones of Last Stand Hill, searching for the museum's discussions of forces that led to Custer's 1876 campaign against the Sioux and Northern Cheyenne, but I could not find any. There is a five-minute video that describes the actual military strategy of the campaign and the movements of Custer's Seventh Cavalry at Little Big Horn; there is a copy of the famous Cassily Adams–Otto Becker lithograph *Custer's Last Fight* that Anheuser-Busch placed in nearly every barroom in turn-of-the-century America; and there is a diorama of tiny sculpted figurines battling an invisible foe atop Last Stand Hill. But the museum does not discuss the reasons that the cavalry and the Indians were fighting there.

Of course, questions about the purpose and motivations of the U.S. army's campaigns against American Indians in the post–Civil War era are among the most volatile in the United States' collective reckoning with its national past. It is hard to blame any museum—particularly one with limited funds and space in Custer's former home—for wanting to avoid such controversy. The drawback to this approach is that it leaves the museum patron feeling as though some crucial piece has been left out from the puzzle. It is one thing to learn what kind of uniform Custer wore, another to learn that he kept the speeches of Abraham Lincoln and Henry Clay in his library, and still another to see the black dress that his widow wore, but none of these experiences help someone to understand *why* Custer was killed. Without that explanation, the final, climactic moments of his life—the reason that Custer has become such a central figure in the first place—become vague and distant, like an old joke or a fairy tale that no one tells any more because it has grown hoary. Instead of tackling the complexities of Custer's demise, the museum puts forward the aging Becker-Adams print—not to encourage patrons to believe in the mythic hero at its center but rather to remind them that the history of the Little Bighorn has been repeated too many times to require a new iteration.

What disappears, most obviously, when one treats Custer as a "Midwestern phenomenon" are the Indians who killed him—and their reasons for doing so. The exhibit case that includes the Last Stand diorama does not include, for instance, portraits of the Indian leaders whom Custer fought against, maps of the lands that the U.S. forces sought to occupy, or even the accounts of American Indian depredations against white settlers that were used to justify the military campaign against them. Rather than justify or damn the actions of the U.S. cavalry, the museum sidesteps judgment by such a wide margin that it avoids giving the impression that there might even be a judgment to be made.

Curiously, at the very place in the exhibit where one might expect some kind of explanation or account of Indian resistance to the U.S. military, the museum gives its patrons something that almost represents Indians without quite doing so. Below and to the left of the Last Stand figurines are a series of Indian-made objects that Custer acquired during his Western travels: a peace pipe found among his possessions and a buckskin vest and trousers decorated with porcupine quills that Custer sent to the mayor of Detroit for the collection of the Audubon club there. And above the vest, between the front page of the *Monroe Commercial* announcing Custer's death and a copy of the written orders Custer received before marching to his death, is a white placard about eight inches wide and ten inches long. The placard reproduces a well-known photograph of Custer in fringed buckskins and a brimless fur hat. He is holding a rifle and posing in front of photographer's scenery devised to represent the wilds of the West. Having traded in his black velvet for buckskin, his oiled curls for a beard, the frontier Custer revises his persona of knightly honor for a hostile, virile landscape. The photo, apparently, was selected by someone as an appropriate illustration to accompany an oft-cited quotation from Custer's 1874 memoir, *My Life on the Plains:* "If I were an Indian, I often think I would greatly prefer to cast my lot among those of my people adhered to the free open plains rather than submit to the confined limits of a reservation, there to be the recipient of the blessed benefits of civilization, with its vices thrown in without stint or measure."[68]

I suspect that this quotation appears here to counter the charge—reinforced often by popular culture—that Custer bore some deep-seated malevolence toward Indians. Yet placing this passage so close to the artifacts related to Little Bighorn also makes Custer seem almost absurd—for he fought and died in the service of his country's efforts to extinguish the very independence that he so earnestly claims here to admire. The collected artifacts, photograph, and memoir quotation come as close as anything in the Custer exhibit to registering an Indian presence by making legible the contradictions of the attitudes that he shared with many of his contemporaries.

For Custer supporters, the seeming gap between Custer's professed approbation for the Indian life of the "free open plains" and his participation in military campaigns aimed at foreclosing that way contributes to the Last Stand an aura of tragic irony. Custer, they claim, respected the way of life practiced by tribal peoples away from the reservations, but he understood that the time for this manner of living was coming to a close. The paragraph from Custer's memoir quoted by the museum exhibition continues by describing "civilization" as an "insatiable monster" devouring Indian land; the Indian "must yield, or like the car of Juggernaut, it [civilization] will roll mercilessly over him, destroying as it advances. Destiny seems to have so willed it, and the world looks on and nods its approval."[69] Custer participated in the realization of this destiny, he believed, even though he understood that it exacted a terrible cost on those who resisted it. By his own logic, his death became part of the price—one that Custer was willing to pay for the ultimate triumph of civilization.

Regardless of whether this passage from *My Life on the Plains* yields an accurate understanding of Custer's own mindset, this writing does help one to grasp how the choices that white Americans presented to tribal peoples in the second half of the nineteenth century were, by the whites' own admission, wholly unpalatable. Like nearly all the observers of the West during his time—particularly the military men—Custer considered those Indians who lived on reservations or near army forts to be a degraded, miserable lot stuck between the nobility of "the free open plains" and the genuine blessings of white civilization.[70] Just as typically, Custer doubted that Indians would ever be successful in moving from the former to the latter. The Indian, he writes in *My Life*, "cannot be himself and be civilized; he fades away and dies. Cultivation such as the white man would give him deprives him of his identity."[71] But Custer's own actions show what would happen to those who rejected the path to "cultivation" altogether: they would become the targets of military action by the nation that they defied.

In other words, though the quotation that the museum reprints suggests a kind of affection on Custer's part for Plains Indians (at least those who lived the way he thought they should), it also reminds us that he believed that Indians had little to no chance of continuing to live *as Indians,* with their "identity" intact, into the twentieth century. Custer's opinion was far more the rule than the exception of his time, when those who wielded power in the United States constantly attempted to force Native peoples to make a simple—or so it seemed to whites—choice: assimilate or die. Custer, at least in this quotation from his memoir, indicates that he saw the second option as the more attractive one, perhaps more fitting with his notion of honor.

There is also something significant in Custer's willingness to imagine himself—at least for a rhetorical moment—as an Indian. "If I were an Indian . . . " he begins, and when these words are placed among the tribal objects that Custer collected, we understand that he did, at times, like to imagine himself as an Indian living on the "free open plains." Philip J. Deloria, a historian of Dakota Sioux descent, has produced a thorough study of this phenomenon of "playing Indian." From the Boston Tea Party to New Age wannabes, Deloria explains, white Americans have taken pleasure in dressing and even acting as Indians as a way of participating in the "absolute, anarchic freedom" that Custer extols. Deloria writes that non-Indians have persisted in believing that "aboriginal freedom was not freedom within a system. Rather they perceive this type of freedom as rejecting every restraint—politics, society, language, meaning itself." [72] Although nineteenth-century observers, Custer included, described Native cultures as brutal and uncultivated, they also admired the kind of pure democracy and absolute liberty that they saw there.

But unlike the patriots who dumped English tea in the Boston harbor or the "Indian Dead" who beat drums and proclaimed universal love outside Grateful Dead concerts, Custer was actively involved in curtailing the same aboriginal liberty that he found appealing. This combination of attraction and violent suppression is even more complex than the emotional state of a hunter who cherishes the animal he kills. Rather, Custer and his peers on the Western frontier often imagined themselves as the inheritors of the values—at least the admirable ones—of the tribal peoples that they believed would soon disappear. Dressed in buckskins, hunting rifle in hand, casually leaning against the wilderness props, the Custer of the photograph that the museum displays with the quotation appreciates those qualities and practices of Indian life that were valuable enough to preserve, even as he bears the sad burden of ending them among Indians themselves. The U.S. army may have fought the Indians of the Western Plains in 1876, but in the twentieth century the children and grandchildren of those soldiers would imitate those same Indians in the Boy and Girl Scouts and at summer camp. [73]

The net effect of this exhibit, with Custer's Indian curios and his professed desire for the "free" Indian life, is to mark the Battle of the Little Bighorn and the Sioux Campaign of 1876–77 as the historical moment when the United States would complete its military incorporation of living tribal peoples and initiate a new era in which whites would be free to pose as Indians and to claim them as their national ancestors. The Custer of this exhibit stands on the bridge between two eras—he was a necessary casualty of the first and a prescient forerunner of the second. Regardless of whether they were the objects of military conquest or playful imitation, the Indians themselves would vanish from the Plains.

Yet Indians did not disappear from the Plains—nor are they absent entirely from the Monroe County Historical Museum. On the first floor, near the stairs where one ascends to the Custer exhibit, stands the kind of visual display that anyone who has patronized a local museum of this size will recognize immediately. At its center, a mannequin of a young woman in an animal-skin dress bends forward, dutifully, to her never-completed task of grinding corn; she fronts a peaceful scene of woodland fishing, and she is surrounded by glass cases that tell the history of Indians living in the region, from the "paleo-hunters" who came to the Great Lakes following caribou and mammoths eleven thousand years ago to the changes in Native life brought on by sustained contact with French traders in the seventeenth and eighteenth centuries. Canoes, cradleboards, baskets, arrowheads, snowshoes, fishing nets—these are the paraphernalia of tribal life that have become the standard overture to the local history of nearly every community in the United States.

Just as there is no sign in Monroe's Loranger Square to mark the location of the Indian bones once buried there, the museum provides no link between these material artifacts (collected from the Potawatomi, Huron, and Ottawa [or Odawa] Indians who once lived in the region) to the Custer exhibit upstairs from it. In fact, the separate floors for the exhibits spatialize a temporal distance between two kinds of local inhabitants—seventeenth-century Indians and nineteenth-century Indian fighters—separating them to the extent that the patron has no reason to uncover a relationship between the two. The Custers of the 1870s and the Indians of 1670s, though, do share a common denominator in the larger colonial struggle between European powers and indigenous peoples in North America. There are historical reasons for the presence of bones beneath the town square, the presence of Native material artifacts in museums, and, equally important, today's absence of a visible community of Potawatomi Indians within the city or the county to care for either. The processes that resulted in the dislocation of tribal groups from the eastern half of Michigan in the early nineteenth century would continue to unfold—with crucial differences, to be sure—fifty and sixty years later on the Great Plains. If one could somehow rearrange the Monroe museum so that the exhibits on Native inhabitants and on Custer's life sat side by side—or, even better, in parallel lines of glass display cases—then the patron might understand these two slices of local history in a different manner, as related to one another and to a vast North American history of negotiations, compacts, tensions, and conflicts between those who have descended from the indigenous inhabitants of North America and those who have not.

The closest that the Monroe Museum may come to forging such narrative links between the history of Indians in the region and the fate of Custer occurs in an unlikely place, a large mural hanging in the main hall—a room so full of historical bric-a-brac that one part of it is actually called "Grandmother's Attic." The mural, called *Romance of Monroe*, was completed in 1938 under the auspices of the New Deal Public Works Administration; it has the angled lines and earnest visages common to the social realism of the Great Depression (figure 7).[74] The left-hand side of the mural portrays a troubled past, in which a bare-chested, mohawked Indian raises his hatchet in what can only be a symbol of the River Raisin massacre. (As far as I can tell, the only possible victim in sight is not an American soldier but a woman whose skin has been painted a shade of brown that leaves her racial identity obscure. She does appear to be in anguish. The Indian, on the other hand, appears only mildly irritated.) The right-hand side of the mural offers a glimpse of the prosperity that is presumably near at hand—clean, muscled white laborers and a young white girl clutching flowers, eyes closed in satisfaction.

At the center of the *Romance of Monroe*, standing as a bridge between the terrors of history and the honest pleasures of tomorrow, are the Custers. Libbie is seated; George is standing; behind them is their Monroe home. With this arrangement of its subjects, the mural's visual iconography provides the historical connection that is missing from the museum as a whole. Custer's actions out on the Plains were, in some way, a continuation of and a response to the violence shown on the left-hand side of the mural. As suggested by the mural, Custer fought against the Indians not because of some irrational personal hatred but because the country that he served feared that events like the River Raisin massacre represented a savagery incompatible with the scenes of peace and prosperity on the right side of this painting. In fact, in the *Romance of the Monroe*, Custer seems neither disdainful nor admiring of the Indians who share the canvas with him. Instead, with his arms crossed in front of him, his golden hair falling to his shoulders, and the two stars signifying the rank of major general sewed securely to his sleeve, Custer looks in the direction opposite to the Indians. If he glimpses his demise at Little Bighorn, he does not show it; he appears composed, placid, stolid.

The *Romance of Monroe* mural dramatizes how the figure of Custer yokes an ideal of martial manhood—the ability to produce his brilliant

Figure 7. *Romance of Monroe,* a WPA mural by Ralf Henricksen, 1938. (Photograph by Kim Brent; reproduction courtesy of photographer and *Monroe Evening News.*)

Civil War charges—with a narrative of the triumph of "civilization" over North America. Custer's continuing appeal is not, though, that he simply rolled across the Plains like the "car of Juggernaut," to use his phrase. Rather, Custer represents the possibility that one could have a kind of sympathetic longing for Indians, in fact a longing to *become* an Indian, but still participate in the heroic story of their conquest in the name of progress. It is a fantasy driven by the love of self-making, a fantasy that rests on the theatricality and flamboyance that were Custer's trademarks from the time of his first commission to his death on the Little Bighorn. And it is a fantasy that constantly, sometimes surprisingly, returns to the relationship of Americans to the indigenous peoples who once inhabited and who continue to inhabit the land they claim as their own.

Custer, in fact, imagined a romantic fable of the vanishing Indian long before he ever knew that he would be called upon to reinvent himself as an Indian fighter. One of the surviving products of his education at West Point is a brief essay he wrote for an ethics class in 1858 titled "The Red Man."

> The Red Man is alone in his misery. The earth is one vast desert to him. Once it had its charms to lull his spirit to repose, but now the home of his youth, the familiar forests, under whose grateful shade, he and his ancestors stretched their weary limbs after the excitement of the chase, are swept away by the axe of the woodman; the hunting grounds have vanished from his sight and in every object he beholds the hand of desolation. We behold him now on the verge of extinction, standing on his last foothold, clutching his bloodstained rifle, resolved to die amidst the horrors of slaughter, and soon he will be talked of as a noble race who once existed but have now passed away.[75]

With hindsight, the dramatic arc of Custer's career—seemingly scripted with the care of a novel or, more anachronistically, a Hollywood film—demands that the boy who wrote these words would confront American Indians on their own land to participate in the bloody work of "slaughter" and "extinction" he describes. The Civil War may have been the most crucial national conflict of Custer's generation, but what occurred west of the Mississippi became the cornerstone of America's imagination of itself for the century that followed. The West was the only stage large enough to supplant the drama of the Civil War, and Custer was as much an actor as a soldier. Being Custer always meant searching for the right part to play.

<hr />

When the current museum building was erected in the early twentieth century as a post office, it displaced the family home of Elizabeth Bacon Custer, but that house did not disappear from Monroe altogether. Today it stands about six blocks away, at the corner of Seventh and Cass, where it is becoming a kind of second, unofficial museum dedicated to Monroe's most famous military hero. Since 1999, the two-story gray building has

been the residence of Steve and Sandy Alexander, who have worked as-
siduously to restore it to something like what it might have been during the
time that the Custers lived there. The Alexanders have installed flooring,
ceilings, and wallpaper that accurately resemble their counterparts in the
postbellum Gilded Age, and they use cabinetry, when possible, to hide
their modern appliances. On the exterior, they have rebuilt a veranda appearing in nineteenth-century photographs of the Bacon house that had
been long lost by the time they purchased the house.

The most accomplished work of historical imitation, however, is not
part of the house but the man who lives in it. Steve Alexander describes
himself on his calling cards as the "Foremost Custer Living Historian"—
a title that has, in fact, been ratified by resolutions of the state legislatures
of Michigan and Ohio. For more than a dozen years, he has appeared as
Custer in reenactments of the Battle of the Little Bighorn, local history
celebrations (both in Monroe and elsewhere), and television productions.
His wife participates as well. Before meeting Steve, Sandy Alexander had
been involved in Civil War reenactments as a Southern belle. Her marriage to Steve in 1996, though, transformed her into Libbie Custer, and
their joint efforts to restore the Bacon-Custer home in Monroe have made
them the paragon of Custer enthusiasts: dedicated, meticulous, and by all
visible signs as devoted to each other as George and Libbie claimed to be.
Indeed, when I talked to Steve it sometimes seemed that his loyalty to his
wife and his loyalty to the Custer story they portray together are so inter-
twined that it would be impossible for him to extricate fully one from the
other.

This kind of historical passion can be intimidating, and I admit that
I was relieved when, during my first visit to the house, the Foremost Custer
Living Historian greeted me at the door wearing a sweatshirt and jeans
rather than his uniform—or, to be more accurate, *one* of his uniforms, for
he owns replicas of every uniform that Custer ever wore. Given Custer's
penchant for dress, this is no small feat, but the uniforms form only one
part of the extensive collection of Custer-related objects that fill nearly every corner of the living space of the house. The Alexanders own photographs, medals, weapons, saddles, hats, coats, maps, and not just one but
two different tables like the one from Appomattox that Sheridan sent to
Elizabeth. Their home contains a replica of Elizabeth's wedding dress, an
original croquet set owned by the Custer family, and a nineteenth-century
shaving kit like the one that Custer probably used on his final Montana
march. They sleep in a bed that is a replica of one the Custers had in
this very house; Steve works in his study at a replica of Custer's field desk

from Fort Lincoln while the mounted heads of a buffalo, an antelope, and a deer look down upon him; and portraits of George and Martha Washington hang in the dining room because, as the Alexanders point out, the Custers lived under the false impression that they were very distantly related to the Washingtons.

The result is a decor that, to a surprising degree, actually seems quite representative of the historical period that the Alexanders hope to evoke. The Victorian era was an age of collecting—a time when mantels became crowded with mementos, walls covered by pictures, and scrapbooks stuffed with keepsakes. What the Alexanders most obviously share with the time that they emulate, in other words, is a love of ornamentation and detail. But their enthusiasm moves beyond this to incorporate a devotion to historical fidelity that one can see everywhere in the house. Alexander, for instance, has painstakingly restaged several of the well-known photographs from Custer's life. In one, Alexander and his son-in-law sit in precise copies of the army uniforms that Custer and one of his officers wear in the mirror photograph, hung next to the newer one. In another, Alexander has reenacted a well-known photograph of Custer from one of his expeditions of the 1870s, and he illustrates how careful the reproduction is by pulling a book off the shelf that contains the original. While the newer image is in color and—thanks to a better camera—sharper, everything else has been replicated to perfection: the angle of Custer's slouch in his seat, the costumes of the Indian scouts who surround him, the dog lying at his feet, and even the faint, stenciled "N.P.R.R." (for Northern Pacific Railroad) on the canvas tent behind him.

A crucial component of these visual illusions is the physical resemblance that Steve Alexander bears to Custer even after all of the costumes and props are set aside. He has the same lanky build visible in the photographs of Custer, the same lean face, and the same reddish-blond hair that everyone who knew Custer described. (Sandy Alexander, on the other hand, occasionally has dyed her hair darker when portraying Libbie.) These physical similarities have been the cornerstone of the elaborate historical pantomimes in which the Alexanders have participated. They also have friends ready to play, when called upon, not only George's brother Tom but also Eliza Davidson, the escaped slave who became Custer's servant during the Civil War. Apparently, even the Custer aficionados attending one reception at the Alexander home were unsure how to respond to having the door answered by an African American woman in a nineteenth-century maid's costume.

The desire to replicate the life of someone far removed from one's own everyday world is hardly unique to reenactors or—to use Steve Alexander's own, and more accurate, term for his work—living historians. This kind of theatrical simulation is the premise of countless childhood diversions, of video games, even of adult recreation like the popular fantasy baseball camps that allow bankers and lawyers to pretend they are major-league athletes for a short while. What Steve Alexander stages, though, is a different kind of performance. When Alexander reproduces a Custer photo—itself a copy of the actual Custer—the result is something cleaner and crisper and perhaps even more meaningful than the original photograph because of the labor required to produce it. The significance of the second photograph, though, depends upon the existence of the first, so that it becomes hard to separate the value of the original from the value of the copy. Consider another example: When the collectible toy maker Drastic Plastic decided in 2001 to manufacture a "museum quality action figure" of George Armstrong Custer (complete with not only pistols and rifle but also bullets and cartridges), the company enlisted Alexander as its historical consultant and model. The final product is not simply a representation of Custer; it is a representation of an amalgamation of Alexander and Custer, inseparable and indivisible.

Steve Alexander's interest in Custer, in fact, began as a young child—at the age of three, by his own account. His webpage (www.georgecuster.com) features a series of snapshots that document his performance of Custer from a very a young age. In fact, Alexander's devotion to Custer is a thing that he does not perceive as actually having a beginning; rather, it has simply always been there. He has overflowing scrapbooks that chronicle childhood passion, packed with clippings from magazines, paraphernalia from several Western television series, promotional materials from films that included Custer, pictures from comic books, even Old West coins distributed by Kellogg's cereals as mail-in prizes in the 1970s. When Alexander was about the age of ten, he persuaded his family to take its annual vacation in Monroe—about eighty miles away from their home and dairy farm in Jackson, Michigan—so that he could visit the historical museum and see the Custer-related sights. Alexander still has several souvenirs from that trip, but none more precious than his worn copy of Lawrence Frost's book *The Custer Album,* which he found in the museum store during that trip but had no money to purchase. For the next year, Alexander carefully saved whatever coins might come his way—often begging, he says, for ice cream money that he would then pocket—until he had sufficient funds to send back to Monroe for the hardback volume. From that point, reading history began to occupy more and more of his time. Teenage life on the farm, with the constant labor of milking cows early and late, was full of dull routine—hardly the "independent merry life" that Whittaker ascribed to Custer's own Midwestern upbringing—but it gave Alexander time to read whatever books he could acquire about the object of his historical fixation.

Years later, in 1986, Alexander was making a trip to what was then called Custer Battlefield when he was approached by a woman from the town of Hardin, Montana, who was working with a group trying to relaunch the annual reenactments of Custer's Last Stand (the subject of chapter 6). She had noticed the physical resemblance between Alexander and his hero, and she asked Alexander whether he knew anything about Custer. ("He knows more about Custer than Custer himself," Alexander's traveling companion told the Hardin woman.) By the end of the chance encounter, Alexander had become an official Custer reenactor. Custer's shoe size, he says, was a 9½ B, and his is a 9½ D, "so it wasn't too hard for me to step into his boots." The next step came after he began giving talks about Custer's life. "My first presentations," he recalls, "were Steve Alexander talking *about* General Custer but looking *like* General Custer." Then his uncle gave him an invaluable piece of advice: start speaking about Custer in the first person. "You are up there in front of us," Alexander remembers his uncle telling him, "you've got the regalia on, and you are saying, 'Custer did this, and Custer did that.' You need to say *I* did this and *I* did that." Alexander now calls this shift into the first-person "a revelation." [76] For Alexander, historical reenactment is about not just performing a role but becoming it.

Since he began his portrayal of Custer, Alexander has become a widely sought figure. He has played Custer in both of the Montana reenactments of the Battle of Little Bighorn (one run by the town of Hardin, the other by the Real Bird family on the Crow Reservation); he has portrayed Custer at battlefields and reconstructed forts, in schools and on steamships; and he is one of the few people in the world of Custerology who travel easily between the arena of historical reenactment and the national associations of enthusiasts devoted to the study of Custer and the Battle of the Little Bighorn. Diehard Custer aficionados tend to stay away from battle reenactments, which they believe present a watered-down version of history at best. But Alexander's devotion to historical accuracy and especially his and his wife's devotion to the Custer-Bacon home in Monroe have made him beloved by Custer buffs everywhere. During the time that I spent researching this book, nearly every Custer enthusiast whom I met claimed a friendship with Steve Alexander. Many told me in an awed voice about visiting the Alexanders in their Monroe house.

Historical reenactment is not lucrative. Alexander sometimes receives traveling expenses and perhaps a modest appearance fee, but just as often he receives neither. He has completed most of the renovations on the house himself, with occasional help from fellow Custer aficionados. His performances as Custer take up a large portion of his vacation time from his job as a surveyor. I have seen him ride into battle on Sunday and then tell me that he will be at work the next day. Custer could earn a salary by being Custer full time; Alexander cannot. But being Custer is not a profession for Alexander, it is—as it was for Custer himself—a calling. This sense of vocational mission is conveyed less the actual words that he speaks than in the unaffected gravitas with which he sounds them. Alexander describes the talks that he delivers, the appearances he makes, the interviews he conducts with newspapers and radio stations, as being part of an educational project to help the public move beyond the bumbling, Indian-hating caricature of Custer that they have found in popular media, toward something more nuanced and three-dimensional—if not, at least at first, someone they can venerate, then at least someone whose charismatic appeal and theatrical sense of virtue can be understood. Alexander does not exhibit the extroverted fervor of a proselytizer; he is not about to seek out the doubters and corner them. But there is still an evangelical edge to his belief in Custer that I recognize from my years spent in the company of teachers: a core desire to convert the languid and the disinterested to some small share in one's passions.

To keep up with his subject, Alexander reads *everything* he can find on Custer, and he is a much more generous reader than some of the other Custer partisans I have encountered, finding value even in those books that are skeptical of his hero's abilities. The result is an immense knowledge of the minutiae of Custer's life; he can recite from memory whole passages from *My Life on the Plains* and the orders that Custer received before the Little Bighorn. Equally important, what he understands about the man he portrays goes beyond factual detail. He realizes how much Custer loved *being* Custer—loved the person he created and re-created over the course of his life. Steve Alexander loves being Custer with the same intensity. Whether he is riding around a camp of reenactors, sitting at home among his Custer memorabilia, or talking to his fellow Little Big Horn Associates, one can see how much delight he derives from becoming the man he has studied since he was a child. He can be stentorian, looking over his "troops" before battle; he can be personable, signing autographs and posing for photographs with tourists; and he can be humorous, joking about Custer's ultimate fate or delivering a comic monologue about buffalo hunting that relies on Custer-like hyperbole. ("The largest buffalo on the North American continent!" he exclaims, in a routine that culminates with his pulling out a long "tail" and waving it at the audience as a mock trophy from the beast that has escaped him.)[77] What stands out about Alexander's performance is more than the frisson of theatricality; it is the pleasure he takes from staging an imagined self, a satisfaction in being able to make visible the thing that one wants to be, even if that thing is embodied in a long-dead military hero. Of course, this is precisely what Custer's admirers have always sought, and found, in the general.

While Alexander is an extraordinary example of a living historian, he shares with other reenactors a professed inability to explain his own motivations. Doing so would require him to separate his life-as-Custer from his life-as-Alexander—an almost impossible task at this point. What one can say is that many obvious rationales do not apply. While Alexander may be intensely interested in Custer's guns, for instance, he has little interest in weapons outside of Custer. Ditto for horses—one reason that some become interested in nineteenth-century cavalry life. Nor has he, like many other military reenactors, served in the military himself. Finally, and perhaps most crucially, he consistently and credibly denies that he holds any antipathy toward the tribal peoples whom Custer famously fought. Having met him on numerous occasions, I should emphasize his sincerity on this point. Alexander's interest in Custer does not stem from some closeted—or uncloseted—form of anti-Indianism.

But disavowals of racism are not sufficient to explain what it means to enact the life of someone best known, from the time of his death to the present, as an Indian fighter. For many Americans, and not only Indians, Custer represents a history of white injustice toward Native peoples that they would prefer to denounce or forget rather than reproduce. Steve Alexander is acutely aware of the emotional response that his historical character can generate. He and Sandy both speak of times when complete strangers have confronted them in public places to abuse verbally the long-dead general whom Steve portrays. They talk about such episodes with enough weariness in their voices to suggest that they no longer find this hostility to be annoying or troubling so much as a tiresome but inevitable occupational hazard.

Both Steve and Sandy Alexander believe that Custer is an object of historical prejudice because of the gross misconception that he was an "Indian hater." They both know well the passage of Custer's *My Life on the Plains* in which he professes his affection for the "free open" life of the traditional Plains cultures. When I ask Steve how, as Custer, he responds to questions about his reasons for fighting Indians, he quickly snaps into the first person: "I'm a soldier. I've been trained in the military, and the military pays my bills. I'm out doing a job; maybe I don't approve of it, but as a military man, when I'm told to march, I march. Much as what we've gone through in this country in recent times—a lot of what the military is doing is a thankless task, but they don't decide they're going to go into Iraq or even Vietnam. I mean, when you're a soldier, you do what you are told to do. A lieutenant colonel doesn't make government policy about the treatment of Indians—that's on a higher level."

It is an answer Alexander has clearly given many times, and his care with the words underscores his sincerity. The response suggests something about the attraction of military history and re-creation, a premise that it is possible to disentangle decisions of ideology from those of strategy. Custer, to be sure, would have started from this same premise; even though they believed that American "civilization" would necessitate the erasure of Indian cultures, Custer and his fellow officers frequently expressed regret that they were blamed for policies that they did not design, a matter to which we will return in chapter 3. Alexander's response is equally suggestive in his invocation of Vietnam and Iraq. On the one hand, he is aware that popular responses to U.S. involvement in both Southeast Asia and the Middle East have recast the nineteenth-century Indian Wars as the crucible of U.S. imperialism. On the other, he seeks to access the populist celebration of the men and women of the military that began in the 1980s as redress for the excesses of the antiwar movement of the 1960s and 1970s. The Montana reenactments of the Battle of the Little Bighorn in which Alexander has participated, after all, were discontinued in the first half of the 1970s, when the Vietnam War was at the height of its unpopularity; their revival coincided with popular cultural productions—think of Oliver Stone's *Born on the Fourth of July* (1989)—that valorized Vietnam soldiers and distinguished them from the architects of that war. Separating those who plotted the war from those who fought in it became a way that one could commemorate the service of veterans without focusing on the suffering endured by the Vietnamese.[78] In a similar way, Alexander and others seek to honor the service of the nineteenth-century cavalrymen, even to celebrate their heroism, without focusing on the dispossession of American Indians that their service helped to effect. Just as Custer's version of manliness relied heavily on theatricality, these reenactors hope that their performances can convey the virtues that they see in the nineteenth-century men they portray— virtues that they believe have been swept aside by the widespread discrediting of the political goals for which the frontier army fought.

To pursue this rehabilitation of Custer and the frontier army, Alexander needs Indians; he needs them because Custer needed them as well in order to continue playing Custer after the Civil War. Alexander's performance of Custer therefore requires sharing the stage with Native peoples and recalling the vexed relationship of the United States to the tribes it fought over the course of the nineteenth century. In Alexander's case, this dynamic is most visible at the annual Battle of the Little Bighorn reenactments staged in Montana, both of which use scripts written by Crow Indians. Alexander expresses affection for the Crows involved in the reenactments yet also speaks of his struggles to overcome what he perceives as their anti-Custer bias. In each of the reenactments, he says, he has worked to alter a negative characterization of Custer to something more even-handed. Alexander's opportunities to perform there and portray the general in the way that he wants, of course, depend on an interest in Custer that depends, in turn, on an interest in Indians. While Custerphiles constantly emphasize that Custer's military engagements with Plains Indians were in fact quite few in number, and while places like Monroe, Michigan, prefer to remember Custer as Civil War cavalier rather than as Indian fighter, popular interest in Custer has been refracted through the national—and even international—fascination with American Indians that existed long before the Battle of the Little Bighorn and that has endured to this day.

In January 2005, for instance, Alexander reprised his hero's famous ride into the nation's capital by riding on a float sponsored by the state of North Dakota in the presidential inaugural parade. This time, Custer did not lead his troops or have the chance to make a solo dash in front of the reviewing stand. Instead, he was accompanied by other "legends" of North Dakota history—stationed so that he was deliberately paired with Ron His Horse Is Thunder, a Hunkpapa Sioux man who was at that time the president of Sitting Bull College and would be elected chairman of the Standing Rock Sioux Tribe in the fall. Just as Alexander portrayed Custer in his dress uniform, His Horse Is Thunder portrayed Sitting Bull, from whom he is descended, in nineteenth-century tribal regalia, including the single feather prominent in a well-known photograph of his ancestor. Custer and Sitting Bull, the white American soldier and the Native organizer of resistance, waved and smiled to the crowds together.[79]

Custer has achieved iconic status because his death paired him with a people—the Plains Indians—equally capable of putting the national imagination into overdrive. Native Americans had been objects of fantasy—both fearful and desirous—for decades before Custer's final campaign, and in the years after the Little Bighorn those fantastic yearnings would be sharpened by pulp fiction, by film, and by the increasing number of institutions devoted to making young boys into masculine men. In the late nineteenth century, Indians became the raw material of make-believe for white American boys; they furnished the imaginative vocabulary of back- yard games and summer camps. The popularity of the Western genre in film, television, and fiction attests to the way that white masculinity in the twentieth century relied as much on Indians as it did on soldiers. Custer's emphasis on honor and chivalry may have become less central to the way that young boys imagined becoming men, but he remained a compelling figure because he could bridge both worlds: the soldier who could both fight Indians and imagine himself as one.

The role Custer created for himself, in other words, became the stuff of boyhood play. It is not surprising that Alexander—like so many other Custer aficionados—dates his interest to a very young age. During Custer's lifetime, the young general played to the imagination of the members of the press who wrote about him and of the public for whom they wrote. After his death, Custer's apotheosis occurred because he so neatly fit a boyish notion of heroism that had a patina of antiquated romance but remained contemporary in its calling attention to the costs of pushing the light of so-called civilization into the benighted darkness. Small wonder that Becker's lithograph *Custer's Last Fight,* probably the most widely circulated image of U.S.-Indian warfare, spread through American barrooms in the 1890s, just as the United States turned its imperial attentions from North America to other continents. Thanks to Anheuser Busch, Custer would breathe his last among men who needed to be reminded what their countrymen were fighting for in Cuba or the Philippines—a quest for martial glory as much as geopolitical goals.

Steve Alexander, meanwhile, has long ceased worrying that Custer's story might be troubling to Americans unsure about this imperial legacy. Yet he realizes that his relationship with Custer may have to change some- how in the not-so-distant future. More than one acquaintance of Alex- ander told me that he purposefully withheld his age from his friends be- cause he feared that something fatal would befall him when he reached the thirty-six and one-half years that Custer had attained before his death at the Little Bighorn. Whether that is true or not, Steve often does sound ca- gey on the dates of his own biography, perhaps to obscure the fact that ev- ery day he lives further beyond Custer's own lifespan. He is acutely aware that there will come a time when he will no longer physically resemble Custer. Sandy, he says, has encouraged him to write (in another histori- cal echo, the Alexanders note that Libbie encouraged George's literary pursuits), and he imagines transforming himself again, this time from an historical reenactor speaking in the first person to an historical authority speaking in the third.

That transition remains in the future. For now, Steve and Sandy Alexander live in harmony with their deceased subjects. Near the end of my visit to their house, I asked them what they might ask the actual Custers if some resurrectionist miracle brought them back for a day. After a long pause, Steve spoke in a low, measured voice: "I don't know. Maybe they wouldn't like us." Sandy and I began to laugh, though I do not know if either of us was sure how funny he meant this to be. "Maybe when I met him, he would just think I was a twit and not have anything to do with me." As Sandy and I talked about what she wishes she understood better, Steve sat and thought further about my hypothetical scenario; a few minutes later, he returned to it. "I wouldn't know what questions to ask him," he said quietly—no need to explain which "him" he means. "I don't know that I would have to ask a lot of questions. I just, in a way, and I don't want to sound like I'm being conceited, I know enough [about Custer] that it would be just good to sit—maybe go fishing. Just sit in a boat and fish with him—that's all I would have to do."

Alexander was, I think, trying to explain to me what he regards as his greatest accomplishment—a union with Custer so complete that words are no longer necessary. Nor, he says, does his life as Custer any longer require an audience. Even though he speaks with pride about his efforts to educate the public about the complexity and heroism of Custer's life, he also says that he is no longer concerned about making new conversions. He has worked hard to create a world that revolves around the nineteenth-century frontier instead of twenty-first-century concerns. "I like performing," he admits, "but there's so much satisfaction in where I am at this stage of my life that outside influences really don't affect me. I know it's kind of weird, but if I never had another person call me and bother me about this story, I really wouldn't care."

Everything that Steve Alexander does belies that sentiment. He and Sandy have acted anything but bothered during the hours that they sat and answered my questions; they have extensive plans for future traveling and appearances; and their schedule seems to show no signs of becoming any less rigorous. But I understand Steve's point: he has reached a kind of "serenity" (his word) that cannot be disturbed by the raging controversies that continue to surround Custer's place in American history, or by the more mundane squabbles that too often break out in the local groups that preserve Custer's history and represent it to new generations. What

Steve Alexander has achieved is a pure desire to lose himself in the theatrical personality that Custer himself crafted during the thirty-six years of his life before the Battle of the Little Bighorn. Alexander, though, may have taken Custer even further than Custer himself when he dismisses what the nineteenth-century general so clearly craved: "It's not contingent on an audience," he says, trying to explain his sense of fulfillment. "It's in my mind, in my soul. Even if I never donned my uniform, every day that I wake up in this house, I'm still General Custer."

❦3❧

LIVES ON THE PLAINS

Cheyenne, Oklahoma

THE YEARS IMMEDIATELY FOLLOWING THE 1865 GRAND REVIEW IN WASHING-
ton were not kind to George Armstrong Custer. His career first stalled,
then shifted into a steady decline. Following the review, he traveled to
posts in Louisiana and Texas, where he was charged with enforcing the
new peace against the smoldering embers of Confederate resistance. Later,
he was mustered out of the volunteer army at his rank of major general,
which left him a captain in the regular army and without command. He
briefly considered an overture by representatives of the Mexican army,
who were searching for an adjutant general, and during the summer of
1866 he accompanied President Andrew Johnson on a disastrous political
tour—a "swing around the circle"—during which the president attempted
to explain the policies of Reconstruction, only to be met repeatedly by
heckling.[1]

By the fall of 1866, Custer had received his new commission: the lieutenant colonelcy of the newly organized Seventh Cavalry, part of the frontier army authorized by Congress for the post–Civil War era. (Custer, notably, had written to Johnson saying that he preferred not to command
one of regiments of African American soldiers being organized at the same
time.)[2] He reported for duty at Fort Riley, Kansas, but the transition to
frontier duty was not an easy one. He participated in a campaign led by
General Winfield Scott Hancock from April to July 1867, designed to
impress upon belligerent Cheyenne and Lakota Sioux Indians the necessity of submitting to the authority of the United States. In fact, the campaign only exacerbated the violence and tension in the central Plains, and

Custer's own part was less than glorious. He spent much of the summer fruitlessly chasing enemies he could not find, battling desertion within his own ranks, and missing his wife. The last of these led him to leave his command under questionable circumstances, for which he was court-martialed and sentenced to a year of suspension without rank or pay. He and Libbie spent the winter at Fort Leavenworth and then departed in the spring of 1868 for Monroe.[3]

The army needed Custer, though, too badly to leave him in Michigan for the full year of his sentence. Phil Sheridan, commander of the Department of the Missouri at that time, called Custer back to duty after only nine months and set him on a course that would rehabilitate his career and return his image to the larger public of the United States. Acting under orders from Sheridan, Custer led the Seventh Cavalry south from Fort Dodge, Kansas, first to a temporary post named Fort Supply and then farther south into Indian Territory, where the regiment searched for villages that Sheridan believed were harboring both Indian men who had violently attacked Kansas settlers and white women whom they had taken captive. Under Custer's command, a force of approximately eight hundred men—mostly Seventh Cavalry soldiers but also non-Indian civilians and Osage Indian scouts—located and followed a trail that led to an Indian village along the banks of the Washita River. Most of those in the Washita camp that night were Cheyennes, though there were also families of their tribal allies the Arapahos and several visiting Lakotas. The morning of November 27, 1868, found Custer charging into battle in a daybreak assault that he coordinated from four different directions.[4]

The attack threw the sleeping Indians into chaos. Some grabbed their weapons and tried to stop the soldiers pouring into their camp; others fled to nearby ravines or the riverbed seeking protection. The fighting within the village itself did not last long, as Custer's men first established control of the main camp and then pursued outlying snipers and those attempting to escape. The Seventh Cavalry was under orders to avoid harming women and children, but Custer later admitted that it was impossible to do so during the frenetic fighting. In his initial report, Custer claimed that the cavalry killed 103 warriors; he later said that the Cheyennes reported losses of more than 140. However, lists of the Cheyenne, Arapaho, and Lakota men killed compiled by witnesses to the conflict lead to dramatically lower casualty estimates. Jerome A. Greene, whose book on the fight offers the most authoritative account to date, states that a 1916 figure of twenty-nine killed "does not appear unreasonable" and suggests that probably sixty Indians from the village were wounded.[5] Regardless, no one disputes that among those killed early in the fighting were Black Kettle, the leader of the village and a peace chief, and his wife Medicine Woman Later.

Twenty soldiers also died in the fighting. One was Captain Louis Mac-Lane Hamilton, grandson of Alexander Hamilton. Most of the casualties, however, belonged to a detachment that rode away from the village with Major Joel Elliott (no relationship to the author) to chase a group of Cheyennes fleeing downstream. The soldiers rode for approximately two and a half miles and then were surrounded by warriors from other villages. The bodies of all sixteen were later found in a defensive circle, scalped and mutilated.

Custer, meanwhile, was preoccupied with the village itself. He ordered the prisoners—fifty-three women and children—gathered into a central location, and he attempted to communicate to them that they would not be harmed. He then ordered that the material possessions of the villagers be destroyed in large bonfires. Edward S. Godfrey, a second lieutenant then only a year out of West Point, later recalled holding a bridal gown "adorned all over with bead work and elks' teeth on antelope skins as soft as the finest broadcloth. I started to show it to the General and ask to keep it, but as I passed a big fire, I thought, 'What's the use, "orders is orders,"' and threw it in the blaze."[6] Custer himself apparently kept a few souvenirs; he later sent to the Detroit Audubon club a shield, a dress, a bow and quiver, and the scalp of the Cheyenne chief Little Rock, reported by Custer to be "second in rank to Black Kettle."[7] Although at least one Seventh Cavalry soldier recalled scalping a fallen warrior, Custer's had probably been taken by one of the Osage scouts, who performed brutal mutilations on the Cheyenne and Arapaho bodies, including beheadings.[8] The official reports of Custer and Sheridan would emphasize the evidence they found in the camp of Cheyenne participation in the Kansas raids: white scalps, photographs, and unopened mail stolen from wagon trains.[9]

But the most significant property that Custer captured was the herd of horses belonging to the village. Even after selecting horses for the prisoners, replacements for the soldiers who had lost their mounts, and other horses simply claimed by the officers as spoils of war—one of the scouts recalled that Custer took "four fine mules"—there were hundreds of horses corralled near a bend in the river.[10] Custer offered the precise number of 875. In the account of the Washita fight that he wrote for his memoir, *My Life on the Plains, or Personal Experiences with Indians,* Custer lingers over the dilemma of what to do with the herd, stretching out his decision over two chapters, noting that the issue became more significant as the officers of the Seventh Cavalry noticed a growing number of Indians watching the destruction of the village from overlooking bluffs. The watchers, the soldiers learned from the captives, were from other downstream villages of Cheyennes, Kiowas, and Arapahos. "We did not need the ponies," Custer writes, "and the Indians did." After realizing the impossibility of driving the herd back to Fort Supply and the undesirability of leaving the herd there for other Indians to capture, Custer ordered all 875 horses to be killed, an act he called in his memoir "cruel but necessary."[11] The scout Ben Clark later remembered that the horses were crowded against a steep bank; one group of soldiers on the slaughter detail stood above them firing down, the other stood in the valley and fired up into the herd. "It took nearly two hours to kill the ponies," Clark continued. "The hostiles who were gathered on the hills witnessed their destruction and with shrill cries derided the soldiers as cowards and dared them to fight."[12] Moving Behind Woman, a Cheyenne in her early teens who escaped capture by hiding in the tall grass, would later say that the wounded ponies "would moan loudly, just like human beings."[13]

Custer, his soldiers, and his prisoners departed the Washita as darkness fell—feinting first toward the villages downstream to frighten the warriors watching from the hills, then reversing course and heading north to the wagon trains and Fort Supply. At least some of the relatives of those killed in the attack would return to the site of the village in the following days to attend to the bodies of the slain Cheyennes. They would eventually depart as well; when Custer brought Sheridan to the scene of the conflict weeks later, the villages along the Washita were abandoned. These bends of the Washita River—called the Lodge Pole River by the Cheyennes—were not part of the subsequent communities where they and the other tribes in the region settled; some Cheyennes have more recently suggested that there was little enthusiasm for returning to the scene of such violence in the decades that followed.

The bones of the 875 horses killed by Custer remained. In 1891, Hugh L. Scott, a first lieutenant serving with the Seventh Cavalry at Fort Sill, was determined to find the site of the conflict and traveled there with a small group of soldiers. He wrote that "many of the bones had been carried away and sold," but enough remained for him to identify the spot.[14] Scott used some of the bones in constructing a makeshift monument topped by a red sandstone slab, engraved by a sergeant who had once worked as a stonemason (figure 8)—a far cry from the eighteen tons of granite that had been transported from Massachusetts to the site of the Little Bighorn in 1881 for the obelisk atop Last Stand Hill. Scott photographed the Washita site and wrote to newspapers in the region urging residents to recognize its his-

Figure 8. In 1891, Lieutenant Hugh L. Scott supervised the construction of this makeshift monument of stones and horse bones at the site of Custer's attack on Black Kettle's Cheyenne and Arapaho encampment on the Washita River. (Photo courtesy of Little Bighorn Battlefield National Monument.)

torical significance. In 1918, the sandstone marker was still there—though the monument had been knocked down and rebuilt several times—and so were some bones of the pony herd.[15] While stories persisted that the bones were being shipped to Texas and sold for fertilizer, a visitor in 1933 found "still enough left to leave proof that there once lay the equine victims of Custer and his band."[16]

Today, the exact location of the Seventh Cavalry's execution of the pony herd remains uncertain. The best guesses place the spot near a railroad grade, where rock and dirt have been constructed into an elevated bed that traverses the valley floor. The railroad track itself is gone—the line has been abandoned for decades—but its former bed is lined with rows of elm trees that were planted to shelter it. The land where the Washita fight occurred was cleared for pasture in the 1970s, and nonnative grasses now grow in the red earth alongside the plants that would have been there in the time of Black Kettle and Custer. The river itself has changed course and now runs about a quarter of a mile from the site of the pony kill. Subject to flood control since the 1950s, the Washita no longer floods the valley floor or cuts a new channel. The muddy water is no more than ten to twenty yards across here; tamarisk and willow trees rise up on the river's banks. In the spring and fall, the morning air is filled with birdsong, and the thickets by the riverbed hum with insects in the summer. But the bones of the horses are gone.

During the last half-century, and especially the last decade, the land where those bones once lay has received increasing attention as a site of historical geography. In the 1960s, the state of Oklahoma constructed an overlook and a large interpretive sign on the side of the state highway that skirts the land, and in 1996, Congress passed legislation incorporating the Washita Battlefield National Historic Site into the National Park System. A new visitor center has been in phases of planning and construction for several years and is scheduled to open by the time this book is in print. The story that the National Park Service is charged with telling here is in many ways much more typical of the conflicts of the Indian Wars than what would later occur at the Little Bighorn, though perhaps it is no less complicated. That single morning on the banks of the Washita River transformed George Custer into one of the best-known Indian fighters of his age, but it also reveals the uneasiness of the nation that employed him with the harsh violence and moral ambiguity of his mission against the Indians of the southern Plains. Eight years later, the U.S. army rushed to Last Stand Hill to bury its dead there, and the American public followed; the carcasses of the 875 horses killed at the Washita were left for scavengers and temporary memorials—the presence of their owners as well as the men who killed them barely legible on the landscape. This chapter investigates the history of what occurred at the Washita River in 1868—the events that led up to the violence there, the reaction of the public at the time, and the failure of the nation to commemorate that violence as Little Bighorn would be memorialized. I am not only seeking to understand what Indian fighting meant in Custer's time but also to show how the increasing visibility of Washita in the American historical landscape is the product of recent, dramatic shifts in the ways that Americans, Indian and non-Indian, regard the violence of their shared past.

———⇒►◦◄⇐———

By the middle of the nineteenth century, the Cheyennes, like most tribes west of the Mississippi river, had accumulated a history of contact with the white descendants of Europe.[17] Members of the tribe met with the Lewis and Clark expedition, signed their first friendship treaty with the United States in 1825, and later traded at places like the post known as Bent's Fort, in present-day Colorado, where the trader William Bent lived with his Cheyenne wife, Owl Woman. Cheyennes hunted and camped with relative freedom over a broad territory from the Platte River in the north and the Arkansas River in the south and continued to conduct intertribal raiding and warfare, even though they also participated in an intertribal peace agreement reached by five tribes of the southern Plains in 1840. A combination of a council of forty-four chiefs and military societies governed the tribe, which lived in ten different bands, each composed of unrelated families. Bands might live and hunt close to one another or disperse, depending on the season, the ability of the land to provide for concentrations of men and horses, and the threat of danger from outside the tribe. Sometimes they traveled with Arapahos, who had been close allies of the Cheyennes since at least the turn of the eighteenth century.[18]

The structure of the tribe was in the process of changing, however. Beginning in the 1820s, the Cheyennes had begun to divide themselves into northern and southern halves. (The Arapahos underwent a similar division.) Historians are not clear on how rapidly this process occurred. For at least part of this period, the entire Cheyenne nation continued to regularly assemble as a full circle for renewal of the medicine arrows, sacred objects that protected the tribe. In spite of these occasions and other less formal traffic, by the 1850s the Cheyennes were constituted as two divisions, a northern one that frequently camped along tributaries of the Platte and Missouri rivers (mostly in present-day Nebraska, Colorado, and South Dakota) and that was an ally of the Lakota Sioux and Northern Arapaho, and a southern division that often camped along the Cimarron and Arkansas rivers (in present-day Colorado, Kansas, and Oklahoma) and that continued its close relationship with Southern Arapahos. During the same time that this separation was evolving, the Dog Soldiers were emerging outside the usual band structure. The Dog Soldiers were originally one of the Cheyenne military societies, with members in several bands, but they became their own band sometime before the middle of the century. They were governed by their military leaders rather than the traditional chiefs of the northern and southern bands, and they often occupied the terrain between the two.

The increasing presence of white Americans on the Plains during and following the United States' war with Mexico in 1846–48 intensified both the division of the Cheyennes and the consolidation of the Dog Soldiers as a separate military force. In 1859 and 1860, gold rushes in the Rocky Mountains increased the number of emigrants into Cheyenne country, and new settlements blossomed in the Colorado Territory, organized in 1861. That same year, some chiefs among the Southern Cheyennes signed the treaty of Fort Wise with the United States, in which the tribe agreed to cede much of the land designated in earlier treaties and live on a smaller reservation within the Colorado Territory. The Dog Soldiers were among those who refused to sign the treaty, and other prominent chiefs soon claimed that they had not signed it either—or that the terms of the agreement had been grossly misrepresented to them. In fact, it soon became clear that the Fort Wise treaty would not work for either side: for the Cheyennes, it was too little land, too far from their hunting grounds; for white Coloradoans, it left the Cheyennes too close to the settlements and wagon routes. Later, during the U.S. Civil War, the Lincoln administration sought to secure the political loyalty and mineral wealth of white Americans in the West. Frontier settlers, in turn, realized their opportunity and sought to take advantage of the militarization of the nation by calling on the federal army to defend against, and even eradicate, the threat of Indian violence.[19]

These calls were particularly loud in Colorado, and the men issuing them often had political ambitions tied to the prospects of statehood. In the winter of 1863, territorial governor John Evans became convinced that the Cheyennes were preparing for a major war, even though the Cheyennes believed themselves to be at relative peace. A series of U.S. military campaigns during the following year, though, actually increased Cheyenne attacks upon white Americans and raids upon property, with each incident generating, of course, further calls from the Coloradans for military action. The rage and panic boiled over in June 1864, when the bodies of the Hungates, a family of white farmers who had been killed and mutilated, were brought to Denver for public exhibition. The murders, committed by a group of four Northern Arapahos, were attributed to the Cheyennes.[20]

The U.S. military expeditions in the months that followed frightened those Cheyenne and Arapaho leaders who sought peace, and a delegation of them met with Governor Evans in a council held at Camp Weld, near Denver, in September. Among the Cheyennes was Black Kettle, a principal peace chief; and among the Coloradans was Colonel John M. Chivington, a former Methodist minister who was Governor Evans's military ally. What occurred at the conference is considered by some historians to be one of the worst examples of deliberate deception in the history of official negotiations between the United States and the Indians of North America. What Black Kettle and his fellow Cheyenne leaders understood from this meeting was that they could avoid war by bringing their bands to Fort Lyon, in southeastern Colorado, to surrender. What Evans and Chivington actually said was that the Cheyennes' only hope was to negotiate a peace with the U.S. army and that Fort Lyon was a place where such a possibility might exist. Evans and Chivington failed to make clear that they, in fact, were not acting as authorities of the federal army, that they were not dictating to the Cheyennes the terms of an actual surrender, and that they would continue, until Washington otherwise ordered them, to regard the Cheyennes as enemies and legitimate military targets.[21]

Black Kettle arrived at Fort Lyon in early November and explained that his village of approximately one hundred lodges was camping about forty miles away, on Sand Creek. The officers of the fort informed Black Kettle that the post had neither sufficient provisions nor the authority to accept the surrender of the Cheyennes, and therefore they suggested that Black Kettle return to his camp and remain there until the proper rations and authorization could be secured. A band of Arapahos were sent away to hunt as well. Fort Lyon's commander, Edward Wynkoop, was about to leave to meet with his superiors and address the situation; Black Kettle trusted Wynkoop and accepted his assurances that the Cheyennes would be safe on Sand Creek.

Not long after this meeting, however, Chivington began moving units of the Third Colorado Cavalry to Fort Lyon. Both Chivington and the "Bloodless Third" had suffered abuse from the Colorado press for their failure to inflict a major defeat upon the raiding Indian tribes, and Chivington had decided that the Cheyenne and Arapaho camps near Fort Lyon offered the best targets. He marched with seven hundred men to Sand Creek and—at dawn on November 29, 1864—surrounded and attacked Black Kettle's village of approximately five hundred Cheyennes and Arapahos. Chivington and his men fired indiscriminately on the camp with both small arms and howitzers. Many of the Indian men were absent, hunting. Those who remained fought back—killing some twenty-five soldiers—and then tried to shield the women, children, and elderly. Some fled along the streambed and attempted to dig defensive trenches to hide; a few managed to reach their horses and ride away. Black Kettle raised both an American flag and a white flag to signal the peaceful disposition of the camp, but to no avail. Black Kettle himself would survive, but at least 150 Cheyennes and Arapahos were killed by Chivington's men, who then proceeded to mutilate and dismember the corpses. They took scalps, ears, even genitalia, some of which were later publicly displayed onstage at a Denver theater.

The events at Sand Creek shaped the world that Custer encountered on the Plains in 1867–68 at multiple levels. The reported brutality of the violence and the perceived treachery of Evans and Chivington increased the stature of those Cheyennes who had urged all along that the growing presence of the United States in the region be met with armed resistance. The Dog Soldiers became even more independent of traditional Cheyennes, and peace chiefs like Black Kettle had to rehabilitate their standing among their people. Rather than frighten the Cheyennes into submission, the unprovoked attack on Black Kettle's village at Sand Creek ensured that the raiding by Cheyennes seeking to defend their territorial claims would continue.

Equally significant, Chivington's actions also outraged white citizens of the United States to the point that Sand Creek became a national scandal. Wynkoop, in whose assurances Black Kettle had trusted, called Chivington an "inhuman monster" and began collecting testimony from officers and soldiers present at Fort Lyon. Two different committees of the U.S. Congress (the House Committee on the Conduct of the War and a joint special committee on Indian affairs) conducted damning investigations. The army launched its own investigation as well, all the more dramatic because the military commission conducted its hearings in Denver. While none of these investigations produced any formal charges against Chivington, who resigned his commission in January 1865, or Chivington's followers, they firmly affixed opprobrium to "fiendish," "foul," and "dastardly" deeds.[22] For those white Americans who considered themselves sympathetic to the interests of American Indians, the Sand Creek Massacre became, in the words of one historian, "a cause célèbre, a never-to-be-forgotten symbol of what was wrong with the United States treatment of the Indians, which reformers would never let fade away and which critics today still hold up to view."[23] The federal army disavowed the actions of Chivington and his voluntary militia, but the taint of the massacre and the suspicion it engendered among the white American public extended to the frontier regulars in the years that followed the Civil War.

Custer was among those acutely aware of the way that Sand Creek had aroused the conflicted feelings of non-Indian Americans about the military effort to contain and combat the indigenous tribes of the Plains in the United States. The successful Indian fighter, he explained in his memoir, "can feel assured of this fact, that, that one half of his fellow-citizens at home will revile him for his zeal and pronounce his success, if he achieves any, a massacre of poor defenseless, harmless Indians; while the other half, if his efforts to chastise the common enemy are not crowned with satisfactory results, will cry, 'Down with him. Down with the regular army, and give us brave volunteers.' "[24] Custer positions himself here as an innocent caught in an impossible bind, as part of his effort to burnish his image in the years following Washita. Yet his point about the contradictory desires of the American public does evoke something of the incoherence of U.S. policy, including military policy, regarding American Indians from the period of the Civil War until the full-scale acculturation program of allotment and boarding schools that ascended in the 1880s. On the one hand, the United States clearly asserted its right to dictate the terms of existence (and even nonexistence) to the indigenous peoples it found living within the territory it claimed. On the other, the United States also evinced a constant desire to convince itself that it acted with a sense of justice, that its actions were intended to do more than unilaterally enforce its own naked power. One result of this ambivalence was a series of treaties in the eighteenth and nineteenth centuries that, at least on their face, recognize Indian tribes as independent entities, nations even, freely selling their lands to the United States, usually in exchange for promises of money and the recognition of the tribal right to occupy other land.

The 1860s was the last full decade of treaty-making between the United States and Native peoples. The treaty system failed to resolve the conflicts between the indigenous tribes west of the Mississippi and the United States for a variety of reasons. Most obviously, the treaties involved complex matters of geographic boundaries and the transfer of wealth, and negotiations were burdened by the difficulties of linguistic translation. But the obstacles went beyond honest or even dishonest miscomprehension. The negotiators from the United States required approval from the House of Representatives, which sometimes amended the treaty, failed to approve it, or delayed action for a year or more—a cumbersome process that often baffled Indian leaders. Tribal negotiators, meanwhile, frequently did not possess the kind of political authority that the U.S. government presumed. Both *tribe* and *chief*, after all, were terms devised by European colonists to impose their own structures on what seemed to them to be chaotic social and political systems. In the case of the Cheyennes, for instance, the influence of a peace chief could wax and wane and might even be limited to his own band.

On the mid-nineteenth-century Plains, the problems of the treaty system went even deeper. Simply put, the settlements reached by the treaty councils very rarely offered sustainable solutions to allow the continued co-existence of U.S. settlers and Indian peoples. Regardless of the intentions of those who negotiated and signed the treaties, all but a few of the treaties seem obviously untenable to most historians now as long-term agreements for either side. The United States constantly hoped that it could concentrate the Plains Indians on plots of land out of the paths of white emigration and settlement, but it rarely considered whether the land would be suitable to a people who had little interest in developing the agricultural habits that the United States hoped to inculcate. For their part, tribal leaders sometimes neglected to make clear their sense of entitlement to the use of land beyond that specified in the particular treaty; they badly overestimated the willingness of the United States to fulfill its promises of material compensation in a timely manner; and they rarely had complete control over the young men who sought more violent resistance. The result was that treaties produced short periods of peace, followed by renewed incidents of violence, followed by further rounds of treaty-making. With historical hindsight, the treaties seem less like solemn, binding compacts to be followed in perpetuity and more like moves on a chessboard in which each side sought a comparative advantage before the next turn. How could either side view the treaty process as enduring when the peace chiefs of the Southern Cheyenne entered into not one but three treaties with the United States within a single decade (in 1861, 1865, 1867)? None of these treaties, after all, sufficed to prevent either the violence of Sand Creek or Custer's attack on Black Kettle's Washita camp.

In 1871, the U.S. Congress decided that no future treaties would be made with American Indians (though it continued to execute "agreements" with Indian tribes structured in almost the same manner as earlier treaties).[25] For non-Indians, the treaties had been intended as steps toward the gradual disintegration of American Indian tribes. Sympathetic whites believed the reservations set aside by the treaties to be places where Indians could learn the habits of "civilization" so that future generations descended from them would become absorbed into the general population. A less sympathetic understanding considered the reservations to be holding pens where Indians would simply die out over time.[26] Many white Americans believed that Indians rejected this incorporation into civilized modernity because of an innate love of anarchistic freedom. "The exigencies of modern civilization point to the inevitable doom of the aboriginal people of the United States," a journalist reporting on the Indian wars of the southern Plains wrote. "Their savage natures, incapable of restraint, render them by instinct foes to progress and the cause of humanity."[27] While the emerging group of reformers known as the Friends of the Indian might replace "doom" with *dissolution* or the later term *assimilation,* and might argue that this "instinct" could be overcome with careful teaching and training, the fundamental reasoning of white Americans would remain constant: tribal Indian life revolved around a kind of premodern freedom that made it incompatible with American modernity.[28] This premise guided the Indian policy of the United States.

Those indigenous leaders who negotiated treaties and agreements, as well as those who led their people into battle, started from a different premise: Indians needed to find a way to survive as tribal peoples. Of course, they frequently differed among themselves—both from tribe to tribe and within each tribe—about how this could be accomplished. Among the Cheyennes, for instance, Black Kettle and other peace chiefs hoped that the reservations agreed to in the treaties could be the path to such a future; the Dog Soldiers and others believed that military resistance and raids on white settlers were better means to defend their territorial claims. Neither Black Kettle nor the Dog Soldiers, though, imagined a time when men and women of Cheyenne descent might live without thinking of themselves as and acting in ways that they considered to be Cheyenne. In fact, Plains Indians sometimes perceived their growing conflicts with the United States as reasons to *heighten* their sense of themselves as discrete peoples. A (translated) sentence from Black Kettle's speech during an 1865 treaty council is telling. One year after the slaughter of Sand Creek, he said, "We consider that we are living as in the olden time when we were one people together for the fear of other troubles." For Black Kettle, the growing intensity of contact between Cheyennes and others meant that the Cheyennes would regard themselves as "one people together" for a common defense, "as in the olden time," not that they would disperse as men and women individuated and separate from the "people."[29]

At the time that Black Kettle made this speech, many non-Indians believed that the conflicts between the United States and the Plains Indians hinged on innate racial instincts that rendered the Cheyennes and other Natives "foes to progress." More recently, a popular interpretation of the Indian Wars has cast them as the result of differing cultural attitudes regarding labor and the use of land, a product of the discrepancy between hunting societies and an agricultural one. Black Kettle's words suggest a third manner of understanding U.S.-Indian warfare: Black Kettle observed that the Cheyennes were acting with and for *political* power. What was at stake, from this perspective, was the ability of Plains tribes to continue to constitute themselves as a political people distinct from the United States, rather than as a conglomeration of individuals who were becoming—or whose children would become—new members of the U.S. body politic. The tribal peoples of the Plains were not searching for a route to civic equality within the United States but for the continuation of themselves as independent and autonomous.

Significantly, the white Americans of the nineteenth century who understood best the political nature of these conflicts may have been the soldiers of the U.S. army. General Philip Sheridan—the man who summoned Custer back to the Plains and whose orders would lead Custer into battle against the Cheyennes on the Washita River—later wrote of the Plains Indians: "We took away their country and their means of support, broke up their mode of living, their habits of life, introduced disease and decay among them, and it was for this and against this they made war. Could any one expect less?"[30] Sheridan, whose statement about the only "good Indians" being dead ones may be the most frequently quoted line on the Indian Wars, could hardly be said to be an Indian apologist. Here, though, he puts the actions into a context too frequently missing from discussion of U.S.-Indian violence. The point was not that Plains Indians wanted to hunt instead of farm or preferred war to peace. Rather, Sheridan realized that Black Kettle and other Cheyennes were engaged in a defense of the conditions—the "means of support" and "mode of living"—that would allow them to survive as "one people," an autonomous nation. But from Sheridan's perspective, that defense would have to be overcome.

⟫ ⊙ ⟪

In October 1867, Southern Cheyennes, Kiowas, Comanches, and Arapahos were meeting with the U.S. Peace Commission at Medicine Lodge Creek, in Kansas, for a treaty conference. Approximately five thousand Indians gathered for the treaty council, in which the negotiators doggedly pursued a policy of concentration and acculturation. If the tribes would agree to live to the south, in the Indian Territory, they would be out of the way of the major routes of U.S. emigration and settlement—and then, the U.S. negotiators hoped, they could be induced to give up hunting and warfare for sedentary farming. The Cheyennes were particularly wary of the treaty, but some, like Black Kettle, were eager for peace; others were placated by treaty provisions that allowed Cheyennes to travel outside the reservation to follow the buffalo. In the end, even Bull Bear, a Dog Soldier, signed.

While the members of the peace commission claimed success, not everyone was so sanguine. Alfred Barnitz, a captain in the Seventh Cavalry, described the scene in his journal with foreboding. The Cheyennes, he wrote "*have no idea that* they are giving up, or that they have ever given up the country which they claim as their own. . . . The treaty all amounts to nothing, and we will certainly have another war sooner or later with the Cheyennes" (emphasis in original).[31]

By the summer of 1868, the peace agreement was falling apart, and Barnitz's prediction was coming true. Congress, tied up with the impeachment of Andrew Johnson, was slow in appropriating funds for the goods promised to the Cheyennes, and the discontent of the Dog Soldiers, who had been skeptical of the treaty from the beginning, erupted into violence. In August, a party of Cheyennes that had started out on an intratribal raid against their Pawnee enemies changed its mind and instead ripped through the white settlements on the Saline and Solomon rivers, killing fifteen men and raping five women in the process.[32] The attacks on white settlements continued throughout August, and by the next month, Sheridan, whose command of the Department of the Missouri gave him military jurisdiction over the southern Plains, estimated that the Cheyennes and other Indians had killed one hundred citizens, raped thirteen women, and stolen over a thousand head of livestock. Sheridan's military attempted to respond in September with a show of force, but the campaign only contributed to further violence, and a series of Cheyenne and Kiowa attacks on wagon trains and homesteads in early October became especially newsworthy because they included the kidnapping of two white women.[33]

By the time of the kidnappings, Custer had been reunited with the Seventh Cavalry. Sheridan planned a strike against the winter camps of the hostile Indians, with one force heading east from Fort Bascom, New Mexico, another heading southeast from Fort Lyon, Colorado, and the third force heading south from Fort Dodge, Kansas. Custer and his Seventh Cavalry constituted the bulk of this third force, to be augmented by a newly raised regiment of Kansas Volunteers. In mid-November, the Seventh Cavalry marched one hundred miles south, into the Indian Territory, where it established Fort Supply, a base camp and rendezvous point for the Seventh Cavalry and the Kansas Volunteers. Plagued by poor weather and even poorer scouts, though, the volunteers failed to show in time, and on November 23, in the midst of a snowstorm, Custer led a contingent of approximately eight hundred cavalry, a dozen Osage scouts, and a handful of civilians on a mission to find the camps of the Indians, kill the warriors, and take prisoner as many women and children as possible. The band—Custer preferred to bring the regimental band on his campaigns—played "The Girl I Left Behind Me."

As the Seventh Cavalry marched south, Black Kettle was traveling north and west from Fort Cobb, the Indian Territory military installation charged with distributing goods to "friendly" tribes. With three other Cheyenne and Arapaho leaders, Black Kettle had asked the commander of the post, Colonel William B. Hazen, if he could bring his camp to the region surrounding the fort. He explained that he could not speak for the Cheyennes north of the Arkansas River—meaning the Dog Soldiers—and he even admitted that some who participated in the recent violence might have been members of his band. "I have always done my best to keep my young men quiet," he told Hazen, according to a transcript made by an army captain, "but some will not listen and since the fighting began, I have not been able to keep them all at home." Black Kettle hoped that his honesty and his earnest desire for peace would persuade Hazen to invite Black Kettle's and allied bands of Cheyennes to move southeast to Fort Cobb. Hazen, however, feared that Sheridan—whom he called "the great war chief"—would still regard the Cheyennes as hostile, and he did not want to repeat the error of Sand Creek by extending protection to Indians who might be attacked by the military soon after. "Therefore you must go back to your country," he told Black Kettle and the others, "and if the soldiers come to fight you must remember that they are not from me, but from that great war chief, and with him you must make peace." [34]

Four days later, Black Kettle arrived back at his camp on the south side of the Washita River. Black Kettle's band of approximately 50 lodges and 250 Cheyennes and Arapahos had set up their winter camp a few miles west of a larger cluster of Indian camps: Arapaho, Kiowa, Kiowa-Comanche, and Apache villages encircled by a sweeping bend in the river. Taken together, around six thousand Indians were camping along the Washita, whose topography provided water, wood, game, and protection from the bitterest winter winds. [35] This land was not included in the territory designated for the Cheyennes in the Medicine Lodge treaty; that territory was to the north, between the Cimarron and Arkansas rivers. However, the Cheyennes hoped that camping farther south, farther away from the Kansas violence, would yield more protection, and the treaty reserved the Southern Cheyennes' right to hunt and camp on lands south of the Arkansas River as long as sufficient numbers of buffalo justified their doing so.

Of course the same treaty also stated that the Cheyennes would no longer "attack any persons at home or traveling, nor molest or disturb any wagon-trains, coaches, mules, or cattle"—a stipulation that Sheridan and Custer believed the Cheyennes had violated, nullifying the agreement.[36]

That night, Black Kettle conferred with other leaders in his band. They agreed that when the snow cleared, they would send emissaries to the "great war chief" of the north in order to identify themselves as peaceful; equally important, they decided that they would move their camp the next day to be closer to the other Indian villages. One Cheyenne woman later said that Black Kettle's own wife—Medicine Woman Later, who bore the scars of nine wounds inflicted at Sand Creek—urged that the village move that very night, but the chiefs thought that the recent blizzard and deep snow had made travel for soldiers difficult enough that they could afford a short delay.[37] The chiefs were wrong, and the Seventh Cavalry charged into the camp the next morning in a day of violence and destruction that would leave its denizens scattered, imprisoned, and deceased. Both Black Kettle and Medicine Woman Later would die early in the fighting, just days short of the four-year anniversary of Chivington's attack on their camp at Sand Creek.

The 103 prisoners taken by the Seventh Cavalry (figure 9) suggests something of the difference between Custer and Chivington, who reminded his men of the white women and children killed in recent raids and allowed them to take their vengeance accordingly.[38] The triumphant

Figure 9. This photograph of Cheyenne prisoners captured at the Washita by the Seventh Cavalry was taken at Fort Dodge, Kansas. (Photograph courtesy of Little Bighorn Battlefield National Monument.)

parade that the returning Seventh Cavalry staged under Custer's direction for Sheridan at Fort Supply four days later also illustrates the distinction. Instead of brandishing the corpses of the victims as some of Chivington's men did after Sand Creek, Custer put his command—and himself—on as extravagant a display as resources would allow. Lieutenant Godfrey said the procession "rivaled and no doubt was the prototype of the modern Wild West Shows." [39] Custer's one-sentence description of the procession reveals both his desire to please his superiors and the aesthetic quality of the military glory he sought:

> In speaking of the review afterwards, General Sheridan said the appearance of the troops, with the bright rays of the sun reflected from their burnished arms and equipments, as they advanced in beautiful order and precision down the slope, the band playing, and the blue soldiers' uniforms slightly relieved by the gaudy colors of the Indians, both captives and Osages, the strangely fantastic part played by the Osage guides, their shouts, chanting their war songs, and firing their guns in [the] air, all combined to render the scene one of the most beautiful and highly interesting he remembered ever having witnessed. [40]

Custer, indeed, had returned.

Considered within the broader history of conflicts between the tribes of the North American Plains and the United States military, what might be most remarkable about the Battle of the Washita—as it came to be known—is how largely unremarkable it is. Both Sheridan and Custer emphasized the novelty of a winter campaign when discussing the battle and the military operations that followed, but this tactic had been used before, in campaigns as recent as General Patrick Connor's attack on a Shoshone-Bannock village in 1863 and the final, "scorched-earth" campaign against the Navajos led by General James Carleton and Colonel Kit Carson in 1864. [41] Moreover, the perceived success of the Washita fight meant that the offensive deployment of troops during the winter would become more common in the years that followed. (For instance, the planners of the 1876 campaign that included the Battle of the Little Bighorn originally hoped to begin the campaign immediately after the winter, before the summer months.)

In his book on U.S. military tactics in the post–Civil War period, Perry D. Jamieson notes that even though there was no formal statement of doctrine for conducting campaigns against Indians, there were a number of common, widely advocated practices, including the necessity of offensive, preemptive strikes, the use of Indian scouts, the deployment of advance and flanking soldiers to protect the main contingent, and the encirclement of an Indian camp so as to be able to assault it simultaneously from multiple directions. Custer's attack on Black Kettle's village—as well as the larger offensive campaign conducted by Sheridan—used every one of the tactics named by Jamieson as characteristic of this larger pattern of U.S.-Indian fighting.[42] Underlying these strategies was the decision to import the "total war" philosophy that had emerged in the fighting of the U.S. Civil War. The purpose of that philosophy, as Jerome Greene explains, was to punish the populace as a whole with an aggressive campaign that instilled terror "among noncombatant as well as combatant populations by any means possible, including indiscriminate destruction of their homes and property and rooting out and killing all warriors and others who might give opposition."[43] As Sheridan put it in an 1870 letter to his superior: "During the [Civil] war did anyone hesitate to attack a village or town occupied by the enemy because women or children were within its limits? Did we cease to throw shells into Vicksburg or Atlanta because women and children were there?"[44] For Sheridan, the noncombatant casualties at Washita were the standard, not the deviation.

Just as Sheridan and Custer conformed to the military norms of their time, Washita also became typical in another way, by provoking controversy. The controversy in fact started before the actual military engagement. "In all these movements," Thomas Murphy, a superintendent of Indian Affairs on the central Plains, wrote about the mobilization of troops under Sheridan, "I fancy I see another Sand Creek Massacre."[45] Sand Creek was also on the mind of Colonel Edward Wynkoop, who tendered his resignation from his appointment as the commanding agent at Fort Cobb just days after the Washita fight. Wynkoop had not yet learned of the battle, but he feared that once again Indians who believed that they were under the protection of the army would be attacked. He also objected to the use of volunteer troops from Kansas and Native American scouts recruited from the enemies of Southern Plains Indians, both of whom he believed would engage in excessive violence. Four years earlier, Wynkoop had mistakenly urged the Cheyennes to camp near Fort Lyon, and he remained troubled by the role he had played then. "I most certainly refuse to again be the instrument of murder of innocent women and children," Wynkoop wrote in his resignation letter.[46]

When news of the Washita fight began to circulate in the press, the comparison of Washita to Sand Creek continued. Wynkoop and others made the comparison implicit when, in the course of denouncing the battle, they dwelled upon the figure of Black Kettle, a leader who "desired to remain at peace, only to meet his death at the hands of white men, in whom he had too often fatally trusted and who triumphantly report the fact of having his scalp in their possession."[47] Those who defended the army's Washita attack, including Sheridan's superior, General William T. Sherman, dismissed the similarity to Sand Creek. Sherman stated that the "cases are widely different" and made reports about the white possessions found in Black Kettle's village and accounts of the meeting between Black Kettle and Hazen available to the press.[48] He explained in a letter to Sheridan that he hoped the documents would counteract assertions "to the effect that Black Kettle's was a friendly camp, and that Custer's battle was a second Sand Creek affair."[49]

By late December, at least some newspapers were reporting that Hazen's warning to Black Kettle meant that "Custer's attack differs essentially from Chivington's, at Sand Creek, the Indians in the latter case, being at the time, under the protection of the United States military authorities."[50] By early January, the *Army and Navy Journal* had picked up the argument as well: "We are told that Black Kettle's band was friendly, and, accordingly, that Custer is a second Chivington. That is not the fact. . . . [Black Kettle's] camp has been a rendezvous for young warriors, who start from it as a 'base,' and return to it with booty."[51]

Custer himself later noted that he anticipated the reaction that his attack on Black Kettle's camp would bring. "Before setting out on the [Washita] expedition, I had stated to the officers in a casual manner that all parties engaged in the conduct of the contemplated campaign against the Indians must reconcile themselves in advance—no matter how the expedition might result—to becoming the recipients of censure and unbounded criticism." Failure to find the Indians, Custer recalled himself saying, would enrage frontier whites; a successful strike would prompt "horrified humanitarians" to accuse the soldiers "of attacking and killing friendly and defenseless Indians." As Custer anticipated, his predictions proved true; "no sooner was the intelligence of the Battle of the Washita flashed over the country than the anticipated cry was raised." Two different groups, he said, protested the Seventh Cavalry's attack at Washita. The first were "humanitarians" whose intentions were honorable but who worked from "sentimental," mistaken notions about the nobility of the Plains Indians. More sinister opposition, in Custer's opinion, came from whites "actuated by pecuniary motives alone," men whom Custer and others often referred to as the "Indian Ring"—dishonest traders, brokers, and agents who profited from the status quo on the Plains by smuggling weapons or alcohol or by illegally selling government contracts crucial to the civilian Indian Bureau.[52] Between the idealism of the humanitarians and the corruption of the Indian Ring, Custer and most of his fellow officers thought, stood the army, the only party able and willing to recognize what was necessary to bring the Indians into submission.

Custer allocates only a few pages of his memoir, *My Life on the Plains,* to the negative reaction to the Washita fight, but they are significant ones, for they reveal that the self-consciousness that had marked his Civil War career would continue to matter as he reshaped his persona to fit the frontier army. He would present himself as a professional soldier who valued pragmatism over philosophy and who therefore understood the ambiguities of waging war against indigenous peoples in ways that neither panicked settlers nor doe-eyed reformers could. The entire first chapter of the memoir is devoted to his characterization of American Indians, and his writing there reads today as a kind of catalog of the conflicting beliefs about Indians held by Americans during the time. He claims to be "shocked and disgusted" by Indian "traits and customs" but also finds "much to be admired and still more of deep and unvarying interest." He says that Indians are the products of their environment—"not worse, perhaps, than his white brother would be similarly born and bred"—yet they also stand outside the laws of humanity altogether—"a race incapable of being judged by the rules or laws applicable to any other known of men." This chapter is also where Custer makes the subjunctive profession of sympathy that I have quoted in earlier chapters: "If I were an Indian, I often think I would greatly prefer to cast my lot among those of my people adhered to the free open plains rather than submit to the confined limits of a reservation, there to be the recipient of the blessed benefits of civilization, with its vices thrown in without stint or measure."[53]

"Shocked and disgusted," but still able to imagine himself as an Indian, Custer does not shy away from the moral ambiguity that many non-Indian Americans felt about the conquest of indigenous peoples. Instead, he presents the Indian fighter as the person who knows those ambiguities best. He subtitled his memoir *Personal Experiences with Indians* and presented himself as someone who trafficked on the frontier between white and Indian life—the oiled curls and black velvet of the Civil War left behind in favor of a beard and buckskins (figure 10). Far from ignoring the controversies that surrounded the campaigns of the U.S. army on the Plains, Custer embraced them by positioning himself as a seasoned professional, a student

Figure 10. This photograph, taken in 1869 at Fort Sill, Indian Territory, shows how Custer appeared on the Washita campaign. (Photograph courtesy of Little Bighorn Battlefield National Monument.)

of Indian life who would perform his duties with a tough-minded fairness required by the very national uncertainty that made his Washita attack on Black Kettle's village the subject of debate.

However, a large segment of the public in the United States was already weary of that debate in the late 1860s, tired of making judgments about the necessity of U.S.-Indian violence. "The Indian question is evidently a very difficult question," a *Harper's Weekly* editorial printed in response to the Washita fight begins. "It is also very uninteresting one, and few care to understand it." In time, even fewer would choose to understand it. The spectacular last stand at the Battle of the Little Bighorn would offer an image of white America as a victim of the violence of the frontier that, while shocking, was also comforting because it offered the United States a stance of moral righteousness in the face of a vicious foe. The fight at the Washita, by contrast, brought into resolution a more problematic picture that many Americans chose to avoid rather than scrutinize: an attack on a village with civilian casualties, women and children held prisoner, and a dead Indian leader who had been on record as a seeker of peace. That Sheridan and Custer may have had good reasons to believe Black Kettle's band, as well as the other villages camped on the Washita, had harbored some of the perpetrators of the raids on Kansas settlers did not ameliorate the moral murkiness but only added to it. Even though the Washita attack established Custer as an Indian fighter of renown—it was his most significant victory in battle against the Plains Indians—white Americans later chose to remember the conflict in which he died.

While the Battle of the Little Bighorn became the subject of paintings, novels, and Wild West shows, the fight at the Washita—sometimes, as I will discuss, referred to as a "battle," at other times as a "massacre"—received little attention in popular culture.[54] It does not appear in films like *They Died with Their Boots On;* the image of Custer attacking a village that included women and children would not square with the portrait of heroic sacrifice required at the time the film was issued, when the United States stood at the brink of another world war. Interestingly, Washita—or something like it—does figure in John Ford's *The Searchers;* John Wayne looks for his white niece among recently captured Indian prisoners being held by the Seventh Cavalry after a winter attack on a village, but the name and location of the fight are not given.[55] Instead, the first mass media introduction to Washita for most Americans would be Arthur Penn's film version of *Little Big Man,* in 1970. In the film, the attack on the Cheyenne village is wholly without provocation; the Cheyennes (including Jack Crabb, a white man who has chosen to live with the Cheyennes, played by Dustin Hoffman) believe themselves entirely safe because they are camping on "Indian land." As the Seventh Cavalry rides into the village and wreaks unexpected havoc, the regimental band stands in neat rows in the distance, coolly filling the air with the strains of "Garryowen." The music gives the scene an absurdist quality, but the attack is also the most graphically violent scene in the film, with slow-motion shots of women and children gunned down as they flee from burning lodges.[56] The evocation of U.S. atrocities reported in Vietnam is not subtle.

Released during the Vietnam War, *Little Big Man* demonstrates something of the difficulty of commemorating an event in which the United States was largely understood to be the aggressor—something that had become evident about the Washita conflict in the century since it had transpired. The sites of Black Kettle's camp and the other Indian villages were part of the Cheyenne and Arapaho reservation designated in the aftermath

of Sheridan's southern Plains campaign, but both tribes avoided that particular part of the Washita valley and gravitated toward the eastern half of
the reservation. The Cheyennes and Arapahos resisted dividing the reservation through allotment, but government officials used subterfuge in
1890 to achieve the appearance of tribal consent.[57] As a result, the reservation was opened to a land run in 1892—becoming in the process part of
the Oklahoma Territory—and approximately fifty white settlers raced to
found a town about two miles distant from the scene of the Washita fighting. In spite of the town's name, Cheyenne, it had no Indian residents,
and during the first decades of its existence, the agricultural community
displayed only occasional interest in commemorating the region's history
of violence.

That interest was momentarily heightened in 1930, when a writer
named Charles J. Brill traveled with two Cheyenne survivors of the Seventh Cavalry, Magpie and Little Beaver, to the Washita River so that they
could identify the site of Black Kettle's village and tell their stories of what
occurred there. During the trip, the group learned that the remains of an
unknown Indian had been unearthed near one of the Indian village sites
some fifteen years previously—and that they were being housed in the office of the town's newspaper. That November, after Brill published both
Magpie's story of the attack and the account of their recent journey to the
Washita, both returned to the site of Black Kettle's village for an interment
ceremony that attracted thousands and sparked a short-lived campaign for
a memorial to the Indians who died there. Along with several non-Indian
speakers, Magpie addressed the crowd in a manner that would have been
familiar to anyone who had attended the burial of the hatchet held just
four years previously at the fiftieth anniversary of the Battle of the Little
Bighorn. "He told the crowd that he forgave General Custer," stated one
newspaper account, "and that he asked God to forgive Custer for the part
he had in the Battle of the Washita."[58]

While members of the community eventually placed a granite marker
at the gravesite of the Cheyenne who had been reinterred, there seemed to
be little interest in developing a larger memorial, museum, or park, as had
been originally called for during the commemoration. Given the emerging
consensus in the 1930s on the Washita fight, it seems hardly surprising that
white Oklahomans elected not to memorialize it. Brill, for instance, took a
deeply skeptical attitude toward Custer and the Seventh Cavalry; he later
published the first book-length account of the Washita fight, *Conquest of
the Southern Plains* (1938), which casts Black Kettle as the victim of U.S.
duplicity at both Sand Creek and the Washita. Even John Casady, the edi-

tor of Cheyenne's weekly newspaper and one of those who supported the commemoration of Washita, wrote in 1932 that what occurred there had come to be "regarded as a massacre rather than a battle"—nomenclature to which we will return later.[59]

Cheyennes, meanwhile, may have been reluctant to engage in public commemoration of the Washita conflict for other reasons. After the town of Cheyenne was established in the 1890s, the land where the fighting occurred had been settled by non-Indian farmers and ranchers, and therefore staging events would have involved a degree of cooperation unusual for that time. A line from Casady's account of the 1930 reinterment ceremonies hints that little interaction took place between the white residents of Cheyenne and the people for whom the town was named. Noting that several Cheyenne families had camped along the Washita River valley during the 1930 ceremonies, he writes that the Indians "enjoyed visits from people of Cheyenne [the town] to the camp and were communicative"—implying that such interactions were rare enough to deserve commentary. If the social divide had not been a barrier, the suffering experienced by the Cheyenne Indians at that place may have been. Recent interviews with descendants of Cheyennes who were present in Black Kettle's village suggest that those who lived through Custer's attack were sometimes (though certainly not always) reluctant to talk about it and that some Cheyennes regard their family stories of the violence as not to be shared with outsiders.[60]

It was not until the 1950s—after economic depression and a cycle of droughts and floods had prompted Oklahoma to turn to heritage tourism—that more formal efforts to commemorate Washita yielded lasting results. In 1958 the state opened the Black Kettle Museum, a ranch-style brick building built to house Indian artifacts and exhibits about the battle, in the center of Cheyenne. (The Black Kettle Museum has remained open as of this writing until the National Park Service completes its new Washita Battlefield visitor center.) In the early 1960s, Oklahoma constructed a large granite interpretive marker telling the story of the Washita fight next to the nearby state highway and then purchased a three-acre parcel for a small park overlooking the site of Black Kettle's village. In 1965, Secretary of the Interior Stewart Udall was present at the installation of a marker designating the land as a National Historic Landmark (a move that requires a presidential proclamation but not an act of Congress).

This series of memorial activities was punctuated by an elaborate centennial anniversary that the town of Cheyenne staged in 1968. The day began with a parade that included covered wagon trains and, in the words of one resident, "real Indians, in traditional dress," for a "spectacular flavor."[61] The town's citizens hosted a free lunch for residents and visitors alike, nearly two thousand in all. The focus of the commemoration, though, was a reenactment of Custer's attack on Black Kettle's village at the original location west of the town. The organizers of the event had persuaded Cheyenne Indians to portray their forebears in tepees arranged in a circle, and the core of the U.S. regiment was portrayed by a group of California reenactors who had traveled to Oklahoma for the event. The reenactment began with a reading of Magpie's 1930 speech (or at least a translation of his speech) urging forgiveness for Custer and justice for Indians, and then proceeded to the mock fighting introduced by the regimental tune that Custer's band had tried to play one century earlier, "Garryowen," only to have the initial notes freeze in the morning air.[62] "From behind the screening hills came the galloping horses—pandemonium broke loose in the hills," one observer wrote. "The grandsons of the 7th Cavalry, outfitted as their sires[,] had been added for authenticity. Mercilessly they sacked the Cheyenne village as soldiers fell from their horses, dead in their tracks."[63] A visiting newspaper reporter focused her attention on the estimated thirty-five hundred spectators who had come to watch the event. The audience, she wrote, "was a quiet and pensive crowd, their thoughts doubtlessly going back one hundred years, to the time the scene was a grim reality and not harmless pageantry."[64]

One observer to whom the pageantry seemed anything but harmless was Lawrence H. Hart, an ordained Mennonite minister and, in his midthirties, one of the younger peace chiefs of the Southern Cheyennes. Hart had been one of those to whom the town citizens had turned for help in recruiting Cheyenne Indians for the reenactment. His older brother, Alvin, portrayed Black Kettle, and his children were present in the village. Decades later, he recalled that he did not know that the town had recruited such realistic cavalry reenactors, with authentic period uniforms—and weapons. As he watched them firing blanks into the village, the effect became disturbing. "It became real for me," he recalled in a 1999 interview. "I just had all kinds of feelings—not very good feelings—about these Grandsons [of the Seventh Cavalry], especially since my children were down there."[65]

The day did not end, though, with Custer's victory over Black Kettle. Hart and hundreds of others returned to the center of the town for the reburial of the remains of another Cheyenne Indian believed to have been killed in the battle, whose skeleton had been unearthed more than thirty years previously during a bridge excavation project on the Washita. Hart and other Cheyennes had insisted on being able to bury the remains properly as a condition of Indian participation in the reenactment. The ceremony was held on the grounds of the Black Kettle Museum, and as the procession carried the coffin through the crowd, a young Cheyenne woman draped a blanket over it. Hart was surprised to find the Seventh Cavalry reenactors at the ceremony as well, saluting the coffin as it was carried past them—and even more surprised as he was instructed by, in his words, "the older and wiser peace chiefs" to remove the blanket from the coffin and present it to the regiment's captain. Hart followed the instructions and believed that his elders were instructing him in the ways of Sweet Medicine, the Cheyenne prophet whose teachings of righteousness and justice remain foundational to Cheyenne political governance. The Seventh Cavalry and the other non-Indians in the crowd understood the gesture as an overture of reconciliation, and the captain presented Hart with a pin from his uniform. "Never again will your people hear 'Garry Owen,'" he told Hart.[66]

Nearly thirty years after this ceremony, Hart found himself again confronting the legacy of Washita. This time, he was speaking in front of a congressional committee that was evaluating the possibility of incorporating Washita into the National Park system as a National Historic Site, and he was able to explain the significance of what occurred in 1868 in terms of an event that had occurred the previous year in Oklahoma City: "The view we [Cheyenne Indians] hold about that ground can best be understood in the context of the Oklahoma City bombing," Hart said. He went on to describe his participation in the ritual reading of the victims' names at the one-year anniversary of the bombing of the Murrah Federal Building and how that experience led him to understand the similarities between the site of the bombing and the site of Black Kettle's village. Both places, he explained, have become "hallowed ground" by what transpired there—"a holy space"; both events were "highly traumatic" and "highly emotional"; and both deserved protection and public commemoration.[67]

Hart's language represents a turning point in the commemoration of the Washita fight at the turn of the twenty-first century. Most obviously, his comparison identifies the position of Black Kettle's village with the kind of innocence ascribed to the victims of the Oklahoma City bombing— though Hart was careful to avoid suggesting that the Seventh Cavalry had the kind of impulses that drove the 1995 terrorists. No longer is Washita treated as a strategic military engagement in a part of a larger war fought by the United States, but rather as an event of spectacular violence that remade the consciousness of the people who survived it. It would be impossible to accept the terms of this comparison in any manner and still find the kind of reenactment staged on the centennial anniversary within the bounds of taste. If anything, Hart's testimony offers a much belated explanation of why he found the dramatic repetition of the Seventh Cavalry attack in 1968 to be so unsettling. Freud's word for this kind of emotional disturbance was *unheimlich*—a word that is usually translated into English as "the uncanny" but that more literally means "the unhomey." [68] Lawrence Hart saw in the reenactment of the Washita fight an assault on his home, his family, and his land, so powerful that the Cheyennes were still coping with its significance—just as citizens of the United States saw the Oklahoma City bombing as an attack on their homeland beyond comprehension.

While the bombing of the Murrah Building in Oklahoma City may not have altered the significance of the Washita fight for the Cheyennes, it played a role in shifting how and to what extent Americans were willing to publicly acknowledge acts of violence through commemoration. The elaborate ceremonies held in Oklahoma City in the aftermath of the bombing, as well as the immediate drive for appropriate memorialization, signaled a consensus that the public commemoration of violence plays a crucial role in aiding affected communities struggling to cope with their collective loss and in providing civic instruction on the need to prevent future suffering. [69] With its rows of empty chairs and towering "gates of time," the Oklahoma City National Memorial (dedicated in 2000) would be only one in a chain of permanent memorials to violence of this kind—a chain that includes the Vietnam Veterans Memorial (the "Vietnam Wall") on the National Mall (dedicated in 1982) and the United States Holocaust Memorial Museum (dedicated in 1993) in Washington, and that will include the "Ground Zero" memorials currently being planned and constructed at the site of the World Trade Center attacks in New York City.

Although a much smaller presence in the commemorative landscape of the United States, the 1996 legislation authorizing the creation of the Washita National Historic Site is another link in this same chain. Many of the key players in the legislative process were non-Indians who were eager for federal aid to preserve the village site and the Black Kettle Museum in the face of budget cutbacks from the state of Oklahoma, as well as some residents of the town of Cheyenne and other nearby communities who believed that a unit of the National Park Service would produce a much-needed economic boost to an area whose population had been in decline since the 1930s. [70] The latter were surely encouraged by a report attributed to the Oklahoma Historical Society in the early 1990s stating that a National Park Service visitor center could attract as many as

100,000 visitors per year and generate over $12 million in annual economic activity.[71] The first attempt to pass legislation creating the Washita Battlefield National Historic Site failed in 1994, however, in part because private landowners objected to a provision that would have placed conservation easements to prevent development on some three thousand acres adjacent to the site itself.[72]

When the legislation was introduced again in 1996 (with much more modest conservation easements), the intervening events in Oklahoma City made possible the comparison that Hart articulated for Congress. Moreover, the bill that President Bill Clinton signed into law that year incorporated a particular relationship between contemporary Cheyennes and Arapahos and the development of the site by the National Park Service. The bill states that one of the purposes of the site will be to "provide opportunities for American Indian groups including the Cheyenne-Arapaho Tribe"—the present name of the tribal entity that includes the Southern Cheyennes and Arapahos of Oklahoma—"to be involved in the formulation of plans and educational programs," and it mandates that the Park Service "consult regularly with the Cheyenne-Arapaho Tribe" in its formulation of a management plan for the site.[73]

Four years later, in 2000, Congress authorized the acquisition of land for the Sand Creek Massacre National Historic Site—the only unit of the Park Service to include the word *massacre* in its title—with language that even more explicitly instructed the Park Service to accommodate the needs of descendants from those tribes who suffered there.[74] In both cases, the U.S. government has seen fit to commemorate its violent conflicts with Plains Indians with the purpose of recognizing and articulating some measure of the losses suffered by American Indians during the nineteenth-century expansion of the United States. Just as at Little Bighorn, these historic sites are being commemorated in ways that emphasize the experience of the defeated—but at Washita and Sand Creek, it is the Cheyennes, Araphaos, and other Plains Indians who occupy that role, not the Seventh Cavalry.

It was not until 2005 that the National Park Service could acquire the land necessary for the Sand Creek Massacre National Historic Site—and it did so with the help of the Cheyenne and Arapaho Tribes, which purchased more than fourteen hundred acres of land that it transferred to the National Park Service in trust.[75] Backers of the Washita Battlefield site in Oklahoma, on the other hand, were able to purchase the 326 acres designated in the 1996 legislation soon after it passed by using state and foundation funds and then transferring the land to the federal government.[76] The land contained within the park's boundaries at Washita includes the over-look constructed by the state in the 1960s and the land to the north that descends to the river. The Park Service commissioned both an archaeo-logical study and surveys of the land and vegetation. The river channel has changed over time; the abandoned railroad bed has altered the terrain as well. Flood control and other human activity have meant that the canopy of tamarisk, elm, and willow trees remains close to the river and other sloughs that occasionally hold water, rather than extending farther across the valley to provide the shelter that Black Kettle's followers sought.[77]

Yet once the visitor begins walking into the valley via the one and a half miles of trails maintained by the Park Service, it is easy to ignore the signs of human intrusion. In recent years, this National Historic Site has received around 15,000 visitors a year—compared with the approximately 400,000 visitors who come to the Little Bighorn Battlefield National Mon-ument. It is possible to walk down to the Washita River and back with-out seeing another person. Custer's attack here has little of the historical capital that the Battle of the Little Bighorn has accumulated in the last 125 years. There are no national organizations devoted to dissecting it, and the books devoted solely to Washita fit comfortably on a single shelf. (Indeed, the most comprehensive book on the Washita conflict was writ-ten by a Park Service historian as a result of his efforts to assess available resources for interpreting the site to the public.) The physical location of Black Kettle's village has surely played a role in the relative obscurity of Washita as well. While the Washita and other nearby river valleys were once important corridors for east-west travel by both Indians and Europe-ans, twentieth-century commerce largely passed this area by. The nearest major cities (Oklahoma City and Amarillo, Texas) are more than one hun-dred miles away; the railroads that passed through the region were built as spur lines and no longer run; and the interstate, which travels the path of the famous Route 66, is twenty-five miles in the distance. The 2000 census pegged the population of the town of Cheyenne at 778; the entire county has fewer than 3,500 residents.

The result is a historical landscape that remains relatively uncluttered by comparison to places like Little Bighorn or many Civil War battle sites. The lack of attention that has been paid to what occurred at Washita pre-sents a challenge to Park Service officials charged with generating inter-est and increasing the numbers of visitors to the site, but it also offers an opportunity. At the battlefield of the Little Bighorn, the commemorative activity of the last century has shaped the physical and cultural terrain to such an extent that the tangible markers of that commemoration have themselves become objects of veneration—which resulted in the outcry at the change of the battlefield's name as well as concern that the new Indian Memorial would detract from the older obelisk erected to honor the men who died with Custer. More recently, Custerologists have been outraged by plans to expand the Park Service visitor center at the Little Bighorn Battlefield National Monument; they fear further physical intrusion into a landscape that they would prefer to restore to its 1876 appearance. By contrast, the Park Service can start anew at Washita; for the last several years, it has been planning and constructing a visitor and cultural interpretive center located approximately one-quarter a mile away from the park itself. From the center, visitors can see the land where the fighting between the Seventh Cavalry and the Indian village took place, but the building itself will have little direct impact on the physical environment there.[78]

The decision about the location of the visitor center has interpretive consequences: the choice reflects an aesthetic of preservation and seeks to allow the visitor access to the physical land where the violence of 1868 took place with little direct mediation. That decision, though, is only one strand in the larger web of interpretation that the Park Service has been asked to spin. The legislation that created the Washita Battlefield National Historic Site stated the need to "recognize the importance of the Battle of the Washita as a nationally significant element of frontier military history and as a symbol of the struggles of the Southern Great Plains tribes to maintain control of their traditional use areas."[79] However, it contains no specific details mandating how to convey that significance to a public that has chosen largely to ignore it for more than a century. For that task, the Park Service staff is still working on contending with old conceptual models and deploying new ones—remaking what Custer called "the determined and unceasing warfare" between civilization and savagery into something more palatable for an age when Washita can be made to stand as an unsettling prolepsis of Vietnam and Oklahoma City.[80]

———»•«———

Historians' discussions of the events at the Washita River in 1868 frequently have been framed by the question of whether the violence that occurred there should be designated a "battle" or a "massacre." As I have tried to show, this argument has its origins in Custer and Black Kettle's own time, when non-Indian observers attempted either to connect Custer's offensive strike to Chivington's at Sand Creek (and thus characterize it as a massacre) or to distance the two (making it a battle). Biographers of Custer have tended to emphasize the fighting as two-sided, pointing out that

Custer's regiment sustained casualties and that Custer, unlike Chivington, issued orders to take women and children prisoner. Those historians who have focused in more depth on the Washita conflict itself have stressed that the attack occurred on a sleeping village that included noncombatants and that the village was under the leadership of a noted peace chief, Black Kettle. In the 1930s, Brill contended that Custer "killed more Indian women and children than warriors" and titled a chapter of his book "The Washita Massacre."[81] Two amateur Custerologists held a debate in 1948, on the sixtieth anniversary of Custer's attack, that has been printed three times under the title "The Battle of the Washita, or Custer's Massacre?"[82] Nearly thirty years later, in 1976, Stan Hoig titled his book *The Battle of the Washita* but coupled Washita and Sand Creek on its very first page, where he says they must both be called massacres "by any accepted use of the word."[83]

This question of nomenclature has become prominent again since Congress has designated Washita a National Historic Site. Following their forebears in Custerology, the Park Service organizers of a 1998 symposium called "Washita: Past, Present, and Future" staged a panel discussion titled "Battle or Massacre?" The participant who most decisively answered the question was the only Cheyenne on the panel, Henrietta Mann, who opted for the latter. By contrast, Edward Linenthal said it would be the "height of arrogance" for him to answer the question on his first visit to Washita, Paul Hutton stated that the question went "to the very heart . . . of why this national monument has been established" and that it was integrally tied with the struggle over the "control" of this history—but did not overtly signal his own preference.[84]

In his book-length history of the Washita conflict published in 2004, Park Service historian Jerome A. Greene calls the question of terminology "the most enduring controversy emanating from the Washita" and with typical evenhandedness explains the case for both nominations. "For the tribesmen who experienced the early morning attacks on their homes and families, wherein bullets from the charging forces ripped through the lodges," he writes, "every army assault must have seemed like a massacre." Furthermore, he notes that the scalping performed by the Osage scouts and a few of the Seventh Cavalry soldiers lends weight to the case for using that label. On the other hand, Greene is careful to note that Washita "was not an indiscriminate slaughter" and that "the troops evidently took some measures to protect the women and children." In the end, Greene follows the course adopted by Linenthal and Hutton at the 1998 symposium by not articulating a decisive choice between the two terms.[85] Lawrence Hart advocated a different path in an article he wrote after that symposium, suggesting that "a combined view—that both a massacre and a battle transpired that morning" would enable reconciliation.[86]

The current Park Service custodians of Washita would like to go even further than Greene's judicious weighing of the scales or Hart's comprehensive proposal. Both Wendy Lauritzen, the current superintendent of Washita Battlefield National Historic Site, and Alden Miller, the chief of natural and cultural resources, emphasize that they would prefer to move beyond the question of nomenclature altogether. Lauritzen compares the debate over terminology to the crack in the Liberty Bell: each is something that cannot be ignored but each is far from the most significant story about the history that has occurred. Miller goes even further, suggesting that posing the question whether Washita was a battle or a massacre turns interpretation into a debate with clearly drawn, antagonistic divisions. In such an atmosphere, he points out, those who visit the site would have "no room to add future information" or to learn more about the forces that actually produced Custer's attack on the Cheyenne and Arapaho village.[87]

Lauritzen and Miller are keenly aware of the significance of terminology, because the name that this unit of the Park Service bears has necessarily furthered this controversy rather than doused it. The legislation that incorporated Washita into the National Park Service named it "Washita *Battlefield* National Historic Site"—in part because its sponsors were hoping to take advantage of the efforts of the American Battlefield Protection Commission (later renamed the American Battlefield Protection Program) and others in the 1990s to protect battlefields, particularly Civil War battlefields, from commercial development.[88] No evidence exists that the architects of the legislation intended to adopt a particular historical interpretation by choosing to call the site a battlefield, but some members of the Cheyenne-Arapaho Tribes of Oklahoma have objected to the name precisely on those grounds. Many of the Cheyennes interviewed in 1999 as part of an ethnographic study commissioned by the Park Service voiced sentiments that the park had been misnamed. "When a man attacks a sleeping Cheyenne camp and kills women and children," Melvin Whitebird asked, "how can you call it a battle?" Larry Roman Nose said that he would prefer the name Washita Massacre Site and predicted that a more rigorous survey would reveal that a majority of Cheyennes would want the name changed. Both veterans of the U.S. armed forces, Whitebird and Roman Nose are among those who believe the "battlefield" moniker incorrectly portrayed the actions of Custer's regiment as being within the bounds of proper military conduct. For some Cheyennes, the choice of nomenclature fed into deeper concerns that the Park Service's development of the site would demean the suffering of those who died there. When asked what visitors should take away from their experience at Washita, Frances Beard responded that she did not agree with the principle of a historic site of any kind. "I think it's a place where our people are killed, . . . and I just don't think it should be a place where you show something off: 'Come over here and see this, this is where you killed my people,' you know. No I wouldn't do that. . . . I think it should be kept just the way it is, just leave it alone. Let them rest."[89]

Lauritzen is deeply sensitive to these reactions, and she says that she emphasizes the word Washita when introducing herself, rather than the word that follows in the official title of her historic site. She even uses business cards that name her affiliation as "Washita BNHS" rather than spelling out the words that the initials, particularly B, represent. The official management policies of the National Park Service, as both she and Miller point out, require historical interpretation to be factual and free of bias—a difficult task when one segment of the site's constituency regards its very name as representing a particular slant. "Interpretation," the policy reads, "will encourage dialogue, and accept that visitors have their own individual points of view."[90]

In the case of interpreting the historical violence of the nineteenth-century Indian Wars, the National Park Service frequently attempts to achieve this goal by deploying the phrase "clash of cultures" to describe events like Custer's attack at Washita. The first "interpretive theme" named in the Final General Management Plan adopted by the Park Service for Washita explains: "The events at Washita were a product of a *clash between two cultures* whose beliefs were so different and incompatible that violent conflict ensued" (emphasis added).[91] This "clash of cultures" rubric has emerged in recent decades as a popular strategy for placing the U.S.-Indian violence of the nineteenth century into a context that extends beyond the minutiae of the battles (or massacres) themselves. The phrase made its first appearance in National Park Service materials on a slender paperback written by Robert M. Utley and published by the Park Service in 1977, titled *A Clash of Cultures: Fort Bowie and the Chiricahua Apaches.* As the title suggests, Utley wrote the book to narrate the historical conflicts that occurred in the vicinity of the Fort Bowie National Historic Site in Arizona between the U.S. military and the Chiricahua Apaches, a history that culminated in Geronimo's surrender and capture in 1886. However, Utley does not explain the significance of the title that he has chosen or even repeat it in the text of the book.[92]

In time, "clash of cultures" became a popular paradigm for interpreting all of the military conflicts of the nineteenth-century Indian Wars, especially the Battle of the Little Bighorn. The earliest application I have found of the phrase to the Little Bighorn occurs in a paper delivered by Elizabeth Lawrence at a Monroe, Michigan, meeting of the Little Big Horn Associates only one year after the publication of Utley's book. Lawrence held a doctorate in veterinary medicine, and at the time she delivered the paper was working on a second doctorate, in anthropology. (She would go on to become a pioneer in the study of animal-human relations as a veterinary anthropologist—and would also write a book about Comanche, the Seventh Cavalry horse famously found wandering among the bodies on Last Stand Hill.)[93] The paper, "Clash of Cultures—The Issues behind the Battle of the Little Big Horn," shows Lawrence's anthropological training as she attempts to use the term *culture* to illuminate the forces that she believes generated the violence of the Indian Wars. She discusses the different worldviews of Plains Indians and Euro-American settlers (the former understood the universe as "circular and dynamic," the latter as "linearly progressive and time-de-marcated"), describes radically distinct attitudes toward the occupation and use of land, and even addresses the kinship and political systems that organized indigenous societies. "Two divergent cultures meant two diametrically opposed perceptions," she concludes, resulting in the "long and tragic drama" of conflict that culminated at the Little Bighorn.[94]

Whether or not Lawrence's paper ever caught the attention of Park Service officials, in the 1980s the "clash of cultures" rubric began circulating around what was then called Custer Battlefield National Monument. By the 1990s, when the site was renamed, the phrase had become a staple of ranger talks and other interpretive programs.[95] The brochure that visitors receive as they enter the National Monument uses the phrase as a title for its discussion of the battle, even if the brochure does not parse out the significance of the phrase in the way that Lawrence does. What the brochure *does* say suggests something, though, of why the "clash of cultures" language became so heavily used to discuss the Battle of the Little Bighorn:

> The Battle of the Little Bighorn was but the latest encounter in a centuries-long conflict that began with the arrival of the first Europeans in North America. That contact between Indian and white cultures had continued relentlessly, sometimes around the campfire, sometimes at the treaty grounds, but more often on the battlefield. It reached its peak in the decade following the Civil

War, when settlers resumed their vigorous westward movement. These western emigrants, possessing little or no understanding of the Indian way of life, showed slight regard for the sanctity of hunting grounds or the terms of the former treaties. The Indians' resistance to those encroachments on their domain only served to intensify hostilities.[96]

As in Lawrence's paper, the "clash of cultures" model serves to situate the Battle of the Little Bighorn in a deep historical context ("centuries-long") that extends far beyond the lives of any of the individuals who fought there. The language emphasizes the failure of intercultural comprehension ("little or no understanding") and is evenhanded in its assessment. "Contact" is a two-way process; the settlers may have showed "slight regard" for Indian land claims, but indigenous resistance "only served to intensify hostilities." The "clash of cultures" is not a single event but a process that is relentless, tragic, and inevitable.

As an interpretive lens, this model has clear advantages. Like the social history that has been in vogue among academic historians since the 1970s, the "clash of cultures" approach privileges the experiences of large populations rather than the virtues of individuals, whether Custer, Crazy Horse, or Sitting Bull. Equally significant, the "clash of cultures" model offers the kind of interpretive neutrality to which the National Park Service aspires. Rather than focusing attention on blaming or valorizing those who fought in a conflict, the Park Service asks the visitor to understand it as the result of forces beyond the control of any single person and to realize that comprehending it in a historical context will require inhabiting multiple perspectives. Speaking about his interpretive work at Washita, Alden Miller uses the phrase "360 degrees of perspective" to describe his interpretive aims of the site. Rather than thinking of what occurred there as a two-sided story, he prefers to think of it as a circle—and his goal is to offer the visitor the chance to travel the entire circumference.

Talking to Miller—who has both served in the U.S. military and worked at the Little Bighorn Battlefield National Monument—one can see why the "clash of cultures" rubric has become so ubiquitous in the Park Service. He talks about trying to impress upon visitors the myriad forces that intersected in Sheridan's campaign on the southern Plains in 1868: Cheyenne migration and strategies of resistance in the aftermath of Sand Creek; the crumbling treaty system; the building of railroads that accompanied and encouraged immigrants who arrived on the Plains, both from the eastern United States and more directly from Europe. For Miller, Lauritzen, and the others staffing the new Washita visitor center, the "clash of cultures" is an interpretive passageway that makes it possible to connect the palpable human losses that occurred at Washita to these larger forces. It is a flexible pedagogical strategy that leads away from the debate over whether Sheridan's orders or Custer's attack was justified and toward other kinds of connections. Miller points out that the twenty-first-century visitor to Washita sees cultural conflicts each night on the evening news; this interpretive approach to Washita, he contends, makes Washita even more relevant to the world that they know.[97]

However, at Washita and elsewhere, this mode of interpretation has been only moderately successful. One of the main constituencies of battlefields—even those like Washita, where that term is in dispute—are those who are interested in the strategies and action of the fighting itself. While the brochure of the Little Bighorn Battlefield National Monument places "The Clash of Cultures" on one side, the other provides a large color map of the kind that battle aficionados know well, with red and blue arrows depicting the movements of the Seventh Cavalry battalions and the Indian resistance; numbers on the map correspond to narrative explanations that allow the reader to reconstruct the sequence of events. For many enthusiasts, this kind of military reconstruction is what makes military history compelling; they are not interested in the social or anthropological contexts that Miller has in mind. Washita, though, may have a comparative advantage over Little Bighorn in this regard: the action of the fighting was simpler and shorter—and historians can offer much more definite accounts of the physical actions there. The new visitor center will feature a large electronic map to detail the movements of the fighting, but because Washita involved less action than did conflicts like the Little Bighorn, perhaps it will be possible to pull would-be strategists into the other exhibits being planned, such as displays devoted to contemporary Cheyenne culture.

Even if strategy enthusiasts can be pulled into other modes of historical interpretation, there are limits to what this emphasis on "culture" and its clashes can teach. As Timothy Braatz has recently argued, privileging the term *culture*—an amorphous concept that anthropologists have long considered ill-defined—detracts from the political decisions made by individuals on all sides of the Indian Wars that produced its violence. "Cultures do not clash; cultures do not even act—people do," he writes.[98] In the case of Washita, these decisions include those made by Cheyenne warriors to conduct raids on the Kansas settlers, the decisions made by officials of the United States to attempt to confine the Cheyennes and other tribes to the Indian Territory, and the decision made by Sheridan and his military colleagues to bring the "total war" strategy of the Civil War to the southern plains. These decisions were all certainly culturally determined insofar as they reflected unconscious beliefs about the way that land should be used and the modes of living that should be defended—but they were also political decisions about governance, territory, and authority. Treating the violence of Washita or Little Bighorn as the inevitable result of a "clash of cultures" diminishes the role that agents played on both sides, including their calculated election of violence at various moments to achieve their political ends. The Southern Cheyennes in 1868 were seeking a degree of political autonomy; the United States was seeking territorial consolidation. This was not the fated product of culture. After all, as Braatz points out, the frontier army was itself a multicultural force by any definition of the term: native-born Americans from northern cities and farms fought alongside sons of the formerly slave-owning South; a significant percentage of men were recently arrived immigrants from Europe; four regiments of African Americans served on the frontier as "buffalo soldiers"; and all of these troops were joined regularly by Indian scouts—Osages at the Washita; Crows, Arikaras, and Santee Sioux at the Little Bighorn. It took more than culture to forge such a coalition.

During the course of the ethnographic study commissioned by the Park Service for the Washita Battlefield National Historic Site, Eugene Blackbear Sr., an elected chief who is deeply involved in Cheyenne ceremonial life, made a historical comparison different from the others that I have seen, a comment that speaks to how the "clash of cultures" model suffers from its own weaknesses in capturing the historical experience of violence. Instead of pointing out the similarities between Washita and the Oklahoma City bombing, or between Washita and Vietnam, Blackbear compared the Seventh Cavalry's strike on Black Kettle's village with Japan's bombing of Pearl Harbor: "Everybody was sleeping, they were surprise attacked, just like Pearl Harbor, Japanese did the Americans. Same tactics were used on our Cheyenne people."[99] The comparison, of course, only goes so far—most obviously, there was a history of Cheyenne-U.S. violence antedating Washita that had no analogue in U.S.-Japan relations in 1941—but Blackbear's choice of words brings into relief certain characteristics of the campaign against the Cheyennes. Like Japan in 1941, the United States in 1868 was attempting to assert its dominance over a region, and like the Japanese military, Sheridan's army sought to surprise the enemy by executing an attack where the enemy had not thought one possible. (For the purposes of this rudimentary comparison, I will leave behind the theory that the United States chose to ignore intelligence of the Pearl Harbor attack.)

Like Pearl Harbor, Washita resulted in the killing of noncombatants even if the primary purpose was to strike military targets—the fighting men of the village and their horses. Moreover, both offensive strikes were designed to provoke fear, and both were successful at doing so. Neither the United States after Pearl Harbor nor the Southern Cheyennes after Washita would feel secure in their homeland for years—and cultural difference does not provide an adequate explanation for either conflict. Indians and non-Indians understood that the violence of the Plains was part of the struggle for control over land and that the violence was committed in a way that its implications could be understood across cultural borders. As Alden Miller said to me, in spite of their divergent worldviews, everyone who was present at the Washita in 1868 knew why Custer killed the horses.

Miller's comment, in fact, leaves me hopeful that the "clash of cultures" at Washita could be transformed, or at least supplemented, by an explanation of what occurred there as a "clash of politics"—a military conflict that resulted from competing political groups who had irreconcilable visions for the land on which the National Historic Site is located. Washita was part of a process that was intended to make the Cheyennes disappear as a distinct political entity. When the Cheyenne-Arapaho reservation was dissolved in the 1890s, the two tribes lost approximately six-sevenths of their land, about three million acres. By the 1930s, the combined populations of the Southern and Northern Cheyennes reached its lowest point, about two thousand people. However, in 1937, the Southern Cheyennes and Arapahos formed the "Cheyenne-Arapaho Tribes of Oklahoma" under the Oklahoma Indian Welfare Act, and since that time they have experienced a resurgence. While their land holdings are still small when compared to the reservations designated by nineteenth-century treaties, the tribal government has been successful in winning reservation status for the land it has acquired and has initiated cultural and economic enterprises. In 2000, the total enrollment of the Cheyenne-Arapaho Tribes of Oklahoma was 11,800.[100] For them, the commemoration of Washita and Sand Creek by the U.S. National Park Service is an act that they hope will contribute to their recognition as a distinct people, both by themselves and by the United States.

When he addressed the 1998 National Park Service symposium on Washita, Lawrence Hart spoke about the events of the Washita with a nationalist pride. He cited a list of some twenty-five U.S. army generals who had been at war with the Cheyennes, noted that the Cheyennes had suffered two of the most devastating attacks in the history of U.S.-Indian warfare, and claimed that both offered proof of the Cheyennes' ability to endure. "There might be another tribe that suffered two or more such attacks," he said, "but they are likely extinct as a result. We Cheyennes are still here, thanks to the warriors and the peace chiefs." [101]

The Park Service seeks to register the presence of the Cheyennes both by consulting with them during the design of the new visitor center at Washita and by portraying contemporary Cheyenne life within that center. Lauritzen estimates that the visitor center will pull in approximately 35,000 visitors a year—a far cry from the 100,000 once hoped for by some Oklahomans and even further still from the 400,000 that Little Bighorn attracts. However, those who do come will be able to confront a history of conflict that does not allow white Americans the moral luxury of assuming the role of romantic defeat. In fact, even in the materials they already have at their disposal, the Park Service interpreters of Washita are trying to remind those who come of the political complexities of the relationship between the United States and the indigenous tribes of the Plains. On one side of the brochure produced for the National Historic Site since 2005, a gray box lists dates and tribal signatories of approximately 375 treaties signed by the United States and the Indian nations of North America between 1778 and 1871 and ratified by the U.S. Senate so that they became, in the words of article VI of the U.S. Constitution, "the supreme law of the land." Six of those treaties are in bold-face type to indicate that Southern Cheyennes and Arapahos were among the signatories, highlighting their ongoing struggle to establish nation-to-nation relationships with the United States. [102] With its central image of a slain Custer atop Last Stand Hill, the Little Bighorn turned out to be a battle that provided an ideal icon for the United States during its confident expansionism in the twentieth century. With the text of these failed treaties in the foreground, Washita could become a conflict more useful for the more complicated politics and ethics of the century to come.

⟹ ◦ ⟸

One name that is not mentioned in either the new Park Service brochure for the Washita Battlefield National Monument or in the short film that the Park Service has produced for its visitor center is Monahseetah. Monahseetah—also spelled Monahsetah or Meotzi—was the daughter of Little Rock, the second most prominent Cheyenne leader killed in the Seventh Cavalry attack at the Washita and among those Cheyennes taken prisoner. Together with the other captives, Monahseetah rode north with the cavalry to Fort Supply. There, according to his account, Custer selected her and two other female captives to accompany him as intermediaries on his subsequent expeditions to the remaining camps of Southern Cheyennes "hostiles," who had fled westward into the Staked Plains of Texas. Since that time, Custer's biographers and detractors alike have speculated that he chose her as his sexual partner.

A leading source of such rumors was Frederick Benteen, a captain who believed that Custer had needlessly abandoned Joel Elliott in the Washita fight and who sharpened his hatred of Custer to a razor's edge in a series of posthumously published letters to a retired enlisted man, Theodore Goldin. In one such letter, Benteen describes the "informal invitation" issued by Custer to his officers "to avail themselves of the services of a captured squaw. . . . Custer took first choice, and lived with her during winter and spring of 1868 and '69."[103] Ben Clark, the chief of Custer's scouts, independently (and with less malice) reported the same facts in a 1910 interview.[104] At least some of the Cheyennes with memories of the 1868–69 campaign told similar stories of Monahseetah, which in the twentieth century found their way into the works of non-Indian historians.

Even Custer's memoir seems alive to the possibility of a liaison. He calls Monahseetah (a name he spells "Mo-nah-se-tah") "an exceedingly comely squaw, possessing a bright, cheery face, a countenance beaming with intelligence, and a disposition more inclined to be merry than one usually finds among the Indians." Moreover, Custer dwells on Monahseetah's social position ("the cream of the aristocracy, if not royalty itself") and comments that her status placed her beyond the reach of the common would-be Cheyenne suitor. To cap off his portrait of this female appeal, he details the story of her first marriage, in which Monahseetah fired a pistol into the knee of an abusive husband in order to precipitate a divorce.[105] In one of *her* memoirs, Elizabeth Custer records meeting Monahseetah after the conclusion of the Washita campaign, in the stockade at Fort Hays, Kansas, and she tells the same story about the Cheyenne woman's first marriage. In Libbie's hands, though, the tale makes her fearful of Monahseetah: "How could I help feeling that with a swift movement she would produce a hidden weapon, and by stabbing the wife, hurt the white chief who had captured her, in what she believed would be the most cruel way[?]"[106] As Louise Barnett has commented, to a modern reader the sentence is so obviously loaded with sexual rivalry that it is difficult to know whether Elizabeth Custer was fully conscious of its emotional resonance.[107]

The question of what Elizabeth Custer may have known about the rumors regarding Monahseetah and her husband offers an explanation of the choice by the staff of the National Park Service not to foreground the relationship in their interpretive work at Washita. The story would move them into the realm of conjecture and innuendo; even if the most careful historians—such as Utley and Greene—suggest that the evidence points to Custer's taking Monahseetah as his sexual partner, it is still not conclusive.[108] Perhaps more important from the Park Service perspective, though, the story of Monaseetah and Custer returns history to the level of personality, focusing once again on the personal failings of a single soldier rather than the larger forces that created conflict on the southern Plains. The Southern Cheyennes of Oklahoma may not be interested in dwelling on this story in a public setting, either. Monahseetah does not figure in any of the ethnographic interviews of Southern Cheyennes conducted by the Park Service since Washita was named a National Monument. One park ranger there told me in 2003 that the Cheyenne families related to Monahseetah would neither confirm nor deny the rumors of her relationship with Custer. One can understand such a stance easily: what matters to the Cheyennes is the fate that befell their whole people, not the possibility that one of their tribe shared a bed with the man who led the attack on their camp.[109] If one imagines Monahseetah as a willing partner, then there is plenty of embarrassment in this story to go around, both for the Custerphiles who want to stress the devotion of their hero to Libbie and for tribal nationalists who want to emphasize anticolonial resistance.

But the story of Monahseetah and Custer continues to resurface. Two American Indian poets, Charlotte DeClue (Osage) and Maurice Kenny (Mohawk), published poems in recent decades about the Cheyenne woman, turning to her as a way of thinking about the historical violence suffered by indigenous women. DeClue's speaker imagines herself trying to heal the spirit of Monahseetah; Kenny's concludes by chastising her: "Custer strutted your grave to glory, foolish girl!"[110] Even more recently, the historical questions that surround this relationship appeared in an entirely different arena, when Gail Kelly-Custer delivered a paper at the 2004 meeting of the Western History Association entitled "General Custer's Secret Indian Family, or How I Discovered My Heritage." As the title suggests, Kelly-Custer told the audience at the conference that she had found evidence that she was a descendant of the union of Monahseetah and George Armstrong Custer.

Many, though not all, of the Cheyenne stories about Custer and Monahseetah have included the suggestion that the Cheyenne woman conceived a child with Custer after having delivered the baby she was carrying when she first met him. Brill, for instance, incorporated this possibility into his history of the Washita, where he stated that the child was named Yellow Swallow as a consequence of his fair hair and skin; one of his readers, Mari Sandoz, popularized the Yellow Swallow story by including it in her well-received *Cheyenne Autumn* (1953).[111] Even Gregory F. Michno, who states that he is skeptical that such a child was conceived, includes in his *Lakota Noon: The Indian Narrative of Custer's Defeat* (1997) a Cheyenne account that insists not only upon the relationship between Custer and Monahseetah and upon the existence of a child but also that both Monahseetah and Custer's son—here named Yellow Bird—were present in the Indian village of Lakotas and Cheyennes that Custer fatally attacked at the Little Bighorn River in 1876.[112]

Kelly-Custer's account goes further in detailing what happened next to the boy, whom she believes was named Yellow Hair.[113] According to her, George Custer had made arrangements with a half-brother, Brice, to raise the child in Ohio in the event of his death. Brice did so, calling him Josiah Custer and hiding his origins. After graduating from high school, Josiah Custer/Yellow Hair moved to Oklahoma to live with his mother, who had since married a white man named John Isaac. He later married and became a farmer; from what Kelly-Custer has learned he was thought to be a quiet and eccentric man who kept his long hair in a braid. But Kelly-Custer encountered resistance from her own father when she began to inquire about family history, and it took her years of research before she located a record that, she claims, indicates the parentage of Josiah Custer, her great-grandfather, as being George Armstrong Custer and Monahseetah. When she found this, other relatives began speaking about the stories that they had kept quiet. The family had kept the secret, Kelly-Custer says, mostly because of the shame of Josiah Custer's being born out of wedlock.

Kelly-Custer has attempted to contact the descendants of Custer's brothers, she says, to arrange for DNA testing, but they have refused to deal with her. While the audience at the Western History Association at least gave her a hearing, she felt they were disbelieving as well. Likewise, Peter Harrison—an amateur historian from England who will soon publish a biography of Monahseetah—doubts the historical accuracy of Kelly-Custer's story based on what he has heard of it, though he stresses that, like me, he has not had the chance to examine her evidence firsthand.[114] In the face of this skepticism, Kelly-Custer has resorted to writing a novel, *Princess Monahseetah: The Concealed Wife of General Custer,* which she hopes to publish with an author's note explaining that she is a descendant of the union between the two figures named in the title. Both will receive sympathetic treatment in the book. Like so many others immersed in Custerology, Kelly-Custer bristles at the notion that her ancestor was motivated by cruelty or racial hatred toward Indians. "He fought them and he killed them," she says, "but he didn't loathe them. I'm proof."

A comment like this one suggests something of how Gail Kelly-Custer's genealogical recovery efforts differ from the relationship of contemporary Southern Cheyennes to the history of the Washita conflict. For the Cheyennes, remembering Washita is significant because it epitomizes the violent attempt that was made in the late nineteenth century to make them disappear as a people. This history includes not only the military attack at the Washita but also the land run that removed it from their collective ownership. By coming back to the Washita River to honor survivors and victims, the Cheyennes hope that they are participating in a process that will reverse this history of tribal dissolution. Kelly-Custer's recuperation of her ties to Custer and Monahseetah, on the other hand, is steeped in romance, a potential hidden history of interracial partnership that has been closeted by a century of suspicion and fear. In bringing it out into the open, she could do more than articulate an unbroken family narrative; she could, like the descendants of Thomas Jefferson and Sally Hemings, offer another example of how the history of the United States is more integrated and multiracial than has been previously acknowledged. Her Washita, in other words, would be a site to recall not Cheyenne independence but rather mutual dependence (and dependents) among Indians and whites. Even if tribal nationalists would prefer the first kind of relationship with the United States, the second is a reality they cannot ignore.

The Washita fight can be incorporated into both the Cheyennes' and Kelly-Custer's perspectives on history because the event has always, from the moment it occurred in 1868, had a kind of double historical life: It was the site of Custer's biggest victory over Indians yet also the place that earned him the scorn of those who believed the attack to be unnecessarily cruel. The event secured Custer's fame in his own lifetime but became a marginal aside after his death. Washita became a place of hallowed memories for the Cheyennes, and yet it was not a place to which they returned. It was where the U.S. army dealt the Cheyennes a devastating blow to their sense of security and independence, but language recognizing the autonomy of the Cheyenne-Arapaho Tribe was later written into the legislation that created the National Monument.

Curiously, one judgment that has remained consistent over time among white and Cheyenne historians alike is that the seeds of Custer's later defeat on the Little Bighorn lay in Washita. The former are likely to emphasize that Custer followed several of the same techniques in Montana that he had in the Indian Territory: he attacked a village of unknown size, without conducting reconnaissance, by dividing his troops into several forces—a strategy that, of course, would have disastrous results the second time he employed it.

Cheyennes, on the other hand, are likely to connect Washita to the Little Bighorn by recalling that in the months after his offensive strike against Black Kettle's village, Custer led the Seventh Cavalry to a Cheyenne village on the Staked Plains of Texas that included many of the survivors of the attack. There he was invited to smoke with tribal leaders—one of whom, named Stone Forehead (or Rock Forehead), spilled the ashes on Custer's boots, pronouncing in Cheyenne that Custer would be destroyed if he should ever walk contrary to the peace pipe again.[115] Eight years later, that prescription was realized in the hills above the Little Bighorn.

Speaking in the 1920s, a Cheyenne woman named Kate Bighead—who had been present at both Custer's successful Washita attack and his failed one at the Little Bighorn—told a story about Custer's body lying on Last Stand Hill. Several Southern Cheyenne women were among those scouring the battlefield in the aftermath of the fighting, and they recognized Custer from his earlier campaign on the southern Plains. Thinking of Monahseetah, they told the Lakotas that Custer was a relative of theirs and that his corpse should not be mutilated. "The women," Bighead's translator later recorded, "then pushed the point of a sewing awl into each of his ears, into his head. This was done to improve his hearing, as it seemed he had not heard what our chiefs in the South said when he smoked the pipe with them."[116] Bighead did not say if Custer was a better listener in the next world.

4

INTO THE BLACK HILLS

Rapid City, South Dakota

IT IS A COOL SUMMER MORNING, AND I AM DRIVING NINETY MILES SOUTHEAST from Rapid City, South Dakota, toward the Pine Ridge Reservation of the Oglala Lakota Nation, to visit the site of the Wounded Knee Massacre. In December 1890, the Seventh Cavalry, which still included veterans of the Battle of the Little Bighorn, was escorting a camp of Lakota Sioux under the leadership of the Minneconjou Big Foot to the nearby government agency on the reservation. Big Foot's followers had been adherents of the Ghost Dance, a pantribal religious movement that held out the promise of cultural and political revitalization for the tribal peoples who practiced it. Dance the Ghost Dance, the messengers from the Paiute prophet Wovoka had said, and the buffalo will return, the whites will vanish, and the *oyate*—a word that means at once nation and people—will be restored. To the United States, the Ghost Dance brought fears of renewed violence, especially from the Lakotas; the army was ordered to put an end to it. On the morning of December 30, the Seventh Cavalry was in the process of disarming Big Foot's followers before marching them to Pine Ridge Agency. One of the Indians' guns fired—whether on purpose or by accident remains unclear to historians—and the surrounding soldiers let loose volley after volley of gunfire into the crowd, chasing those who fled to a nearby ravine and ultimately killing between 150 and 300 men, women, and children. They were not the only casualties: 25 soldiers were also killed, at least some, historians presume, from friendly fire.[1]

As I drive toward the scene of this historic violence, sitting next to me in the rented car is Father Vincent Heier, who has been a Catholic priest for the last twenty-seven years and a Custer aficionado for even longer. We follow two-lane roads that skirt the crags and canyons of the badlands and bring us to the reservation. The winter snow and spring rains have been heavy this year in South Dakota, and the tall grass of the prairies, blowing now as a thunderstorm arrives, are greener than usual. There is not much at Wounded Knee to mark the location of the event except a large historical marker at the side of the road that gives an outline of the history. The sign has been altered to call the episode a "massacre" instead of a "battle"—a board with the harsher term nailed over the blander one—but the text itself is surprisingly vague about who is to blame for what happened. As the army was disarming Big Foot's band, it states, "a gun went off and all hell broke loose." Indeed.

On the other side of the road, a small Catholic cemetery sits at the top of a hill. Heier and I walk up to see a monument erected to honor the victims who have been buried there. We stay a few minutes to look at the crosses and memorials that mark the graves of other Lakota men and women, including veterans of World War II, the Korean War, and Vietnam—even a few who served the frontier army as Indian scouts.

At the foot of the hill, Gary Rowland, a Lakota, runs the Fire Lightning Visitor Center. It is housed in a circular building, and the inside walls have been painted with slogans proclaiming the sovereignty of Indian nations: "Indian Pride on the Move / Decolonization / Independence / Freedom," "The Indian Wars Are Not Over." There are pictures of the victims of the Wounded Knee Massacre, as well as a display devoted to the events of 1973, when the American Indian Movement seized control of several buildings in the hamlet of Wounded Knee, leading to a seventy-one-day standoff with the FBI. There is a familiar object as well: the metal plaque that Russell Means and AIM planted in Last Stand Hill in 1988. That plaque had once been on display in the visitor center of the Little Bighorn Battlefield National Monument, and it was placed in the center of the Indian Memorial, next to the open microphone, on the day of the memorial's dedication in 2003. After the dedication, the plaque was not returned to the visitor center, and I was not sure where it had gone. Now I had an answer. When it was first unveiled by Means at the then–Custer Battlefield, the plaque was a protest against a one-sided presentation of history. Here at Wounded Knee, that protest is situated as a small part of a larger history of anticolonial struggle; the rhetoric of "Homelands, Treaties and Sovereignty" used on the plaque fits right in. There is also a poignancy in the juxtaposition of the plaque's declaration of victory—"In honor of our Indian Patriots who fought and defeated the U.S. Calvary [sic]," it begins—with a grainy black-and-white photograph of mangled bodies lying in the snow at Wounded Knee. Together, the objects serve as a visible reminder of how the efforts of tribal activists to memorialize history require acknowledging the pain of loss as well as celebrating triumph.

Heier and I take pictures of the cemetery and the visitor center, and Heier asks Rowland if there are any postcards for sale. There aren't. Instead, he buys a poster of Sitting Bull and a bumper sticker that reads, "Vote Russell Means [for] President." On our way back to Rapid City, our conversation ranges from what we have seen at Wounded Knee to the exhibits at the Little Bighorn visitor center—Heier wishes it displayed more popular culture—to Heier's work in St. Louis, where he is both the pastor of a small parish and the director of an archdiocese office for ecumenical affairs. We talk about my teaching, and he asks me about my family. I can see that Heier must be a valuable counselor to his parishioners: as much as he likes to talk, he is a skilled listener. The return drive, as return drives often do, seems to take less time than the outbound journey. As we pull into the parking lot of the hotel where we are both staying, Heier looks around and notices that the parking lot is filling. "Well," he says, "the nuts are starting to arrive."

The "nuts," among whom Heier counts himself, are the members of the Little Big Horn Associates gathering for their annual meeting. (The organization uses the older, three-word spelling of the battle instead of the one currently preferred by historians, "Little Bighorn.") The LBHA was founded in 1967 with twelve charter members, including Lawrence Frost of Monroe, Michigan, and Robert J. Ege, an army veteran, radio commentator, and newspaperman from Great Falls, Montana, whom Frost later credited as the group's founder.[2] "The purpose of this monthly letter," Ege wrote in the first LBHA newsletter, "is primarily to afford the members of the association a medium or outlet in which to 'air their views,' seek information, and volunteer information beneficial to other serious historians of General George A. Custer, the 7th United States Regiment of Cavalry and the Battle of the Little Big Horn."[3] At its inception, the LBHA was organized to enable historical enthusiasts to correspond with one another via a newsletter, which is still published ten times each year. Within a year, the organization had 260 members; by the 1990s, the membership hovered at approximately one thousand, where it remains today, with members from every U.S. state (except Rhode Island) as well as from six other countries. The newsletter continues to print reviews of new books about Custer and the Indian Wars, short articles by members about their historical research, and announcements of upcoming events of interest to Custer buffs. In addition to the newsletter, the LBHA publishes a semiannual *Research Review*, featuring longer articles, glossy illustrations, and a production value that surpasses that of many academic journals; more recently, the organization launched a website with a message board where members can thrash out their arguments about Custer and his most famous battle.[4]

In 1974, the LBHA held its first convention in Louisville, Kentucky. Fifty-nine people attended that meeting, and the LBHA has sponsored a conference every year since. The LBHA has always been distinct from its "sister" organization, the Custer Battlefield Historical and Museum Association. The CBHMA was once a cooperating organization that aided the National Park Service in its administration of (what was then called) Custer Battlefield, and it still remains focused on the Battle of the Little Bighorn and the preservation of the land where it took place. By contrast, the LBHA has a broader topical range that includes the whole of Custer's life and the regimental history of the Seventh Cavalry. The annual meetings of the two organizations bear the mark of this difference: while the CBHMA always convenes in Hardin, Montana, near the battlefield, the LBHA travels throughout the United States to locations somehow associated with the Custer story, alternating between meetings west and east of the Mississippi River. It has met twice in Louisville, near where Custer served Reconstruction duty; it has met in both Amarillo, Texas, and Oklahoma City, so that members could visit the Washita battlefield; it has met in Canton, Ohio, near the place of Custer's birth, and at West Point, New York, where Custer's body is buried.[5] It has even met in Lawrence, Kansas, where the only significant link to Custer—aside from its proximity to Forts Riley and Leavenworth, where the Seventh Cavalry was stationed—is the stuffed and mounted body of a horse, Comanche, the famous survivor of the Last Stand that was found on the battlefield by the army, now housed in the natural history museum of the University of Kansas.

Heier is one of a handful of LBHA members who have been to every one of these annual meetings over the last thirty-two years. In 1974, Heier was in his first year of study at Kenrick Seminary in St. Louis, and he skipped a class retreat to drive to Louisville. He recalls being thrilled at the chance to meet the Custer buffs whose words he had read and remembers paying twenty dollars for an old edition of the muckraking biography *Glory-Hunter*. "From that moment on," he says, "I was hooked."

Now Heier lives in a small two-story rectory adjacent to his parish church near the campus of Washington University. The first floor houses the business office of the parish, but the upstairs holds what Heier calls "the shrine": four rooms of living quarters that have been filled to capacity with Custeriana, from serious historical artifacts and scholarship to pop culture ephemera. A neatly arranged library holds more than three thousand books related to Custer and the Indian Wars. Nearly every inch of wall space is covered with a map or a painting or a poster: framed portraits, memorabilia, Custer sitting, Custer charging, Custer departing from his wife, Custer in his camp, Custer posing for a photograph, Custer in newspapers, advertisements, and political broadsheets. (Heier keeps a poster with Vine Deloria Jr.'s slogan "Custer Died for Your Sins" behind a door, where the archbishop cannot see it.) Every spare inch of flat surface is littered with magazines, comic books, journal articles. He has folk art, ashtrays, belt buckles, statues, plastic figurines, and stuffed dolls. There's a wall of videotapes and DVDs, as well as record albums and compact discs that contain—Heier thinks—the most complete collection of Custer-related songs that anyone has assembled.

When I visit him there at the rectory, he plays for me what he considers to be the worst piece of Custer music ever recorded, "Custer's Last Stand" from Harry Belafonte's 1970 album *Calypso Carnival*. He is gleeful as the sound of bongos, mimicking an Indian war dance, fills the apartment. Heier is right; it's a *terrible* song. "This is what I love," he exclaims. "What other American has had this much bad music made about him?" [6]

Now, when we enter the lobby of the Rapid City hotel where the LBHA is meeting, Heier's enthusiasm bubbles over once more. Even before checking into his room, he's circulating among the arriving conferencegoers, inquiring after their families, asking whether mutual friends will be coming as well. He is eager to tell them about what we have seen at Wounded Knee and even more eager to hear that the book dealers who have brought their wares to the convention will soon be open for business. This will be Heier's condition for the next three days: ebullient, irrepressible, and in constant motion as he rekindles the relationships that he has built over the last thirty-odd years and cultivates new ones. Everyone knows about Heier's profession: they often call him "Father Vince," and he dons his clerical collar when he celebrates Mass for any LBHA Catholics. Heier spends the rest of his time, though, wearing an assortment of Custer-themed T-shirts and hats and indulging in his lifelong passionate pursuit of all things related to the slain general of the Last Stand. Here, in other words, he is not so much the "Custerpriest" (Heier's eBay handle) as simply one of hundreds of Custer aficionados, a buff among the buffs—or, to use his own characterization, a nut among the nuts.

But it would be a mistake to take Heier's self-mockery too seriously. The men and women who meet each year at the LBHA conventions are not a fringe cult of hobbyists who have taken leave of their senses. They are, in fact, meticulous, careful historical enthusiasts whose shared intelligence crosses into the realm of the scholarly in its depth and detail. The members of the LBHA often refer to themselves as outliers, as being on the margins of contemporary popular culture. In one sense they are right; the number of people who will eagerly devour a new biography of, say, Tom Custer (one of George Armstrong's brothers)—let alone the two biographies that came out in a single year—is quite small. The number of people who want to travel and devote a weekend to discussing those biographies is even smaller. However, I have come to see the LBHA as less of a distinct phenomenon disconnected from the larger public and more of a representative group that has helped me to understand the process that transforms an abstract and intangible idea—history, the past—into an emotional force in contemporary life. Paradoxically, one of the things that make Custer enthusiasts typical is the way that they articulate themselves as a kind of aberration. Like other forms of social affiliation—hobbies, clubs, fan groups, even political organizations—that seek to carve out a niche of differentiation by distinguishing themselves from the public at large, an engagement with history is a kind of self-fashioning that produces for its participants a distinction from the masses through an identification with the past.

This identification with the past hinges upon an approach to history that emphasizes the empirical—the factual—and that treats these historical facts almost as a kind of material item that can be collected, collated, and stored. In their study of Colonial Williamsburg, Richard Handler and Eric Gable point out that a favorite metaphor of this "objectivist" or "realist" approach to history represents the past "as a shattered object whose surviving pieces must be put back together. To put the puzzle of the past back together requires the problem-solving skills of a detective searching out mysteries and hunting through minutiae for clues."[7] This description fits most military history enthusiasts, and the members of the Little Bighorn Associates are no exception. Moreover, one can extend the metaphor further in this case; for Custer aficionados, the past is a puzzle with pieces that can never be found—in particular, the missing history that would reveal what actually happened to Custer and the men who died with him at the Battle of the Little Bighorn. The permanence of the "mystery" of the Little Bighorn and the impossibility of ever solving it is what makes Custerology, for its participants, a pleasurable activity.

In this chapter, I seek to offer a glimpse into that pleasure and to show that it has a greater complexity than what a noninitiate might at first imagine. I will also contend, though, that the aficionados' emphasis on the small pieces of the puzzle, both those that are missing and those that have been found, serves to draw the attention of these historical enthusiasts away from certain larger frames that surround the nineteenth-century Indian Wars. Microhistory can obscure macrohistory—particularly the political consequences of that larger historical narrative. As I have tried to suggest, my point is not that the Custer enthusiasts are exceptional in this regard; rather, they embody an approach to history that values authentic, tangible details—and that privileges those details to the near-exclusion of the political contexts of both the past and present. In the case of the history of U.S.-tribal conflicts on the North American Plains, that exclusion has consequences for how one thinks, or does not think, about contemporary tribal peoples.

There is perhaps no better place to unravel the complexity of what and how—the nineteenth-century history of warfare means for contemporary Americans, both Indian and non-Indian, than the ground where the LBHA convened in 2005: the Black Hills.[8] We will follow the Little Big Horn Associates in this chapter, but I will tell their story by moving back and forth in history from the time of their visit to the nineteenth-century expedition whose steps they followed. Doing so will allow us to go slightly beyond the purview of these historical enthusiasts to get a glimpse of a broader, or perhaps longer, historical landscape, one that connects the nineteenth-century past to the twenty-first-century present.

——➤◦◄——

Following its practice of locating annual conventions in places with a Custer connection, the LBHA met in Rapid City, South Dakota, because Custer had been there. In 1873, after three years of Reconstruction duty in Kentucky and other southern states, the Seventh Cavalry was reassigned to the northern Plains, to be stationed first at Fort Rice and then at Fort Abraham Lincoln, across the Missouri River from Bismarck, capital of the Dakota Territory. Custer and his men spent their first summer back on the Plains escorting a surveying party for the Northern Pacific Railroad into the Yellowstone valley, where the Seventh Cavalry skirmished with some of the Lakota warriors whom they would face two years later at the Little Bighorn River: Rain in the Face, Gall, possibly Crazy Horse, all under the leadership of Sitting Bull. That fall, though, railroad construction halted when the banking firm Jay Cooke and Company, the primary backer of the Northern Pacific, closed its doors in bankruptcy. Cooke's failure touched off a financial panic so severe that the New York Stock Exchange closed for ten days, and it left Custer at Fort Lincoln—near the terminus of the rail-road line constructed thus far—without a definitive mission in the offing for the following summer.

The solution came in the form of an exploratory expedition into the Black Hills, which lay to the south and west of Fort Lincoln. An oval-shaped, forested uplift that rises out of the surrounding prairie, approximately 120 miles long north to south and 40 miles east to west, the Black Hills take their name from the dark appearance of the ponderosa pine on their slopes when viewed from a distance. For decades, rumors about gold in the Black Hills had been in circulation, but they had remained unsubstantiated. Two different military expeditions had skirted the region in the 1850s, but nei-ther had traveled into the heart of the hills themselves. In the 1860s, white settlers in the Dakota Territory had attempted to organize exploring parties, only to be frustrated by the U.S. army, which refused to offer protection in a region where mining would require a constant military presence. The Black Hills were in the middle of the territory that the Lakota Sioux claimed as their own; in fact most of the whites who considered exploration of the Hills recognized that the Lakotas attributed special significance to them. In 1868, the treaty signed by the U.S. Peace Commission and more than one hun-dred Lakota Sioux leaders, including Red Cloud, created the Great Sioux Reservation, which extended west from the Missouri River over half of what is now South Dakota, including the Black Hills.

The treaty, commonly referred to as the Fort Laramie Treaty of 1868, was negotiated in the wake of Lakota attacks on the U.S. forts along the Bozeman Trail, which ran from Fort Laramie in present-day Wyoming north and west to the gold fields of Virginia City in Montana Territory. As part of the treaty, the United States agreed to abandon the forts, and the Lakotas largely considered the treaty a capitulation to their claims of dominion over their tribal lands. Railroads, though, had rendered the Boz-eman Trail less crucial to U.S. expansion into the northern Plains. For the U.S. Peace Commission, the Fort Laramie Treaty—like the Medicine Lodge treaty negotiated on the southern Plains during the previous year— was a step toward confining the Lakotas and introducing them to the arts of "civilization," including agriculture, through government agencies es-tablished throughout the reservation. In other words, the government of the United States thought of the treaty as a temporary expedient toward the incorporation of the Lakota Indians; the Lakotas, on the other hand, believed that the treaty recognized them as a sovereign political entity, a Sioux Nation (as they were called in the nineteenth century) with at least some autonomy.[9]

The Fort Laramie treaty prohibited white Americans from settling within the boundaries of the Great Sioux Reservation, but article 2 retained for the U.S. government the right to authorize its "officers, agents, and employés" to enter the reservation in the performance of their duties.[10] The official purpose of Custer's Black Hills expedition was to find a suitable location for a new military post that would help the U.S. army in the case of future conflicts. But even General Phil Sheridan admitted that his authorization of the expedition had other motivations. "I set to work," he wrote in his annual report for 1874, "to make a reconnaissance of the country about which dreamy stories have been told."[11] Those "dreamy stories" were about gold, and the mineralogical quest of the expedition seems to have been a kind of open secret as the Seventh Cavalry readied for departure. At least some white Americans believed the expedition violated the Treaty of 1868 in both spirit and letter, but Custer and his superiors all stated in correspondence with one another and in interviews with the press that the treaty allowed for this kind of exploring party.[12] Their manner of addressing the treaty suggests that the U.S. army continued to regard it as important enough to consider with care, even if it did so in order to evade its provisions.

Custer set out from Fort Abraham Lincoln on July 2, 1874—only weeks, in fact, after completing the final installment of *My Life on the Plains*. He had nearly a thousand men under his command. Ten companies of cavalry and two of infantry made up the main force. The 110 wagons that carried supplies for the expedition required civilian teamsters, and the column traveled with its own herd of cattle in case game was scarce (it was not). The expedition included seventy Indian scouts; they were Arikara and Santee Sioux, and among them was Bloody Knife, who was reportedly Custer's favorite Indian scout and who would die by Major Marcus Reno's side two years later at the Little Bighorn. The scientific corps included a young George B. Grinnell (later the editor of *Forest and Stream*) who came to collect fossils and wildlife specimens, as well as a geologist, a botanist, and a photographer, William H. Illingworth. Four newspaper reporters accompanied the expedition, as did two miners who had not been officially appointed to the expedition but who had, at the very least, Custer's sanction in being there. Frederick Grant, the president's son and a second lieutenant three years out of West Point, managed to find a place on the expedition as Custer's acting aide; one of Custer's brothers, Boston, landed a position as a civilian guide (another brother, Tom, already commanded Company L of the Seventh Cavalry). The expedition also counted a lone woman in its ranks: Custer's cook, an African American woman named Sarah Campbell, known to the men as Aunt Sally.

The expedition took more than two weeks to reach the Black Hills, and this initial leg of the journey was arduous; the thermometer repeatedly topped 100 degrees Fahrenheit as the long column churned out the miles through a dusty landscape where wood and water were often scarce. Little wonder then that the pens of the newspaper correspondents, as well as of Custer himself, gushed with acclaim once the expedition breached the Black Hills and entered their cooler, greener climes. On July 24, 1874, the expedition reached what was soon nicknamed Floral Valley. "Such brilliancy, such beauty, such variety, such profusion!" Samuel J. Barrows, reporting for the *New York Tribune*, wrote. "All the glories of color, form and fragrance which Flora could command had been woven into a carpet for our feet. The whole valley was a garden, teeming with creation. Yes, an Eden of the sky without the forbidden fruit."[13] Custer, in a field report that would be reprinted by newspapers, said that the officers held a contest to see "how many different flowers could be plucked without leaving our seat at the garden table."[14] The military expedition had turned, at least temporarily, into a picnic.

But it was a military expedition still. One reason for its size was to intimidate any Indians who might oppose it, and reporters told their readers to expect conflict. Private Theodore Ewart, who kept a diary of the expedition, wrote on July 14, "Every member of the camp is expecting a battle within the next few days as war and warpath are the only two words talked about."[15] War never came to the expedition, and the absence of armed resistance would be interpreted by some of its participants in a manner portentous for those Lakotas who wished to retain their dominion over the Black Hills. A few days before the expedition reached the Floral Valley, Lieutenant James Calhoun, Custer's brother-in-law, had written in his diary: "As I gaze upon this particular spot, I think that it is a great pity that this rich country should remain in a wild state, uncultivated and uninhabited by civilized men. Here the wheel of industry could move to advantage. The propelling power of life in the shape of human labor is only wanting to make this a region of prosperity. . . . For the hives of industry will take the place of dirty wigwams. Civilization will ere reign supreme and throw heathen barbarism into oblivion."[16]

The "heathens" in question would interpret even the flower picking as an intrusion into their domain, and the botanical collecting was simply a prelude to the more ominous activities of the explorers. According to the *Tribune* report on Floral Valley, the natural beauty of the landscape meant that the "greed for gold was forgotten. We ceased to look only for the nuggets which would make us suddenly rich."[17] The members of the expedition would not, though, cease their pursuit of gold for long.

————— ➤ ◦ ◄ —————

More than 130 years after Custer and his officers picked wildflowers around their dinner table, the Little Big Horn Associates are following his expedition in the Black Hills. Four buses pull up to the hotel where we are meeting, and the two hundred or so participants in the convention climb aboard to spend a day tracing the expedition's path—or at least as much of it as the roads and our air-conditioned coaches will allow. With a population of about sixty thousand, Rapid City sits at the northeastern edge of the Black Hills, sprawling down into the surrounding plains. The hills themselves are probably best known to most Americans as the home of Mount Rushmore, which logs more than two million visitors each year. Coincidentally, Gerard Baker, the Mandan and Hidatsa Indian man widely considered by Custer buffs to be their least favorite superintendent of the Little Bighorn Battlefield (especially because he allowed young Indian men to "count coup" on Last Stand Hill), was appointed the previous year to oversee the Mount Rushmore National Memorial. The LBHA will not be going there on its field trip.

The construction of Mount Rushmore complemented a regional bid for tourism that began when South Dakota lured President Calvin Coolidge to spend his summer vacation in the Black Hills in 1927, the same year that Gutzon Borglum began blasting away to create the monument. Driving in the hills, particularly on the highways that connect the interstate to the north with Mount Rushmore, one can see the evidence of a long history of road-trip tourism: petting zoos, reptile gardens, mini golf, crystal caverns, wildlife parks. Nearly every other store in the area sells T-shirts commemorating the annual Sturgis Rally, held each August, when tens of thousands of motorcycles clog the streets of the small town sitting at the northern edge of the Black Hills. Within the hills themselves are a series of small towns straddling narrow valleys, all at some stage of the transition from an economy based on mining and logging to one revolving around tourists, particularly summer tourists, since downhill skiing opportunities are limited. Leading the charge in this respect is Deadwood, with a recently refurbished historical downtown, casino gambling, and a gritty HBO series bearing its name.

The main attraction, though, remains the dramatic scenery that captivated the men of the Custer expedition. An isolated, unglaciated range of mountains, the Black Hills rise more than three thousand feet above the surrounding plains, a lone outpost of verticality in a region of flatness. The roads into the Black Hills take travelers past the "hogbacks"—rounded ridges of pine-topped sandstone encircling the hills—to an interior of steep mountains covered with pine and spruce and winding defiles carved out by small, clear creeks. The most striking features are the cliffs and pinnacles of rock, exposed and eroded over centuries, that crop up everywhere in the landscape in the center of the Hills.[18] One of these offered Borglum a presidential canvas, and others—with names like the Cathedral Spires and the Needle's Eye—line the surrounding mountain roads. In fact, the original idea of Doane Robinson, the state historian who brought Borglum to South Dakota, was not to spread presidential visages across a hillside but to use the rounded knobs of the Needles to sculpt historical figures along an already existing highway.[19] In the southeast corner of the hills, the seventy-one-thousand-acre Custer State Park now hosts an ambitious buffalo (or more correctly, bison) breeding program, and offers the chance for visitors to catch glimpses of a herd that usually totals around fifteen hundred animals—a sight much less common in our time than in Custer's.

The LBHA, though, has not come to the Black Hills for zoology or geology but to track the general. Our leader in this pilgrimage is Paul Horsted, a soft-spoken photographer in his mid-forties who lives in the southern Black Hills near the town of Custer. Horsted is not a lifelong Custer aficionado, but beginning in the late 1990s, he and his coauthor, Ernest Grafe, became involved in a project that attempted to trace the exact route of the 1874 expedition through the region. In particular, Horsted and Grafe sought the precise locations where William H. Illingworth, the expedition photographer, shot his fifty-plus photos. Illingworth worked with wet glass-plate negatives and a camera with two lenses, positioned side by side, which he used to produce stereographs—cards with nearly identical images that one could look at through a steropticon viewer for a three-dimensional effect, much like the red plastic Viewmasters of the 1950s and 1960s.[20] Working with the diaries, letters, and maps produced by members of the expedition, Horsted and Grafe labored over a three-year period to find the Illingworth photo sites so that Horsted could re-shoot the contemporary scenes using modern equipment.

The juxtaposition of Illingworth's and Horsted's photographs forms the centerpiece of *Exploring with Custer,* the book that Horsted and Grafe eventually produced. Part guidebook, part narrative history, part photo essay, *Exploring with Custer* is an impressive feat of bookmaking at every level.

The book provides topographical maps, GPS coordinates, and detailed driving and hiking instructions, so that the dedicated tracker can follow each step that Custer and his men took through the Black Hills, including the precise spots where Illingworth took his photos. This visual and textual guidebook is integrated with a compilation of historic quotations from primary accounts—the words of the newspaper reporters, scientists, diarists, and even Custer himself—that describe the same topography. And the book culminates with full-page photography: Illingworth's in black-and-white, Horsted's in color. Designed by Horsted's wife, Camille Riner, and published by Horsted and Grafe themselves, *Exploring with Custer* is easily the most accomplished and most aesthetically pleasing volume published thus far on the 1874 Black Hills expedition—and arguably one of the richest books of any kind on the Black Hills themselves. Even the *New York Times,* not usually a reviewer of self-published regional works, managed to find (and praise) this one.[21]

Horsted came to his first LBHA meeting in 2003, the year after *Exploring with Custer* was published; he gave a presentation on the project and sold copies of the book, as well as larger prints of the photos. Now, two years later, the book is in its second edition, and Horsted is one of the two "project officers" for the LBHA convention. When I call him a few weeks before the meeting, he is more concerned about the arrangement of tables in the book room and finding out whether the toilets on the buses will work (they will) than about Custer or the Black Hills expedition. When I ask him about Custer, he chooses his words with care, pointing out that he had only a vague idea about who Custer was and what his expedition accomplished before he began doing the research for the book. Horsted knew, though, that Custer spelled controversy. "I have friends here who are Native American," he says, "and who revile Custer. I'm very sensitive to that." He said that he and his coauthor came to respect Custer's tenacity and skill in managing the day-to-day business of a massive expedition, but he emphasizes that they are "definitely not cheerleading for Custer."[22] Horsted seems as though he is used to making this point, and indeed a virtually identical sentence—"We do not intend to glorify Custer"—appears in the preface to the book.[23]

In spite of that qualification, at the time of the Black Hills tour Horsted has scores of Custer buffs on his hands, many of them carrying a copy of *Exploring with Custer.* As the bus climbs slowly into the mountains, those of us riding on Horsted's bus are alerted each time that we cross paths with the expedition route, and especially when we pass some feature that Illingworth captured on film. Those who have the book with them flip to the relevant page and scan the passages of nineteenth-century prose describing the scenery of a century ago. In the intervening moments, the bus fills with idle chatter about past conferences, future travel plans, and the hotel restaurant. My seatmate is a college student from California who is attending the convention—his first—with his parents. He is a history major and plans to teach someday. I ask him if he has studied this period of U.S. history in his classes. He tells me that he has but that his professors don't bring up Custer or the Indian wars. "It's still a bit touchy," he says.

I am not entirely sure what "it" is, but I miss my chance to ask, because we have arrived at our first stop: Castle Creek valley, so named for the weathered limestone ridges that the expedition found on the hilltops. The Custer expedition camped here after two days of marching from Floral Valley, and it is where the expedition engaged in its only encounter with Lakota Indians in the Black Hills. Signs of Indian activity were visible everywhere, according to the records of the expedition. "We became aware," Private Ewart wrote, "that we had now, in real earnest, entered the red man's sanctum sanctorum, that this portion of his allotted ground was to have been kept sacred from the prying paleface." [24] Ewart and others mention finding stacks of tepee poles, stakes used for stretching and tanning hides, and other signs of recent camps. Fred Power, writing for the *St. Paul Press,* fell back on notions of the noble, natural savage that had long been the stock-in-trade of the American writer: "One would judge from these trails that the Indian is an admirer of all that is grand and beautiful in nature. They always select the wildest spots for camp ground, surrounded by the most romantic hills and dales, and bounded on one side by the prettiest of rippling streams—a fit place for student or lover." [25] It was easier, of course, to admire the Indian penchant for natural beauty when the Indians themselves were absent.

But they were close. While Custer's men were setting up camp, Arikara scouts began following the trails, and one of them discovered an encampment of five lodges in a valley two to three miles farther downstream. The Arikaras were delighted. Not long before the expedition, an Arikara village belonging to their band had been attacked by Lakotas; Bloody Knife had lost a son, and another scout, Bear's Eye, had lost a brother. "These deaths," as one reporter put it, "they were anxious to revenge, and the prospect of an opportunity gave us a glimpse of the old-Indian war-spirit." [26] Custer, on the other hand, was not interested in settling intertribal scores. He took a company of cavalry with him and rode to the camp with the eager Arikaras. Once there, he sent a guide and some of the Santee scouts into the village under a flag of truce, all the while ordering

the Arikaras not to attack unless fired upon first. Bloody Knife would remain angry at Custer for some time. Two weeks later, at an Elk Dance held
by the scouts as the expedition exited the Black Hills, he made a speech
chiding Custer for forcing this restraint. Ewart recorded Bloody Knife's
words as interpreted by one of the guides: "The Ree [Arikara] warriors felt
bad," Ewart's account concludes. "They returned to Fort Lincoln without
a single scalp."[27]

The Lakota Sioux who were camped downstream from the expedition were a small band under the leadership of One Stab, an Oglala, who
was out hunting at the time of Custer's arrival. When One Stab returned,
Custer explained the purpose of the expedition and asked if One Stab's
camp would travel with the expedition to help it navigate the Black Hills.
One Stab was reluctant but suggested that someone, perhaps himself,
could stay with the soldiers for a few days and tell them about the region.
Later that afternoon, One Stab and three other adult men came to the
expedition camp, found Custer's headquarters, and received gifts of sugar,
coffee, and bacon for their band. While the army officers were busy trying to organize a party to deliver the rations downstream, the Oglala men
began riding away into the woods, one by one, as if to avoid being noticed.
Later, Custer's Indian scouts would return with news that the Oglalas had
abandoned their camp, cutting up their tent poles and making holes in
their kettles so that their enemies could not use them. The visit of One
Stab and his men to the expedition camp was clearly a diversion to allow
the village time to disband and move on—with one exception. One Stab
himself was captured and kept prisoner in the expedition camp as a hos-
tage and guide. He would stay with the expedition until Custer released
him ten days later, sending him off in the night so that his Arikara enemies
would not notice his departure.[28]

Today, the ground where One Stab and his band camped is under
Deerfield Lake, created when Castle Creek was dammed by the Civilian
Conservation Corps to create a 414-acre reservoir. Horsted points this out
to us as the bus climbs past the lake, mentioning that the expedition itself
later camped in the same place, though only after One Stab had taken
Custer's men on a lengthy detour to the north, probably to give his people more time to make their escape. We are off the main highway now,
winding past heavily forested hillsides on a two-lane road that follows the
creekbed. The buses then enter Castle Creek valley itself, where the expedition camped for two nights while Custer dickered with One Stab and
restrained Bloody Knife from exacting retribution. The entire gaggle of
Little Big Horn Associates assembles on the valley floor while Horsted,

speaking into a portable microphone, talks about the events that occurred here and points to the various locations where Illingworth took photos. We then split up into groups to walk to two of the photo sites. One follows Horsted to the creek, to walk downstream along the valley floor; I join the second group, led by Don Schwarck, which clambers over a barbed-wire fence and climbs a grass-covered hill.

Schwarck, a recently retired middle-school science teacher from Michigan, has been active in the LBHA since he began coming to meetings in the mid-1980s. He has edited the newsletter and chaired the organization's executive board. This year, he is working with Horsted as the second program officer arranging the convention in Rapid City. Like many other members of the LBHA, he pursues his own historical research, but his primary subjects are tangential to the life of Custer, the Battle of the Little Bighorn, or even any of the better-known officers of the Seventh Cavalry. For instance, he has been researching K.C. Barker, the Detroit mayor and president of the city's Audubon club, to whom Custer sent wildlife specimens and Indian artifacts during his time on the Plains. Schwarck has also focused his research energies on Illingworth and the Black Hills expedition, which first attracted his interest when his wife picked up two of the Illingworth stereograph cards at a flea market about twenty years ago. Since then, he has amassed a collection of more than two hundred of Illingworth's stereoviews, including many of the fifty-five-card series that Illingworth produced from the Black Hills expedition. Schwarck has researched Illingworth's life sufficiently to write a short biography for Grafe and Horsted's *Exploring with Custer* and even found out that Illingworth, when traveling with an immigrant party from Minnesota to the gold fields of Montana, crossed land now belonging to Schwarck's uncle's farm.[29]

At the top of the hill, someone opens Horsted's book, and Schwarck finds the page with the photograph taken from where we stand. Twenty-first-century trees block part of the nineteenth-century view into the valley, and of course we see none of the tents or wagons in Illingworth's picture. Nor, for that matter, do we see any of the signs of Indian trails or camps that the diarists and reporters on the 1874 expedition described. Instead, the valley rolls out before us, green and peaceful, with a cool, pleasant breeze. The only truly remarkable feature of the landscape is the colorful line of our own members, the other LBHA group, stretched out in the distance. As we compare the past and present perspectives, Schwarck sets up his camera. He is pursuing his own photo project. Like Horsted, he is trying to reproduce the Illingworth views, but his plan goes even beyond what Horsted has accomplished in two respects. First, he hopes to find the locations of all the photos that Illingworth took on the expedition, including those that he took outside the Black Hills, closer to Fort Abraham Lincoln. Second, he is trying to produce his own stereoview photographs so that he can replicate the three-dimensional effect of the nineteenth-century stereographs. He actually owns a stereo 3-D Realist camera from the 1960s, but for this particular photo he needs the wide lens that he has attached to a regular 35mm camera. He has the camera mounted on a wooden slide, so that after taking the photo, he can move it two and a half inches—the span between two eyes—to the right for a second photo. The process requires patience and care, and during the time it takes him to move the camera from the first position to the second a stiff wind can blow all the vegetation out of position, so that the image is blurred.[30]

Schwarck's own photography project helps to explain why Grafe and Horsted's *Exploring with Custer* is so perfect for the history enthusiasts of the Little Big Horn Associates. For these aficionados—many of them, like Schwarck, amateur historians themselves—history is not about looking for abstract patterns or tracing a grand sweep of ideas. Instead, history for them lies in the exact, sometimes mundane particulars of everyday life; it is about the accumulation of detail. Many of the diehard members of the LBHA are collectors of physical objects—nineteenth-century weapons, pop culture ephemera, books—but they are also collectors of historical fact. Schwarck, like others I have talked to in the organization, talks about the pleasures of digging through archives, sifting through documents in search of a new piece of the puzzle. In one sense, this kind of research is analogous to the collecting of historical photographs or other artifacts; it centers on the acquisition and evaluation of objects, whether a stereocard or a census record. As Jean Baudrillard observes, a "collection is never really initiated in order to be completed."[31] The same holds true, in this case, for history itself.

This close relationship between the collection of tangible artifacts of history and intangible historical facts is pivotal to the popularity of Grafe and Horsted's book among Custer aficionados. *Exploring with Custer* assembles all of the requisite pieces, all of the known facts, of the 1874 expedition into the Black Hills, and packages them so that readers can fashion their own relationship to this history. As the day progresses, I notice several of those who had brought their copies of *Exploring with Custer* folding down page corners or otherwise marking the locations we visited or passed on the bus. The book offers a kind of shopping list for heritage tourists. By following the book and traveling to the locations it names, they can assemble a collection of historical experiences that are both shared—

because others can collect them too—and personal. Kevin Melchionne has described collecting as offering a kind of aesthetic cultivation that counters the reigning dictates of mass culture.[32] The same kind of cultivation can take place in relationship to a historical landscape. In this case, readers of *Exploring with Custer* can visit carefully demarcated locations and believe that they are uniquely equipped to appreciate them. This practice of historical appreciation, centered on visiting a geographic location where an event occurred, serves as one of the organizing principles of the LBHA meetings, which offer their members a chance to visit where Custer and his men stood, walked, and fought—all so that Custer aficionados can experience those places as only those with their specialized knowledge can do. Traveling through the Black Hills with the LBHA is like walking through an art museum with a lifelong devotee of, say, Edouard Manet—a specialist who interprets the whole of European art as a series of precursors, echoes, foils, and descendants of her beloved painter.

⊶•⊷

By the time the 1874 expedition reached Castle Creek, the miners on Custer's expedition were already at work looking for evidence of gold. Private Ewart's diary describes the gold fever that gripped the expedition. "As we sat on our horses looking towards the supposed Eldorado," he wrote before the expedition entered the Black Hills, "the conversation naturally turned up on the 'filthy lucre'—Gold. If all accounts would prove true we would find plenty of it, surely. How would we carry it?"[33] Ewart and his fellow enlisted men never had to worry about emptying their saddlebags or sneaking nuggets on the wagons, as they thought they might, but the expedition was relentless in its quest to provide evidence for the rumors of gold that had been attached to the Black Hills for decades.

Success finally came three days after the expedition left Castle Creek, when it arrived at French Creek, in the southern part of the hills. "The few glittering grains, with a slight residue of earth, were carefully wrapped up in a small piece of paper and put in the miner's pocketbook," Barrows wrote in the *New York Tribune*. The camp moved downstream for fresh grass, and the miners dug a grave-sized hole; this time, they had even more cause for celebration. "From the grass roots down," the *Chicago Inter-Ocean* reported, "it was 'pay dirt.'"[34]

In fact, Custer's men scraped together merely forty to fifty pinhead-sized particles of gold—enough, though, to set first the expedition and then the nation abuzz. Within a few days, Custer would send a messenger to ride south out of the Hills to Laramie, and he would carry the dispatches of Custer and the newspaper reporters telling of the discovery. By mid-August, newspapers would be carrying their stories under bold headlines: "The New Gold Country," "The Eldorado," or more simply, "GOLD!"[35] Custer's own widely reprinted report to Sheridan was more cautious, but only slightly. "Gold has been found in several places, and it is the belief of those who are giving their attention to this subject that it will be found in paying quantities."[36] Some of the men in his command organized the Custer Park Mining Company to stake their claims.[37]

What remained unclear was how the organizers would return to work their claims. The same *Chicago Inter-Ocean* article that brought the news of the gold discovery to its readers also sounded a note of uncertainty: "The expedition has solved the mystery of the Black Hills, and will carry back the news that there is gold here, in quantities as rich as were ever dreamed of. The method to reach it is yet to be provided. It is in the very heart of the Sioux territory—in their choicest hunting ground—and they hold the land with as holy reverence as the savage heart can feel. No one can come here with any safety, or with any legal right as long as the treaties that now exist hold good, and the wealth that we have found must be for several years under the ban."[38] Everyone on the expedition understood that the Black Hills had been recognized by the United States as a part of the Great Sioux Reservation, but they shared a tacit understanding that the discovery of gold would begin a process—perhaps peaceful, perhaps not—by which that recognition would cease. In the meantime, the army stated it would enforce the prohibition against entry into the Black Hills by non-Indian civilians, and a year after Custer left the Black Hills, General George Crook was dispatched there to remove the estimated fifteen hundred white prospectors who had contravened the army's ban. Along French Creek, where the gold discoveries had first been made, Crook found a settlement that included a stockade and log cabins. He ordered the settlers to leave but helped them to record their claims so that they could be honored when Lakota title to the land was extinguished, as Crook accurately believed it soon would be. The miners even planned out and assigned the lots of a town near the stockade—and then voted to give the new municipality a name: Custer.[39]

The town of Custer turned out to be on the opposite side of the Black Hills from the most significant gold deposits, the deep veins that would sustain the Homestake Goldmine in Lead—reputedly the richest mine in the Western Hemisphere—for over a century. Now the town's location is also farther away from both the interstate and Mount Rushmore, so the tourist traffic seems more subdued than in some of the other Black Hills towns to the north. With a population of just under two thousand inside the town limits and another thousand or more in the nearby environs, Custer stretches for no more than three miles along the valley carved out by French Creek and then to the north into the surrounding hills. The town offers impressive views of the pre-Cambrian granite outcrops distinctive to the region, two grocery markets advertising buffalo meat for sale, and retail outlets that range from quiet galleries displaying Western art to souvenir stores stocked with shot glasses, snow globes, and motorcycle T-shirts for the Sturgis Rally. The LBHA tour buses drive along the streets and to the meadows east of the town, where the 1874 expedition camped and made its more significant gold strikes and where the men staked their claims. We file off to hear Paul Horsted talk more about the photographs that Illingworth made in the area, but everyone becomes nervous as the lightning strikes of a storm seem to be getting closer. Soon, we are back in our seats, the rattling noise of dime-sized hail drowning out any casual conversation.

The final stop on our field trip is the unfinished Crazy Horse Memorial being sculpted out of a mountainside about ten miles north of Custer— a nominal juxtaposition with obvious irony. The Crazy Horse Memorial has been a work in progress for more than fifty years. In 1940, Korczak Ziolkowski received a letter from Henry Standing Bear, an Oglala/Sicangu Lakota chief, who sought a sculptor for a work that would portray a Lakota leader in the same iconic cast as the soon-to-be-completed Mount Rushmore. Eight years later, Ziolkowski touched off the first blast in the six-hundred-foot granite monolith known as Thunderhead Mountain; five Lakota survivors of the Battle of the Little Bighorn attended the dedication. In the years that followed, Ziolkowski continued laboring on the mammoth sculpture that, when finished, will present Crazy Horse sitting on his horse and pointing into the distance (figure 11). More than 640 feet long and 560 feet high, the sculpture will dwarf Mount Rushmore in size and will portray Crazy Horse in the round, instead of in relief. Each nostril of the horse will be more than thirty feet in diameter.

At the base of the mountain, a three-stanza poem written by Ziolkowski will be carved in letters three feet high; the poem concludes:

> For us the past is in our hearts,
>> The future never to be fulfilled
> To you I give this granite epic
>> For your descendants to always know—
> "My lands are where my dead lie buried."

Figure 11. This composite illustration shows the construction on the Crazy Horse Memorial to date, with a model of the completed sculpture in the foreground. (Photograph copyright Crazy Horse Memorial Foundation.)

The final line has been attributed to Crazy Horse himself, who, pointing in the distance, used it as a response when he was asked after his surrender where his lands were. The incident is the inspiration for Crazy Horse's pose in the statue.

Ziolkowski died in 1982 at the age of seventy-four, but his wife, Ruth, and eight of their ten children continue work on the sculpture, using detailed plans that Korczak left behind. To date, the Ziolkowskis have removed more than eight million tons of granite from the mountain. The face of the memorial—unveiled in 1998 to mark the fiftieth anniversary of work—points out from the mountainside. An even shelf, which will eventually be rounded into Crazy Horse's pointing arm, reaches out horizontally. The outlines of the horse he rides have been painted to demarcate where the head will be carved, and a tunnel underneath the arm shows where the bodies of the rider and his mount will eventually be differentiated. The Ziolkowski family refuses to project a completion date for the project, and it is easy to imagine that the work will take another fifty years, or perhaps even twice that. In its current state, the massive unfinished statue seems less like a monument to a nineteenth-century Lakota warrior than a testament to the ambition and determination of an autodidact sculptor—orphaned at age one—and his heirs. From its inception, the enterprise has remained a private one. A nonprofit foundation acquired the land around the mountain through a series of exchanges with the National Forest Service, and Ziolkowski twice rejected possible federal funding during his lifetime. Ziolkowski also planned a larger complex around the sculpture that will include an Indian Museum of North America, the campus of the University and Medical Training Center for the North American Indian, and an airport—all joined together by a wide boulevard of the "Avenue of the Chiefs."

While that vision remains in the distance, the cluster of buildings that make up a combination visitor center and museum—run by the Crazy Horse Memorial Foundation, a nonprofit organization that does not accept government funding—are impressive. They house wide galleries of American Indian art, as well as some historical artifacts. Indian writers sign and sell their books there, and a cultural center provides space to indigenous artists selling their wares. Still, one is likely to leave the memorial having learned much more about Korczak Ziolkowski than about Crazy Horse. The story of Ziolkowski (referred to simply as Korczak) is invoked and repeated constantly: the letter he received from Henry Standing Bear, his decision to portray Crazy Horse pointing to the lands where his people are buried, his decades of selfless, and often solitary, labor on the mountain. And everywhere one looks, one sees miniature representations—scale models, paintings, drawings—of what the sculpture will look like when completed. As for the biography of the man who is being portrayed, that is reserved for a single glass case near the entrance.

Walking through the museum and around the observation deck, many of the LBHA members do not seem to know what to do with themselves here. They are interested in a certain kind of visceral experience of history, particularly the history of the Seventh Cavalry, and not in the spectacle of icon making. Some grumble about the Indian (and therefore, to them, anticavalry) focus of the museum, and a few of us talk about what Crazy Horse, who avoided being photographed during his entire life, would have made of the memorial depicting him.[40] Meanwhile, we are watching the storm clouds—the remnants of the summer storm that hailed upon us— gather and blacken behind the unfinished sculpture as though preparing for another act of meteorological drama. The ghost of Crazy Horse, someone jokes, is conjuring the weather to smite the Custer buffs. Everyone laughs.

For Donovin Sprague, on the other hand, the emerging Crazy Horse Memorial has the same kind of commemorative power as the Little Bighorn Battlefield. Sprague, from the Cheyenne River reservation, is a descendant of the families of both Crazy Horse and Hump, a noted Minneconjou warrior who played a leading role in the military force that defeated Custer. Sprague is also the director of the cultural and education center located adjacent to the visitor center at the Crazy Horse Memorial, where he oversees cultural programming, teaches university classes as an extension of Black Hills State College, and coordinates the Indian sellers of arts and crafts. When we talk a few days before the LBHA convention, we realize that we had both attended the same ceremonies held the previous weekend at the Little Bighorn battlefield to mark the anniversary of the battle. Sprague tells me that he experiences the same sense of pride in his ancestors here at the Crazy Horse Memorial as he does there at the battlefield. Moreover, he says, the commitment of the Ziolkowski family to the welfare of tribal peoples is genuine; he points both to the classes they have paid him to teach and to the experience of the average visitors, who "are first attracted to the spectacle of the mountain, but take away something about the history and the culture of the tribes." It is true that as we are talking, I see a number of tourists in conversation with the Native artists selling their wares at the tables that Sprague offers them free; Sprague himself is at work carving a flute. "If this," he says, gesturing to the tables, "were on the reservation, there's no way that we would be able to draw this kind of audience." I ask Sprague whether other Lakotas share his enthusiasm for the memorial, and he points out that in the ten years he has worked for the cultural center, he has never received a negative comment from an Indian, nor found one written in one of the available comment books. "Of course," he admits, "those who oppose it probably don't come up here."[41]

I am thinking about Sprague's comments about who comes to the memorial and what they learn from it, when I come back, by myself, to watch the nightly laser-light show, "Legends in Light." According to the brochure, "The multimedia program is laser-light storytelling to illuminate our cultural diversity, celebrate our similarities and encourage better understanding and harmony among races and nations." It is hard to argue with goals like these, and it turns out that the lasers illuminating the mountainside offer an innocuous version of multiculturalism. Korczak Ziolkowski's biography is told once more, a roster of famous Native American leaders appears on the screen, and a song titled "The Legend of Crazy Horse" reminds the audience that the Lakota warrior "never signed a treaty / or hung his head in shame." Perhaps the most provocative moment in the show is a kind of "yesterday and today" segment in which scenes from traditional tribal life morph into images from the contemporary world—so that the chiefs in headdresses sitting around a campfire become the modern boardroom of the tribal council. The show includes well-known words of Lakota spiritual leader Arvol Looking Horse, the keeper of the Sacred

Buffalo Pipe, about his people's sense of renewal: "The Lakota prophecy of mending the sacred hoop of all nations has begun."

But before the show is over, the music has changed, and the loudspeakers are filling the air with a familiar song: Lee Greenwood's "God Bless the U.S.A." and its refrain "I'm proud to be an American." At this point the incongruities of contemporary multiculturalism, with one foot in the melting pot and another in cultural separatism, come into relief. The montage of images that accompanies the song emphasizes the service of American Indians for the United States, including Ira Hayes (Pima), who raised the U.S. flag with his fellow Marines at Iwo Jima, and astronaut John Harrington (Chickasaw), who became the first American Indian to walk in space on a 2002 flight of the space shuttle Endeavor. The show concludes with an illumination of the mounted Crazy Horse portrayed to show how the statue will eventually look, but the laser show goes a step further and animates Crazy Horse's hair so that it flows in the wind.

This finale reveals the sustaining contradiction of the Crazy Horse Memorial and perhaps even our larger cultural moment at the turn of the twenty-first century. We now live at a time when it is possible to celebrate the life of a man who bitterly fought the United States, who considered himself an enemy of the United States, who "never signed a treaty"—all the while participating in the fervor of Lee Greenwood's U.S. patriotism. Whatever Crazy Horse may or may not have been during his life, there is no evidence that he was ever proud to be an American.

—————⇒⋅◦⋅⇐—————

Article 12 of the Fort Laramie Treaty of 1868 mandated that any future cession of the land designated for the Lakota Sioux would be invalid "unless executed and signed by at least three-fourths of all the adult male Indians, occupying or interested" in the reservation land.[42] So in the fall of 1875, after General Crook had labored to clear the Black Hills of prospectors (an act designed as a show of good faith to the Lakotas), a commission headed by Senator William Allison arrived at the Great Sioux Reservation to buy or lease them. At least some Lakotas argued that their tribe should never sell the Black Hills, and Little Big Man—a close friend of Crazy Horse—threatened to kill any Indian who did so.[43] The Lakota leaders with whom the commission met, however, took a different tactic. Emphasizing the value of the Black Hills, they stressed that selling the hills would require compensation of an extraordinary magnitude. "As long as we live on this earth we will expect pay," Spotted Tail said. "We want to leave the amount with the President at interest forever. . . . The amount must be so large that the interest will support us." Red Cloud more poetically said that the amount must be large enough to take care of the next seven generations of Lakotas.

Fast Bear, meanwhile, recalled to the commissioners the indignities that One Stab had suffered at the hands of the Custer expedition during the previous summer. The commission transcript reads:

FAST BEAR. . . . One of my head men was caught in the Black Hills and scared
   a little last summer. I want the Government to pay him for that road.
MR. ALLISON. What road?
FAST BEAR. That Thieves' Road. (Custer's Trail).

The figure mentioned by more than one Lakota leader was $70 million. The commission proposed $6 million to buy the Black Hills, or $400,000 per year to lease them—and returned to Washington without a deal.[44]

That winter, the Grant administration decided quietly to discontinue interfering with white settlement in the Black Hills and also began laying the groundwork of what would become the Centennial Campaign against those Lakotas and Northern Cheyennes who remained hostile to the United States. When a new commission arrived at the Great Sioux Reservation in the fall of 1876, fifteen thousand non-Indians were already in the Black Hills, and the Battle of the Little Bighorn cast a long shadow over the proceedings; the commission had neither the disposition nor the authority for generous negotiating. Instead, the commission proffered an agreement that included the cession of the Black Hills to the United States, the forfeiture of hunting rights outside the reservation, and even a requirement that a Lakota delegation visit the Indian Territory in the hope that the Lakotas might be relocated there. In exchange, the commission offered a program of annuities and assimilation similar to the treaty provisions that it had failed to fulfill from the treaty of 1868. If the Indians did not sign, the commission explained, they would be cut off from further distribution of rations and subject to military authority at the reservation agencies. The commission did not bother obtaining the signatures of the three-fourths of the Lakotas mandated by the 1868 treaty; instead, the commission's threats and bribes resulted in about 10 percent of the adult Lakota males' signing the agreement. The U.S. Congress ratified the agreement in 1877, and the Black Hills were officially open for business.[45]

Rapid City occupies a small part of the territory that the United States claimed from the Lakotas under the 1876–77 agreement, though there are not many reminders of that historical fact in view. (Perhaps the lone exception is the recently opened Journey Museum, which displays the text of the Fort Laramie Treaty of 1868 as part of an exhibit about the ongoing conflicts over land.) Back at the hotel after a day of tracing Custer's Black Hills route, the Little Big Horn Associates are meeting for their own form of commerce, an annual auction of Custer-related paraphernalia. Part silliness and part seriousness, the auction feeds the acquisitive desires of the LBHA membership and raises money to help stage the next year's conference. Most of the items are books; there are always prints and paintings of nineteenth-century cavalry life and original magazines with articles related to Custer, as well as a few choice items of Custer kitsch. This year, the big-ticket items are a quilt sewed with a Morningstar pattern ($300), a Navajo blanket ($400), and a reproduction of a Civil War overcoat ($155). Horsted has donated a muleshoe that he has found in the Black Hills and that he believes is an artifact of the 1874 Custer expedition; Vincent Heier has contributed a metal engraving of the famous *Harper's Weekly* illustration of Custer charging during the Civil War; and someone who attended the recent Little Bighorn reenactment picked up a bottle of water half-drunk by Steve Alexander—auctioned off as "Custer's last drink" for four dollars. By the time the night is over, the auction has raised over three thousand dollars for next year's convention.

The auction illustrates something of the motives and rewards that draw new members into the LBHA and keep them involved. Many of the members with whom I have spoken and corresponded recall the event that first ignited their interest in Custer or the U.S. Cavalry: a film (*They Died with Their Boots On* or *She Wore a Yellow Ribbon*), a book (many mention Quentin Reynolds' *Custer's Last Stand,* a children's book first published in 1951), or a visit to the battlefield in the course of a family vacation. However, when they speak about the pleasures of the organization, they focus on the camaraderie that the organization provides. Like an academic society devoted to an esoteric subject, the LBHA members revel in the chance to spend a few days among others who speak the same language that they do, who have an opinion about Reno's charge and retreat, Benteen's scout to the left, or Custer's crossing at Medicine Tail Coulee Ford. As one member explains, "During my normal, everyday life, it is difficult to have an intelligent conversation on my historical interests, as very few in the general population share my interests. It is refreshing to be surrounded by 100–200 people with the same passion for history as myself, and be able to discuss or argue the various aspects of the events surrounding Custer and the Little Bighorn battle."[46] Or as I overheard someone say during the field trip: "At home, I'm just a weirdo. Here, there are four buses of us."

The majority of those on those buses, about two-thirds, were male, and of the women who come, many are spouses whose enthusiasm does not match that of their husbands. Yet it is not unusual to find wives who are just as knowledgeable and interested as their husbands, and there are cases where the women gently coerce their male partners to attend the conference, rather than the reverse. The year of the Black Hills conference, two of the seven members of the LBHA board of directors were female, and each year there are a handful of women, between 5 and 10 percent of registered participants, who attend unaccompanied by a male partner.[47] At Rapid City, one of these was Deborah Buckner, a homemaker from the suburbs of Kansas City who drove to South Dakota with her daughter and mother for her second LBHA conference. When she was fourteen, Buckner found *They Died with Their Boots On* playing on late-night television; she was so captivated by the story that she began checking out books from the library: Elizabeth Custer's *Tenting on the Plains,* W.A. Graham's *Custer Myth,* Douglas A. Jones' counterfactual *Court-Martial of George Armstrong Custer.* She even wrote a fan letter to Olivia de Havilland and, seven years later, received an improbably late reply. The two, says Buckner, continue to correspond.

Buckner has continued to accumulate a collection of books and articles and now claims her own "Custer room" in her house to store them—a common practice among Custer aficionados. Buckner's is decorated with a painted border of buffalo and includes a closet with several period costumes, which she wears when she gives historical talks in the persona of Libbie Custer. She has visited the Custer grave at West Point, and twice each year she decorates the graves of Tom Custer, James Calhoun, and Algernon Smith—all officers who died at Little Bighorn—in Fort Leavenworth, Kansas, not far from her home. However, she has never been to the Little Bighorn battlefield. "I seriously question whether I could stand to do so," she states. "I think it would be too difficult emotionally."

For Buckner, the mechanics of the battle are of interest, but ultimately less important than an affective experience—*spiritual* is her word—that she finds difficult to describe. She returns home after the conference with poems that she has written about Custer, and she sends me two of these. They express a deeply felt longing for a romantic version of history, in which the extraordinary deeds and sentiments of those who engaged in battle—especially Custer himself—are more significant than the mundane, decidedly inglorious realities of the masses that have received so much attention since academic historians turned toward social history. In one poem, Custer's spirit speaks to the reader, instructing us not to look for him on the battlefield—"I do not linger in that land of loss," reads the poem's refrain—but in all of the other places that he lived. In another, "June 25, 1876," the speaker describes Custer bowing to Crazy Horse, just as he once bowed to his opponent during the Civil War: "We both advance / To battle, then, and let those after know: / This was a day when foe respected foe."[48]

Buckner offers a dramatic example of the fact that, as in any hobbyist group, the people who belong to the LBHA do not uniformly act out of precisely the same rationale or even out of similar rationales in the same proportion. (Unlike Buckner, for instance, many LBHA members proudly accumulate visits to the battlefield rather than experiencing emotional difficulty when traveling there.) The members also range from those who are more casual or occasional in their interest to those whose devotion to this subject occupies a large portion of their leisure time. For some of those who have been coming for ten, twenty, or even thirty years, the interest in Custer can become almost secondary during the annual meetings to the chance to see old friends. (The comparison to academic and professional conferences once again seems appropriate.) More than one person uses the phrase "family reunion" to describe the significance of the annual meeting to him or her. In fact, *family* has more than one meaning at the LBHA convention: not only do parents bring young children, or meet their grown ones, but the conference is frequently attended by descendants of those who participated in the Battle of the Little Bighorn. Charles Custer came to the meetings during the 1980s, and more recently Brice Custer has attended (both are descended from George Armstrong's brother Nevin); "Charles Reno, the great-grandnephew of Major Marcus Reno's brother, has come; the last surviving granddaughter of Captain Frederick Benteen, Maria Luisa Steves, regularly participated in the conference until her death in 2001. Her husband, Myron Steves, still attends, sometimes with his son and daughter-in-law. Myron and I share a connection: he is a graduate, class of 1934, of the university where I teach. He still climbs aboard the bus for every field trip and always seems ready to talk. "People get involved in this history in all kinds of ways," he told me once. "I married into it."

The chance to rub elbows with relatives of such historical figures and to talk with the specialists in Indian Wars history whose books they own is just one of the attractions of the meetings. Members frequently speak of their sense of a community and take pride in noting the organization's national scope, often pointing out that the LBHA has led them to develop friendships that span the United States. Moreover, this participation in communal belonging enables LBHA members to distinguish themselves from a larger society that they believe has neglected and misunderstood the history of the Indian Wars and its iconic, golden-haired general. The foil for the LBHA, in other words, is not the indigenous people of the United States who descended from those who fought Custer but rather a popular culture that the members believe has traded historical accuracy for misplaced romantic sympathies for those indigenous people. As one member, a retired military officer, states, "It seems more people today are interested in [being] PC, than in finding out what really happened in history."[49] Such complaints about "political correctness" are common among LBHA members; sometimes they level this charge at the National Park Service, but more often their target is Hollywood. During the mid-1990s, the organization's newsletter regularly included derisive comments about the television series *Dr. Quinn, Medicine Woman*; during the Rapid City conference, I heard similar sneering about the TNT miniseries *Into the West*. Of course, many of the members seemed to be watching *Into the West* closely enough to have ample fodder for their criticism. Custer buffs are certainly not the only group of historical enthusiasts who seem to enjoy demonstrating their expertise by exposing the limits and errors of the media.

The popular culture tastes of the LBHA members tend—and there are many exceptions to this generalization—to gravitate toward the mid-twentieth century, the golden age of Westerns on both the big and small screens. Many, as I have said, mention films such as *They Died with Their Boots On* as their initial gateway into the world of Custerology; when pressed, they will admit the gross historical inaccuracies of the film, but they will also argue that this era of popular culture understood the heroism of Custer and his contemporaries in ways that contemporary works do not. "The Battle of the Little Bighorn," a retired elementary schoolteacher states, "was one of the last acts of chivalry, where men stood alone against the elements and overwhelming odds. It bothers me that too many of our so-called 'heroes' in contemporary society are Hollywood phonies, obscene rap singers, or overpaid athletes. . . . I believe he [Custer] died a hero's death, even if there are some who may not consider him a hero."[50]

However, many of the long-time LBHA members whom I interviewed have also suggested to me that the tone of the LBHA has mellowed in recent years from a more intense antagonism against the perceived "anti-Custer" backlash of the late 1980s and early 1990s, when the organization opposed the change in the name of Custer Battlefield to Little Bighorn Battlefield. The placement of the Indian Memorial near Last Stand Hill also upset some LBHA members. (The LBHA itself never took an official position on the Indian Memorial, and some of its members argued in support of it.) But the decisions about the name change and the memorial placement are now receding into the past. The favorite National Park Service targets of the LBHA during the 1990s—Barbara Booher (now Barbara Sutteer) and Gerard Baker, the first and second Indian superintendents of the Little Bighorn Battlefield, respectively—have moved to other positions, and the LBHA membership seems generally pleased with Darrell Cook, a Lakota man who currently supervises the battlefield. Just one week before the Rapid City convention, Cook had allowed Steve Alexander and several other cavalry reenactors to ride on horseback up to Last Stand Hill in their period uniforms as part of a memorial service held each year by Custer enthusiasts for those killed in the battle, and several LBHA members who had seen or heard about this event spoke of Cook's decision with approval.

The change in tenor may also be the result of the loss of several key members. During the 1970s and 1980s, two of the most central figures in the Little Bighorn Associates were Lawrence Frost and John M. Carroll. Frost, the podiatrist, local politician, and amateur historian from Monroe, Michigan, mentioned in chapter 2, was among the founders of the organization; he brought to it not only a lifetime of knowledge, some of it based on his private collection of primary documents, but also a set of close relationships with the Custer family. Carroll was a teacher who had left the classroom to become a full-time historian of Custer. He was responsible for the publication of more than a dozen books—two dozen, if one counts smaller pamphletlike publications—many of them compilations or reproductions of nineteenth-century source material. Those who knew him speak of his endless supply of energy and of the nearly endless debates about the Little Bighorn that took place in his conference hotel room late into the night—"the ebullient and bellicose monarch of the LBHA," according to one account.[51] Like Frost, Carroll was an unabashed Custer apologist, a self-appointed "keeper of the flame, ever ready to embark on a noisy crusade against any perceived danger to the memory of Custer and his troopers as gallant American heroes."[52] Ron Nichols, who has since written a biography of Major Marcus Reno, recalls that Carroll and Frost's Custerphilia reached the point that those interested in the Battle of the Little Bighorn but skeptical of the general's decisions at the Little Bighorn sometimes felt themselves marginalized within the organization.[53]

More often, though, members who attended the conferences during the Carroll-Frost era recall with nostalgia their galvanizing presence. Chuck Merkel began his membership in the LBHA while he was serving as an army pilot in Vietnam. When he returned to the United States, he toured what was then Custer Battlefield with LBHA founder Robert J. Ege, traveled to Monroe to meet Frost, and attended the first LBHA convention in Louisville. In the years that followed, as his military duties took him across the United States, he would punctuate his travels with visits to fellow Custer enthusiasts. "A lot of my colleagues would go off to the local bar," he says, "but I'd go off to talk about Custer." In the meantime, Merkel turned his passion for the Seventh Cavalry into academic accreditation, eventually earning a doctorate in history with a dissertation on Captain Thomas Weir, who tried to come to Custer's rescue at the Battle of the Little Bighorn. Now he works as a civilian manager on an Air Force missile program, but he also teaches evening and distance classes in U.S. history through a Troy State University program that caters to military personnel. Merkel is still deeply involved in the LBHA, at the center of the hub of activity that makes the organization run: he regularly takes his turn as program officer, serves on the executive board, and has recently been elected to serve as chairman. His wife, Diane, edits the LBHA newsletter, acts as the organization's webmaster, and moderates the organization's burgeoning Internet message boards. Yet Merkel also expresses regret that the meetings are larger and "more formal" than they once were. With Carroll and Frost at the center, he says, the camaraderie had a different character. "I miss some of that intimacy."[54] Both Carroll and Frost died in 1990, one year before Congress approved the battlefield name change that they so vehemently opposed.

If the organization has since softened the tone of its historical partisanship, it nonetheless remains nearly overwhelmingly white. I have often been asked if the organizations of Custer aficionados (which include the LBHA, the CBHMA, and the Friends of the Little Bighorn, a smaller group founded in 1998 to assist the National Monument) have at their core a covert, or even overt, white racism; I hope that this chapter has already shown that the texture of historical pleasure at the center of the LBHA belies the simplicity of such an accusation. Yet just as Custer's death offered to his contemporaries a symbol of white sacrifice as the cost of redeeming the world from the darker races—as Richard Slotkin so persuasively argues in *The Fatal Environment*—whiteness seems to remain a precondition for those who affiliate around Custer's memory.[55] Some of the members of the LBHA with whom I have spoken, such as Vincent Heier, have expressed some regret to me about this. They point out that since the LBHA professes to be open to all possible viewpoints in its pursuit of historical truth, American Indians, as well as other nonwhites, should be able to proffer their interpretations of Custer's battles as readily as anyone else.

In fact, as I will discuss in the following chapter, the Custerologists of the LBHA have in recent years been among the leaders in collecting, printing, and studying the Indian accounts of the Battle of the Little Bighorn. But it is hard to imagine that many Indians, or for that matter African Americans, would be interested in participating in an organization that lavishes such attention on a man who has become (wrongly, most LBHA members believe) the symbol of U.S. colonization of Native peoples. Expanding to include a Native or black membership could require a reorientation of the LBHA away from the meticulous pursuit of the Seventh Cavalry lore and would almost surely have a dramatic effect on the fellowship so central to the group's annual meeting.

But racial homogeneity does not necessarily equal ideological uniformity. At the Rapid City conference in 2005, Lynn Wilke cuts a distinctive figure. Wearing the blue wool trousers of a cavalryman, a buckskin jacket, and a beaded bolo tie, Wilke carries a battered bugle with him throughout our field trip into the Black Hills; he blows "reveille" in the morning and "retreat" to call us back to the buses. Wilke, age seventy-five, is a retired music teacher from Peru, New York, and he is traveling this summer with his wife in a small RV outfitted with ham radio equipment. They may be the only couple at the LBHA meeting who will leave the conference for an extended stay at an Indian reservation. Wilke explains that his mother, an artist, had developed over the course of her lifetime a close relationship with the Crow Creek Sioux, whose reservation adjoins the Missouri River in the center of South Dakota, to the point where she was named an honorary member of the tribe. Now he, too, goes to visit friends on the reservation, and he believes that his LBHA colleagues have neglected Native perspectives on nineteenth-century history. "I like these guys," he says, "These are some of the most intellectual people I've ever known. The only problem is that they fall for everything that the white man writes."

Wilke himself became interested in the Seventh Cavalry when he found out that his grandfather had served in the New York National Guard under Major General Charles F. Roe, who had been an officer in the Second Cavalry during the Sioux campaign of 1876. Roe, in fact, was one of the first soldiers to arrive at the site of the Last Stand after the battle; he supervised the burial of the bodies there and then returned five years later for the construction of the hilltop monument in 1881. After finding this connection to the Little Bighorn, Wilke became an aficionado of the battle and the Seventh Cavalry and has since combined his historical enthusiasm with his musical expertise to develop a program called "Broadcasts from the Little Bighorn," focused exclusively on the bugle calls of the

Seventh Cavalry. He has also found the music of Custer's funeral march, which he played for the LBHA members when they held their conference at West Point. "I'm Sioux on the inside and white on the outside," he tells me. "But I don't hate Custer. . . . He was an adventurer, and I'm an adventurer."

⟹•⟸

The Crow Creek reservation that Wilke will be visiting is one of six created when the Great Sioux Reservation was diminished and broken up by an 1889 act of Congress that attempted to reduce the Lakota land base once and for all by encouraging the allotment of communal lands to individual Indians in 640-acre tracts. According to the 2000 census, more than thirty-six thousand Indians reside on those six reservations, with about the same number of enrolled members of the tribes living off the reservations. The economic conditions of these reservations in North and South Dakota are frequently said to be among the worst of any communities in the United States. The same census revealed an unemployment rate on the Pine Ridge reservation—home of the Oglala Lakota nation—of 33 percent (other estimates have been higher) and said that more than half of its residents live below the poverty line. Buffalo County, which includes the Crow Creek Sioux reservation, is regularly referred to as the poorest county in the United States (1999 per capita income, $5,213); Shannon County, which includes the Pine Ridge reservation (1999 per capita income, $6,286), is listed as the second poorest.[56] This kind of poverty is accompanied by the social problems one would expect. In 2004, for instance, a spate of suicides among young adults and teens on the Standing Rock reservation, where Sitting Bull lived after his surrender, became dire enough to prompt the Senate Select Committee on Indian Affairs to hold hearings there.[57]

Economic decline is not the only legacy of the U.S. appropriation of the Black Hills that followed Custer's 1874 expedition. In the 1890s, Lakotas began holding meetings to talk about the violation of the treaty of 1868, which had provided that land could be alienated from the Great Sioux Reservation only with the approval of three-fourths of adult males. For the Lakotas, the agreement approved by Congress in 1877 was nothing more than an illegal seizure of the Black Hills. During World War I and its immediate aftermath, a time when American Indians were asked to contribute to the U.S. war effort, the grievances of the Lakotas began to win sympathy within the federal Indian Bureau, and in 1920 Congress passed a jurisdictional act that allowed the Sioux tribes to sue the United States in federal court. Over the next half-century, the tribes and their lawyers waged a long legal battle punctuated by minor victories as well as several setbacks that nearly ended the lawsuit altogether. At last, in 1979, the U.S. Court of Claims decided that the transfer of the Black Hills to the United States constituted an illegal taking and awarded the Sioux tribes a judgment of $105 million. A year later, by an 8-1 margin, the U.S. Supreme Court affirmed the decision. Writing for the majority, Justice Harry Blackmun quoted with approval the words of the Court of Claims: "A more ripe and rank case of dishonorable dealings will never, in all probability, be found in our history."[58] (The lone dissenter, then Justice William Rehnquist, said that it was "unfair to judge by the light of 'revisionist' historians or the mores of another era actions that were taken under pressure of time more than a century ago.")[59]

The litigation over the Black Hills then took one more dramatic turn: The Lakotas, through their tribal councils and other groups concerned about the Black Hills, refused the monetary settlement. They insisted that they wanted to recover the land itself, not a cash payment for it. In *Black Hills/White Justice*, a comprehensive account of the legal history that led to the Supreme Court's 1980 judgment, Edward Lazarus (the son of one of the lead attorneys litigating on the behalf of the Sioux) suggests that the Lakotas in the early and mid twentieth century had widely understood that the litigation could produce an award of monetary damages only, and he contends that the Lakotas had been misguided into rejecting the award by a romantic nationalism that became popular in the 1970s. "The Sioux have abandoned any meaningful attempt to control their own destiny in favor of rhetorical claims to sovereignty and independence," Lazarus's book concludes.[60] For those Sioux who advocated for the rejection of a monetary settlement, however, the claims of sovereignty are anything but rhetorical, and they insist that the purpose of the Black Hills litigation has always been the recovery of the land that was illegally taken. In a scathing review of Lazarus's book, the Santee/Yankton Sioux author Elizabeth Cook-Lynn calls the proffered settlement "the ultimate 'buy-out' of an act of criminal expansionist U.S. historical behavior"—and insists that "the return of the Sioux lands *can be accomplished in this century*" (emphasis in original). She points out, for instance, that the United States found a way to do more than offer monetary damages when Iraq stole Kuwait's land.[61]

Cook-Lynn wrote her review in 1992, but the Black Hills claim still remains unresolved. Even at the time that she was writing, the U.S. Congress had already failed twice to pass legislation, sponsored by Senator Bill Bradley, that would have conveyed the federal lands within the Black Hills to the Sioux (leaving private holdings intact). Since 1980, the award has remained undistributed, and the accumulation of interest means that its current value has surpassed, by one estimate, $700 million.[62] Cook-Lynn and others remain adamant, though, that the land itself must be recovered. "The Sioux Oyate [a word, again, meaning both nation and people] believe they now walk with a renewed pride in themselves," she wrote in 1999, "instead of walking around with their heads hanging in defeat and shame, which would have been their fate if they had accepted the monetary award for the Black Hills."[63]

At the Crazy Horse Memorial, Donovin Sprague explains that both the claim on the Black Hills and the rejection of a money settlement are part of the history of tribal sovereignty among the Lakotas. He discusses the provisions of the 1868 Fort Laramie treaty in detail, explaining that it recognized the Lakotas and other Sioux tribes as "sovereign nations." He goes on to talk about the treaty's unilateral abrogation by the United States in the 1870s and the efforts of Sioux for more than a century to have their "inviolable" sovereignty recognized once more. A signal moment, he observes, came in 1970, when the U.S. Congress passed (and then President Nixon signed) legislation returning Blue Lake to the Taos Pueblo of New Mexico, whose members regard the lake and its shores as sacred.[64] It was the first time that the U.S. government had returned disputed land to an Indian tribe, and it gave the Sioux hope that their claim could be successful as well. Tribal sovereignty, Sprague points out, has since had an uneven record across Indian Country. He notes that tribes in places like Oklahoma have been much more successful than the Lakotas in managing their own tribal services and in generating economic security. Mismanagement of tribal affairs on the reservations—and he notes the internal strife of the Oglala Lakotas as a prominent example—is only an invitation for the federal Bureau of Indian Affairs to intervene. "We say we are sovereign nations," Sprague says, "but the United States can always come back in."[65]

Having traveled to tribes and universities across the United States, Sprague is acutely aware of the limited economic opportunities for the Lakota nations. Indian nations in Oklahoma, he points out, are working to elect their members to the state legislature; the Lakotas, on the other hand, are still at a stage where they need to work to get Lakota teachers into schools, clerks into banks, managers into offices, and so on. But he remarks that sovereignty also means that material wealth is not the only marker of national success: "The Lakota are not better off in terms of money, but they are rich in their culture, their knowledge of the world—the things that money can't buy. They sit in poverty, but they see themselves as rich."[66] Comments like these help to explain why the Sioux might be able to resist the temptation of a monetary settlement. For his part, Sprague maintains optimism about the potential for the Sioux to recover at least some of the land, though he thinks it improbable that they will ever own the land on which towns like Custer are built—and in fact he dismisses the fear that whites would be evicted from their homes as nothing more than a political scare tactic. Instead, Sprague says there might be a return of some land with a payment for what the Sioux tribes cannot recover. The return of land might start, he suggested, by having the tribes function first as managers of the land that the federal government owns. "We're good stewards of the land, you know," Sprague remarked. "We have a long history of that."[67]

Sprague's comment suggests how tribal treaty rights and the contemporary environmental movement can converge around threats to the land that tribal nations claim as their own and that environmentalists believe should be free from commercial development.[68] In South Dakota, this intersection has led to the formation of the Defenders of the Black Hills, a group that simultaneously advocates for the recognition of the 1868 treaty boundaries of Sioux land and sponsors efforts to protect the region from ecological harm. Charmaine White Face, an Oglala Lakota writer and a former college teacher of biology and environmental science, founded the Defenders in 2002. Today it has more than five hundred members; most are local, but others hail from other areas of the United States and even Europe. The group has managed to place the Black Hills on an international list of endangered sacred sites, has worked to preserve cultural and religious sites within the Black Hills from development, and has lobbied for the cleanup of areas contaminated by decades of mining.[69]

Several Indian tribes have sacred sites in the Black Hills. The Cheyennes, for instance, share with the Lakotas a special regard for Bear Butte, located on the northern edge of the Black Hills and now designated a state park; the Northern Cheyenne tribe has recently purchased surrounding land in an attempt to limit encroaching development from nearby Sturgis, whose biker bars threaten to impinge on the worship and prayer that take place on the small mountain.[70] White Face's Defenders have been active in protecting Bear Butte, but the ultimate goal of the organization is the return of the Black Hills to the Lakotas. White Face says that she first heard about the 1868 treaty from her grandmother, who told White Face that the treaty gave her the right to live "anywhere I wanted in South Dakota." Now White Face gives lectures explaining the history of the Lakota Sioux and the treaties that cover this territory. White residents in the region, she says, are often "stunned" to learn that their residence in the Black Hills is based upon a violation of treaty law. "They don't want to talk about it. They want to avoid it. They're in denial." She says, however, that she feels sympathy for them as victims of a U.S. government that has deliberately misled its people about the legality of their possession of the land.

Like Sprague, she maintains a sense of optimism, even confidence, about the return of the Black Hills. "Eventually it will come back to us," she says. "It's in our prophecies. But in what condition? I don't know." She laughs. "It's the condition that has me worried." Part of her argument is that U.S. relinquishment of the treaty territory would benefit everyone. "It would heal the integrity of the United States, . . . strengthen their own constitution and help the United States in the eyes of the world."

At the end of our conversation, I tell her about the group of Custer buffs who are coming to the Black Hills to follow the route of his 1874 expedition, and I ask her what she would like the group to know about that expedition. There's a long pause before she answers. "It was illegal trespassing," she finally responds, her voice on the telephone now flat, "and it was breaking the Constitution"—a reference to article VI of the U.S. Constitution, which declares treaties to be part of the "supreme Law of the land." White Face concludes, "That's really all you need to know."[71]

———— ⋙ ◆ ⋘ ————

The word *trespass* does not come up during the Little Bighorn Associates meeting in Rapid City. In fact, no one mentions the Black Hills litigation filed by the Lakota Sioux, the adjudicated monetary settlement, or the continuing demand of the Lakota Sioux that the treaty territory be restored. For someone like White Face, an awareness of the Lakota Sioux legal battle is vital to those who would seek to understand Custer's 1874 expedition, for the expedition—in which Custer and his superiors gingerly stepped around the provisions of a treaty as a precursor to more blatant violations—set in motion a process of dispossession whose material effects are still tangible to Lakotas today. However, the LBHA's focus on the microhistorical rather than the macropolitical means that the Lakota Sioux's outstanding land claims are not within the scope of its members' interests.

On the final day of the annual convention, the LBHA's mode of historical erudition—featuring a detailed knowledge of the facts of military campaigns, battles, and biographies—comes to the fore with a symposium similar to those that one regularly encounters in the academic arena.

Speakers give presentations from the podium using slides and PowerPoint, the audience responds with questions, and on occasion the exchanges become lively, even heated.

The first presentation at the Rapid City symposium, by a long-time LBHA member, focuses on Custer's 1873 battles near the Yellowstone River and features photos that the presenter had taken trying to pinpoint their exact locations. Next, a National Park Service historian describes the theatrical and painted representations of Buffalo Bill Cody's "first scalp for Custer"—an incident in which Cody claimed to be the first to kill an Indian after the Battle of the Little Bighorn. Later, Ron Nichols begins his discussion of Major Marcus Reno's post–Little Bighorn career at nearby Fort Meade with a version of Bob Newhart's telephone stand-up routine. Speaking into his cell phone, Nichols pretends to be Custer atop Last Stand Hill answering a phone call from General Alfred Terry. ("You'll be here when? . . . Tomorrow? . . . Any chance for today?") Vincent Heier gives the last paper of the day: "It Coulda, Shoulda, Woulda Happened That Way: Custer's Last Stand in Alternative Histories." As he explains how alternative history novels speculate about what might have happened if Custer had survived the Little Bighorn—in many versions he becomes president; in others he changes his name; in still others he inhabits alternate universes of dinosaurs and demons—Heier brings the audience back to laughter with the outlandish fantasies of popular fiction, bizarre to those who expend so much effort pursuing the facts of literal history. Regardless, Heier admonishes the conference that these novels have significance, for they help to show "why Custer's Last Stand has remained forever etched in the consciousness of the nation"; the narrative of tragic sacrifice, and of the flamboyant soldier brought to defeat by circumstances beyond his control, he says, remains compelling even when it is altered or inserted into new, strange imaginative contexts. With a little more textual analysis, one could give much the same talk at an academic conference.[72]

In between the talks, the members peruse the book room, where a dozen or so dealers have set up their books, artifacts, and items of Custeriana for sale. It is the kind of place where you can find an original photo of Sitting Bull or a reproduction of a cavalry saber. If you are looking for Lawrence Frost's book *Custer's Thoroughbreds* ($88) or James L. Pope's lesser-known work *Custer and His Dogs* ($45), they are both here. Someone is selling stationery from the now-defunct Custer Motel in Billings, Montana ($10), and another dealer has the original March 19, 1864, *Harper's Weekly* cover featuring Custer leading the charge ($100). A rare copy of William J. Bordeaux's *Custer's Conqueror*—which gives the account of a

Brulé Sioux who claimed to witness the Battle of the Little Bighorn from a tent in the Indian village—is on sale for $500; at the other end of the spectrum, old paperback editions of Jay Monaghan's 1959 Custer biography (and every other Custer biography, for that matter) are available for less than $10. Members can buy shirts and caps embroidered with the LBHA logo or older versions of the commemorative mug issued at each annual convention. Two of the most popular items this year are a pair of books, *Little Bighorn Mysteries* and *More Little Bighorn Mysteries*—large, soft-cover volumes of 350 pages each, written and self-published by Vern Smalley. As the titles suggest, the books are arranged around the unresolved, deeply specific historical questions that Custerologists love to ponder—and Smalley has put forward some surprising conclusions that those well versed in the arcane knowledge of the battle will be able to continue debating for at least another year. It is a small market, but Smalley has pegged it well.[73] The Custer aficionados do not actually want to solve the mysteries of the Little Bighorn but to make sure that the sense of mystery remains—and even proliferates; a complete, definitive historical "solution" to the battle would, like the final piece of a puzzle, put an end to the endeavor and the enjoyment.

This approach to history, which takes pleasure in uncertainty about the minute details of military action, again occupies center stage at the climactic event of the LBHA symposium: a panel discussion titled "Custer, the Indian Fighter." This kind of panel discussion is a regular staple of the LBHA conferences, but this one stands out because of the roster of participants. Two of them are LBHA stalwarts: Don Horn, a former chairman of the organization's board and the author of his own, pro-Custer book, *Portrait of a General;* and William Boyes, a retired aerospace engineer who has served the LBHA in a variety of capacities, including editor of the LBHA *Research Review.* The others on the panel are less regular attendees of the conferences, but each is a kind of celebrity in the world of Custerology: Jerome Greene, a research historian for the National Park Service in Denver and the author of several books on the Indian Wars, including an authoritative history of the Washita conflict; Paul A. Hutton, a professor of history at the University of New Mexico who is the executive director of the Western History Association and a favorite talking head on documentaries about Custer and the Indian Wars; and, finally, Robert M. Utley, the onetime chief historian of the National Park Service whose books on the Indian Wars are treated like black-letter law in the world of Custerology. The rank and file of the LBHA approach Utley with a touch of quiet reverence and awe; prior to the panel, he has been signing copies of his new memoir, *Custer and Me.* In the memoir, Utley tells of driving to Fort Riley, Kansas, with Hutton in 1989, the year after the publication of Utley's Custer biography, *Cavalier in Buckskin.* John M. Carroll, a member of the LBHA prize committee, told Utley that the biography would "undoubtedly" win the organization's annual award for the best book published on Custer, and Utley believed he should accept the award in person. Carroll even arranged to have Utley serve as the speaker at the convention's banquet. However, he had made a mistake about the prize, which was awarded to Roger Darling's *Custer's Seventh Cavalry Comes to South Dakota,* a book of detailed, empirical research of the kind that Custer enthusiasts value, which provided an account of the movements of the Seventh Cavalry in its transition from southern Reconstruction duty to the northern Plains during the first half of 1873.[74] In the memoir, Utley recalls trying not to betray his surprise as he congratulated the winner, as well as enduring Hutton's laughter on their long homeward journey together.[75] Now, sixteen years later, Utley was back at the LBHA to accept a different award, a prize that the LBHA has decided to give annually to a previously published work that the organization failed to recognize when it was first published, a kind of book-prize mulligan. So Utley and Hutton have repeated their history by driving to the conference together.

The panel discussion is supposed to assess Custer's entire career as an Indian fighter, and the opening questions do just that by asking the participants to assess Custer's Civil War record against his record of fighting the Plains Indians or to compare Custer with the other military leaders who participated in the Indian Wars. (Everyone agrees that Custer's Civil War career is far more accomplished than his career in the West and that Nelson Miles was the superior military commander of U.S. troops in the Indian Wars.) Soon, however, someone from the audience asks the panelists to evaluate Custer's tactical decisions during the Battle of the Little Bighorn, and the discussion quickly moves to the favorite ground of the LBHA membership: the actions—both known and unknown—of the Seventh Cavalry during the battle. Within a matter of minutes, Utley is speculating on what might have occurred if another officer had been in charge of Reno's column, Horn is proffering his theory that Custer was wounded early while trying to cross the Little Bighorn River, and everyone is arguing about what could have happened had the Indians begun to panic and flee from the cavalry.

In the middle of the debate, Hutton suggests that there may have been something larger at work in the fighting:

I'm probably the least spiritual person on the planet, but I don't think it was possible for Custer to make any right decisions that day. And the emotional power of what was going on in that village is what turned that tide, because they *didn't* run. . . . That was a different summer, and that was a different group of Native people than had ever existed at any place, at any time, and Custer, I think—because he did embrace the West, he did embrace the romance of war—was the perfect soldier to go against them. And it results in the one Indian Wars battle[field] that you can go on the field as a white American and walk across and have a romantic notion of it. . . . It [the Little Bighorn battle] is really that last great moment of all of European expansion. There are a lot of Indian wars after that, but here is the perfect, beautiful, symbolic moment. Maybe it was all written in the stars. Maybe nothing could have saved him that day.

Hutton has it, of course, exactly right. The secret to the historical power of the Battle of the Little Bighorn is that the defeat of the Seventh Cavalry means that twentieth-century and now twenty first-century whites can commemorate the violent work of Western expansion without having to feel entirely guilty about the fate of the American Indians whom the United States attempted to conquer. Custer's loss so sharply resists the tides of history, as commonly understood, that it has seemed to one generation after another as though it were the outcome of some unknowable, preternatural force. The spectacle of defeat explains why generations of Custerologists have pored over the arcane details of this one conflict in the Indian Wars when so many others remain relatively neglected; why Custer continues to exert power as a romantic hero even when the larger public sympathizes with his foes; and how a historic event can be transformed into an object whose aesthetic appeal rivals that of artistic masterpieces. For a moment, the discussion pauses as the audience digests what Hutton says—and then someone steps forward to ask a new question.

As I sat and listened to the LBHA members argue about whether Custer should have accepted the Gatling guns that Terry offered him, about how far north Custer and his battalion marched before their demise on Last Stand Hill, I tried to imagine how the descendants of the Lakota resistance that defeated the Seventh Cavalry—people like Gary Rowland at Wounded Knee or Donovin Sprague at the Crazy Horse Memorial—would have responded to this discussion. My guess is that their reaction would have been primarily indifference, perhaps laced with some frustration. From the perspective of someone devoted to the cultivation of tribal sovereignty, particular theories about the mechanics of the battle are beside the point, insignificant compared to the broader role played by the nineteenth-century Indian Wars in a history of political resistance to U.S. colonialism that, from this point of view, confers legitimacy on contemporary tribal nations. Elizabeth Cook-Lynn has expressed her annoyance with the "inexplicability" of the Battle of the Little Bighorn. "The truth of the matter," she writes, "may be that the defeat of Custer on the Montana prairie is imminently explainable. Very simply, he meant to wipe out the United Sioux, a superb military force, a nation of people who had signed solemn treaties with the United States of America as sovereigns and who, within a decade, began to understand the perilousness of the treaty process and were now desperate to defend themselves, their way of life, their homelands."[76] In other words, the Lakotas were attempting to defend their right to political separatism; they were successful; and there is nothing more, for Cook-Lynn, that needs to be said about the Battle of the Little Bighorn. Inexplicability is a red herring.

Even though the Custerologists of the LBHA might want to preserve the inexplicability of the Little Bighorn, they would not dispute Cook-Lynn's account of the "United Sioux" as a people who, in 1876, considered themselves foreign to and at war with the United States—nor would they contest her characterization of the Sioux as a "superb military force." In the late 1970s, for instance, John M. Carroll objected when the National Park Service affixed to the battlefield visitor center a quotation attributed to the Oglala holy man Black Elk: "Know the power that is peace." Carroll pointed out that, by his own account, Black Elk had participated in the battle and helped to kill Seventh Cavalry soldiers; at least on that day, "the power of peace" was something that he did not wish to know, at least not peace on the terms of unconditional surrender being offered by the U.S. government.[77] Cook-Lynn, I think, would agree with Carroll here. If, as Cook-Lynn argues, the Plains tribes were sovereign nations defending their homelands, then it makes sense that they elected to know the power of war (as Carroll contended) rather than peace (as the quotation suggests). At least some Native nationalists believe that tribes continue to enjoy that power. Recall the slogan painted on the wall of the Wounded Knee visitor center: "The Indian Wars Are Not Over."[78]

That phrase may, in fact, be the key to the distinction between those who, like the members of the LBHA, take a microhistorical approach to the Indian Wars and those who, like Cook-Lynn, are interested in the macropolitical. The difference is not so much about the way these groups perceive past events; both groups understand the nineteenth-century Indian Wars as primarily a political conflict over territory instead of relying on the "clash of cultures" formula that has become popular in public history, as we have seen in the last chapter. Rather, the central difference is in the way the groups view that past in relation to the present. For those whose primary purpose is the articulation and restoration of tribal sovereignty, the nineteenth-century conflicts between the United States and the indigenous peoples of the Plains are worthy of commemoration because one can trace threads of continuity between those historical struggles and contemporary ones. They want to close the distance between nineteenth-century resistance to U.S. colonialism and the twenty-first-century lives of American Indians. Custer buffs, on the other hand, want to preserve the distance between the history they study and the contemporary world that they see around them, because this distance enables them to fashion a kind of resistance to a mass culture that they believe is increasingly devoid of value. For them, the Indian Wars represent a world of uncomplicated virtues and vices all the more attractive because of its foreignness; these conflicts marked the end of an era in which sacrifice and heroism seemed clear-cut and well defined. As much as these hobbyists might invest their time and energy in immersing themselves into that foreign time, they do so because of its disparity from the contemporary world, because its details of everyday life must be studied and learned, because it holds secrets that cannot be easily discovered, and because it represents sentiments that seem out of place in our postmodern, ironic age. As much as they may work to recover the history that they study, they also insist on—indeed, revel in—the pastness of the past.

The reader of this book will have already realized that I am sympathetic to the political agenda that Cook-Lynn and other tribal nationalists advocate. Yet I also have come to appreciate the passionate antiquarianism of the Custer aficionados. They obsessively investigate the minutiae of the historical past to derive a distinctly nonutilitarian pleasure that, as a research scholar in the humanities, I find quite familiar. During the course of the LBHA convention in Rapid City, I heard several members—including Vincent Heier and Paul Hutton—voice concern that the LBHA membership is aging and not being replaced by younger members. Both Heier and Hutton were students when they attended the first LBHA meeting more than thirty years earlier, and Hutton recalls that about half of the participants then were in their twenties or early thirties. Perhaps taking up the hobby of Custer and the Indian Wars no longer appeals as an opportunity for self-fashioning as it did in the early 1970s—notably, a moment when Red Power and *Little Big Man* had made Custer particularly unfashionable. Unfortunately, the LBHA does not keep age statistics on its membership, but even a casual observer at a convention will realize that the member under the age of forty is far more the exception than the rule. Whether or not these demographics will ultimately spell the demise of the LBHA is not clear: the organization continues to attract new members, and though they are in the minority, there are at least some younger ones, such as the college student—my onetime bus seatmate—who came to the convention's closing banquet in the dress uniform of a nineteenth-century cavalry officer.

The collective enterprise of the LBHA may be missing something crucial in its neglect of the continuity between the nineteenth and twenty-first centuries, a continuity epitomized by the Lakota Sioux's ongoing efforts to recover the very land through which Custer's Seventh Cavalry traveled in 1874. But the labors of Custerology have also sustained the pleasures of history, and have done so in a way that mines the complexity of military conflicts between the United States and the indigenous tribes of North America. As the next chapter shows, one result has been an unusually rich archive of American Indian expression about the Indian Wars, whether they are over or not.

⚛5⚛

TESTIMONY IN TRANSLATION

The Library

ON JUNE 26, 1876, THE SHALLOW-DRAFT STEAMBOAT *FAR WEST* WAS MOORED in the Bighorn River, about a half-mile upstream from the mouth of the Little Bighorn. Under the command of Captain Grant Marsh, the *Far West* had navigated up the Missouri and Yellowstone rivers in support of the U.S. army's campaign against the Lakota Sioux. Less than a week earlier, while the *Far West* was anchored where the Powder River feeds into the Yellowstone, it had been the site of a conference between Brigadier General Alfred Terry and his subordinates, including Lieutenant Colonel George Armstrong Custer and Colonel John Gibbon. Now the steamer waited as Gibbon and Terry led their troops south into the Little Bighorn valley, where they had planned to rendezvous with Custer's Seventh Cavalry.

Marsh and some others from the boat were fishing nearby when they were surprised by a young Crow Indian who rode into their midst. The Crow was exhausted, and he held his rifle aloft in a gesture of peace. They brought him—a seventeen-year-old named Curly—on board the boat and attempted to learn from him the news he carried. Without an interpreter, Curly resorted to iconography. First, he picked up a handful of sticks, stood them on their ends, and knocked them down. Then someone offered him a pencil, and he drew two concentric circles, marking dots inside the smaller one to indicate soldiers, and then more dots between the two circles—so many dots that he nearly filled up the space between them as he repeated: "Sioux! Sioux!" It was the first written record of what befell Custer and his men at the Battle of the Little Bighorn.[1]

Curly's dramatic arrival at the *Far West* catapulted him into the mythic history of the Little Bighorn. As we shall see, the account of the battle that he eventually gave, with the aid of an interpreter, and the story he told about how he rode from the battlefield to the steamer became recurring topics of dispute within the world of Custerology. But Curly was not necessary for the army to learn of the battle. At the very moment that he arrived at the *Far West*, Gibbon and Terry were closing in on the aftermath of carnage. Nor was Curly the first Indian to try to tell of the battle. The previous evening, three of the other five Crow scouts who had ridden with Custer signaled to soldiers patrolling from the steamboat. Using sign language, they tried to explain that there had been a large battle downstream, one with disastrous consequences for the bluecoats; after attempting to relay this news to the men on the steamboat, the scouts rode away, traveling to their own villages. No one aboard the *Far West* gave the information much credence; the meaning, the soldiers assumed, must have been garbled through such an awkward means of transmission.

Curly, on the other hand, stayed long enough to get his story—or at least its broadest outlines—across. In doing so, he initiated a long history of American Indians speaking to whites in order to reveal the history of the Battle of the Little Bighorn. As the meeting of the Little Big Horn Associates shows, a crucial element of the appeal of the Little Bighorn for its enthusiasts is the conception of the battle as a puzzle that has, and always will have, significant pieces missing. The Little Bighorn enthusiasts compare the battle to an unsolvable crime novel and revel in debate about the final actions of Custer's battalion, the plan that he may or may not have carried to his death. They sift through the contradictory evidence, the layers of historical dust that have been accumulating for over a century, hoping to unearth solid clues that have not yet seen the light of day—or to fit together old ones in new ways.

Ever since Curly tried to scribble out his message about the fate of the Seventh Cavalry, Indian testimony has offered Custerologists chances to fill in the missing gaps in their knowledge of the battle. But what makes this testimony so important to the history of the Battle of the Little Bighorn is that it raises as many questions as it answers. Consider what happened next aboard the *Far West*. Having drawn his circles and his dots, Curly (whose name is also commonly spelled "Curley") began to beat his own breast and repeat the word "Absaroke," the Crows' word for their own tribe. As he would explain years later, Curly believed that if the men aboard the *Far West* could be made to understand that he was Crow, then they would realize that he had come from Custer's force. Unfortunately, no one present on the boat had any idea of what the word meant; at least one of them surmised that the word meant "soldier."[2] Walter Camp, who interviewed Curly in 1910, wrote in his notes that "scholarly men about Washington and elsewhere are still studying the archives to find out what Curley meant." Camp's notes continue, "When I told Curley in 1910 that the historians were still doubtful as to the translation of the world Absaroke, he had a hearty laugh."[3]

This kind of mistranslation has made the testimony of Indian eyewitnesses to the Battle of the Little Bighorn, not only the Crow and Arikara scouts serving with the U.S. soldiers but also the Lakota and Cheyenne who fought them, a problematic source of data for historians. The obstacles of linguistic translation were the most obvious difficulty, particularly since the translator might have little knowledge of the topic under discussion and the nuance of a single word could matter a great deal in the reconstruction of the complex motion of the hundreds of men riding over the battlefield. Moreover, interviewers frequently asked specific questions designed to test or support a particular theory; rarely did they simply ask their Indian informants to recount the events of the day in their own narrative style. Historians have also surmised that Indians from the "hostile" Lakota Sioux and Cheyenne tribes might have been reluctant to tell all they knew of the battle for fear of reprisal, or they may have simply decided to tell what they supposed the white investigators wanted to hear.[4]

The history of Custerology is filled with examples that illustrate the limitations of Native testimony. On the tenth anniversary of the battle, several prominent survivors from Reno's battalion met at the battlefield with Gall, a noted Hunkpapa warrior who had been among those fighting Custer's forces at the Little Bighorn. As Gall was telling his story, he became suspicious about the work of his interpreter. One of the cavalry veterans, Edward S. Godfrey, recalled: "From the volubility of the answers by the interpreter nearly all, including Gall, became satisfied that the interpreter was 'padding' and I could see that Gall was becoming quite restive." Eventually Gall became so frustrated that he rode away from the veterans to the top of Last Stand Hill, where he continued his narrative without the aid of a translator by using hand gestures, speaking the "occasional interpolation of an English or Sioux word," and pushing Godfrey around the terrain to represent the movements of the soldiers. Godfrey was thrilled with the account ("The old Chief was himself again—it was intensely dramatic!") and claimed that he received a more accurate understanding of Gall's memory about the battle. A careful reader of Godfrey's account must wonder, though, exactly how perfect a translation these gestures and movements could provide. Little wonder that Gall's story of the final phase of the battle quite neatly supports Godfrey's own.[5]

Or consider the story of Brave Bear, a Cheyenne man also among the warriors who defeated the Seventh Cavalry. In 1909, Joseph K. Dixon, a photographer and historical entrepreneur working under the auspices of retail magnate Rodman Wanamaker, assembled a group of notable Indian men for "the Last Great Indian Council."[6] During the council, Dixon offered a reward for the Indian who would come forward as the killer of George Armstrong Custer. No one knew who actually fired the fatal bullet at Custer; given the dust and smoke, it is likely that the warriors failed to recognize him until after the fighting ended. But Dixon wanted to know, so the Indians who had been present at the battle deliberated on the matter and eventually decided to choose Brave Bear. A Southern Cheyenne, Brave Bear had been present at the Washita in 1868 when Custer attacked Black Kettle's village, and he had been present the following spring when Stone Forehead had poured the ashes on Custer's boots as a curse. Given that history, the council reached the conclusion that Brave Bear deserved the mantle of Custer's killer. Twenty years later, in 1929, the white doctor Thomas Bailey Marquis was introduced to a group of elderly Cheyennes that included Brave Bear; eager to hear more about the Battle of the Little Bighorn, Marquis tried to introduce the subject by praising Brave Bear to a Cheyenne friend of his. "Some white people," Marquis said, using sign language, "say this man Brave Bear killed General Custer." The reaction was swift and unanimous. "The whole group of Cheyennes there, including Brave Bear himself," Marquis later wrote, "burst out into roars of laughter."[7] Whether Brave Bear ever received the reward from Dixon remains unclear.

Because of incidents such as these, nearly every historical study of the Battle of the Little Bighorn includes a cautionary note about the obstacles to using Indian testimony. "Most of the Indian testimony is so confused, contradictory, and weirdly divorced from known reality," Robert M. Utley wrote in his first foray into Custerology, "that one is tempted to ignore all such evidence."[8] Yet Utley, like others, succumbs to the temptation and proceeds to evaluate the historical merit of accounts of the battle by several of the better-known Indian participants. Native testimony is simply too alluring to ignore altogether, particularly since these statements are often the source of many of the most shocking historical innuendos made about Custer and his men: for instance, the suggestion that Custer believed a dramatic victory would make him a presidential candidate, which comes from remarks that an Arikara scout reported hearing him make before the battle, or that at least some his soldiers committed suicide rather than suffer at the hands of the Lakota and Cheyenne.[9] Custerologists seem to delight in refuting such stories, even if doing so means repeating them. Another weakness of Indian accounts as historical evidence—their focus on an individual's experience to the exclusion of a larger narrative of the battle—plays into the hands of military enthusiasts who delight in attempting to reconstruct the minutiae of the hundreds of movements that made up the battle. The "confused" and "contradictory" nature of Indian testimony, especially when one takes it as an aggregate, is not a frustration to Custerology but a welcome invitation to further deliberation. Paradox, contradiction, and inscrutability are the ideal grist for a mill that desires to keep grinding interminably.

Testimony by Indians about the Battle of the Little Bighorn also supplies an impressive *quantity* of grist. Using only the print sources currently available, I have counted more than 250 different accounts produced from interviews with Indians who either participated in or witnessed the battle—or who could relate second- or even third-hand information from those who did. More exist in newspaper clippings, historians' notes, and archives. Several participants were interviewed on multiple occasions; there are at least seven different published interviews with the Cheyenne leader Two Moons, for instance. Two Moons' experience also illustrates the range of people interested in recording Indian stories of the Little Bighorn. He was interviewed by Hamlin Garland, a well-known writer of regional fiction, for *McClure's Magazine*; by an unknown writer for the *Harness Gazette*, a magazine devoted to Western life (particularly, as its title suggests, its equestrian aspects), by Joseph Dixon during "the Last Great Indian Council"; twice by Richard Throssel, a Crow photographer and writer who published one of the interviews in the *Billings Daily Gazette*; by J. M. Thralls, a self-styled "Kansas pioneer" and historical enthusiast, whose interview of Two Moons was not published until the 1920s; and by an unidentified interviewer during a trip that Two Moons made to Washington, D.C.—an interview that was published for the first time in 2004.[10]

Garland, Throssel, and Thralls made only occasional forays into the world of Custerology. For others, the accumulation of Indian testimony of the battle was a more sustained endeavor. In the preface to his novelistic account of the Battle of the Little Bighorn, *Custer's Fall: The Indian Side of the Story* (1957), David Humphries Miller claimed to have interviewed "seventy-one aged Indians who had actually participated in the Battle of the Little Bighorn"—fifty-four Sioux, sixteen Cheyenne, and an Arapaho. He also interviewed the relatives of several of Custer's Crow scouts. Miller conducted most of these interviews between 1935 and 1942, and he stated that the conversations were "carried on in their language. This resulted in my learning to talk fluent Sioux and Plains Indian sign language." Unfortunately, though Miller also says that he made "copious notes" from the interviews, those notes have vanished from the public historical record.[11]

Walter Camp's notes, on the other hand, have become increasingly central to the textual corpus of Custerology. Born in Pennsylvania in 1867, Camp was a civil engineer who became the superintendent of track construction for the Englewood & Chicago Railway. In 1897, he became the engineering editor for the *Railway and Engineering Review,* and writing and editing became his life's work, even though the only book he published in his own lifetime was a two-volume textbook on railway construction and maintenance, *Notes on Track,* published in 1903. During this same period, Camp became interested in the Indian Wars of the nineteenth century. He could use railroad passes to travel to the West during the summer, and he began visiting battlefields regularly. By his own count, he visited the sites of more than forty conflicts between the U.S. army and Plains Indians, even finding some sites that had not yet been marked. In 1908, he began interviewing veterans of the Indian Wars, particularly witnesses—both whites and Indians—of the Battle of the Little Bighorn. He was relentless in tracking down his informants, and he occasionally used surrogates whom he supplied with questionnaires. In 1917, he wrote to Elizabeth Custer that he had interviewed "more than sixty survivors of Maj. Reno's command, including eight officers, and more than 150 Indian survivors of the battle."[12]

The questionnaires that Camp received back from his accomplices reveal the lines of inquiry of interest to him, topics that are still of interest to Custerologists today. Camp asked about whether the Indians had foreknowledge of the Seventh Cavalry's attack, about the length of the fighting, and especially about the movements of the troops. He asked informants to look at a map of the battlefield labeled to identify the places where Custer's men may or may not have traveled—whether, for instance, Custer attempted to ford the river and charge into the village. He asked whether any of the soldiers' bodies were taken back to the village after the fight, whether the Indians recognized "Long Hair" (as the Sioux and Cheyenne called Custer), and which Indians took part in the fighting. While the interviews may have differed in format when Camp himself was present, these notes suggest how rigorous and detailed an interviewer he could be. Yet the notes he compiled were anything but methodical. As one of his recent editors puts it, "For a man who conducted scores of interviews, Camp never seemed to have the proper paper on his person. He would record the account on whatever scrap of paper he could obtain at the time. Some of the interviews are literally written on old envelopes, the reverse side of due bills, and the back of blank pre-printed forms which had been discarded." [13]

This kind of record keeping may explain why the book that Camp had planned to write on the Battle of the Little Bighorn and the Indian Wars remained unwritten at the time of his death in 1925. However, I also consider Camp's lack of completion as an illustration of the Sisyphusian pleasure of Custerology—a pleasure that requires constant deferral of completion in the face of an unending task of assembling every possible shred of evidence. In this case, Camp worked so hard to procure the recollection of every possible participant of the battle available that the work of reconciling the accounts into a smooth and coherent narrative may have overwhelmed him, or at least seemed much less appealing than the gathering and questioning that had occupied him for so many years.

Camp's labors epitomize an era of collecting the eyewitness testimony of Indians who participated in the Battle of the Little Bighorn, an era that began the moment that Curly stepped onto the *Far West.* In the second half of the twentieth century, though, the effort to gather all available first-hand accounts of the battle changed to the different, but related, endeavor of bringing these accounts into print. Since 1976, four volumes alone have been published based solely on Camp's interview notes; three other edited collections draw on Camp's interviews as well as those conducted by his contemporaries; and a major trade publisher has even offered a coffee-table size book filled with stories of descendants of Indian participants in the battle. [14] Gregory Michno's *Lakota Noon: The Indian Narrative of Custer's Defeat,* published in 1997, assembled excerpts of the Indian accounts in a way that produces a coherent narrative of the battle, and it did so successfully enough to win the Little Big Horn Associates' prize for the best book published on Custer or the Battle of the Little Bighorn for that year. The interest of Custerologists has also extended to visual representations of the battle by Indian witnesses, many in the form of what is called ledger art (figure 12). A publisher of Custerology released a volume that reproduces and analyzes the works of twelve such artists with the purpose of extracting from these graphic representations new historical information about the fighting at Little Bighorn. [15]

Indian accounts of the Battle of the Little Bighorn have been sought after and dismissed, prized and scorned, by both amateur and professional historians to varying degrees for more than a century; it is a cycle of

Figure 12. This muslin painting of the Battle of the Little Bighorn—created by One Bull, a Hunkpapa Lakota who participated in the fight—is one of the Indian representations of the battle that have received attention from Custerologists in recent years. (Reproduction courtesy of the Minneapolis Institute of Arts, Christina N. and Swan J. Turnblad Memorial Fund.)

discovery and disavowal that has become central to the larger enterprise of Custerology. It is hard to think of another single event in the history of the United States about which the firsthand testimony of so many American Indians has been collected and scrutinized. It is the history of this archive of Indian accounts and the archive's place within Custerology that interests me in this chapter. Instead of offering a complete catalog of these accounts, I will begin by focusing on the attempt to record the perspective of Sitting Bull in the late nineteenth century and will then proceed to the twentieth by highlighting the treatment that Curly receives in key works of Custerology. Unlike historians of the battle, here I do not aim to evaluate the accuracy or insights of the statements made by Curly, Sitting Bull, or any of the other Native witnesses to the event. Rather, I hope to understand what it means that Custerology, which began in a military assault upon Indians, has come to rely so heavily on Indian accounts of that military action. For Custerology needs Indian speech both to illuminate the mysteries of the Battle of the Little Bighorn and to perpetuate them.

⇒▶◀⇐

The Euro-American practice of transcribing, printing, and reading the English translation of speech of North American Indians has a history that extends back to the seventeenth century. The Puritans produced records of Indians professing their conversion to Christianity. Benjamin Franklin printed and sold accounts of treaty councils that included American

Indian oratory. The best-known examples of such recorded speech, though, have been tragic lamentations of defeat. In his *Notes on the State of Virginia* (1787) Thomas Jefferson included the speech that the Mingo chief Logan purportedly made upon his surrender to the British, to provide an example of the "eminent" oratory of the Indians. In the speech, Logan grieves for his family, "murdered" in "cold blood" by the British. "There runs not a drop of my blood in the veins of any living creature. . . . Who is there to mourn for Logan?—not one?"[16] In the century that followed Jefferson's publication, Logan's was among the most frequently reprinted speeches by any American, Indian or not, and was even included in the McGuffey readers that taught literacy and rhetoric.[17]

Reading and repeating Logan's words, though, did not necessarily equate to taking his political position in opposition to colonization and conquest. As David Murray has pointed out, Jefferson's interest in the emotional effects of the speech were part of a longer tradition in which whites became impressed with the oratorical abilities of American Indians— viewing this ability as a product of their "natural" nobility—at the moment that they were being removed from and colonized by the United States. Reading such speeches (or hearing versions of them on stage in the many plays that featured vanishing Indians) was structured by a dramatic irony, a distance between the defiant, tragic Indian and an English-literate audience of European descent secure in the knowledge of British or U.S. conquest. It was easier to ascribe classical eloquence to the Indians when one knew that, like the Romans with whom Logan was compared, they would be passing from the historical stage. During the nineteenth century in particular, it is almost possible to chart a direct relationship between, in Murray's words, "the upsurge of interest in Indian material generally, both at popular and scholarly anthropological levels," and "the actual decline in autonomy and independence of Western Indians."[18]

The collection of Indian speech that began in the immediate aftermath of the Battle of the Little Bighorn is both connected to and distinct from this tradition. On the one hand, the whites who have participated in Custerology have long agreed that the Lakota and Cheyennes who fought the Seventh Cavalry "won the battle, but lost the war," to reiterate the usual formulation. On the other hand, the Indian accounts of the Battle of the Little Bighorn have been sought by historical aficionados to illuminate an Indian victory and a U.S. defeat. Moreover, as the first Native accounts of the battle were published, the duration and human cost of the larger conflict between the United States and the Lakota resistance was not yet certain. As an example of the kind of Indian rhetoric that appealed to Euro-

Americans, recall that in the year following the Battle of the Little Bighorn, Chief Joseph of the Nez Percé made one of the most famous speeches in Native American oratory as he surrendered to General Nelson Miles. "Hear me, my chiefs," Chief Joseph reportedly said. "I am tired; my heart is sick and sad. From where the sun now stands I will fight no more forever." Joseph's speech was instantly seized upon by the print media of the United States, and in the twentieth century it replaced Logan's as the verbal epitome of a noble Native eloquence, submitting to its fate.[19]

Sitting Bull, the Hunkpapa Sioux constantly identified as the leader of the Lakota and Cheyenne resistance, has never been widely quoted as speaking with the same emotional force of Joseph's elegiac surrender; none of Sitting Bull's words have attained anything like the degree of popularity enjoyed by Joseph's. Yet in the aftermath of the Little Bighorn, the print media of the United States sought to publish his perspective of that battle and his account of his own life. They printed pictographs he had supposedly drawn (including some he did) and subjected them to lengthy interpretations; published lengthy interviews when they could obtain them; and even manufactured comic hoaxes. Sitting Bull's role at the Little Bighorn became hotly disputed, and he was variously described as a shrewd strategist, a savage enemy, and a buffoon. Perhaps he remained such an object of fascination because he never delivered the kind of eloquent admission of defeat that has been attributed to Joseph.

In the summer of 1876 Sitting Bull was in his mid-forties. As a boy, he had been named "Slow," but when he was fourteen his father gave him a new name after the youth achieved his first success in battle, during a raid against the Crows. His deeds as a warrior accumulated, and in his adulthood he also became known as a holy man, a *wichasa wakan*. Later, in the wake of the Fort Laramie Treaty, which he did not sign, Sitting Bull became the center of a plan by his uncle, Four Horns, to create a Lakota federation of Hunkpapas and other Lakotas living away from the U.S. agencies. Leaders from five Lakota tribes as well as the Northern Cheyenne met in an extraordinary conference in which they chose Sitting Bull as their leader. "For your bravery on the battlefields and as the greatest warrior of our bands," Four Horns reportedly said, "we have elected you as our war chief, leader of the entire Sioux nation. When you tell us to fight, we shall fight, when you tell us to make peace, we shall make peace."[20]

The details of this conference were not known to the United States, but over time the military and the press came to identify Sitting Bull as the leader of the "hostile" Indians on the northern Plains. In fact, the press coverage of the 1876 campaign and the Battle of the Little Bighorn against the Lakotas and Cheyennes probably overplayed Sitting Bull's importance as a political and military leader in complete command of the Indian resistance. "The whereabouts of Sitting Bull," the *New York Herald* quipped in an article published a week before the battle, "is now as much a conundrum to the military as the hiding place of Boss Tweed to the New York police."[21] The *Herald*'s initial headline describing the battle even used Sitting Bull's name as a synecdoche for the entire confederation of Lakotas and Cheyennes—"A Bloody Battle / An Attack on Sitting Bull on the Little [Big] Horn River / General Custer Killed / The Entire Detachment Slaughtered"—and in the weeks that followed the press used the phrase "the camp of Sitting Bull," "Sitting Bull's band," or "Sitting Bull's army" to denote the Native village near the Little Bighorn and its warriors.[22]

Sitting Bull's name quickly became equated with Native treachery and violence. "He defies the government and hopes that he can get the Sioux nation to join him," said a Montana politician in an interview widely reprinted in the weeks after the Little Bighorn story broke. "If they will only do this he promises to drive the white race into the sea, out of which they came." But Sitting Bull was also an object of deep curiosity within the United States. Newspapers printed rumors that he had been taught French in Jesuit schools and modeled his military strategy on what he learned of Napoleon's, that he was white or at least partly white, or that he was a disaffected West Point graduate who had traveled West to lead the Indians.[23] (Frederick Whittaker, Custer's first biographer, would later make use of these stories in a dime novel that portrayed Sitting Bull as a highly educated member of a global "Black Order.")[24] Such fictions demonstrate the overactive imagination of the nineteenth-century print media, but they also show how coveted any verifiable detail of Sitting Bull's life—or death, mistakenly reported on more than one occasion—had become.[25]

Even better than Sitting Bull's deeds were his own words, or at least his own representation of himself. Only two days after printing its first story on the Battle of the Little Bighorn, the *New York Herald* splashed a two-column-wide pictograph across its pages under the headline "Sitting Bull's Autobiography: Scene in the Life of the Sioux Chief from a Picture-Language Book Drawn by Himself." The story explained that Sitting Bull had drawn more than fifty illustrations ("rude pictures," the *Herald* called them) denoting "the story of Sitting Bull's career up to six or seven years ago." The "literary work, now likely to be famous," was obtained by an army surgeon, who in turn sent the drawings to the Army Medical Museum in Washington.[26] In fact, the fifty-five drawings include fifteen illustrations of deeds performed by Sitting Bull's adopted brother, Jumping

Bull, and the whole set obtained by the doctor was a copy of the original made by Sitting Bull's uncle, Four Horns.[27] Such distinctions were not of interest to the newspaper. Rather, the report reveled in the sanguinary history that the autobiography reveals—and in the forthrightness with which the author portrayed his own violent actions. "Sitting Bull," the *Herald* explained, "is not at all modest in committing to posterity the story of his great deeds. Whether it be the scalping of a solder in battle, the killing of a Crow squaw, counting 'coup' upon an adversary, that is striking him, killing and scalping a white woodchopper, lancing a Crow Indian, or the sly theft of a mule, he brags equally of his prowess in his curious autobiography."

Three days later, the *Herald* published an even wider selection of drawings—nineteen in all—from what it started calling the "Autobiography of the Napoleon of the Sioux"; *Harper's Weekly* followed later in the month by publishing fifteen of the drawings attributed to Sitting Bull, together with an article that provided analysis of them. Both the magazine and newspaper articles highlighted the significant interest that surrounded Sitting Bull and overstated the uniqueness of the drawings as a historical record of Indian life. "When everybody is anxious to know everything that can be known of the daring Sioux chieftain," the *Herald* gushed, "these contributions to his history will be examined with great curiosity as specimens of the only extant autobiography of an American Indian ever prepared."[28] Moreover, the publication of the drawings built upon and developed further the sensationalistic stories of violence that were circulating as accounts of the Battle of the Little Bighorn became more elaborate. In fact, both the *Herald* and *Harper's Weekly* provided narrative explanations for the illustrations that far exceeded the brief commentary accompanying the original in the army Medical Museum (which the writers for both publications clearly read). For instance, this short description written by the surgeon who obtained the drawings—

> In a warm engagement with the whites, as shown by the bullets flying about, Sitting Bull shoots an arrow through the body of a soldier who turns and fires wounding Sitting Bull in the hip.[29]

— becomes, in the hands of *Harper's Weekly*, this:

> It never rains but it pours, and our hero with his band soon meets a party of whites in battle. Although Sitting Bull and his antagonist are the only figures represented, the fury of the action is shown by the numerous pen marks over the field of the picture, indicating the flight of arrows and bullets. In this

fight he charges the enemy with his usual spirit, and sends an arrow through the body and lungs of a retreating soldier. Mortally wounded, with the blood spouting from his breast, back, and mouth at the same time, the soldier turns and delivers his last shot, wounding his slayer in the hip, which, judging from the flow of blood, must have been a damaging and dangerous hurt. But our red brethren have tough hides and mighty healing flesh.[30]

The magazine's narrative transforms the pictographs into the stuff of dime-novel derring-do, but the *Herald* took even greater liberties. The newspaper mislabeled an illustration depicting Sitting Bull lancing a Crow Indian of indeterminate, but probably male, sex as definitively showing the Hunkpapa warrior killing a Crow *woman.* "Sitting Bull's Gallantry," the newspaper titled the drawing, which it followed by another—"Another Exhibition of Woman's Rights"—that did, in fact, show Sitting Bull lancing a female Crow Indian.[31]

However, the publication of Sitting Bull's "autobiography" was as much a harbinger of an interest in aesthetic primitivism as a reflexive exercise in vilification. *Harper's Weekly* called the artwork "child-like" to praise a "rude and laborious sincerity of purpose, a simple and earnest appeal to our indulgent understandings" that produced a "peculiar combination of the baby artist and the savage warrior." The obvious tone of condescension even gave way in a few instances to words of appreciation: "The composition of some of his driving scenes is worthy of the antique, and will compare favorably with the Elgin Marbles," stated *Harper's Weekly*, which also claimed that the "principal interest" of the drawings was in the "peculiar combination of the baby artist and the savage warrior."[32] In an unsigned editorial published the same day as the second installment of illustrations, the *Herald* expressed its own version of qualified praise: "There is character in these rude drawings which shows that the mind which conceived and the hand which executed them are capable of something more heroic than the vulgar murders in which this coarse savage delighted to paint himself as the hero." The Battle of the Little Bighorn, the editorial suggested, had demonstrated that Sitting Bull possessed "cunning, courage, dash—everything which pertains to a soldier, including, perhaps, even magnanimity."

This characterization of Sitting Bull—which is as generous as anything that appeared in the U.S. press immediately following the defeat of the Seventh Cavalry—reveals a significant purpose of the reproduction of the autobiographical drawings, and in Sitting Bull generally. In order to complete the apotheosis of Custer and install him, as the *Herald* hoped to do, into a national pantheon of military heroes, he needed to be vanquished by a foe worthy of the deed. While later accounts of the battle would emphasize Crazy Horse as the more significant military leader at the Battle of the Little Bighorn, Sitting Bull was consistently presented as the mastermind of the Lakota and Cheyenne resistance, an enemy of historic proportions who deserved the intense scrutiny that the press focused upon him. "He is a savage after the kind whom our ancestors found on the shores and rivers of the Atlantic when they first came to make their homes in the wilderness," the *Herald* continued, "a chief as bold, as brave and as cruel as any warrior that preceded him."[33] Little wonder that *Harper's Weekly* sought to recast his personal narrative as a thrilling epic.

Sitting Bull's autobiographical drawings offered a kind of ideal substitute for his own account of the Battle of the Little Bighorn because they afforded so much room for interpretation. Not only did the illustrations invite discursive commentary, but the life history presented in the pictures stopped well short of the events leading up to the battle. Yet the drawings did not quell the appetite for news, and especially speech, from the Hunkpapa leader. As the campaign against his Lakota followers continued throughout the year and into 1877, newspapers continued to report any scrap of information they could find about him and his whereabouts. They seized upon the story of Kill Eagle, a Blackfeet Sioux man who surrendered in September 1876, and reported that he and his followers had been held in Sitting Bull's camp throughout the summer against his will.[34] They printed jokes about his name (calling him "Gen. S. Bull"), his cruelty (one story has him learning to scalp cats as a child), and his ability to elude the U.S. army: "One leg is a little longer than the other or the other is a little shorter, I forget which"—ran a satirical account—"this deformity sorter bothers the military, as it gives him an uncertain warbling gait, and they can't tell whether he is bound for the Big Horn mountains or the British Possessions."[35]

Sitting Bull did indeed head north to the "British Possessions" of Canada, and it was not until over a year after the Little Bighorn that newspapers could offer their readers his own account of the battle. In October 1877, a group of United States commissioners traveled to Canada to meet with Sitting Bull and, in a conference facilitated by the British military, to attempt to persuade him to return to the United States and live on a reservation. The commissioners failed, but two reporters, Charles Diehl of the *Chicago Times* and Jerome Stillson of the *New York Herald*, succeeded in securing interviews that were widely reprinted by other newspapers.[36] Both of the reporters understood the value of Sitting Bull's own words to their readers, and they approached the Hunkpapa leader with, if not sympathy, at least a more respectful attitude than many of their more virulent peers working for newspapers in the West. The interviews offered a chance for Sitting Bull—albeit in a highly mediated fashion, via the vagaries of translation, reportorial transcription, and editorial intrusion—to offer his rationale for refusing to return to the United States, declare his desire to remain independent of the U.S. government, and, of course, give his own account of the Battle of the Little Bighorn.

The interviews of Sitting Bull that Diehl and Stillson published included questions about Little Bighorn that would become typical of the scores of similar interviews conducted with Indian participants in the decades that followed. They offered Sitting Bull a map of the battlefield and then interrogated him about the movements of troops and the timing of the different phases of the battle. Diehl and Stillson also tried to find out what Sitting Bull knew about Long Hair—Custer—during the battle. Did Sitting Bull see Long Hair? Where did Long Hair die? How did he die? Who killed him? Dozens of the Indian veterans of the Little Bighorn would later hear a virtually identical list of inquiries from a parade of historical enthusiasts desperate to establish the definitive history of the battle and especially of the final moments of Custer's life. In this case, it may have seemed particularly appropriate that the putative leader of the Lakotas and Cheyennes might provide an account of the death of the Seventh Cavalry's famed general. Sitting Bull told the reporters that he did not participate in the fighting himself and that he had never seen Long Hair before; nonetheless, he did not disappoint them in their questions about Custer's death. Stillson, in particular, reported that Sitting Bull claimed "the Long Hair stood like a sheaf of corn with all the ears fallen around him," laughing as he fired his final bullet.[37]

Diehl's failure to report a similar story suggests some selective embellishment, though Sitting Bull may be just as likely the origin of this figurative speech as Stillson. Moreover, this kind of language illustrates a dynamic between Sitting Bull and his interlocutors that was different from the relationships between other Indian informants and white interviewers. As the embodiment of Indian resistance to the U.S. colonization of tribal peoples, Sitting Bull was expected to yield an extraordinary account. Yet one way that reporters characterized Sitting Bull as an exceptional figure was to emphasize his ability to remain at least partly inscrutable, to give up his secrets with only the greatest of struggles. Stillson, for example, portrays himself as having to employ a long series of questions in order to coax gently Sitting Bull into describing his own position of leadership among the Lakotas—indeed, both interviews report that Sitting Bull flatly refused to call himself a "chief"—a cat-and-mouse game that makes Stillson appear all the more impressive for so successfully engaging in verbal parry with the Hunkpapa holy man. Diehl, meanwhile, concludes his article by stating that Sitting Bull "has in his village an ordinary sketch-book filled with rude drawings, in his own hand, of the battles in which he has been engaged. . . . In addition to this the interior of his tepee is covered with illustrations of the Custer massacre."[38] But Diehl could neither purchase the book from Sitting Bull nor acquire permission to visit Sitting Bull's camp—so both the existence and the content of these sources of information would remain only tantalizing possibilities. Sitting Bull, these reports suggest, possessed knowledge about the Little Bighorn that he had yet to divulge.

This fuller disclosure would come in other forums. Days after the articles by Stillson and Diehl appeared, a third interview of Sitting Bull was published by the *New York World,* courtesy of an unnamed "regular correspondent" who met with Sitting Bull in the holy man's own lodge ("well skinned and with a hissing fire of poplar sticks very comfortable"). The interview offered Sitting Bull a chance to expound upon the relationship between whites and Indians, on his desire for a permanent peace with the United States, and, once more, on the defeat of Custer. According to the reporter, Sitting Bull seized this opportunity to provide long, florid expositions on these topics—in fluent French. "Les Grand Espirit a fait l'homme blanc et l'homme rouge frères, ets ils doivent se predere tous led deux par let main," the *World* reports Sitting Bull saying (and provides an English translation: "The Great Spirit has made the white man and the red man brothers, and they ought to take each other by the hand").[39] The article includes more directly reported speech of Sitting Bull—more than fifteen hundred words in all—than the interviews by the *Chicago Times* and *New York Herald.* That Sitting Bull did not, according to any other credible source, actually speak French so fully or fluently is only one sign of the article's fraudulence. Just as significant are some of the sentences that the "regular correspondent" put into Sitting Bull's mouth, which contained notions more in line with the popular version of a noble spokesman of a disappearing people than the truculent, cagey speech quoted in other articles. "If sometimes we cannot live by the chase or by the land, why then let him"—the "Great Father [the U.S. president]"—give us food," Sitting Bull supposedly said. "Then we shall be quiet and die off quietly."[40]

At least one publication, the *Army and Navy Journal,* noted "certain peculiarities" about the *World*'s Sitting Bull interview and identified it as "an object of suspicion," even though the *Journal* also reprinted portions of the interview for its readers.[41] Whether the hoax was perpetrated by the editors of the *World* or by someone who submitted the fictional interview to them is not known, nor can one be certain that many of its readers recognized the "peculiarities."[42] No one, though, could miss the joke of two pamphlets printed in Chicago during the year that followed the commission's visit to Canada: *The Works of Sitting Bull in the Original French and Latin, with Translations Diligently Compared* and the sequel, *The Works of Sitting Bull, Including Part II.*[43] Both of the pamphlets purport to offer the written words of Sitting Bull, letters and dramatic poetry, in which the Hunkpapa holy man declaims the virtues of Canada ("This land of the Great Mother"), worries that he will soon be forced to return to the United States, and invites the U.S. president to negotiate. What *The Works of Sitting Bull* lacked in plausibility it made up for in linguistic bravura. The pamphlets include writings in the "original" languages of Latin, French, Greek, German, Spanish, Italian, and even the occasional English, which is also the language used for translations of all of the documents included in the Works:

> Great Father! and beloved Chief Magistrate!
> Who rulest wisely all the mighty state
> Composed of many peoples! here, where I write,
> Let me your honored presence dare invite,—
> Here at my cap by which the Red Deer flows,
> And where I dwell, oblivious of my foes,
> In lodges,—the skins of buffaloes the chief in size.
> In these the home of all my people lies.
> Between us two it might improve the case
> Could we but see each other face to face,—
> Commissioners I do not highly rate,—
> But let us meet and talk together straight,—
> I tell you, straight I always do take mine;
> And purer here the samples in that line
> where the Great Mother rules, than th' Union boasts
> As sold about its military posts.[44]

The Works of Sitting Bull makes sense as a humorous hoax only if one recognizes it as an exaggerated version of the articles that had appeared in newspapers since the Battle of the Little Bighorn claiming to tell Sitting Bull's story through his own pictures and language. The object of the satire is not simply the intelligence and education that had been attributed to Sitting Bull but also the journalistic desires that drove this characterization—a quest for the authentic medium of Sitting Bull's self-representation. Significantly, these articles frequently rely, as *The Works of Sitting Bull* does, on a process of translation and interpretation in order to reveal the hidden truth to the reader of English, so that the promise of full disclosure is necessarily accompanied by the possibility of mistranslation, misinterpretation, and even misinformation. As much as U.S. readers may have wanted to unravel the mysteries of the infamous Hunkpapa holy man, in the years that followed the Little Bighorn they still also wanted to preserve the sense that some secrets remained.

The relationship of Sitting Bull to the mass culture of the United States would change after his return and surrender to the U.S. government. Sitting Bull's tour with Buffalo Bill's Wild West Show in 1885 inserted him into a production that told the glorious story of U.S. "civilization" coupled with the tragic decline of American Indians. But Sitting Bull did not actually participate in any of the show's dramatic historical reenactments; rather, he paraded before the show and then sold pictures and autographs.[45] He was not dramatizing his life either on the stage or the page. Yet the longing of at least some Americans to hear Sitting Bull's own story, particularly his account of the Battle of the Little Bighorn, remained. By the time that Stanley Vestal published his biography of Sitting Bull in 1932, the desire of Custerology to have his perspective had become so pronounced that Vestal's prose attempted to reconstruct the mental response of Sitting Bull to the events of the battle through a confident indirect discourse. "Sitting Bull thought Reno was acting like a fool," Vestal writes in a typical passage. "But Sitting Bull was much too intelligent to underestimate his enemy. He wondered what was up."[46]

The last instance that I wish to present of Sitting Bull's being treated as a source of information about the Battle of the Little Bighorn was actually printed four years before Vestal's biography, in the 1928 memoir of Luther Standing Bear, *My People, the Sioux*. Standing Bear was born in the late 1860s on the Pine Ridge reservation, and in 1879 his father enrolled him in the Carlisle Indian School in Pennsylvania, the Americanizing endeavor guided by Richard Henry Pratt's maxim "Kill the Indian, and save the man." Standing Bear succeeded so well at Carlisle that Pratt selected him to work in Philadelphia's Wanamaker department store (whose fortunes would later underwrite the "Last Great Indian Council" convened by Joseph Dixon in 1909). While working there in the mid-1880s, Standing Bear learned that Sitting Bull would be appearing in Philadelphia, not with Buffalo Bill's Wild West show but in a separate appearance. In his memoir, Standing Bear recalls hearing Sitting Bull speaking to the audience in Lakota about his desire to meet with the president so that he could talk about his impressions of the parts of the United States he had visited and express his desire for a peaceful future between the United States and the Sioux. The white interpreter, though, told the audience that Sitting Bull was describing the Battle of the Little Bighorn, including "how the Sioux were all prepared for battle, and how they had swooped down on Custer and wiped his soldiers all out." The interpreter then invited the audience to line up and meet "the man who had killed Custer." Standing Bear, probably the only person present (other than the putative interpreter) who understood both Lakota and English, recalled his surprise at the enthusiasm with which the audience heard this account and then proceeded to greet Sitting Bull himself. His reaction serves as a commentary on the larger history of attempting to produce Sitting Bull's account of the Little Bighorn: "It made me wonder what sort of people the whites were anyway," he wrote. "Perhaps they were glad to have Custer killed, and were really pleased to shake hands with the man who had killed him!"[47] For white Americans to make Custer their symbol of tragic sacrifice, they needed an iconic antihero who could be at once recognizable and inscrutable, explained and mistranslated. Sitting Bull's words—both those he did not speak and those he did—fulfilled that dual purpose.

<hr />

Sitting Bull was an exceptional figure among the thousands of Indians present at the Little Bighorn and even among the hundreds who would later be interviewed by whites about that day. His leadership position made him the object of sensational journalism and even more fanciful fiction; at the same time, his failure to witness up close the combat between Custer's battalion and the Lakota-Cheyenne resistance has meant that his statements about the actual fighting have been peripheral to Custerologists' efforts to collect, print, and endlessly sift through Indian speech reconstructing the actions of Custer and his men. The goal of being able to produce a definitive account of what happened to Custer's soldiers—how they deployed, what strategies they attempted, where and how they were actually killed—compelled Custerologists to seek out witnesses for decades after the time of the battle and has fueled debates among them ever since.

Curly, the Crow Indian scout who first reported news of the battle to the *Far West,* offers an instructive example, albeit an unusual one, of the treatment of the testimony of Indian witnesses. Curly gave several interviews throughout his own lifetime, and the treatment that his words have received from white historians and journalists demarcate distinct phases of Custerology: enthusiastic collection and wonder, then skepticism, then careful investigation of the details by correlating them to other accounts of the battle. The dramatic rendition by Curly after the battle quickly turned him into the "sole survivor" of Custer's battalion; he gained fame as the last living person to have seen Custer alive. The most sensational versions of Curly's account can be traced to newspaper reports that first appeared in the weeks following the battle. In a *Helena Herald* article reprinted by other newspapers, Curly remained until the battle was nearly concluded; he saw that Custer remained alive until the very end and that "the field was thickly strewn the dead bodies of the Sioux who fell in the attack—in number considerably more than the force of soldiers engaged." According to the story as first reported by the *Herald,* after seeing Custer die—the *Army and Navy Journal* has Curly reporting that Custer was first wounded in the left side and then in the breast—the Crow disguised himself by wrapping himself in a blanket in the manner of a Lakota and rode through the lines of their warriors to safety.[48] A *New York Times* article heightened the drama by having Curly rush to the Little Bighorn River, wash, and change the style of his hair before making his escape.[49]

Frederick Whittaker's speedy, hagiographic biography of Custer went even further than the newspaper accounts in spelling out Curly's heroism. The officers aboard the *Far West* who questioned Curly supposedly told Elizabeth Custer—who, in turn, told Whittaker—that they learned more details from the Crow scout about the final moments of Custer's life than the newspapers had reported. In this version, Curly realizes that Custer's men are about to be overwhelmed and begs Custer to escape with him. "General Custer dropped his head on his breast in thought for a moment, in a way he had of doing," Whittaker wrote. "There was a lull in the fight after a charge, the encircling Indians gathering for a fresh attack. In that moment, Custer looked at Curly, waved him away and rode back to the little group of men, to die with them."[50] As in some of Sitting Bull's interviews, Indian testimony serves to verify the heroic sacrifice of the white general.

The amateur historians who would replace Whittaker in the decades that followed recognized the spurious nature of this version of the battle; the interviews that Curly gave in subsequent years were much more modest in their claims regarding the timing and manner of the battle. Curly himself later tried to point out the absurdity of the story of his asking Custer to escape with him: "The fact that I could speak no English and Custer not a word of Crow shows how ridiculous the story is."[51] Moreover, the legacy of the newspaper accounts published in the immediate aftermath of the battle made his later testimony to more reliable investigators suspect. At the 1886 gathering of white and Indian veterans of the battle, the Lakota warrior Gall had heard at least some of the stories attributed to Curly, and he called Curly a liar. "You were a coward and ran away before the battle began," Gall reportedly told the Crow man; "if you hadn't, you would not be here today."[52] By the early twentieth century, a prominent historian of the Indian Wars, Cyrus Townsend Brady, would say in his book *Indian Fights and Fighters* that Curly's account was "generally disbelieved"; Brady questioned the authenticity of Whittaker's version even as he summarized the most sensational elements of the story for his own readers.[53]

For those devoted to collecting eyewitness testimony of the Battle of the Little Bighorn, though, Curly was too valuable a source to ignore. Written records exist for eight different interviews with Curly between 1881 (five years after the battle) and 1923 (the year of Curly's death). Four of these interviews were conducted by Walter M. Camp between 1908 and 1913 as part of Camp's relentless collection of firsthand accounts of the battle. The interviews reveal the shift in Custerology from Whittaker's time to Camp's. Rather than evoking heroic episodes, Camp quizzed Curly on the specific locations and movements of the Seventh Cavalry. Two of the interviews took place on the battlefield itself, where Camp, through an interpreter, could ask Curly exactly what he saw in 1876. Where did Custer separate his men? When did they begin firing? Where did they travel mounted? Where did they dismount? Which ridges were crossed in retreat? In attack? Unless one is intimately acquainted with the geography of the battlefield and the organization of Custer's command, Camp's interview notes are difficult to comprehend; they contain a proliferation of logistical details rather than a narrative that will be comprehensible to those uninitiated in the nuances of the battle. Whittaker's version was popular theater; Camp's interviews pointed toward an intricate history (a history that Camp never actually wrote) for specialists. Little wonder that Camp's Curly interviews would later be published through the efforts of the Custer Battlefield Historical and Museum Association as part of its centennial commemoration of the Battle of Little Bighorn.[54] The Camp interviews constitute a kind of insider language: Custerology for Custerologists.

Camp was not, though, the only person interviewing Curly during this period. In 1909, Curly and the other three surviving Crow scouts from the Battle of the Little Bighorn were invited to participate in Joseph K. Dixon's "Last Great Indian Council," the undertaking sponsored by the retailer Rodman Wanamaker. The council was a gathering of approximately one hundred notable men from throughout the West whom Dixon assembled for the purpose of restaging their traditional tribal life to be recorded by his notebooks and cameras. Alan Trachtenberg explains, "He had them don full regalia, build a council lodge, light signal fires, powwow with each other in sign language, reenact Custer's last stand as their own moment of glory." Throughout, Dixon saw the enterprise as a kind of theatrical re-creation. "The aim," writes Trachtenberg, "was to make of the already vanished people a spectacle of sunsets, empty saddles, burial sites, last arrows, a spectacle in the manner or guise of a record." [55]

The resulting book, *The Vanishing Race,* is a hodgepodge of tribal history, folklore, personal testimony, and photography, with a tone exemplified by the elegiac title (see figure 13). A prefatory note explains, "In undertaking these expeditions to the North American Indian, the sole desire has been to perpetuate the life story of the first Americans and to strengthen in their hearts the feeling of allegiance and friendship for their country." The "council," in other words, would help make "Indians" into "Americans" and record the Native ways of life that necessarily would dis-

Figure 13. William Dixon took this photograph atop Last Stand Hill, titled "Here Custer Fell," during the "Last Great Indian Council" that he convened in 1909. The photograph shows four of the Crow scouts who served with the Seventh Cavalry; Curly is third from the left. (Photograph courtesy of William Hammond Mathers Museum, Indiana University.)

appear in the process. In this respect, Dixon's efforts to record the speech of Curly and other Indians was part of a long history of transcribing the language of Indian warriors in order to mark their transition from military opponents to historical artifacts. Early in the volume, Dixon writes: "The wonderful imagery of the Indian orator—an imagery born of his baptism into the spirit of nature—his love of his kind, and the deathless consciousness of the justice of his cause made his oratory more resistless than the rattle of Gatling guns, and also formed a model for civilized speech. It was an oratory that enabled a few scattering tribes to withstand the aggressions of four great nations of the world for a period of several centuries, and to successfully withstand the tramping columns of civilization." But *The Vanishing Race* shows that successful resistance to be a thing of the past. "An Indian world revolves for the last time on its axis," the book states in the final chapter. "The Indian cosmos sweeps a dead thing amid the growing luster of the unfading stars of civilization and history." [56]

The council was staged at Crow Agency, near the Little Bighorn battle-field, and a substantial portion of the book is devoted to the recounting of the battle by participants, not only the Crow scouts, but also Cheyennes and Lakotas. Dixon, though, was less interested in the accuracy of historical reconstruction than in placing the battle at the center of a romantic history that was all the more tragic because modernity would soon erase its final traces. While the topography of the battlefield—Last Stand Hill surrounded "by barren landscape so forbidding that it is a midnight of desolation"—might last into the future, the Indians will not. "The camera has recorded the scene," Dixon writes of his photographs, "a last vision of the red man standing above the grave of his conquerors, a pathetic page in the last chapter of Indian warfare." [57]

This tragic narrative frame changes the significance of recording Indian testimony about the Little Bighorn. Instead of data waiting to be mined by military historians, the accounts provided in *The Vanishing Race* come across as rhetorical performances that supplement, perhaps even supplant, the defense of land that took place at the battle. The book even characterizes the Crow participation in the battle as an attempt to recover a tribal homeland. Custer, according to White Man Runs Him, told the scouts before the battle, "If I die, you will get this land back and stay there, happy and contented, and if you die, you will be buried on your own land." Curly, meanwhile, is restored to his role as Custer's final witness, the person who can verify that "Custer was the last man to stand." [58] The battle, though, does not result in the preservation of either Crow or Lakota independence;

instead, in Dixon's account it is, like his photographs, an object whose power crosses from the historical to the aesthetic. *The Vanishing Race,* for instance, introduces Curly by quoting an "eloquent speech" that he made in 1907 against the opening of reservation lands to white settlement:

> I was a friend of General Custer. I was one of his scouts, and will say a few words. The Great Father in Washington sent you here about his land. The soil you see is not ordinary soil—it is the dust of the blood, the flesh, and bones of our ancestors. We fought and bled and died to keep other Indians from taking it, and we fought and bled and died helping the whites. You will have to dig down through the surface before you can find nature's earth, as the upper portion is Crow. The land, as it is, is my blood and my dead; it is consecrated, and I do not want to give up any portion of it.[59]

The context of this speech is the combined effort of a substantial number of Crow Indians to resist the selling of "surplus lands"—that is, land not allotted to individual Crow Indians under the Dawes Allotment Act—to non-Indians who wished to purchase them. The policy of allotment and this kind of land sale were part of the Americanization program that Dixon and Wanamaker's project endorsed, a transformation of American Indians into "civilized" U.S. citizens. But Dixon includes this protest against the policy because of its poetics of tragedy, an imagery that ties the death of tribal peoples to the landscape itself. The intent of Curly's speech is beside the point; Dixon does not even tell us whether his protest had practical consequences or whether the reservation was preserved. It is a speech to be admired, not acted upon.

This kind of Indian speech would become popular in the second half of the twentieth century among environmentalists, but Custerologists have had little interest in it. Instead, they are drawn to the factual details contained in the multiple interviews that Curly granted, many of them in response to the same questions asked over and over again by different interviewers of the Crow man. The writers who produced the major histories of the Battle of the Little Bighorn during the twentieth century all took the opportunity to evaluate the statements attributed to Curly about what he saw during the battle. The responses range from curt dismissal of his fantastic escape—as in W. A. Graham's *The Story of Little Big Horn* (1926), which dispenses with Curly in a single note and a photograph—to elaborate interpretations of the testimony.[60] In *The Custer Tragedy* (1939), Fred Dustin considered Curly important enough to the Little Bighorn that he devoted a section of his "prelude" to answering the question "Where Was Curly, the Crow Scout?" "After going carefully over the testimony, the Arikara narrative, the Scott interviews, and other relations by the Crow scouts, my final conclusion is that Curly was the last survivor to see Custer close at hand," Dustin announces triumphantly at the outset of his book, before going on to discuss the evidence in detail.[61] Charles Kuhlman (a historian of the French Jacobins whose academic career was cut short by deafness) gave Curly's interviews an even more thorough treatment in his book-length narrative of the battle, *Legend into History* (1951). Kuhlman subjects Camp's interviews of Curly to careful scrutiny that reveals, he thinks, as much about Camp's assumptions as about Curly's knowledge, and he devotes a three-page footnote to explaining how he has used Curly's testimony to chart the movements of two different companies.[62]

It is Robert M. Utley's *Custer and the Great Controversy* (1962) that best encapsulates the role that Curly has assumed within Custerology. Noting that the most fantastic elements of the Curly story had recently found their way into *Life* magazine, Utley writes, "So deeply imbedded are the Curley myths in the legend of the Little Bighorn that it is now difficult to evaluate Curley's genuine role in the battle."[63] Yet that is precisely what Utley goes on to do in the pages that follow. What makes Curly's testimony so attractive to Custerology is not only the possibility of recovering a factually correct, firsthand account of the battle's action but also the opposite: an archive of contradiction that is impossible to understand without the expertise of the Custerologist. Claims about the myths that have surrounded Curly, or about the previous misinterpretations of his testimony, are not simply rhetorical preludes in these histories of the battle; they are part of the shared tradition of reconstructing the Battle of the Little Bighorn—a part of the glue and binding that hold Custerology together. The transubstantiation of Custer into the national iconography required American Indians as foils; the historians of Custerology require the corpus of Indian accounts of the battle in order to prove their mettle.

In fact, Curly's posthumous career among the still growing Little Bighorn literature has recently taken a dramatic turn. In 1991, John S. Gray published *Custer's Last Campaign: Mitch Boyer and the Little Bighorn Reconstructed*, the cumulative result of decades of study of the battle. Gray, a professor of physiology at Northwestern University, had first turned to Western history in the 1940s when his administrative position as department chair prevented him from conducting biomedical research, and he brought his scientific methodology to bear on the reconstruction of historical events.[64] His first book, *Centennial Campaign* (1976), revolves around collecting and plotting empirical data on charts, graphs, and tables in order to produce a painstakingly detailed account of the campaign that culminated in the fight at the Little Bighorn; Gray devotes an entire chapter to calculating the fighting strength of the Indian village.[65] In *Custer's Last Campaign*, Gray returns to the battle in order to create a "time-motion" study of movements of the Seventh Cavalry. An exhaustive account of who-was-where-when, this is history for the empirical-minded military enthusiast, and Gray's careful attention to detail has made the book highly regarded by Little Bighorn aficionados.

Surprisingly, one of the heroes of *Custer's Last Campaign*—not as a soldier but as a historical source—is the Crow scout Curly. Gray admits that the testimony of the "oft-maligned" Curly "baffled" him at first. "But when I systematically used maps to maintain geographic orientation, and time-motion analysis to maintain a temporal orientation and to provide feasibility checks, his accounts began to blossom as a unique display of valuable information."[66] An entire chapter of Gray's reconstruction of the actions of Custer's battalion—a chapter that, with his usual chronological precision, Gray states covers the time from 4:04 to 4:46 p.m. on June 25, 1876—revolves around Curly's testimony, including thorough, line-by-line comparisons of the clues provided by his multiple interviews with Camp. In particular, Curly allows Gray to show how Custer feints to buy time at a place called Medicine Tail Coulee Ford, how Custer divides his five companies there, and how they later reunite "all under engagement and facing death within the next 39 minutes."[67] Gray is so grateful to Curly for helping him to unlock the mysteries of this hotly debated (among Custer-ologists) phase of the battle that he feels "justice demands" that he focus the following chapter on mapping Curly's escape to the *Far West*, before the book returns to the narrative account of Custer's battalion and a consideration of the evidence on their final demise.[68] Gray, who died the same year *Custer's Last Campaign* was published, seems to have made a second life for Curly among his final gifts to Custerology. "I trust that the old image of 'Curley the liar,'" he concludes, "will fade in favor of 'Curley the reliable.'"[69]

Gray's proposed rehabilitation of Curly is part of a larger trend exhibited by the books and articles published within the world of Custerology during the last few decades. Not only have historians of the Battle of the Little Bighorn—both amateur and professional—turned to Indian accounts in their work, but there has been a pronounced effort to collect the interviews conducted during the late nineteenth and early twentieth centuries for book publication. As I have stated earlier, hundreds of accounts are now available to the Little Bighorn enthusiast, most of which were accessible only in manuscript collections or periodical collections during much of the twentieth century. Indeed, the fact that I have been able to write this chapter working with sources in print, instead of traveling extensively to archives and begging private collectors for access to their manuscripts, illustrates the success of these publication efforts. Richard G. Hardorff alone has published three different collections—*Lakota Recollections of the Custer Fight* (1991), *Cheyenne Memories of the Custer Fight* (1995), and *Indian Views of the Custer Fight* (2004)—each of which was first printed by a small publisher of Western Americana and then reprinted by a university press. The endeavor of retrieving and publishing Native American speech meshes nicely with late-twentieth-century multiculturalism, which placed increased value on the recovery and circulation of nonwhite voices in the history of the United States. Such publications, however, also constitute a logical continuation of an earlier phase of Custerology. Little Bighorn enthusiasts once scoured the reservations for Indian informants to interview; now they scour the archives for interviews to publish.

Moreover, recent works in Custerology have attempted to reconcile Indian accounts of the battle with other empirical methods, as part of Custerologists' constant quest for a definitive historical reconstruction of its action. The attention that John S. Gray devotes to Curly offers one example of this tendency; a more visible one, though, has been the work of Richard Allan Fox, whose theories have been disseminated not only in print but also via cable television programs on the battle, making him one of the leading—and most controversial—contemporary interpreters of the Battle of the Little Bighorn. The seminal event in Fox's personal involvement with the battle occurred in 1983, when an accidental grassfire swept over the battlefield. Fox, a long-time resident of the area, conducted an initial reconnaissance and proposed a more extensive archaeological survey of the battlefield to the National Park Service. During the following two years, he and Douglas Scott led a team of nearly one hundred volunteers in combing the battlefield for artifacts: bullets, shell casings, parts of rifles, human remains.[70] The result was a new set of empirical data that has generated a new body of esoteric knowledge for Custerology to assimilate, debate, and ponder. Scott even published an entire volume devoted to evaluating the forensic evidence recovered in the dig: *They Died with Custer: Soldier Bones from the Battle of the Little Bighorn* (1998).[71]

Fox, though, has emerged as the leading interpreter of the data gleaned from the archaeological data. In *Archaeology, History, and Custer's Last Battle* (1993), he extrapolates from the firearms, bullets, and casings found on the battlefield to establish the firing patterns of both cavalry and Indian warriors in the battle—so that he can combine the archaeological evidence with historical research to produce a coherent, detailed narrative of the final hours of Custer and the men who perished with him. One of Fox's central arguments is that Custer sent several companies downstream much farther than had been previously considered, probably in an attempt to surround the Indian village or to cut off the warriors from the noncombatants who were fleeing the initial charge by the battalion of the Seventh Cavalry that was under the command of Major Marcus Reno.[72] This claim by Fox has been largely accepted by Little Bighorn enthusiasts, but his other central argument remains hotly debated. Fox contends that Custer's men buckled under pressure rather than maintaining their discipline and composure in the heat of battle. "Indeed," he writes, "tactical stability broke down early; panic and fear, the prime ingredients in collapse during combat, spread throughout the tactical units. The battalion quickly lost its ability to fight." In his account, the tactical disintegration of Custer's soldiers contributed to their total defeat—and the battle did not conclude with a defiant hilltop "last stand."[73] For at least some Custer enthusiasts, this is akin to heresy.[74]

Fox does not base these claims solely upon archaeology. Rather, he stresses throughout the book the usefulness of Indian accounts of the battle in corroborating the physical evidence he considers. In fact, in a footnote, Fox chides Gray for relying too much on the testimony of Curly and not enough on the interviews of Cheyennes and Lakotas who were Custer's adversaries.[75] More than once, Fox suggests that the keen attention he pays to Indian accounts of those who fought against the Seventh Cavalry is almost as significant a methodological innovation as the use of archaeological data. "Custer battle interpretations of every kind," he states, "with but a few exceptions, have altogether or substantially ignored these indispensable resources on the grounds that the many Indian stories cannot be reconciled."[76] The history that I have surveyed in this chapter suggests that Fox's examination of Indian accounts is not quite the radical breakthrough that he maintains it to be. While his integration of historical and archaeological evidence surely does constitute something distinct in studies of the Battle of the Little Bighorn, Fox's use of Indian testimony to support his narrative of the battle is a strategy continuous with the past of Custerology—a methodological difference of degree, not kind.

In fact, Fox's theories about the battle recall those put forward by a Custerologist of a much earlier period. Thomas Bailey Marquis was a medical doctor who, after serving in France during World War I, lived on both the Crow and Northern Cheyenne Indian reservations during the 1920s. During that time, Marquis learned Plains Indian sign language and began to befriend Indians who could tell him about the Battle of the Little Bighorn. Whenever possible, he accompanied Cheyenne veterans to the battlefield, so that they could tell him what they recalled. Marquis aspired to become recognized as a leading authority on the battle and Indian life, and his friendships yielded books and articles related to both, including full-length "as told to" books telling the life stories of Wooden Leg, a Cheyenne who fought at Little Bighorn, and Thomas LeForge, a "white Crow Indian" (that is, a white man who had married a Crow woman and lived among the Crows) who was among the first men fluent in Crow to interview Curly after the battle.[77] Marquis was also the writer who recorded the story of Kate Bighead, the Cheyenne woman who claimed that the Cheyennes recognized the body of Long Hair after the battle and punctured his ears so that he could hear better in the next world.

But Marquis was never able to find a publisher for his book-length work on the Battle of the Little Bighorn during his own lifetime— a book that Marquis titled "The Custer Soldier Suicide Panic." This working title points directly to Marquis's thesis. "The intention is to prove that the most astounding military tragedy in the annals of our western frontier warfare was caused by an unbridled collapse of soldier morale resulting in general self-extinction," he announced at the beginning of the book.[78] The white soldiers, Marquis wrote, had been frightened by stories of Indian torture and taught to avoid capture at any cost; suicide pacts among them had even been reported. When confronted by the overwhelming numbers of hostile warriors at the Little Bighorn, the cavalrymen panicked and ended the fighting prematurely. As evidence, Marquis relied on the few suicides that Indians claimed to have witnessed, as well as the relatively low number of Indian casualties. (He arrived at thirty-one as the total number of Lakota and Cheyenne fatalities.) Moreover, he contended that the Cheyenne accounts express a shared bewilderment at the behavior of the soldiers that could best be explained by suicide, a possibility that would have perplexed them at the time; "no Indian could see why any Custer soldier would kill himself," he explained, "since the Indians had no thought of trying to capture them alive."[79] Indian stories about soldiers' being drunk, or about supernatural forces, Marquis thought, had been generated by this incomprehension.

Fox repeatedly cites the testimony of both Wooden Leg and Bighead, not only for their stories about the soldiers' confusion but because their accounts of the soldiers' movements and the sequence of the battle support the narrative that he derives from archaeological evidence.[80] However, he refuses to go as far as Marquis does and believe their assertions that soldiers with Custer committed mass suicide. "Quite simply," Fox states, "the contention is nonsense."[81] My purpose here is not to endorse either Fox's theories or Marquis's, but the rhetorical force of Fox's refusal seems curious to me, particularly given the extent to which he relies on Wooden Leg and Bighead's other testimony to support his own ideas. He refers to the story of mass suicide as the stuff of the *National Enquirer,* yet for most readers, it is only a short step from believing (as Fox does) that Custer's soldiers lost because they panicked and failed to hold formation or fire their weapons, to believing that Custer's soldiers lost because they panicked and decided they would rather die at their own hands than undergo prolonged torture.[82] Of course, many Custerologists consider both theories preposterous, and that has surely something to do with the tone of Fox's disavowal. Like Marquis, Fox is willing to follow Wooden Leg and Bighead, but he also wants to keep some distance.[83]

I linger on this moment in Fox's book because it is emblematic of something larger in the way that Custerology treats Indian speech. For 130 years, whites seeking a definitive account of the Battle of the Little Bighorn have valued Native testimony. But they have been more resistant to Indian interpretations of the larger causes of the Battle of the Little Bighorn, the historical significance of the battle, and what the battle might mean for the future of Native peoples. Fox's detailed account reconstructing the battle ignited a lively debate among Custerologists that has lasted more than a decade. By comparison, consider the lukewarm reception of James Welch's *Killing Custer* (1994). Welch, a Blackfeet Indian and highly regarded novelist, combines in this book an account of Little Bighorn with his personal narrative about making a documentary film about the battle. Welch asserted that the film—and presumably the book as well—would tell "the Indians' side of the story," but what he means by that phrase is different from what Custerologists poring over Walter Camp's interviews have in mind.[84] The provocative, original parts of Welch's book are the personal ones: Welch's discussion of what it means for him as an Indian man trying to document this violent past.

The most memorable passages in *Killing Custer,* in fact, do not directly involve Custer or the Little Bighorn but another historical event: Colonel E. M. Baker's January 1870 attack on the Blackfeet village of Heavy Runner, a peace chief, camping on the Marias River in the Montana Territory. Baker had incorrectly identified the camp as belonging to a hostile band and ended up killing 173 Indians who believed they were at peace with the United States. Welch, whose great-grandmother survived the attack, describes at the beginning of *Killing Custer* his own expedition to locate the site of the Marias massacre, a place without monuments or memorials. "As I looked up the gentle slope to the top of the ridge, I thought, This would be where the children had played on their sleds," Welch writes. "Perhaps Heavy Runner, or my great-grandmother Red Paint Woman, had stood on this very spot and watched them." [85] Welch contends that Baker's successful assault on the Blackfeet was more typical of the wars between the United States and the Plains Indians than was the Battle of the Little Bighorn, even if Custer's unsuccessful attack on the Little Bighorn village is what most whites, drawn by the romanticism of a tragic defeat, and Indians, seeking to recall a spectacular victory, have chosen to remember.[86]

Welch's mode of reflecting on the legacy of historical violence, in which he emphasizes the continuity of nineteenth-century colonialism and the experiences of Indians over a century later, is not what Custerologists seek from Indian testimony. Their reaction to *Killing Custer* was less hostile contempt than indifference. One of the few printed remarks I have been able to locate is Wayne M. Sarf's dismissive note in the preface to the revised edition of his short history of the Little Bighorn Campaign: "It [*Killing Custer*] denounces the alleged distortions of white historians while leaning on them for source material to the point of embarrassment."[87] Sarf is correct that Welch is much less interested than Gray or Fox or many other Custerologists in delving into the archive of firsthand testimony collected from Native participants; Welch simply does not know the minutiae of the battle as Gray, Fox, or the diehard aficionados who devour each new book on the Little Bighorn. But Welch is not concerned with reconstructing a detailed historical narrative of the action of the battle, either. His is not a kind of Indian testimony that Custerology—with its focus on empirical reconstruction to the exclusion of moral or even political questions—seems likely to value any time soon.

Since the time of the battle, Little Bighorn enthusiasts have gone further than most other devotees of U.S. history, whether professional or amateur, in their careful treatment of the memories and life stories of American Indians. While the advocates of the "New Western History," for instance, have attempted during recent decades to give Indians and other nonwhite peoples central roles in the revision of older historical narratives, they have produced little scholarship about the military experiences of tribal peoples—and have practically ignored the vast archive of American Indian testimony that Custerologists have collected, published, and scrutinized.[88] However problematic, the interviews of Little Bighorn witnesses might be as windows into the lives of the Lakotas, Cheyennes, Crows, or Arikaras—framed as they are by the interests of investigators and hampered by the limits of translation—these documents bring onto the written page the conflicts among Plains tribes and U.S. government. Their textual nuances represent continuities between the military fighting of the nineteenth century and the disputes over historical interpretation in the twentieth and now twenty-first centuries.

Sometimes the interviews serve this function in surprising ways. As a final example, I turn to the interview of He Dog by General Hugh L. Scott, conducted during Scott's 1919 tour of Indian reservations and printed in 1991 by Richard Hardorff in *Lakota Recollections of the Custer Fight*. He Dog, an Oglala Sioux, was an experienced and honored warrior by the time of the Battle of the Little Bighorn, and in his later years he was frequently sought out by historians of the Indian Wars.[89] Scott, meanwhile, had a long-standing interest in the Indian Wars; as a lieutenant, he was the one who had located the site of the Washita conflict in 1891 and erected the first monument there (see figure 8 in chapter 3). By the time of their 1919 conversation, He Dog had already spoken with whites on several occasions about the Little Bighorn and was ready to return Scott's questions with some of his own. Why, He Dog asked, didn't Custer send someone to talk the Lakotas and Cheyennes before attacking them? He Dog suggested that some of them, at least, might have returned to their Dakota agencies in peace. Scott wrote in his notes, "The Indian view of the matter is that they were living on their own ground, making their living hunting buffalo as they had always done. . . . Those Santees [Sioux] and other Indians had come out to hunt buffalo and not to fight, and the Sioux only fought when attacked."[90]

He Dog was even more perplexed as to why army officers kept asking him questions about the details of the battle. He told Scott that he had been interviewed previously by an officer acquainted with Elizabeth Custer, and he wanted to know what the officer and Elizabeth Custer could have been seeking. "Were they trying to get paid for [the] killing [of] these soldiers?" Scott summarizes the conversation that followed: "It was explained [to He Dog] that all with Custer had been killed and no one could tell what happened. There were many disputes in consequence, and Mrs. Custer was only trying to settle some of the disputes. He Dog said he had told the officer if he wanted to know the cause of that trouble, he would have to look in Washington—Custer did not come out himself; someone there gave him orders and he had to come; that Washington was the place all those troubles started."[91]

In one way, He Dog's response here foreshadows what Custer enthusiasts would say decades later: Custer "had to come" and therefore should not be blamed for the violence he inflicted on the Indian village or the carnage his own troops suffered. He Dog, though, is also saying something subtler here, something more resistant to the entire enterprise of Custerology. The larger truth of the battle, he suggests, is not in whether Custer attempted to ford the river, or how many companies he deployed upstream, or which location on the battlefield the fighting finally concluded. What matters about the battle are the things that brought Custer and his men there in the first place, forces that had little to do with the physical fighting itself. If Scott understood He Dog on this point, his notes from the interview do not show it. Instead, he continued by following up with more questions about the size of the Indian village, Custer's strategy, and the actions of Crazy Horse following the battle.

For generations, Little Bighorn enthusiasts have been coming back to interviews like this one for answers to similar questions, just as they return to the battlefield itself to pay homage to this history. So in the final chapter we, too, will return to Montana, where audiences arrive each summer to hear "the Indians' side of the story"—and to see the Battle of the Little Bighorn staged for the twenty-first century.

⚜6⚜

LITTLE BIGHORN FOREVER

Hardin, Montana • Garryowen, Montana

LOCATED JUST STEPS FROM THE INTERSECTION OF THE TWO MAIN STREETS of Hardin, Montana, the Four Aces does not have much to distinguish it from other bars in this corner of the high Plains. There's a jukebox, a pool table, a few video games. The bartenders are friendly, and the waitresses will bring ribs and chicken drenched in barbecue sauce to your table. The bottled beer is domestic and reasonably priced. During the day the barroom sits largely empty, with maybe a few regulars trading their seasoned stories or a couple of ranchers grabbing a late lunch. On summer nights, the business picks up. Singles in their twenties, marrieds in their thirties and forties, grandparents in their fifties—they are all here. There are ranchers who have washed off the week's work, white-collar professionals from the town, some teens trying to look older than their age. Cigarette smoke and blue jeans are everywhere.

For one weekend each year in late June, the crowd at the Four Aces packs in a little closer and the clientele becomes more diverse: a network news producer from New York City; a Mexican-born professor of art and architecture who now lives in Louisiana; travel writers from across the United States; an engineer from Glasgow; independent filmmakers from Alabama; a 250-pound Scot named George Stewart, who sports a shaved head, a goatee, and a kilt. I am there, too: a thirty-something literature professor worrying about my sunburn and my footnotes. I sit with the other "foreigners"; we trade stories about the people and places we know in common, including the Four Aces and its regulars. George Stewart alternates between complaining about the pallid taste of American beer, ordering more, and boasting about his stint bouncing for an Amsterdam brothel. As the night progresses and the empty bottles accumulate, I try to work my way closer to Stewart. If a fight should break out in the Four Aces, I have decided, I want to be near him. But Stewart has the kind of presence that keeps potential brawlers from crossing the line, and before the bar closes, all of those who have made Hardin—and the Four Aces—into a kind of annual pilgrimage have promised to return next year for another round of Little Bighorn Days.

Little Bighorn Days is much like any other local history celebration staged by communities the size of Hardin. The town holds a parade, merchants push their wares onto the sidewalks, church groups hold pancake breakfasts and bake sales. There is a "Grand Ball" with nineteenth-century costumes on Thursday night, a bull-roping contest on Friday, bed races and a street dance on Saturday. What sets Little Bighorn Days apart is that for a single, long weekend, the small town of Hardin is transformed into the center of the Custer universe, the crossroads of Custerology. Many of the hardcore Custer aficionados come for the meeting of the Custer Battlefield Monument and History Association—the CBHMA—an organization similar to the Little Big Horn Associates, which holds its own symposium every year on the weekend nearest to the anniversary of the battle. The more casual tourists might stop by the mock court-martial of George Armstrong Custer staged at the junior high school by a group of lawyers from Sturgis, South Dakota. The trial features a guest judge, and every year the prosecuting and defending lawyers try out new arguments to decide whether Custer would have been found guilty by a military tribunal if he had miraculously escaped.

What Hardin and the Little Bighorn Days have become best known for, however, is a reenactment—or, rather, a pair of reenactments: one run by the town that takes place four miles west of Hardin, the other by a Crow Indian family on its land adjacent to the National Monument itself, about fifteen miles southeast of the town. The reenactments are what bring the exotic "foreigners" to the Four Aces and pull the RVs off I-90, which stretches west here into the Yellowstone River valley and south across the Crow reservation and into Wyoming. Hardin is not much to look at from the road. The most striking visual feature is composed of two buildings that dominate the skyline north of town: a sugar beet factory that has been closed since the early 1970s and a power plant whose construction was completed only recently. Agriculture—wheat and barley—still drives the local economy, though many hope that tourism will play an equal role in the town's future. Recent censuses have described the town population as holding steady at about 3,400—roughly 60 percent white and 35 percent American Indian—and the town serves as the seat of Big Horn County (population 12,700), which includes the 37,000 square miles of the Crow Indian reservation and the approximately 7,000 Crow Indians who live there. The nearest city of any size is Billings, more than forty-five miles away, where many families do their shopping. With so much space and so few people, Hardin is the kind of place where a tourist can imagine the frontier of the American West; in the high arid Plains, one finds wide vistas—studies in brown and green beneath the bright blue sky—that can be overpowering in their stark simplicity. The land is the stuff of films and fiction.

But economics are another matter. In 2004, the unemployment rate for Big Horn County stood at 9 percent, more than double the state average.[1] The situation is more distressing if one concentrates on the population of Crow Indians living on the reservation or even in off-reservation towns like Hardin. In 2003, the state of Montana pegged the Crow Indian unemployment rate at 18.5 percent by using a standard methodology that excludes potential workers who are no longer actively seeking work. The federal Bureau of Indian Affairs, on the other hand, calculates tribal unemployment rates using a far more inclusive method, one that takes account of so-called discouraged workers. For the same year, 2003, the BIA reported that among those Crow Indians eligible for the workforce who were living on or near the reservation, 62 percent were without employment. More than a third of those who were employed fell below the poverty standard as set by the federal government. On the Northern Cheyenne reservation, some forty miles to the east, the numbers are even worse: 16.9 percent unemployment in 2003 by the state of Montana's reckoning and 72 percent by the BIA's.[2]

You cannot see any of this from inside the Four Aces, not during Little Bighorn Days. The barroom—like nearby motels and campgrounds—is full of people who have come to take part in or watch the spectacle. But you will not find many of those who will ride with the Indian resistance; most of those who come from afar to reenact the Battle of the Little Bighorn march with the U.S. Cavalry. They include dedicated Civil War reenactors for whom the Montana and the Little Bighorn are a step off their usual battlefield path, especially equestrian buffs who relish the chance to ride—the Little Bighorn reenactments are among the few that feature cavalry. There are more casual participants, often from nearby cities and towns, who have come to give reenacting a try. The core group of cavalry reenactors, though, are devoted to this single battle and rarely engage in any other historical re-creations. These are people like Nicola Sgro, a Detroit coffee salesman who portrays Lieutenant Charles DeRudio, who, like Sgro, was born in Italy. Sgro traces his fascination with the Little Bighorn to a young age, when he would compose "Dear General Custer" letters as an American child might write to Santa Claus. Now he comes to the Little Bighorn each year to ride into battle with the "Band Box Troop" that surrounds Custer during one of the reenactments; when Sgro can, he brings his family, including the aging Italian parents who once wrote back to him in the persona of a deceased American general.

This chapter, however, does not focus on Sgro's story or the story of any of the individuals who participate in the dueling reenactments of Custer's last battle. As compelling as these personal histories might be, the reenactments have a complexity and force of their own. They are visual spectacles that manage to command an audience using stagecraft that, by the standard of contemporary technology, seem almost deliberately antiquated. They tell the story of a two-sided conflict at a time when the judgments of professional historians have come to value relativism, mediation, and negotiation over the wins and losses of battles. Finally, they focus on a military campaign designed to reduce American Indians to a state of dependence at a moment when the American public—at least on its surface—has become more sympathetic than ever to the desire of tribal peoples to achieve a state of political, cultural, and autonomy within and from the United States. In these respects, the reenactments of the Battle of the Little Bighorn may be profoundly out of step with the current moment. Yet their anachronistic quality, their aura of belatedness and nostalgia, may be what makes them so revealing, for they bring into relief the complicated ways that American Indians and non-Indian Americans alike have used the military history of the West to map out their paths into the future.

Assessing the impact of the reenactments of the Battle of the Little Bighorn on their audiences is made more difficult by the variety of constituencies who attend them: casual tourists from both the United States and abroad; enthusiasts of Western history, including diehard Custerologists; a significant number of local residents, both white and Indian—and in the case of the latter, from both the Crow and nearby Northern Cheyenne reservations; and the actors and production staff of the shows themselves, who constitute a demanding internal audience that evaluates each annual iteration of the reenactments against their predecessors.[3] Even for the first-time spectators, the emotional package offered by the performances is neither neat nor tidy. They evoke admiration and nostalgia for the heroism on both sides, forms of guilt over the violent colonization being portrayed, and a variety of patriotisms. The ways in which the reenactments fuse together these disparate kinds of historical emotion for their audiences tell us less about the history of the Indian Wars than about the current relationship between Indian Country and the United States. At the turn of the twenty-first century, there are still white Americans who want to come back to the Little Bighorn to watch Custer die—or even to perish with him on mock versions of Last Stand Hill—but the obsession with Custer is hardly one-sided. There seem to be plenty of Indians who are willing to ride into battle to kill him.

≫◦◦≪

In the United States, historical reenacting is largely associated with the reenactment of Civil War battles, a hobby that gained national attention with the centennial of the Battle of Bull Run (or Manassas) in 1961. The so-called Third Battle of Bull Run took place on the actual Virginia battlefield, featured nearly twenty-five hundred mock soldiers, and attracted an estimated crowd of fifty thousand.[4] In the decades that followed, Civil War reenacting mushroomed, fostered by publications such as the *Camp Chase Gazette* ("the voice of Civil War reenacting since 1972"), the growing interest in "living history" as a mode of pedagogy, and, of course, Ken Burns's wildly popular Civil War documentary series, which first aired on PBS in 1990. Articles on the reenacting hobby typically place the number of Civil War reenactors at between twenty and fifty thousand nationwide, and towns the size of Hardin across the United States have sponsored Civil War reenactments as a means of generating tourism revenue.[5] However, the nineteenth century is hardly the only period subject to military re-creation. The Revolutionary War has long been a popular source of public spectacle in the Northeast, and in *War Games: Inside the World of Twentieth-Century War Reenactors,* Jenny Thompson documents the growing number of people who gather to re-create World War I and II battles.[6] There are even groups that stage events from the Vietnam and Gulf wars.

No one has been able to explain precisely why reenactments have surged in popularity during an age when scholars and public leaders frequently bemoan the "historical amnesia" of the American public. Most who have tried end up positing that historical re-creation is a reaction to the postmodern conditions of social fragmentation, geographical mobility, and media saturation. In the face of this chaos, the conventional academic wisdom runs, reenactors respond with a desire to experience a coherent narrative of historical experience rooted in a particular landscape.[7] Perhaps the most provocative version of this assessment comes from someone who writes about neither the United States nor historical reenactment, Pierre Nora, a French historian who directed a monumental project on his nation's history entitled (in its English translation) *Realms of Memory*. Nora contends that the late twentieth century generated a new relationship between us and our history. A gap, he argues, has opened up between the historical and the contemporary, a gap that has created anxiety and actually increased interest in a certain experience of history: "Paradoxically, distance requires rapprochement to counteract its effect and give it emotional resonance. Never have we longed more for the feel of mud on our boots, for the terror that the devil inspired in the year 1000, or for the stench of an eighteenth-century city. . . . If the old ideal was to resurrect the past, the new ideal is to create a representation of it."[8]

Reenactments of military battles offer precisely the kind of representational frisson that Nora describes. While they take place in a specific place and time, their real location is a state of mind, an almost aesthetic experience of something that seems historical—culminating in the moment of "period rush," when the present recedes and the reenactor becomes immersed in the simulation of the past.[9] While the props of the reenactment—the uniforms, guns, and other equipment that reenactors so scrupulously research and collect—might create the necessary conditions for the emotional climax of the period, the real payoff is something far less tangible; it is the participants' sense of being on intimate terms with the historical. Jenny Thompson points out that battle reenactors have difficulty explaining their love of history and their passion for their hobby; my own experience speaking with participants at the Custer reenactments led me the same conclusion.[10] Some of the most devoted reenactors have few words to articulate their devotion to history or the pleasure they receive from reenacting it. To them, the experience cannot be reduced to language.[11]

Nora refers to sites where contemporary humanity acts out its fear of historical loss as *lieux de mémoire*, "sites of memory." For him, these places have a goal distinct from that of the museums and archives of an earlier age. This new purpose hinges on what he calls "representation." According to Nora, it is no longer sufficient to produce an intellectual interpretation of the past or to hold on to select artifacts. Rather, the contemporary world is so bewildered by its own place in time that it seeks to produce something that allows the illusion of historical immersion. *Lieux de mémoire* do not offer, as historical places once did, the opportunity to reflect upon the historical process that have brought us the fragments of former ages, the ruins of time that have been preserved. Instead, our age of hypercommemoration offers the chance to escape the present. Nora writes: "Unlike historical objects, *lieux de mémoire* have no referents in reality; or, rather, they are their own referents—pure signs."[12] Nora would argue, in other words, that reenactments such as those staged near Hardin each June do not really re-create what occurred on the Little Bighorn battlefield in 1876. Instead, they get caught up in their own history—reproducing, simulating, and improving upon other re-creations.

The antecedents for contemporary Little Bighorn reenactments begin with the Wild West shows popularized by Buffalo Bill Cody and others in the late nineteenth century. Cody himself boasted that he took the "first scalp for Custer" in revenge for the slain general when he killed—and scalped—a Cheyenne Indian named Yellow Hand (or Yellow Hair) weeks after the battle. Cody soon after relived the episode in a stage drama, and it became a pivotal episode in his 1879 autobiography. For the rest of Cody's career, Joy Kasson writes in her book on Cody and American popular culture, he would draw on his association with Custer to augment his own popularity.[13] Cody first added "Custer's Last Stand" to his Wild West Show in 1887, an alteration that he hoped would create repeat customers by offering them something new. In 1893, when Cody performed his show just outside the grounds of the World Columbian Exposition in Chicago, "Custer's Last Stand" became part of the show once again. The show presented Cody as Custer's successor, for Cody would ride into the arena after the general had died his famous death—too late to save Custer but in time to make sure that the drama of Westward expansion continued. Buffalo Bill, Kasson points out, helped to recast the resolution of the battle as a morality tale. The martyred Custer died so that the work of conquest could go on, and Buffalo Bill would participate in that work as well as its historical preservation.[14]

One element of Buffalo Bill's Wild West Show remains a crucial element of contemporary battle reenactments: the idea that visual spectacle can conjoin entertainment and education through authenticity. An 1886 article on Buffalo Bill's company in a New York newspaper used the term "educational realism" to name this principle.[15] By giving the audience the chance to see real cowboys, soldiers, horses, and especially Indians, the Wild West Show claimed that it did more than just thrill its spectators, it offered them the chance to learn about history firsthand—and in fact learn more than they might learn from simply reading books. The modern reenactments of the Battle of the Little Bighorn promise the same combination of pleasure and pedagogy. However, the Wild West shows are not their only antecedents, for the reenactments owe as much in their visual style and narrative to another historical form of public theater: the local history pageant.

Local history pageants were staged by communities throughout the United States during the first half of the twentieth century, though their popularity peaked during the 1910s and 1920s. While these pageants were backed by a more genteel class than Buffalo Bill's, one that took its mission of community "uplift" more seriously, they shared the Wild West Show's premise that cultivation and emotional pleasure could be united in a visual spectacle for a mass audience. What differentiated the pageants from entertainment such as Wild West shows or circuses was the emphasis not only on history but on the locale that produced the show. Tourists might come from the outside to see the town's pageant, but the events that the pageant portrayed, the setting of the pageant, and even the actors belonged to the community. The goals of the pageant were to enable the community to tell its own story to itself in a compelling manner, to produce civic pride, and to teach the community about its own past as a way of galvanizing it for the future. In the process, organizers often hoped, the pageant might contribute to the financial health of the community by bringing in both immediate revenue as a tourist attraction and long-term revenue by rendering the locale attractive to investors.[16]

Local history pageants fed the public's appetite for historical tableaux and dramatizations that had been met in the recent past by the Wild West shows and other forms of public theater, but the pageants went further by stringing episodes together in a way that emphasized narrative continuity. The result was a series of dramatic scenes that were at once mimetic (presenting things as they actually occurred) and figural (symbolic of the larger populations and histories at stake)—and that were united by a dramatic arc of progress and community development. In fact, the towns frequently incorporated into their pageants some representation of Indian inhabitants before the coming of white settlers, and many included a dramatization of white-Indian conflict. (The American Pageant Association issued a bulletin with "three typical pageant plans" in 1915; all three included some clash between Native Americans and non-Natives.)[17] The goal of the productions was to show how the community emerged over time and then overcame its struggles—first Indians, then the Civil War, then, perhaps, new European immigrants—in a way that showed it ready to meet its current challenges. Each episode was part of the larger story.

Over the course of the twentieth century, film superseded the local history pageant as the central visual medium representing historical narrative, and the classic westerns of the mid-twentieth century fueled the interest of reenactors and their audiences for staged performances of cavalry-Indian warfare—and shaped expectations about how those performances should appear. In fact, Errol Flynn's 1941 biopic *They Died with Their Boots On* plays a particular role in the history of reenacting the Battle of the Little Bighorn that goes beyond aesthetic influence. In the late 1930s, Joseph Medicine Crow—a Crow Indian studying for his master's degree in anthropology at the University of Southern California—was lured to the Warner lot by an advertisement for Indian extras. When he arrived, he learned that the studio was making a film based on Custer's life, including, of course, his death at the Battle of the Little Bighorn. Medicine Crow already had more than a passing interest in the battle. He is a descendant of White Man Runs Him, one of the Crow scouts who served with Custer and the Seventh Cavalry during that campaign. He grew up near the battlefield and was often present when White Man Runs Him and others who had firsthand knowledge of the battle were interviewed by white reporters and historians.

By Medicine Crow's account, when the studio learned of his expertise, it decided he would be more of an asset behind the camera than in front of it. He was assigned to work with the scriptwriters, but his Hollywood career was soon nipped in the bud. A producer, seeing an Indian at work with the writers, stopped Medicine Crow and asked him what he thought of Custer. Medicine Crow is now over ninety years old, and he still relishes telling the story of what happened next. "I told the man," he recalls, "that my grandfather always said Custer was very foolish. He didn't listen to them [the Crow scouts]. He didn't wait for the other columns to arrive." When Medicine Crow stated that he agreed with his grandfather, the producer summarily fired him. Medicine Crow laughed at first but then realized it was not a joke. "So I was heading to the door, and I turned around and said, 'You people here in Hollywood, you mess up good stories, and that is what you are doing here. And I'm glad to get out of here. But someday I'm going to write my own Custer story and tell it like it was.'"[18]

More than twenty years passed before he acted on those words. In 1964, Medicine Crow—working at that time for the Bureau of Indian Affairs—walked into a conversation between the Crow tribal chair and a state official coordinating the year's events in commemoration of Montana's territorial centennial. Medicine Crow proposed reproducing the most famous military encounter in the state's history. "Custer is still out there," he remembers saying. "So is Sitting Bull. Let's bring them back together—let them have it out again."[19] Soon after, Medicine Crow began writing the script for the "Custer's Last Stand" reenactment, and the venture began to take shape. Members of the Crow tribe formed an alliance with whites from the town of Hardin to form Big Horn County Special Events, Inc., the official producer of the reenactment. The organizers hired an experienced director from out of state, ordered costumes, and solicited volunteers. The adjutant general of Montana's National Guard agreed to play the part of Custer, and several of the Indian figures would be portrayed by men with personal ties to the battle; the Northern Cheyenne leader Two Moons, for instance, was played by his own grandson. In the end, everyone agreed that the reenactment was a smashing success: more than twelve thousand people, including the governor of Montana, attended one of the four shows produced during the weekend of the battle's anniversary.[20]

The reenactment continued to generate similar attendance figures throughout the 1960s, with an occasional dip in patronage due to bad weather. Newspaper and magazine accounts emphasized not only the success of the visual spectacle—the horses, painted warriors, and thousands of rounds of blank ammunition—but also its novelty. "What made the Custer re-enactment special," said *Newsweek* in 1964, "was that the Battle of the Little Bighorn unfolded entirely from the Indian's point of view."[21] The magazine also mentioned that the production was an example of cooperation between Hardin whites and reservation Crows—presumably a novelty as well. The *Saturday Evening Post* emphasized the same point with its lead sentence two years later: "In Hardin, nothing has brought the white citizens of the town and the Indians of the neighboring Crow reservation closer together than a full-scale re-enactment of the worst licking the Indians ever gave us."[22] Restaging old battles seemed, curiously, to hold the key to racial reconciliation, even if the *Post* left no doubt as to which side of the racial divide "us"—its readers—stood.

In the early 1970s, the mood surrounding the reenactment changed. Native American political activism, led by the highly visible American Indian Movement (AIM), reintroduced racial tension to the production of the show. In 1972, vandals destroyed a press box that had been constructed at the arena, and "Indian activists" claimed responsibility, demanding that an outstanding loan of $10,000 made to the reenactment by the Crow Tribe be repaid immediately. Equally important, attendance at the performances declined.[23] At a time when Indians were occupying government buildings in Washington, fewer people were interested in seeing them refight the battles of the old West. Some time after the 1973 performances, Big Horn County Special Events decided to fold the show—and Custer remained without reanimation for more than fifteen years.

The mid-1980s were especially cruel to this region of Montana, which had not been, by economic measures, particularly prosperous at any point in the twentieth century. Low agricultural prices and a bust in the oil market compounded the local effects of a national economic downturn. During this period civic leaders in Hardin began their efforts to develop a tourist economy. The town applied for and was awarded a series of grants to help it refurbish the storefront blocks of its small, Main Street–style town center—and the chamber of commerce decided to bring back the Custer's Last Stand reenactment.[24] The timing could not have been better. The first year of the revived production, 1990, coincided with a resurgence of interest in the American West. Kevin Costner's *Dances with Wolves* would be released that fall, and a television miniseries based on Evan Connell's *Son of the Morning Star* was filming in Montana that same summer, to air the following February. The number of visitors to what was then called Custer Battlefield National Monument increased a staggering 84 percent from June 1990 to June 1991.[25] The legislation changing the name of the national monument would soon make newspaper headlines across the country and generate even more interest in the battle. Custer and the Little Bighorn became historically hot properties once again, but the production of the reenactment did not work in entirely the same way as in its earlier iteration. This time there would be no formal partnership with the Crow Tribe, and the reenactment would take place west of the town rather than on a site closer to the battlefield.

Not long after the town of Hardin revived the Custer's Last Stand show, a rival appeared. In 1992, the Real Bird family, Crow Indians, staged a small reenactment called "The Battle of the Little Bighorn" on its land adjacent to the national monument administered by the National Park Service. The Real Birds own part of the land where the Lakota Sioux and other Indians were camped along the banks of the Little Bighorn River, including the Medicine Tail Coulee Ford, where Custer may have tried to cross the river (Custerologists debate this point) in a failed attempt to charge into the Indian village. The land designated as the Little Bighorn Battlefield National Monument and owned by the federal government for that purpose, in fact, includes only a portion of the terrain on which the action of the battle took place. The most notable part of the park includes a national cemetery and Last Stand Hill, where Custer and the other casualties of the battle were hastily buried in 1876; the National Park Service also owns the hilltop depression five miles distant where Reno, Benteen, and their troops awaited rescue for three days in a defensive position. Today, tourists who wish to travel from Last Stand Hill to the Reno-Benteen hilltop do so on a road traversing, in part, Real Bird land. In fact, just

weeks before their first reenactment in 1992, the Real Birds allowed Lakota activist Russell Means to hold the Sun Dance, described in chapter 1,
that temporarily closed that road to tourists.

In the years that followed, the Real Bird reenactment of the Battle of
the Little Bighorn has become an annual event that is still gaining momentum. The Real Birds attract fewer spectators than the Hardin reenactment does (without any national advertising, the Real Birds rely on word
of mouth and chance tourists), but each year they add more seating to the
riverbank land where they stage the event. The Real Bird reenactment has
also become part of "Native Days," sponsored by the Crow Indian Tribe
at the nearby town of Crow Agency—a three-day festival that coincides,
deliberately, with the anniversary of Little Bighorn and therefore Hardin's
"Little Bighorn Days." At the reenactment itself, Richard Real Bird, the
eldest of the Real Bird brothers who run the event, appears to enjoy tweak-
ing his Hardin rivals—mentioning at every chance he can find that his
reenactment is simply a "family show" and not a "fancy, professional production." His brother, Kennard Real Bird, recently offered more pointed
criticism of the Hardin organizers in an interview with Hardin's weekly
newspaper, the *Big Horn County News*. "I felt they should have more respect of for the Indian community," he said. "Indians have made the effort
to bridge that gap [between whites and Indians] over the last 200 years,
but the white community has not tried to bridge that gap." [26]

Comments like Kennard Real Bird's often frustrate those associated
with the Hardin reenactment, particularly those who feel that they are
working hard to make their production inclusive and cooperative. After all,
without the participation of a large number of Native volunteers, both on
the stage and off, Hardin's reenactment of Custer's Last Stand would fail.
But the Real Birds seem to understand that the rivalry between the two reenactments may in fact benefit both groups. Battle reenactments are inher-
ently excessive, for they are superfluous as reproductions of the historical
past; unlike the military action that we might read about in the newspaper
or watch on television, reenactments serve no actual purpose beyond the
emotional pleasure of seeing a violent history re-created. Having two reenactments of the same event taking place simultaneously, only miles apart,
increases that sense of excess and its pleasures even further. In the second
half of the nineteenth century, companies staging *Uncle Tom's Cabin* would
sometimes have two actors play the same character simultaneously, on the
same stage, as a way of increasing the visual spectacle of their productions. [27] Now, instead of seeing two Little Evas or Uncle Toms, the visitor
to the Hardin area can watch, in a single weekend, two Custers lead two

Seventh Cavalries against the superior numbers of two forces of Indian warriors (guided by the visions of two Sitting Bulls and led into battle by two Crazy Horses) and, of course, die a glorious death—twice. In fact, thanks to Montana's generous speed limit, a real die-hard can squeeze both reenactments into a single day, a Custer doubleheader.

Neither the Hardin nor the Real Bird reenactment focuses entirely on the Battle of the Little Bighorn, however. Both reach back much further in history, following a narrative structure that makes them similar to the local history pageants of the early twentieth century. The reenactments begin with Native life, include the exploration of the Lewis and Clark expedition, portray episodes of settlement and then conflict—all culminating in a representation of the Battle of the Little Bighorn itself, which actually makes up only a small part of each performance. The way that pageantry governs the visual style of these reenactments means that they differ in a significant way from most other contemporary presentations of "living history." Whether a Civil War battle reenactment, a park such as Colonial Williamsburg, or even a PBS reality show, the re-creation of history today focuses most often on a single period of history, perhaps even a single day; it is *synchronic* in orientation. On the other hand, presentations like those of Hardin and the Real Bird family are *diachronic* in orientation; they span decades as they move forward in time. This structure seems so out of step with the way that history is more frequently dramatized that one almost feels as though one is watching a historical play from an earlier era, a performance that has been preserved in amber.

The genealogy of the shows offers a reason for this: Joseph Medicine Crow wrote his script in 1964, and he seemed to have had in mind an earlier tradition of pageantry and film when he wrote it. When telling the story of his initial proposal for a reenactment, he even refers to the idea as a "pageant."[28] Medicine Crow's script is still the basis for the Hardin production—and served as a reference point for the Real Birds since they began staging their reenactment in the 1990s. But there may also be something about the Custer story itself that lends itself to an antiquated form of public theater. The frontier was already a type of historical artifact, an object of nostalgia, when Buffalo Bill brought it to the arenas of his Wild West Shows. For more than a century, the Battle of the Little Bighorn has been so effectively appropriated by the practitioners of "living history" because it has been regarded by most Americans as a purely historical event, even at the moment when it actually occurred. Custer's Last Stand was a thrilling spectacle that offered Americans a new chapter in an historical narrative that revolved around a clear lesson about the costs of triumphing over savagery. This lesson presumes a sense of inevitable white superiority that, for many white Americans, has long become unpalatable. Yet this same spectacle continues to compel audiences and reenactors alike in a multicultural age, a time when the "clash of cultures," instead of the course of empire, governs the popular interpretation of U.S. history.

–––––––––»-0-«–––––––––

The Custer's Last Stand reenactment sponsored by the Hardin Chamber of Commerce takes place four miles west of the town itself.[29] To get there, tourists follow spray-painted signs on a two-lane highway through rolling farmland, then turn onto a dirt road that cuts through fields that have yet to show the results of their spring planting. A ridge obscures the site itself from the main road, as if geology had been enlisted to separate the reenactment from the modern world from which spectators and actors are escaping. Flag-topped bleachers built to hold three thousand spectators face the "stage"—really nothing more than the yellow and brown earth with a few slight mounds in the foreground that offer a platform for the reenactment's most dramatic moments. In the distance, the hills rise up to meet a sky that during the Montana summer can change from bright blue to threatening gray in a matter of moments. "Stage right" is bounded by a facade of a frontier fortification, "stage left" by a group of white tepees that constitute the "Indian Village."

Spectators begin arriving more than an hour before the actual performance begins. Some are day-trippers from Billings or other Montana towns; most are from some other part of the United States—or even abroad—and are here as part of a larger trip to "the West." They have heard about the reenactment from a newspaper or radio story, read about it on the Internet, or seen an advertisement when they stopped to buy gas near the Little Bighorn Battlefield. You can often pick out those in the audience who have a long-standing interest in Custer; they wear Seventh Cavalry baseball caps and shirts embroidered with the red and blue Seventh Cavalry standard. The atmosphere as the crowd gathers is equal parts rodeo and Fourth of July. Vendors sell food and drink—hot dogs, frybread, even a coffee called Custer's Last Brew. Some years you can strike up a game of chance with Calamity Jane or maybe handle the antique pistols of the Single Action Shooter Society. "Living historians" display the equipment of an Indian Wars–era soldier, and with little prodding they will tell you grim tales of frontier medicine. And the usual souvenirs are for sale: programs, posters, T-shirts, videotapes, even stuffed dolls in the likeness of Custer and Sitting Bull.

The noise and commotion around the arena is generated as much by those who are about to participate in the reenactment as by those who have come to watch it. The reenactment program lists well over a hundred different names of people involved in staging the production, including actors, stage managers, narrators, and masters of the various props. Since there is not an actual "backstage" to the event, many of these people are scurrying among the tourists as they race through last-minute preparations. Mounted cavalry soldiers ride past; Indian children are having their faces painted; mountain men help carry sound equipment to the broadcast booth; Custer himself can usually be spotted granting an interview to one of the local television stations. Just beyond the arena itself are the corrals where the horses are kept and an impromptu campground where some of the participants stay during the long weekend. The air smells of sweat, sunscreen, and horse manure. The hubbub reminds the spectators that what they are about to see is not a professional production in the usual sense; these are not people who perform every day, but rather, like performers in the town pageants of the early twentieth century, they are people who have invited the world in to see their local history. Most of the actors have participated in the show for several years—long enough that they know their part well and are resistant to changing it. Stories circulate about directors who have tried to alter the show substantially, only to find the longtime participants unwilling to change what they have done in the past.

The hum of preshow activity serves to whet the appetite of the members of the audience, many of whom have been sitting in the sun for over half an hour by the time that the director finally strides forth to meet them. The Hardin reenactment has had four different directors in the last five years, but the opening speeches remain much the same: praise for the cast, testimony to the privilege of "witnessing history," and short, but serious, warnings about safety precautions when attending a show featuring charging horses and blank ammunition. Frequently—though not always—the director introduces Joseph Medicine Crow to the audience. Medicine Crow's poor hearing makes it difficult for him to address a large audience, but he seems delighted that the show he authored forty years ago still draws a steady crowd. Those who direct and produce the reenactment are fond of emphasizing Medicine Crow's role as the originator of the script. His name is frequently used in the show's publicity, and when the director and actors talk to the press, they often mention Medicine Crow and his famous ancestor, the scout White Mans Run Him. They understand the appeal of a reenactment of the Battle of the Little Bighorn written by someone who serves as living link to the actual experience of the battle, particularly when that person can legitimately claim the title of Crow tribal historian. In the post–*Dances with Wolves* era, an Indian perspective has particular cachet, even if the Indian belongs to a tribe that fought *with,* not against, the U.S. Cavalry.

The staff and participants of Hardin's Custer's Last Stand value Medicine Crow for more than the indigenous imprimatur that he places on the show. In spite of his age, he remains a captivating storyteller and something of a showman himself. When he appears before the reenactment audience, he brings four young men with him, a drum circle; they join him in singing a song that Medicine Crow has written, an honor song for Custer. They sing with the drum and then stop between verses so that Medicine Crow can translate the words into English:

> Will everyone look at me
> I am Son of the Morning Star
> Always look at me
>
> Will everyone look at me
> I am a soldier chief
> Look at me—remember me always
>
> Will everyone look at me
> I fought at the Little Bighorn
> Look at me—remember me always
>
> Will everyone look at me
> I fought the mighty Sioux and Cheyenne
> Look at me—remember me forever and ever

As Medicine Crow and the others sing, the actor who plays George Armstrong Custer stands by in his cavalry blue, red necktie, and buckskins and nods solemnly as the man he portrays is honored. At one performance, Medicine Crow tells him to dance to the song, and he complies, stepping carefully in a circle in the style of Plains Indian dancer. "Custer," Medicine Crow guffaws, "you are a pretty good dancer."

The respect that Medicine Crow pays to Custer is the first of several overtly symbolic acts that serve as the prelude to the reenactment itself. After the narrator comes on the loudspeaker with the cheery enthusiasm of a theme park—"Let the history and legend begin!"—the notes of what I have come to think of as the anthem of Custer's America begin to fill the arena: Lee Greenwood's "God Bless the U.S.A." (a.k.a. "I'm Proud to Be an American"). Custer himself reappears now before the audience;

this time he is on horseback, leading the Seventh Cavalry, which bears the U.S. colors in a slow procession that comes closer to the bleachers than anything else will in the performance. As he passes, the spectators rise, and Custer repeatedly salutes the crowd in a measured, serious gesture. It is a moment that the cavalry reenactors mention among their favorites; more than one director has tried to replace Greenwood's well-known song with a more historically appropriate anthem, only to be rebuffed by the cast.

The procession of the Seventh Cavalry does not conclude the prelude to the action. Next, as the narrator speaks about honor and courage among Native peoples of the Plains, Custer rides alone toward the center of the arena to meet the person who figures as his adversary in this reenactment, the Lakota leader Sitting Bull. Custer carries an American flag, Sitting Bull a "medicine lance." When the two riders converge, they circle, trade their iconic objects and then ride back to their respective "sides"—Custer to the fort and Sitting Bull to the tepees. The meeting and exchange signify a kind of mutual recognition, like opposing team captains shaking hands and wishing each other luck before a football game. But that analogy also highlights something puzzling about the one-on-one encounter. It is not clear whether the audience is supposed to interpret the moment as being a representation of the historical Custer and the historical Sitting Bull showing respect for one another—as if the war between the United States and the Plains Indians were in fact a sporting event—or whether the spectators should view the exchange as taking place between two twenty-first-century actors who want to acknowledge the contribution of the man whom the other will portray, or simply want to acknowledge the other actor himself. Is this a representation of nineteenth-century history or a self-conscious attempt at twenty-first-century reconciliation?

The answer is that the exchange attempts both things, history and revisionism simultaneously, and in so doing puts into play a dynamic that resurfaces during the dramatic action that follows. The attraction of a historical reenactment is authenticity, whether in the details of the actors' costumes, the accuracy of the script, or, in this case, the identity of the script's author. The aim of this mode of history is, as Nora has argued, to reproduce the sensations of a historical moment for audience and participants alike. Yet the Custer's Last Stand reenactment also includes moments that are so over the top in their symbolism that the audience cannot help but be aware that it is watching contemporary actors playing historical roles, rather than the historical participants themselves. This sensation continues as the reenactment unfolds, for its action often depends upon using the actors as metonyms: a dozen or so "settlers" cross the stage to stand in for the thousands of Western migrants from the United States; twenty to thirty Indian adults and children demonstrate the domestic life of an Indian camp—the figuration of not just a single larger camp or even a single tribe, but all of Plains Indian life. The pageantry of the reenactment, at such moments, rests at the convergence of a mimetic mode that depends upon historical authenticity and a more symbolic one that depends upon the audience's familiarity with the stagecraft of representation. Joseph Medicine Crow displays indigenous authenticity by singing an honor song to an actor playing Custer; the actor playing Custer, in turn, is never more genuine than when he leads out his soldiers and his flags accompanied by a song that would not be recorded until more than a century after his death. At moments like these, the reenactment generates a kind of emotional power by bridging domains of representation—the actual and the figural, the real and the pretend, the historic and the mythic—that we normally consider distinct.

Another kind of contradiction is also at work in these opening moments of the Hardin reenactment. When the Seventh Cavalry parades with the flag to command the attention of the entire audience, it underscores a vision of patriotism that Custer himself would have recognized, a vision of the United States entirely united by a single government and protected by a military whose leaders, if not all of its soldiers, were white. With the words of "I'm Proud to Be an American" hanging in the air, the implication of the patriotic spectacle is that this vision has indeed prevailed. Yet when Custer rides alone out to meet Sitting Bull as an equal and the two make their ritual exchange, the visual signals are different. The audience is asked to regard the two forces that will join in mock battle as separate from one another, and even to respect that separatism. In the first of these two events, the U.S. flag appears without any Indians present; in the second, an Indian carries it off as a trophy, not as a symbol of his national loyalty. In neither visual representation—one with the United States triumphant, another with the United States tolerant—is it clear what the relationship between the American Indians and the United States is supposed to be in either the nineteenth or the twenty-first century.

When Medicine Crow first drafted the reenactment script forty years ago, he hoped that it would serve as an antidote to the Western films that had been popular for decades. Those films, he points out, are always told from the perspective of the white soldier, cowboy, or settler. By contrast, he hoped that the Custer's Last Stand show would put the white spectator "inside that Indian camp" on the Little Bighorn—long before Hollywood decided that a sympathetic stance toward Indians could be profitable. To illustrate this goal and his success in achieving it, he frequently tells a story about one of the initial performances of the reenactment in 1964. Medicine Crow and the others working on the show used all the stagecraft they had at their disposal to heighten the emotion of a scene in which Sitting Bull performs the Sun Dance. During the course of this ritual, Sitting Bull suffers more than a hundred self-inflicted wounds and, as a result, receives a vision of the Little Bighorn fight to come. With ketchup streaming down his back as fake blood, a rising crescendo of singing and drumming, the actor playing Sitting Bull captivated that initial audience, at least according to Medicine Crow's account:

> Finally, he [the actor playing Sitting Bull] pitched forward and he hit the ground. He shook. He lay still. And a little boy near the stage—about five or six years old, a little white boy, he jumped up and said, "Oh, Mama, Mama!"—you could hear him all over—"What are we going to do?" *We.* "Sitting Bull is dead!" And he burst out crying. His mother joined him, and I figure I joined him, too. Well, I did it. For that one psychological moment I converted the white man into that Indian camp. I was very pleased. That was my reward for writing this.[30]

This account of the white boy using the first-person plural to refer to himself, his mother, and Sitting Bull is perhaps Medicine Crow's favorite story from his years of association with the Custer's Last Stand reenactment. It suggests that the show could provide more than entertainment by changing, literally, where a white spectator sat and viewed the violence of the Plains Indian Wars. Medicine Crow's choice of words—"*converted* the white man"—betrays not only a kind of evangelical mission but also a sense of the total transformation that his show aspires to effect. A less sympathetic interpretation of the same crowd reaction, though, might be skeptical about how much had changed when the white boy cried out in 1964. After all, white Americans have been lamenting the suffering of American Indians for centuries without doing much to recognize Native territorial claims or desires for political autonomy.

Regardless, Sitting Bull's sacrificial Sun Dance no longer delivers the dramatic punch that Medicine Crow ascribes to its initial performance. Perhaps the scene suffers from the spectators' being farther away from the actors than they once were; perhaps the music accompanying Sitting Bull's actions is no longer as effective; or perhaps white audiences in the twenty-first century simply react differently to a Native American performance. In 1964, after all, the vast majority of Indian roles in film and television were being played by non-Indians, like Sal Mineo, the well-known "Hollywood

Indian" who starred in John Ford's *Cheyenne Autumn* that year—or even, more absurdly, like Elvis Presley, who played Indians of mixed heritage twice (*Flaming Star*, 1960; *Stay Away, Joe*, 1968) during that decade. With foils such as these, little wonder that the Custer's Last Stand reenactment of 1964 could offer its audience a genuine reconsideration of the images of "Indians" that had saturated their imaginative lives.

But in the years after the advent of the American Indian Movement, multiculturalism, and even films like *Dances with Wolves*, the notion of a Custer's Last Stand reenactment written by and featuring American Indians no longer has the same power to surprise and shock as it did in its early performances. In fact, rather than offering a radical alternative to popular Westerns, the reenactment now seems like a reincarnation of them. The nostalgia of the show arises less from the nineteenth-century history that it dramatizes than the mid-twentieth-century films and early-twentieth-century Wild West shows that its visual iconography evokes. The show begins by telling the story of exploration and settlement as a familiar epic. Lewis and Clark appear to cross the dusty Plains—two whites guided by an Indian woman (called Sekakawea or Sacajawea) and a black servant (York). A soundtrack that could have been borrowed from *Rio Bravo* accompanies them, and most of the scenes that follow could have come from a local history pageant in 1910: Indians peacefully hunting and gathering; a cadre of pioneers heading west; a discovery of gold and the rumbling of wagon trains. The narrator's voice over the loudspeakers dutifully supplies the narrative outline that links these events, which culminate in a scene that Buffalo Bill himself employed: an Indian attack on a wagon train, complete with the U.S. cavalry coming to the rescue. True to the pageant tradition, the reenactment offers a story of progress in which the conquest of Plains peoples and the incorporation of their land into the United States figures prominently. Manifest Destiny rides again.

The script that Medicine Crow has written, in other words, relies so heavily on the established narrative forms of the American West that the show comes close to replicating them. Yet the show does add new wrinkles to the old story of expansion and conquest. For instance, Medicine Crow has scripted a lengthy scene that dramatizes the Fort Laramie treaty negotiations of 1868. As chapter 4 discussed, the Fort Laramie Treaty is crucial to the history of the U.S.-Sioux conflicts of the 1870s and beyond, because the Lakota Sioux believed that its terms were violated when white settlers began streaming into the Black Hills in search of gold—and because the treaty sustains contemporary land claims of the Sioux. Were the articles of the treaty to be enforced today, approximately half of the state of South

Dakota would be under the domain of the "Great Sioux Reservation." The Custer's Last Stand reenactment attempts to stage the treaty negotiations as one of its most dramatic scenes. With the exception of the battle scenes, more actors are on "stage" for the treaty scene than at any other moment in the performance. Blue-coated soldiers form one half of a large circle; the other half belongs to the men who portray Sioux leaders. The narration provides detailed information about the negotiations and their result, including lengthy speeches by each side that are spoken from the sound booth while the actor in the arena mimes the appropriate gestures. First, the Oglala Lakota leader Red Cloud:

> I am Red Cloud, head chief of the Sioux. I speak with one tongue. Only a few winters have passed since I smoked the peace pipe with you. The great white father in Washington knows that I never break my word. What about the word of the white man? This is the way you treat your words: you break them all. We were faithfully promised that the great white father's children would stay away from the Sioux hunting grounds. Before long many white men came in white-topped wagons. They frighten away the game; they come to search for yellow metal and dig ugly holes in our sacred mountains. We tell the great white father to stop, but he has no ears for us. Instead, he sends the pony soldiers to build houses along the medicine roads. Soldiers come to live on the Tongue River, Big Piney Creek, and the Big Horn. They kill our young warriors. You say the white man wants peace? Then prove it. Let him give up the roads and the forts. Why do the white men keep crowding up near the setting sun, where there is no room to turn?

Then General Sherman makes his concessions:

> I shall try to be brief and concise with my representation. The government of the United States sends best wishes to our red brothers. Within ninety days this land will be abandoned as requested, and the roads leading to them closed. *No* white person will be permitted to settle or occupy any portion of the Sioux land, or pass through it, without the consent of the Sioux governing councils.

The words printed above are, in fact, only a part of what the audience hears, for each of them is spoken twice—once by a speaker of English, and another time by a speaker of Crow. For Red Cloud's speech, the Crow narrator, speaks, pauses, waits for the English translation to catch up, and then moves on; when Sherman "speaks," the narrators work in reverse order, as though translating the general's words for Indian auditors.

Given the antagonistic relationship between the Lakota Sioux and the

Crow in the nineteenth century, the substitution of one tribal language for the other is not only historically inaccurate but grossly inappropriate.[31] Most spectators, though, are unlikely to be able to distinguish one Plains language from another, and to them the Native speech enhances the aural realism. In fact, the treaty scene strives for authenticity on every level. It is the only episode in the reenactment that portrays historical figures speaking at such length, and even though the narration includes a caveat ("The council portrayed before us is a representation of all of these great meetings and their consequences"), it purports to reproduce the actual words spoken by Red Cloud and Sherman to each other.

Yet the scene does not make compelling theater. The lengthy portrayal of the treaty council is long on historical information provided by the narrators and short on the spectacle of physical action—a combination that makes audiences restless, particularly when it comes two-thirds of the way into the show on a hot Montana afternoon. Joseph Medicine Crow states that he was the one who decided that the scene should include a portrayal of translation, and it is one of the innovations of which he is most proud. But moving back and forth between two languages also slows the pace of the drama. More interesting, its effect is the opposite to the effect that the dramatization of Sitting Bull's Sun Dance once had on the audience. In the latter case, according to Medicine Crow's account, the non-Native audience is invited to sympathize or even empathize with the Native leader; in the case of the treaty council, the foreignness of the Native language distances the spectator who does not speak it. All of these elements—the slow pace of the speeches, the language that requires translation, and recitation of factual details—mean that the reenactment proves to be its least compelling to its non-Indian spectators at the moment that it presents its strongest case for contemporary claims of tribal self-determination. On the other hand, the scene puts the brakes on the narrative engine that drives the reenactment's pageantry long enough to force the tourists who have spent their recent days driving through large expanses of Western land—including, most likely, reservation land—to think about the nineteenth-century history that divided and assigned its ownership. Sympathizing with Sitting Bull is one thing, but recognizing why his descendants continue to claim legal rights to the Black Hills is quite another. This reenactment of Custer's Last Stand gives its audience the opportunity, at least, to do both.

The narrators conclude the treaty council with Sherman's ominous judgment that the United States made "an error in judgment in trying to make peace with the Indian," and the reenactment springs back to life, quickly presenting a series of scenes that form a prelude to the Battle of the Little Bighorn: the discovery of gold in the Black Hills, the elevation of Sitting Bull to leadership, the decision of his followers and allies to resist calls to return to their reservations, and then Sitting Bull's Sun Dance, bringing him a vision of military victory. Finally, the reenactment reaches the military clash that the audience has come to see. Custer and his men appear on the ridge in the distance, waving their flags and peering down into the "Indian village." They ride slowly at first, and then, as the music builds in tempo, they break into a gallop to charge down the hill as a full-throated voice—sounding suspiciously like Richard Mulligan, the actor who played Custer in *Little Big Man*—urges the soldiers on: "Onward, to the Bighorn, and GLORRRY!" As the men reach the base of the hill, the Indian warriors ride out to meet them, and the two forces circle each other, firing blanks and stirring up just enough dust that the figures seem less like real men of the present and more like shadows of the past they are trying to re-create. Clouds of smoke from gunpowder linger in the air, and a few men fall, "wounded." The soldiers ride back toward the hill, only to turn and regroup in a defensive position, the last stand so famous that thousands of spectators, including me, have all come out on a summer day to see it staged once again.

The actual fighting between Custer's battalion of the Seventh Cavalry and the Lakota, Cheyenne, and Arapaho warriors probably consumed less than an hour. At the Custer's Last Stand reenactment, the battle takes less than fifteen minutes. With Custer and his men lying on the ground, the smoke and dust lift, the warriors ride off, and Indian women and children run into the arena to inflict final blows and strip the fallen of their possessions. As they do so, the narrator intones judgment on the battle. The victory "has brought dignity to the red man," he states, even though "some of us of the Mountain Crow tribe will mourn for him. . . . Some of us thought of him as a great man, a military genius, but we knew that day was to be his downfall." The script's evenhandedness then reaches its climax: "We—red man and white man—live in a united fortress of democracy—the United States of America." With that, the reenactment concludes with the national anthem played over the loudspeakers. The bodies of the soldiers lie in repose for a moment longer before coming back to life—so that they, like the Indian warriors, can mingle with the spectators and pose for photographs.

—————⊰◦⊱—————

Members of the audience stream into the arena, as eager to have their pictures taken with Crazy Horse and Sitting Bull as with Custer, and I follow, hoping to learn more about what they will take with them from their afternoon watching Custer die his predictable death. It is hard to have a long conversation with a family of five who are about to climb back into a hot minivan; however, most of the tourists whom I can buttonhole for a few minutes are eager to share their appraisal of the performance, and they are uniformly enthusiastic about what they have seen.[32] Their enthusiasm is perhaps due in part to the fact that they are a self-selecting lot. One does not come to a battle reenactment to hear a complex analysis of historical motives or to hear scholars debate the questions that still remain unanswered about what actually occurred. Yet the spectators with whom I have spoken often use the word *history* when explaining what makes the reenactment so appealing. For them, performances like these bring history alive and offer something "more real"—in the words of a New York tourist—than any book can. But written history is not the only point of comparison. Many of those who come to see Custer die once more say that their affection for Western history was first ignited by Western films, and they rattle off their favorites with glee: *The Searchers, Stagecoach, High Noon.* Unlike Custer diehards who focus on films that feature the long-haired general, those who come to the reenactment are inspired by the larger genre of the Western film. For them, Hardin's Custer's Last Stand reenactment offers an opportunity to connect entertainment to history, to see events that they remember from the screen staged as a living reality.

What makes the impact of the Custer's Last Stand reenactment difficult to judge is the manner in which it concludes. The local history pageants of the early twentieth century, whose general structure the reenactment shares, always emphasized a story of progress that extended to and even included the present.[33] The Custer's Last Stand reenactment alters this tradition by finishing with Custer and his men dead in the Montana sun, with very little overt instruction to spectators about what the event might mean for the present world in which they live. Even though the narrator speaks about both Indians and non-Indians living in a "united fortress of democracy," that unity is not what the audience has just seen. In fact, the popularity of the Battle of the Little Bighorn as a subject for historical re-creation may emanate from the ambivalent position that it allows one to occupy regarding the colonial relationship between the United States and American Indian tribes. The Native victory at Little Bighorn allows white spectators a guilt-free chance to enjoy the spectacle of violence between whites and Indians—and, just as important, it allows American Indians the chance to take pride in their resistance. Even if the ultimate conquest of the Lakota and Cheyenne is implied by the overt references

Figure 14. Tony Austin, right, leads the charge as George Armstrong Custer in the 2005 Custer's Last Stand reenactment, sponsored by the town of Hardin, Montana. (Photograph by Bob Zellar, courtesy of the *Billings Gazette.*)

to patriotism—conquest is how the "fortress of democracy" became "united"—no one at the Custer's Last Stand reenactment sees that conquest performed in the show.

Custer reenactor Tony Austin (figure 14) still puzzles over the way that Custer's demise continues to produce such an abundance of meaning for those who come to watch it recur. A mail carrier living in Vancouver, British Columbia, Austin made an annual journey south and east to Hardin so that he could portray Custer in the Last Stand reenactment and other Little Bighorn Days activities from 1998 to 2005. He was a gracious Custer, whose clipped Canadian accent still carries a hint of his early childhood in England—just distinct enough from the slurred consonants of most American speech that one could hear something of a nineteenth-century general in his voice. His face, particularly with long hair, mustache, and goatee, indeed resembled the well-known images of Custer, and Austin presided over the period dress Grand Ball with an air of gallantry, bowing respectfully to the gentlemen who presented themselves and turning his smile—as Custer surely did—to the ladies. At the reenactment itself, he wore his enthusiasm more plainly, cheerily signing autographs and bantering with tourists. At one performance, he met an elderly couple from Switzerland with the surname Coster and could barely contain his glee over this encounter with people who traveled across the globe to watch his portrayal of a man who, he presumed, must have been a distant, distant relative of theirs.

Austin describes himself as a "student" of Custer, and he can speak about his historical doppelgänger with an air of intellectual detachment. "The other day," he tells me, "I was driving along the freeway that follows the Little Bighorn River and parallels the ridges of the battlefield." We are talking after one of the reenactment performances, and Austin has not changed or washed. Dust clings to his face, hands, and uniform: black boots, fringed white pants, a blue cavalry blouse, and the red felt tie that Custer famously wore. "And I'm thinking, 127 years ago, a man with two hundred of his followers were on that hill over there, fighting and dying. And I was thinking, if Custer, as he was breathing his last breaths, looking down into that Indian village and fighting for his life, if he could have visualized that 127 years later there would be a freeway along here, and there would be a guy driving down it in a Japanese-made van dressed as *him*, going to a reenactment of *his* death . . ." Austin's voice trails off. "That's such a strange feeling."

Austin was born in Brighton, England, and as for his fellow Custer-double Steve Alexander, his interest in the American West and the Indian Wars actually predates his conscious memory. For him, "cowboys and Indians" were an exotic addition, perhaps even an antidote, to the ubiquitous knights and armor. In fact, he thinks that Westerns may have inspired his family's decision to emigrate from England to Canada. He says, "I remember going together in Brighton to see *How the West Was Won*"—the John Ford epic that aspires to tell the nineteenth-century history of Western expansion through the experiences of a single family. "It was in Cinerama, projected across three screens. And it was the Civil War; it was the pioneers; it was Indians and the railroad. I think we all sat there and thought, 'That's the place where we've got to go.' Two years later we emigrated." In 1967, at the age of twelve, Austin moved with his family to Vancouver. Austin's father worked for Canada's Bureau of Indian and Northern Affairs, and he would take Austin with him on trips to Canadian

Indian reserves, trips that further cultivated Austin's interest in the history of conflict between whites and Indians in North America. Austin dressed as Custer for his first Halloween in his new country, and in the summer of 1968 the whole family traveled to visit what was then called Custer Battlefield. The Austins even attended the Custer's Last Stand reenactment in its original location.

By 2005, Austin has had multiple chances to star in the reenactment as his boyhood hero. He readily testifies to the devotion of the other cast members who return each year, and he speaks affectionately about the friendships that he and his wife have developed over their years of traveling to Hardin. He describes the opportunity to portray Custer as an "honor," particularly when he gets to work with descendants of those who participated in the battle. Austin claims that hearing the U.S. national anthem at the conclusion of the performance puts "a lump in my throat," even though he is not an American. He also likes to tell stories of the jokes that the actors share, such as the way that Bill Joseph, the Cree Indian man who formerly played Sitting Bull, teased Austin about his Canadian home ("It's a good day to die, you hoser," Joseph would tell Austin on the battlefield), or the line that one of his Indian "attackers" used during Austin's first stint as Custer: "Hi, I'm Max, and I'll be your scalper today."

Austin's sense of humor, however, does not diminish his passion for his subject. In our postperformance conversation, we go over the different ways that Custer has been found lacking in the century since his demise: the charges of military incompetence, personal arrogance, racism. It is familiar ground for both of us, but Austin is happy to travel over it once more. He discusses the orders that Custer issued at the Little Bighorn in detail and laments—with genuine sorrow—the fact that Reno and Benteen did not come to their commander's aid. He explains how Custer's personality led him to achieve such splendid success in the Civil War. He talks about the 1876 election and the possibility that Custer might have become a candidate, had he succeeded at Little Bighorn. (Austin, like most historians, thinks the notion absurd.) As we proceed through these topics, Austin becomes more animated, eager to engage an audience and defend the man he physically resembles. Then he brings up *Little Big Man*. Thomas Berger's novel, he points out, offers a complex Custer, if not one grounded in complete historical accuracy. But the mad, Indian-hating Custer in the film directed by Arthur Penn represents something that Austin cannot abide. "I find it *appalling* that historical figures [meaning Custer and the Seventh Cavalry], that their name can be dragged through the mud with impunity, and that there's *nobody* to stand up for these fallen dead," he says, his voice quivering with emotion. "You know, Custer was no saint, but he's certainly no devil. He is *not* responsible for the ills that have befallen the country and the Native Americans. He was just an instrument of government policy. I admit he's a flawed man—aren't we all?—but he was no devil."

This kind of outrage is representative of the larger community of Custerphiles, of course, who feel strongly that their hero has been a victim of generations of slander, most recently from multiculturalists who oversimplify the story of the American West into a tale of only Native suffering at the hands of greedy, murderous whites—and make Custer into the symbolic colonial oppressor. However, the controversy that surrounds Custer has been generated by the same qualities that have made him, in his afterlife, such a magnetic presence in the American imagination. The flamboyant, brash personality of the young general is what attracts many Custer aficionados in the first place, and one cannot help wondering if the ongoing controversy that surrounds his Indian fighting is not one of the things that keeps them so intensely interested in his life—and his death.

When talking about Custer's experiences with American Indians, Austin summarizes the same passage from *My Life on the Plains* that every other Custer fan knows by heart. "I think he [Custer] respected and admired the Indians," Austin states, "but his was a far more informed opinion of Native Americans" than those held by other white Americans in the decades that followed the Civil War. Austin continues: "He [Custer] said that you can't, quote, civilize the Indian, because he doesn't want your civilization. And really there's nothing that that civilization had to offer the Native Americans. It was just a loss of power, a loss of prestige, a loss of land, a loss of lifestyle. Why on earth would he [the Native American] want to welcome that? . . . Of course Custer said that if he were an Indian, he would have thrown his lot in with the people that lived the free lifestyle. He wouldn't have lived on a reservation."

For Austin, portraying Custer's life means that one can resurrect an attitude toward American Indians that combines respect with combat, admiration with military opposition. This stance corresponds to Austin's own work as an actor, in which he does mock battle with Indians during the performance and then cultivates friendships—relationships characterized by camaraderie and mutual admiration from what I been able to see and hear—with the actors who portray his foes as soon as the show is over.[34]

When talking about the Custer's Last Stand reenactment, Austin is quick to mention the role of Joseph Medicine Crow, whose authorship, he thinks, represents a broad shift in the way that the history of the Battle of Little Bighorn is being told. "The Native Americans, the Indians," he says, "in this area are taking back their story. Ultimately, as victors, they can claim the right to this story." He tells me another anecdote, this time about lying dead at the end of the reenactment. A young Indian boy stood over him and asked, "Hey, Custer! Can I shoot your gun?" From his prone position, Austin managed to convince the boy that he was out of the blank bullets used by the performers, so that stripping him of his gun would be fruitless. But he suggested the boy take and wave the Seventh Cavalry flag that had fallen nearby. "You won the battle, didn't you?" As Austin watched the boy pick up the pole and wave the flag back among the Seventh Cavalry soldiers lying on the ground, the boy's face filled with pride.

"For me," Austin recalls, "that was a great moment, and it's an empowerment thing. You know, the Native Americans, the Sioux and the Cheyenne, they beat the best that the United States army could send against them, and they should be justifiably proud of this." One could tell from the way that Austin told this story that *he* was proud of his participation in something that fostered this sense of "empowerment" through the representation of Native history. Even though Austin always stresses that the reenactment's first purpose is entertainment—"We're here to put on a show; this is not historical purity," he states—he also likes to believe that his performance can change the relationship that those who work with him and watch him have with historical events that have been distorted by Hollywood Westerns and television.

Yet the way that Austin speaks about the reenactment reveals a tension that complicates the work of the performance in recasting history for a new generation. One the one hand, Austin praises the show for establishing common ground between the whites and Indians who participate in it—both in costume and behind the scenes. We spoke during the same summer when the Indian Memorial at the Little Bighorn Battlefield National Monument was being dedicated in 2003, and Austin talked enthusiastically about the dedication's theme of "Peace through Unity." As an outsider to the area, he said, he could recognize that the divisions generated by the nineteenth-century Indian Wars, by years of racism, and by cultural chauvinism, had a profound impact upon the way that whites and Indians interact today, but he was hopeful that the interest in "unity" was genuine and that the Custer's Last Stand reenactment was helping to encourage it. On the other hand, the reenactment also fosters Indian identity by portraying a coalition of tribes prepared to resist the United States through physical force. "I can't speak for them," he said of the Indian riders in the show, "but it must nice to be able to go out there, jump on a pony, put on some feathers, an old war bonnet, and grab a shield—and go after the Wasichu," the whites. Perhaps, indeed, the common enterprise of drama-tizing historical antagonisms can generate a sense of equality and common allegiance. At one rehearsal for the reenactment, Bill Joseph—who is play-ing Sitting Bull this summer—shows up wearing a baseball cap that reads "NATIVE PRIDE" and a T-shirt displaying an American flag above the words "United We Stand." It is an ensemble without irony.

———◦———

Talk to the actors and the spectators who mingle in the arena after a per-formance of the Custer's Last Stand reenactment and their conversation will turn on large and noble ideas that the show evokes for them: "history," "patriotism," "honor," "courage," "sacrifice." Spend the performance be-hind the bleachers talking to the Hardin locals who manage the props, sell tickets, and work the concession stands, and the discussion will quickly turn to matters more mundane. Like any community of its size, the resi-dents of Hardin enjoy a steady trade in gossip, and the reenactment pro-vides its share. Some lighthearted banter and a few questions will yield (off-the-record) stories about directors and actors, past and present: tales of petty jealousy and injustice, of theatrical missteps remembered well by the local cognoscenti, and of dissent among the ranks of the small business owners who sponsor the reenactment. Inevitably the conversation will turn to the topic of the "other" reenactment—the smaller, more recently cre-ated reenactment of the Battle of the Little Bighorn staged by the Real Bird family during the same weekend Hardin produces its Custer's Last Stand show. Since the two shows are in direct competition—for spectators, for actors, for technicians—each year adds a new chapter to the intricate tale of their rivalry.

The land that the Real Birds use for their production includes the Little Bighorn River itself, running south to north here, which gives the terrain an entirely different appearance from that of the Hardin site twenty miles away. Instead of a flat, arid space worn down by years of horse hooves, the earth here is covered with grass up to the bank of the slow-moving river. On the other side of the Little Bighorn, to the east of where the spectators sit, the land rises into a series of hillocks and gullies, culminating in a ridge and road that connect the two parcels of land that make up Little Bighorn Battlefield National Monument. As the performance of the reenactment unfolds, the spectators see battlefield tourists driving back and forth in their station wagons and SUVs and stopping, occasionally, to look down at the historical re-creation unfolding in the valley below.

The location of the Real Bird reenactment is known as Medicine Tail Coulee Ford, and it figures prominently in accounts of the battle, even if those accounts do not agree precisely on what occurred there. By the time that he arrived at this portion of the battlefield, Custer had already ordered Reno to lead a battalion of the Seventh Cavalry to charge into the southern end of the Little Bighorn village. The general then began leading his own troops north along the ridge, trying to look down into the valley just as a tourist might do today. At Medicine Tail Coulee Ford, he led some portion of men down to the river. What remains disputed is what happened next: whether Custer actually entered the river and was repulsed; whether he fired across the river into the village; whether this was a failed charge into the village or simply Custer's attempt to learn more about it. Regardless, nearly all historians agree that Custer withdrew (though how quickly has been debated) and retreated to higher ground so that he could travel further north, possibly still searching for the northern end of the village.[35]

The members of the Real Bird family who stage the Battle of the Little Bighorn reenactment, led by four brothers, know that their site trumps Hardin's. "Mother Earth is the star of the show," they are fond of saying, and those who come to participate in the Real Bird reenactment agree. For anyone invested in the aura of authenticity, the chance to ride on the ground where the action occurred cannot be paralleled. Many of the cavalry reenactors camp among the trees that grow near the river, and some even stage a period camp that includes tents mimicking the nineteenth-century military issue. As with the Hardin reenactment, some of those who don the army blue are involved in Civil War reenacting, so the Little Bighorn is a chance for them to expand their repertoire. There are also a number of reenactors for whom the Little Bighorn is the full extent of their reenacting. Nicola Sgro, who emigrated from Italy to Detroit, comes to portray the Italian-born Lieutenant Carlo DeRudio. Bill Rini, who portrays Captain Myles Keogh, is a history teacher in Queens. Andrew Gallagher comes even farther—from Glasgow, Scotland, where he works as an engineer for the national waterworks. Others are from Montana, Wyoming, California. Many of the years that I have come to the Real Bird reenactment, there have also been two Lakota men—Paul Kicking Bear and Aaron Ten Bears—from southern California, who have traveled to the Little Bighorn to reenact on the side of the Indian resistance. "It gives me a chance to feel closer to my ancestors, in a small way," says Kicking Bear.[36]

As the soldiers prepare for mock combat, Steve Alexander—dressed in his Little Bighorn outfit of cavalry blue, buckskins, and Custer's signature scarlet tie—meanders through the camp on horseback. Alexander played

Figure 15. Steve Alexander, center, portrays George Armstrong Custer in the 2003 Battle of the Little Bighorn reenactment, sponsored by the Real Bird family. (Photograph by John Warner, courtesy of the *Billings Gazette*.)

Custer in the Hardin reenactment in the early 1990s but decided to leave the cast for a year to pursue a film opportunity. In 1998, he returned to the Little Bighorn as the Real Birds' Custer, and he has played the role ever since (figure 15). Alexander never looks so pleased as when he rides among "his" men before a reenactment performance. For a short time, the campground takes on the air of soldiers readying for combat—guns are cleaned and checked, equipment packed and stowed, orders barked. In the midst of the commotion, Alexander slowly rides, receiving and returning salutes, projecting an authority at once stern and benign. Even if Alexander learned his general's manner from the silver screen rather than firsthand experience, his portrayal is more than adequate for those preparing to "fight" with him, including those who are actual veterans of armed service.

The geography of the Real Bird reenactment also makes it an attractive subject for film. Every year since I began attending the reenactments in 2002, the knot of professional (and semiprofessional) media seems to grow larger: documentary filmmakers interested in either Native American affairs or the reenacting phenomenon (or both) are on hand; freelance photographers from travel magazines look for images that will lure first their editors, then the tourists; and the History Channel frequently sends a crew to record footage that it can employ in its programming. The reenactors are all too ready for their moments of fame, eager to be captured on video or to be interviewed by a newspaper reporter. Reenacting is a public hobby, and the presence of media serves to validate the scrupulous

care with which the reenactors have researched their periods and paraphernalia. Many of them carry their own cameras during the performance
so that they can snap photographs for their personal collections. In contemporary reenacting, the re-creation of a battle is not simply about reproducing history; rather, it is an opportunity to stage an event that has its
own intrinsic worth and deserves its own preservation in film and print.
Reenactors frequently note that the spectacle of whites and Indians in live-
action mock combat is a rarity in living history re-creations—a throwback
not only to an earlier period of history but also to an earlier period of historical remembrance.

The Real Bird reenactment is a smaller affair than Hardin's. Spectators
number in the hundreds, not the thousands, and the bleachers have a dozen
or so rows instead of thirty. The Real Birds do not advertise nationally or
maintain a website. They rely on word of mouth, press accounts, and signs
at local tourist stops. There was no printed program until 2005. The Real
Birds, though, understand that the amateur nature of their production is
part of its appeal for audience members, who equate its makeshift quality with its authenticity. When Richard Real Bird takes the microphone
to speak to the spectators before the performance, he constantly reminds
them that they will be seeing a "family show" without professional actors.
"And I'm not a professional emcee," he laughs. The self-effacement is part
of the act, as Real Bird warms up the crowd with the skill of a veteran—
asking the spectators where they come from, telling jokes, and reading lists
of trivia about Custer. He asks for volunteers to play a few of the bit parts
that remain unfilled and conducts a Custer-look-alike contest, with audience applause determining the winner. If any spectators were unsure about
driving onto a family ranch in order to attend a reenactment staged by a
Crow Indian family, Richard Real Bird puts them at ease. To this point,
the show has all of the exoticism, and comforts, of vaudeville.

Richard Real Bird's monologue also has its moments of seriousness. In
particular, he emphasizes that the audience will hear a version of the Battle
of the Little Bighorn that will differ from what is proffered by the National
Park Service at the official monument. The Real Birds contend that their
version of the battle originates from the account of a Cheyenne man, Spotted
Wolf, who participated in the battle. Spotted Wolf's son, Pat Spotted
Wolf, passed on his father's story to the Real Birds' grandfather, Mark Real
Bird.[37] In fact, recent performances of the reenactment have begun by por-
traying Henry Real Bird, the author of the reenactment script, listening to
Pat Spotted Wolf tell the story of the battle to Real Bird's grandfather.[38]
Just as Joseph Medicine Crow appears before the audience at the Har-

din reenactment to remind the audience of his connection to participants in the battle, this scene serves to verify that what will follow in the Real Bird reenactment is an authentic indigenous story, an alternative—or alter-Native—to those that appear in written textbooks or in the visitor center that sits at the base of Last Stand Hill.

What happened at Last Stand Hill is in fact the most crucial point of disagreement between the Real Birds' version of the battle and the more common one. The Real Birds contend that Custer never made it there alive. Instead, they state in their show that Custer was killed in his failed attempt to cross the river at Medicine Tail Coulee Ford, that the Indian resistance staked him to the ground there as the rest of his forces retreated. Only later, this account claims, when the Cheyennes recognized the slain general as Yellow Hair—whom they knew from the Washita fight—did they move him up to the hill where the monument now stands, so that his body could serve as a warning.

To those uninitiated in the arcana of Custerology, the precise location of Custer's death may seem to be a minor point. The Real Birds are not, for instance, alleging that Custer committed suicide or was killed by one of his own men. In fact, my sense is that most tourists watching the event do not even register the distinction between the Real Birds' version of the battle and the Park Service's, especially since the Real Bird reenactment makes this claim most explicitly in the midst of the noise and commotion of the climactic mock battle. However, to those already versed in the Custer story, the revision is significant. As the archaeologist Richard Fox found out when he claimed that no last stand occurred (see the previous chapter), the image of a final and glorious defensive stand is at the heart of the Custer legend. It is also the reason that Last Stand Hill has proven to be such a popular tourist attraction. In suggesting that Custer died on *their* land and not the Park Service's, the Real Birds have reconfigured the symbolic geography of the battle so that their land is at the center.

With their reenactment of the Little Bighorn the Real Birds have found a way to use the history of the battle to issue the kinds of provocation that have made them a controversial family among many local residents. When Richard Real Bird served as tribal chair in the late 1980s, he acted as a staunch advocate of Crow national sovereignty, including political and economic independence from the Bureau of Indian Affairs. His antagonistic relationship with the U.S. federal government began shortly after he took office, when he filed suit against the secretary of the interior, the assistant secretary for Indian affairs, and other officials for, in Real Bird's own words, "breach of trust, arbitrary and capricious conduct, breach of contract, violations of Constitutional rights, and tortious interference with economic relationships."[39] Not long after Real Bird initiated the lawsuit, federal agents raided the Crow Tribal offices and seized the financial records of the tribe. When Richard Real Bird was later indicted on charges of embezzlement of tribal funds—for which he eventually served a year in jail—his defenders believed him to be a political prisoner persecuted by the federal government as an act of retribution for his lawsuit.[40] More recently, many of the Hardin residents involved with Little Bighorn Days feel that the Real Birds have sought to use their own reenactment to irritate and divide the Hardin community. The Real Birds respond that they are only trying to help their own tribe, both by generating economic revenue and by telling its story.

Since the Real Birds began their reenactment in the early 1990s, their performance has included other episodes sure to raise the hackles of Custerphiles. Henry Real Bird, who has written and continues to rewrite the script, says that prior incarnations portrayed Custer as more of an "Indian hater," primarily through a portrayal the Seventh Cavalry attack at Washita. Even recent versions of the reenactment have stated that the Cheyenne present at the Little Bighorn remembered Custer for killing "women and children" in 1868. Henry Real Bird recalls that they once thought about including a scene in which Custer executed Confederate soldiers he captured in the Shenandoah Valley during the Civil War—an incident that he admits was based only on a shaky rumor. The cavalry soldiers refused to portray the incident, however, and the scene was not included.[41] Bill Rini, who plays Captain Myles Keogh, recalls a similar conflict in 2001, when the Real Birds wanted the Indian warriors to stake Custer's body to the ground, then pull out a pig's heart (in lieu of Steve Alexander's) to parade before the audience. Once again, the cavalry threatened to walk out on the production until the Real Birds backed down.[42]

Henry Real Bird is aware that these conflicts have threatened the reenactment, and he says he hopes they are a thing of the past. "The way it is now," he said in 2004, "we've ironed it out to where everybody gets along, so we've just left it like that for a while."[43] Indeed, during the years that I have watched the Real Bird reenactment, there has been little change from one performance to the next. Equally important, the reenactment as it is now performed each year on the Real Bird land substantially resembles the Hardin reenactment in terms of its narrative style. Like the Hardin Custer's Last Stand reenactment, the Real Birds' Battle of the Little Bighorn show is actually much less a representation of the battle than a series of episodes strung together to present a historical pageant. The expedition of Lewis and Clark, Jesuit missionaries, the Fort Laramie treaty council, Sitting Bull's Sun Dance: these are all performed in the Real Bird reenactment much as they are in Hardin's. Even though the Real Bird re-enactors include a longer sequence of mock battle action between the Seventh Cavalry and the Indian camp of Lakota and Cheyenne, the result is the same. The Real Birds do not conclude with anything like Hardin's line about the "red man and white man" living in a "united fortress of democracy," but Richard Real Bird's prefatory remarks include an ample reference to and reverence toward U.S. patriotism. He points to the American flag flying above, leads the crowd in the pledge of allegiance, and then speaks (at least in the years that I have attended) with pride about the number of Crow men and women currently serving the U.S. military in Afghanistan and Iraq. Any antagonism toward the federal government that Richard Real Bird or his family may have felt in the past is not on display during the reenactment. Instead, the Real Bird performance starts with an invocation of a united nation and then marches through a series of historical episodes leading up to the event that took place on that very land.

As with the Hardin reenactment, this straightforward march through Western history echoes, rather than challenges, the story of Manifest Destiny that has reigned over the American imagination since the nineteenth century. Once, according to this story, Native Americans lived peacefully here; then explorers, missionaries, and settlers came; conflict ensued, and white "civilization" triumphed in order to produce a united twentieth- (and now twenty-first-) century country. Both the Hardin and the Real Bird reenactments cut that story off by ending with the spectacular Indian victory at the Battle of the Little Bighorn, but the spectators know the rest of it. Lest they forget, the flags, pledges, and anthems of loyalty to the United States serve to remind them of that chestnut of Little Bighorn wisdom—the Indians "won the battle but lost the war."

However, the Real Bird reenactment also does something else. It slows down and even interrupts that narrative of U.S. expansion and conquest on four different occasions to present something quite different: lyric poetry. The shift in the narrative style of the performance is immediately evident to the audience when the usual narrator—Kennard Real Bird, whose deep, booming voice extends each syllable he pronounces—hands over the microphone to Henry Real Bird, the author of the poetry. Henry is a former rodeo rider and the former president of the tribal Little Bighorn College, and he spends parts of each performance as a stage manager, maneuvering in the wings, directing riders to their stations, and managing the coming and going of the horses. But he returns to the small announcers' table to read his poems in a breathless, staccato voice. There are four poems included in the reenactment performance, each of them serving as aural accompaniment to the portrayal of some element of traditional Plains life, such as women gathering food or men preparing for battle.

Henry Real Bird began writing poetry while in college; since then, he has become a featured reader on the "cowboy poet" circuit, including the National Cowboy Poetry Gathering held each year in Elko, Nevada. He lets me pore over a dog-eared copy of his self-published book that travels in his briefcase while he talks about the role of the poems in the reenactment. "I put them in there," he says, "because I wanted to show the peace and serenity before the coming of the Western world."[44] In some cases, as in "Love and Dreams," the pace of the rhythm and the density of the rhyme give the lines an almost overwhelming force, especially when heard by an audience unprepared for lyric verse:[45]

> To meet death filled with hope
> That life is made of love, and dreams
> Is the war pony rearing to go.
> Spent love and dreams can longer keep the lope
> That the rest of life's remuda steams
> Through their nostril's rhythmic blow.

Other poems are less elliptical and more descriptive. Henry reads "Rivers of Horses" as a dozen or so horses (usually with a few colts) gracefully trot back and forth in front of the audience in synchronized movement. At one point, the poem includes a recitation of proper names that transitions into historical violence:

> Bird Horse, Horse On The Other Side,
> Medicine Tail, Pretty Paint, Rides The Horse,
> Takes the Horse, Horse Herder, Spotted Horse,
> Brings Home Many Geldings, Has a Lot of Colts,
> Lucky With His Horses, Always Rides Horses,
> Gray Horse Rider, Sorrel Horse, Buckskin Horse,
> Black Horse Rider, Lead Horse Rider:
> These are our names from a horse culture.
> Then, there was a day that all my father's horses
> Were killed by the Bureau of Indian Affairs
> And sell-out Indians for 25 cents an ear.
> . . . .

"You don't shed a tear for the horses
For they replace a human being's life."
Said my Grandmother, Everything She Joins,
Florence Medicine Tail Real Bird.
"But that day, I made my tears drop
When they killed all the horses. . . ."

These lines move from the names that connect the contemporary Crows to the "horse culture" that was threatened in the 1920s by the event the poem describes: the systematic destruction of tens of thousands of Crow horses at the instigation of both non-Crow ranchers, who argued that horses were destroying their grazing land, and BIA officials, who worried that the horses retarded the process of acculturation.[46] The pairing of the poem with the presence of the live horses belonging to the Real Bird family offers a vivid illustration, on the one hand, of what the Crows lost during this dark episode in their history and, on the other, of their ability to recover from those losses.

"Rivers of Horses" is, perhaps, a six- or seven-minute scene in a ninety-minute production, and as pleasing as the sight of horses trotting in unison might be, it probably does not rate as high with the audience as the final conflagration of gunfire, dust, and smoke. Elegant horses and poetry are not what the tourists have come to see and hear. In fact, the poem acts as a kind of counterweight to the narrative drive of the reenactment, friction in the machine of pageantry that churns ever onward toward the battle. To some extent, all of the lyric poems included in the reenactment interrupt the linear story that the performance tells. In this case, however, the disruption goes further, because "Rivers of Horse" specifically refers the audience to a historical moment (the 1920s) that postdates the Battle of the Little Bighorn and is therefore outside the temporal frame of the performance. It is as if a Christmas nativity pageant paused momentarily to describe the fate of early Christians in Rome. The chronology becomes confused, if only for a moment, and in so doing, the reenactment forges a link between the lives of nineteenth- and twenty-first-century Plains Indians. For the Crows, the horses serve as an embodiment of that continuity, for the proficiency of the young Crow men in riding and handling horses at the reenactment offers visible proof that the "horse culture" of the Crows survived the threats that Henry Real Bird's poem describes.

Scenes like this one contribute to an emotional complexity of the reenactment that is critical to its success. White tourists pull off the freeway to see Custer—the figure of history and Hollywood—re-created. A performance of Crow horsemanship might draw an audience, as the rodeo at Crow Fair does each August, but not an audience filled with non-Native tourists and historical enthusiasts. Yet those same spectators have come to also see something "Indian," especially when they opt for the smaller Real Bird production over the more professional Hardin reenactment. They want to see the story of U.S. expansion across the North American West in all of its epic glory, but they also want to register their sympathy with the Native peoples who opposed it. One spectator, a man in his mid-forties from Pennsylvania, tried to explain this mix to me after a performance. "Watching the cavalry ride over the hill and charge down—it's just like all the movies, only better. It's brilliant. Of course, the Indians out here got a raw deal. You feel sorry for them . . ." His voice trailed off as he looked up and saw the cavalry soldiers riding past the bleachers toward the campground. "But it's brilliant." The Real Bird production, with the aid of elements like Henry Real Bird's poetry, offers a chance for audience members like this one to have their sorrow for the plight of Native peoples confirmed; they can feel as though their sympathy has been acknowledged by the Indian producers of the reenactment, before they go on to watch the thrilling climax of military conflict. In the case of the Battle of the Little Bighorn, the conclusion sends its own mixed signals: an episode of Native victory that, paradoxically, has come to serve as the symbol for a longer series of conflicts ending in Native defeat.

Finally, for the careful observer, the poem "Rivers of Horses" also serves as an explicit reminder of a dimension of the reenactment that can be easily overlooked. The poem is a specific recitation of a series of events in *Crow* tribal history, and indeed the Real Birds and nearly all of the Native men and women who appear in the Real Bird reenactment are Crow Indians. Yet they portray Custer's enemies at the Battle of the Little Bighorn: primarily Lakota Sioux, some Northern Cheyennes, and a small contingent of Arapaho Indians. Crows were present at the battle only in the six Crow men who scouted for the Seventh Cavalry. Custer's allies, in other words, now portray his enemies, and non-Indians and Indians alike still delight in the spectacle of mock combat between them—even as both groups profess their common allegiance to the contemporary United States. The Battle of the Little Bighorn lives on because reenacting it combines the play-acting of violence with professions of friendship. The hard question is whether one ever trumps the other.

In 1992, not long after Hardin revived the tradition of annual Little Big-horn reenactments, Harlequin Books published *Cody's Last Stand,* a ro-mance of the type made famous by that press. Written by Kathy Clark, Harlequin's contribution to Custerology tells the story of Elizabeth Law-rence, a white historian with a blue-blood pedigree—her father is a U.S. senator—that includes General Custer.[47] Elizabeth (who symbolically has the same first name as Custer's wife) travels to the Little Bighorn to con-duct research for a book that will exonerate her ancestor, and she attends a reenactment of the battle. There she meets Cody, a doctor of mixed Sioux and Crow descent who participates in the reenactment by playing the role of Sitting Bull—*his* ancestor. True to Harlequin conventions, Elizabeth and Cody fall in love, struggle against objections from their families, and, in the end, manage to bring everyone together for a joyous wedding. As the book closes, Elizabeth carries the child of her union with Cody—a child whom the ghostly voice of Sitting Bull has told Cody "would be the one to make a difference."[48] The novel, in other words, could have the same slogan as the recently dedicated Little Bighorn Indian Memorial—"Peace through Unity"—though the last word has a more literal, bodily meaning in the context of a Harlequin novel. The voice of Sitting Bull even speaks directly to Cody about reconciliation: "Custer was not my enemy. He was a warrior, fighting for his people and for personal glory, just as we did. On that particular day, he had the misfortune to lose and we had the misfor-tune to win. It is time the wars ended."[49]

But the wars go on—for anyone willing to pay the price of admission to either the Hardin ($16) or Real Bird ($12) reenactments. Those who stage them argue that they, too, are devoted to the project of reconcil-ing the descendants of the nineteenth-century Indian Wars. For Joseph Medicine Crow, the key to this process has been to give white Amer-icans a chance to understand the history of the West from a Plains In-dian perspective—to "convert a white man into an Indian," as he puts it. The Real Bird family, meanwhile, talks about how the reenactment has helped them to understand and respect those whites devoted to the his-tory of the Indian Wars. Several members of the family even have traveled to Monroe, Michigan, where they dined in Steve and Sandy Alexander's house—the very building that the Custers once called home—and partici-pated in the town's holiday parade.[50] With their salutes to the U.S. flag and emphasis on shared loyalty to the United States, the reenactments actu-ally continue the tradition of friendship ceremonies that have been taking place at the battlefield since the early twentieth century. In 1926, Edward Godfrey of the Seventh Cavalry and several Lakota Sioux chiefs buried a hatchet to profess their friendship; today, the reenactors claim to pursue that same goal by firing their weapons in a pantomime of historical theater.

The reenactment performances, though, do not necessarily make the terms of that reconciliation easy ones. The Hardin reenactment, using Medicine Crow's script, dwells at length on the treaties of the nineteenth century, treaties that many contemporary tribes—including the Lakota Sioux—still insist that the United States honor. The Real Bird reenactment includes its own discussion of nineteenth-century treaties, and it mentions specifically the treaty terms that secured the land that the Crows presently occupy and that have been the basis of legal claims by the Crow Tribe against the state of Montana as recently as 1998.[51] Treaties, after all, are central to the assertion of tribal sovereignty, to the right of tribes to have government-to-government relationships with the United States, and to their conception of themselves as "nations." That desire for self-determination becomes more tangible to the spectators who attend the Real Bird reenactment, where a Crow tribal flag flies next to the U.S. one, where the Crow national anthem follows the U.S. pledge of allegiance, and where, at every moment before, during, and after the show, the outside visitor is aware that he or she is in the midst of a tribal community and on tribal land—represented by the constantly visible presence of the extended Real Bird family.

Both the Hardin and Real Bird reenactments make a series of gestures that, taken together, seem logically incompatible. Their live performances of the Battle of the Little Bighorn promise reunion and reconciliation between the United States and Indian peoples, but they also insist on a kind of tribal separatism, a future in which Indians will continue to exist as separate Indian nations and not simply part of the larger United States. The Custer story itself, the tale of the boy general's glorious defeat at the hands of an enemy he badly underestimated, can sustain this set of contradictions because it has already served for so long as a site of ideological confrontation. Custer's death can at once be a blood sacrifice necessary for the consolidation of the West under the U.S. flag and a symbol of the history of Native American resistance to the colonization of tribal lands and peoples. The Battle of the Little Bighorn can offer a nostalgic trip back to a time when history and its representations in popular culture were simpler and more clearly delineated in a narrative of American triumph and victory, or it can serve as an entry point into a more pluralistic attitude toward history that strives to regard events like these as contests of power in which everyone suffers. Or the Custer story can be all of these things—which is one reason the rival reenactments continue to be performed each June.

One key to this profusion of meaning may rest in who actually performs the reenactments. As I have noted throughout this chapter, Joseph Medicine Crow, the Real Birds, and the majority of the Native men and women who act in the two reenactments are Crow Indians, a tribe that fought with, not against, Custer and the Seventh Cavalry. Crows have had a sustained involvement in the reenactments since their inception in 1964, and Crow Indians have written the scripts for both of the current reenactments. In other words, the white tourist seeking "an Indian perspective" from the reenactments may get one, but it will be the perspective of a Crow rather than that of a Lakota Sioux, Northern Cheyenne, or Arapaho—the tribes whose members battled Custer in 1876. Crows, in fact, feuded and waged war against the both Lakota Sioux and Northern Cheyennes during the nineteenth century; they sided with the U.S. army in 1876 in large part because they hoped to secure their land base against the incursion of these tribes.[52] While only six Crow men rode with Custer, 175 fought with General George Crook at the Battle of Rosebud Creek, eight days before Little Bighorn.[53]

The role of Crows in the 1876 campaign and, especially, the location of their land base surrounding the battlefield have turned them into cultural brokers of Little Bighorn history, people who are able to position themselves as sympathetic to both sides in the conflict and thus uniquely able to tell its story. This practice has a long history dating from the immediate aftermath of the battle, when Curly and the other Crow scouts were among the most prominent witnesses of the conflict, and this history of white interest in Crow accounts of the battle dramatically influenced the young Joseph Medicine Crow in the early twentieth century. Today, the Crows mediate the history of the Little Bighorn as it is told to tourists throughout the region. Not only, for instance, does the National Park Service regularly employ Crows as seasonal and permanent employees at the battlefield, but it has a concession agreement with a Crow tour company tied to the tribal community college. Apsalooke Tours (recall that *Apsalooke* is the Crow language word for "Crow") offers bus tours in which Crow guides lead tourists through the battlefield. The current concession agreement, in fact, is an exclusive one, so that Crows are the only guides, Native or non-Native (outside of the Park Service), permitted to lead paid tours over the ground where the Lakota, Northern Cheyenne, and Arapaho battled the Seventh Cavalry.

Below the official battlefield, on the Real Bird land, the cavalry reenactors with whom I have spoken are all acutely aware that most of the Indians against whom they wage their mock battle are engaged in a kind of cross-tribal performance. Some use the history of Crow service alongside the U.S. military to explain why the contemporary reenactors—whites and Indians—get along so well. Others feel that the zeal of the Crow warriors during the mock combat means that they have "forgotten" on whose side their tribe fought during the battle. Native American critics of these productions have pointed out the discrepancy in tribal identity more sharply. During a recent commemoration of the anniversary of the Battle of the Little Bighorn held at the Indian Memorial there, Leo Killsback castigated those Crows who stage and participate in the reenactments. Killsback, a Northern Cheyenne and a doctoral student in Native studies at the University of Arizona, spoke at the Indian Memorial in 2004 to a small, predominantly Indian crowd that nodded approvingly throughout his remarks. He later repeated his charges in a letter to the *Billings Gazette:* "Members of the Crow tribe are blessed to have close proximity to the tourist attraction [of the battlefield], and they have taken advantage of the economic potential in tourism. However, a select few of the Crow tribe have taken their economic exploitation too far. Though they did not take part in the fight for the sacred Black Hills and the Plains Indian way of life, the Crow tribe proudly boasts of the victory at the Little Bighorn as if they were fighting alongside Sioux and Cheyenne against the United States Empire."[54]

Killsback's charges of "economic exploitation" raise thorny questions about the stewardship of history and the motives of the Crows who recreate the Little Bighorn. The Crows do have the advantage of the land near the battlefield, land that they helped to secure by siding with the United States in its 1876 war against the Lakota Sioux. What Killsback suggests is that this land comes with the obligation to handle the history of the Little Bighorn with careful circumspection, not as a subject for sensational theater. He argues that the integrity of American Indian tribes may require that they recognize certain subjects as the proprietary domain of others—a difficult proposition in a country that has a long history of racial and ethnic theater open to anyone with a convincing costume. Weighing the necessity of intertribal respect versus economic and artistic freedom is a particularly daunting task for someone like me, who lives outside these tribal communities, especially when the communities in question seem to differ among themselves. While Killsback's speech received an enthusiastic response from the Northern Cheyennes in his audience, each year a significant contingent of Northern Cheyennes also travel from their nearby reservation to the Hardin reenactment to participate.[55]

As part of his criticism of the misappropriation of tribal history, Kills-back makes another, more subtle claim: the Crows, he says, are engaging in a kind of wish fulfillment by assuming the roles of the Lakota and Cheyenne anticolonial resistance. At the Indian Memorial, he put it this way: "Today, the Crow wished they had fought along with the Sioux and Cheyenne, but they did not."[56] Indians from the northern Plains have been assuming the role of enemies of the United States since the Wild West shows of the late nineteenth century, and scholars who have studied the history of these performances have found that Indians have done so for a variety of motives. They have sought economic gain, the chance to travel, the opportunity for individual achievement—and they have been attracted by the possibility of receiving these rewards for acting *as* Indians, even if that meant acting out Indian lives from the past rather than their contemporary one. In other words, Indian actors in both Wild West shows and films always understood the historical sleight-of-hand at work in their performances; they presented the past as though it were the present, and enduring, way of the Plains Indian.[57] To complicate the matter further, there is evidence that such performances have been used by Indians to express not only intertribal but *intra*tribal conflicts, as in the case of the earliest documented reenactment of the Battle of the Little Bighorn. This performance did not occur as part of a Wild West show but rather at a Sun Dance sponsored by Crazy Horse in 1877, just one year after the battle. According to a witness, an interpreter named William Garnett, a "sham battle was arranged to represent the Custer fight, and the Crazy Horse Indians who had been in that [meaning the actual Battle of the Little Bighorn] were to take the side they had in that affair, and the friendly Indians"—those who might be called "agency Indians"—"were to stand in for the Custer soldiers." In other words, the reenactment pitted Lakota Sioux who had carried out armed resistance to the United States in the previous year against those who elected to stay on the reservation. This division reflected the tensions among Lakotas in the aftermath of the army's centennial campaign, and the mock battle turned dangerous. "When this fight was on, instead of striking the Custer party lightly as was usual some of the others struck their opponents with clubs and . . . hard blows."[58]

The contemporary cross-tribal performances of the Crows who portray Lakota and Cheyenne warriors contribute a new chapter in history of Indian performance (figure 16). There is an economic dimension to the Crow involvement in the reenactments at the level of both the community (stag-

Figure 16. Crow horsemen cross the Little Bighorn River in the 2003 reenactment
of the Battle of the Little Bighorn staged by the Real Bird family. (Photograph
by John Warner, courtesy of the *Billings Gazette.*)

ing the reenactments generates tourist revenue for the entire region) and
the individual (Crow riders are paid; white cavalry riders are not). As the
employment statistics I cited at the beginning of this chapter suggest, the
opportunity to earn money by "playing Indian" is a significant one for
the Crows. However, Killsback is correct in suggesting that there is more
than money at stake in these performances. The pleasure and enthusiasm
of the young Crow men who ride down the white cavalry and kill them in
mock combat, the way the Real Birds use the first-person plural when describing the nineteenth-century Indians who fought against Custer, the fact
that Joseph Medicine Crow wants to forge an empathic bond between the
audience and the Lakota holy man Sitting Bull—all these suggest a form
of theatrical play in which Crow Indians are able to imagine themselves
not simply as historical Indians but as Indians from a tribe other than their
own. The result blurs tribal identification for the audience and perhaps
for the participants as well; for a moment, being "Indian" is equated with
belonging to the anticolonial resistance of the 1870s. It does not matter
if you are Crow, or Northern Cheyenne, or Arikara—as long as you are
Indian, you can pick up a blank-filled gun and fire off some rounds at the
U.S. Cavalry.

Pan-Indianism—a term often used to describe a common Indian sense of identification that supersedes tribal boundaries—has a long history in the United States. Fostered in places like the Indian boarding schools that brought children of multiple tribes together, pan-Indianism has produced religious movements like the Native American Church, cultural phenomena such as the powwow circuit, and many of the indigenous political organizations of the late twentieth and early twenty-first century, including the American Indian Movement.[59] In fact, the theme of "Peace through Unity" chosen for the Little Bighorn Indian Memorial (see chapter 1) had an intertribal meaning in addition to its call for reconciliation between Indians and whites. Clara Nomee, then chairwoman of the Crow Tribe, emphasized this point in her testimony at a 1990 congressional hearing on the memorial proposal. Noting that "all the involved tribes had their own respective reasons for being there [the Little Bighorn] on June 25 and 26, 1876," Nomee said that the Crows "hope to show, with our support of the memorial, unity among the American Indians. It is fitting for other American Indians to see this is as show of Indian solidarity."[60] In other words, just as the battle had once served to expose tribal enmities, its commemoration at the turn of the twenty-first century could foster cross-tribal allegiances.

At the Real Bird reenactment, Paul Kicking Bear made an equally telling comment about the desire for unity across tribal lines. As one of only two Lakotas participating in the reenactment, Kicking Bear said he had feared "that maybe my Crow brothers might not like me too much." However, he continued, "they've done nothing but make me feel at home, give me lots of respect and kindness, show me lots of kindness. And I get along really good with them."[61] In these reenactments of the Battle of the Little Bighorn, a sense of common Native cause makes it possible for contemporary Crows and Lakotas alike to play the roles of the nineteenth-century resistance.

This kind of pan-Indianism, though, is only one of several forms of Native identity on display during the Hardin and Real Bird reenactments. Both shows are also full of references to the specific tribal identity of the Crows who authored (and authorized) them. Even though the Hardin reenactment has for many years included around twenty Northern Cheyenne men as well, and a Cree playing Sitting Bull, the production emphasizes its affiliation with the Crow tribe. Hardin's narrators, for instance, begin by mentioning that many of "us"—Crows—"admired Custer"; it ends with the message "You are always welcome in Crow country." As I have mentioned, the Real Bird reenactment includes discussion of the boundaries of the Crow reservation as set forth in the 1868 Fort Laramie treaty and constantly reminds its audience that it sits in the middle of Crow land, a fact that would be difficult to forget given the omnipresent members of the Real Bird family. These are all markers of tribal identification that are unique to the Crows. "Rivers of Horses" might tell about an experience common to other indigenous peoples in western North America, but the details of the poem are particular to the Crow people, their horses, and their land. This kind of specificity is necessary to the political existence of American Indian tribes and their claims of national sovereignty. Tribal nationalism depends upon the articulation of a unique political and historical identity—one that is recognized in treaties like those that the reenactments describe—rather than an appeal to a larger sense of indigenousness, and it is distinct from pan-Indianism in its insistence that tribal distinctions are significant. This last point fuels Killsback's criticism of the reenactments. Crows should be Crows, he says, not Lakotas or Northern Cheyennes. While the Crows in the reenactment cross tribal boundaries for the sake of theatrical performance, the productions they inhabit also take pains to remind us that the Indian men and women who have staged the shows are, in a very real way, not "Indians" but *Crow* Indians.

These reenactments seem to be trying to have it both ways, to allow for both pan-Indianism fantasy and tribal-specific history—and there is a still a third way that they address the question of Indian identity in the twenty-first century. Even though the reenactments allow contemporary men to play out the role of historical antagonists to the nineteenth-century American empire, the reenactments also stage overt and dramatic expressions of Native loyalty to the contemporary United States. As I have described, the shows begin by inviting the audience to join with the reenactors in professions of U.S. patriotism. Richard Real Bird refers to the material sacrifices that Crow men and women have made for the United States; Joseph Medicine Crow's script claims that Indians stand beside non-Indians in the "united fortress of democracy." These gestures of allegiance to the United States encourage the spectators to think of the Indians on the stage not as the inheritors of a broad, indigenous anticolonial resistance, nor as tribal separatists, but as citizens of the United States who have an equal claim to American national identity. In this sense, the reenactment presents one episode in the making of a single nation, the history of a common nation that now encompasses the descendants of all of those who fought at Little Bighorn. Local history pageantry, after all, was devised as an attempt to connect the regional with the national and instill a sense of a shared purpose and future. Seen through this lens, the reenactment does not portray a contest between colonists and anticolonists or between nation-to-nation combatants. Rather, the blanket of U.S. patriotism casts the conflict as an unfortunate setback in the making of a unified country, a skirmish between two sets of people who can claim equally to be ancestors to the contemporary United States.

One might say that these different ways of imagining what it means to be an Indian in the twenty-first century—pan-Indian anticolonialism; tribal nationalism; U.S. patriotism—contradict one another, and at the level of abstraction, one would be correct. Taken as a whole, the reenactments present a fiercely incoherent vision of contemporary indigenous identity, one that rearticulates and lays claim to a pantribal history of Native identity forged in opposition to the United States; one that identifies a specific tribal nationalism coterminous with Crow land; and one that also stresses Crow citizenship in and allegiance to the contemporary United States, particularly its twentieth- and twenty-first-century military endeavors. Moreover, the inconsistencies of these various forms of tribal identity may, in fact, be exactly the point. What the Crows involved in the reenactments seem to understand is that the future of tribal self-determination may require the deployment and juxtaposition of forms of tribal identity that are usually, at a theoretical and even practical level, inconsistent with one another. Being Crow in the twenty-first century may require fighting against the Seventh Cavalry as a Lakota one day and honoring your relative fighting in Iraq the next, all the while carefully guarding your rights as a Crow to the land that surrounds the Little Bighorn battlefield—and the economic opportunities for heritage tourism that that land provides.

Throughout this book, I have been arguing that the story of Custer and the Little Bighorn has afforded non-Indians, particularly whites, a way of continuing to think about the place of Indians in the United States. Watching these reenactments, though, has suggested to me that the Custer story has also been crucial to the way that American Indians conceive of themselves in relationship to the United States. When talking to me about the benefits of the reenactment that his family stages, Richard Real Bird stressed that it offers young Crow men the chance to develop the riding and other horsemanship skills that are crucial to being a young Crow man. In other words, the performances helped the performers become Crow. My sense is that the Custer story plays an equally important symbolic role in the process of self-identification for all the Native Americans who are involved in telling it. For those Indians who work in the reenactments—and perhaps in the museums and other sites of historical commemoration as well—the Custer story helps them to think about what it means to be an Indian in the contemporary world. Custer actually enables the imagination of Indianness for the twenty-first century. At times it may be a tentative Indianness, or one rife with contradiction, but it is an Indianness nevertheless.

George Armstrong Custer would have never believed that there would be Indians who thought of themselves *as* Indians in the twenty-first century. Like his white contemporaries, including the most sympathetic observers of Indian affairs, he believed that the "juggernaut" of modernity would crush the indigenous population of the North American Plains, either physically through extermination or spiritually through assimilation. That there would be people living more than a century later who still conceived of themselves first and foremost as Crow, Lakota, or Cheyenne would have seemed impossible to any white person interested in Native America in the late nineteenth century. That there are such people today constitutes one of the great historical surprises in the development of the United States. That such people might actually be using the story of Custer's life and death to help them understand what it means to be an Indian in the twenty-first century constitutes one of American history's most elegant, and least appreciated, ironies.

EPILOGUE

Indian Country

IN THE SUMMER OF 2006, 130 YEARS AFTER THE BATTLE OF THE LITTLE Bighorn, the Real Birds flew a different version of the U.S. flag over the reenactment that they staged. This one had the familiar stripes of red and white, but the fifty stars on the field of blue were replaced with an outline of the New York City skyline, complete with the Twin Towers of the World Trade Center. Text above the image spelled out "September 11, 2001." The flag, Kennard Real Bird told the audience, was a gift to the Real Birds from a New York state sheriff.

My pursuit of Custerology has, in a sense, transpired under this flag. In the United States since 9/11, the historical landscape has become charged with a version of patriotism that emphasizes national unity and cohesion to a greater degree than in any of the years since the dawn of the Vietnam era. After pointing to the flag, Kennard Real Bird said that even though he did not agree with the policies of the U.S. president, he wanted the crowd to know that they were all "Americans first." He then went on to discuss the number of Crow Indian men and women who were serving abroad in the armed forces, and he called attention to reenactors—both white cavalrymen and Indian warriors—who either had returned from or would soon be leaving for service in Iraq. With some variation, this has become a regular feature of the Real Bird reenactment since 2004.

What the aftermath of 9/11, including the war in Iraq, has done to Custerology has been to bring the U.S. patriotism that runs throughout the historical landscape of the Indian Wars, like the rounded bumps of hills on a topographical map, into even sharper relief. This has made Custerology, still reorienting itself after the convulsions of multiculturalism, an even more robust and vibrant enterprise and as useful as it has ever been as a marker of a particular moment in cultural history. If the canonization of Custer's Last Stand in the national iconography signaled an earlier moment of nostalgia for the drama of Manifest Destiny on the part of white Americans, then the post-9/11 incarnation reveals a United States seeking to use its past to forge national cohesion at a time when the world seems newly shadowy, complicated, threatening.

But there is a crucial difference built into the latest chapter of Custerology. More than ever, Custerology has become a venue for the explicit expression of patriotism by American Indians for their tribal nations. As I have tried to show, for many American Indians (though certainly not all), this patriotic allegiance to tribal nations is compatible with patriotic allegiance to the United States, and the commemoration of the Battle of the Little Bighorn has offered an arena in which that compatibility can be articulated. The vocabulary of the post-9/11 era has put an edge on the language of patriotism that sometimes makes this reconciliation difficult to finesse.

To return to the land of the Little Bighorn Battlefield National Monument—where we started our tour of Custerology in the first chapter and which sits adjacent to the Real Bird land—the construction of the new Indian Memorial is not the only alteration to the commemorative landscape that has occurred there in recent years. Since 1999, the National Park Service has been erecting red granite markers on the locations where Indian warriors are believed to have been killed in the battle. These are counterparts to the white markers, resembling small tombstones, that have stood for more than a century to show where the bodies of Custer's Seventh Cavalry were discovered. When the first two markers (for the Cheyenne warriors Lame White Man and Noisy Walking) were unveiled in 1999, they each stated underneath the individual's name: "A CHEYENNE WARRIOR DIED HERE ON JUNE 25, 1876 WHILE DEFENDING HIS HOMELAND AND HIS WAY OF LIFE." Using the language of "homeland" defense, these markers now seem prescient of the political vocabulary that dominated the United States in the years immediately after 9/11. Like the T-shirts claiming that American Indians have been "Fighting Terrorism since 1492" (mentioned in chapter 1), this language inverts the vision of the United States as the victim of armed aggression, an inversion has only become more potent and politically charged since 9/11. In fact, in 2003 the National Monument decided to change the wording of future markers in deference to a request by a Crow Indian, Patrick Hill, who worked there at that time as the lead interpreter on the Park Service staff. The Crows, Hill pointed out, believe that the land along the Little Bighorn was *their* homeland as designated by the Fort Laramie Treaty of 1868. Now the markers simply identify the casualties as having died while defending their tribal "way of life."[1] The political stakes of a word like *homeland* have become high ones, indeed.

Custerology, as I have portrayed it in this book, is a kind of linguistic dialect, a language that some Americans (including some American Indians) have chosen to describe the relationship of the present world in which they live to the past conflicts between the United States and the Indians of North America. The terrorist attacks of 2001, the U.S. response to those attacks, and the war in Iraq have not altered the vocabulary of that language so much as provided it with a new inflection, shifting its accents. A word like *homeland* means something more after 2001, even if the word was chosen two years previously. More pointedly, just as Lawrence Hart once compared what the Southern Cheyennes experienced at the Washita River in 1868 to the bombing of the Murrah Building in Okalahoma City, I have now heard a similar analogy being made between Washita and 9/11 by those who wish to emphasize the surprise and suffering that they believed were experienced by the Cheyennes and Arapahos of Black Kettle's village. The analogy can play out, however, in a very different direction as well. In his recent book on Sand Creek, Greg Michno has argued that Black Kettle "was not immune from attack" in 1864 because of the Cheyenne Dog Soldiers in his village. "Placed in a 21st Century context," Michno writes, "Black Kettle harbored terrorists."[2]

What I have come to realize in the course of writing this book is that the post-9/11 environment has served as a fertile ground for two key developments within the territory of Custerology, developments that have significant implications for the continuing relationship between the United States and American Indians. First, the intense patriotism of our moment has sharpened the complicated relationship between tribal and U.S. nationalisms. To put it another way, the apparent contradictions of Russell Means's speech at the Indian Memorial dedication—where he claimed that Indians "put American first" yet retained the right to defend their tribal sovereignty "by any means necessary"—make a kind of sense after 2001 that they might not have made before. Both the emotional call for American solidarity and the justification for the defense of one's "homeland" have been produced by the political rhetoric that has characterized the years since the 9/11 attacks. In a way, this is a new version of something older: It has long been possible for white Americans to valorize the nobility of Indians while still claiming that the entire continent should be united under the rule of a white-led United States. But 9/11 introduced a new way for American Indians to fuse the political language of tribal struggles for self-determination to the demands of the United States for its national unity. Custerology offers the perfect vehicle for this connection, because from one perspective the Battle of the Little Bighorn serves as a climactic moment in the national U.S. narrative of Manifest Destiny and from another expresses proof of the historical desire of American Indians to resist U.S. colonialism.

The second development that I believe to have emanated from the post-9/11 world is one that I have more advocated as an approach to Custerology than observed in its practice. It is the attempt to reinterpret the nineteenth-century Indian Wars as a series of political conflicts rather than cultural ones. For the last two decades, the "clash of cultures" has been the dominant paradigm for the public interpretation of the Battle of the Little Bighorn and other U.S.-Indian military conflicts. By no means do I wish to shortchange the usefulness of that model, particularly its insistence that we understand this violence within a wider historical context. But this rubric also risks repeating the nineteenth-century reasoning that this violence could not be stopped, that it was governed by an impersonal, unrelenting force that would crush Native peoples under the wheels of History. The clash of cultures replaces the struggle of civilization and savagery with a clash of putatively equal cultures, even as the rubric retains the sense of an inevitable outcome in which the decisions of individuals and institutions could have done little to change the course of events. This thinking has not been the exclusive domain of the National Park Service or white Custerologists. The Blackfeet author James Welch stated in his prologue to *Killing Custer* that the Battle of the Little Bighorn "had to take place. It was as inexorable as any showdown in a clash of cultures which has been historically brought on by the whites."[3]

Several factors have started to push Custerology away from this treatment of the Battle of the Little Bighorn—and indeed all of the conflicts of the Indian Wars—as an "inexorable" cultural event and toward regarding the battle and the series of campaigns against the Plains Indians as political events shaped by very specific decisions made by participants on all sides of the military conflicts. The most significant of the causes of this shift is the Native American intellectual resurgence that has insisted that the treaties ratified by the United States form the basis of a mutual recognition by the United States and the signatory Indian tribes as sovereign nations. Even in areas such as literary studies, American Indian intellectuals have insisted that Indian identity should be defined through the political terms of participation in a tribal nation rather than through the anthropological realm of culture. What this means is that indigenous people in the United States with increasing frequency regard their "Indianness" using a lens of tribally specific political histories. So at the Little Bighorn, in the Black Hills, and on the Washita River, the descendants of the Lakotas, Cheyennes, and Arapahos who fought the U.S. army—and even the descendants of the Crows and Arikaras who fought *with* the U.S. army—demand explanations of the history of U.S.-Indian conflict that refer to the treaties and political agreements that they believe justified their forebears' actions. It is no accident that the most recently created unit of the National Park Service discussed in this book, the Washita Battlefield National Historic Site, is also the one that makes the greatest effort to provide its visitors with information about nineteenth-century treaties in the printed materials that it distributes.

The attacks of 9/11 and the events that followed—the creation of the Department of Homeland Security, the Patriot Act, the deployment of U.S. troops to Afghanistan and Iraq—have forced all Americans to consider the relationship between military violence and politics. To say that an act of military violence is the product of politics is neither to endorse nor to criticize it. Rather, it is to situate that violence in the context of questions of governance, economics, territory. To call the al Qaeda attacks on the World Trade Center and the Pentagon political makes them no less horrific, and to call the U.S. invasion of Iraq political does not necessarily presume that one approves of it or not. Regardless of whether they approve of the actions that have been taken by the U.S. government since the 9/11 attacks, Americans are now acutely aware that those actions are political choices made by individuals in power and the organizations that they command.

What this awareness means for Custerology was first suggested to me by a comment that Steve Alexander made in an interview just weeks after the U.S. army, including the tanks of the contemporary Seventh Cavalry, entered Baghdad in April 2003. Sitting in the home that once housed George and Libbie, Alexander stated that Custer had no more control over the U.S. policy toward American Indians than the U.S. soldiers in Iraq did over the decision to invade that country.[4] In a sense, Alexander was right: Neither Custer's Seventh Cavalry in 1876 nor the twenty-first-century men and women bearing the same regimental designation possessed the power to choose one course of national policy over another. However, what I hope is emerging in Custerology is a sense of necessity of linking Custer's presence at the Little Bighorn to the policies that brought him there, just as Americans from all sides of the political spectrum rightly insist in the twenty-first century that they should understand the decisions that commit their nation's resources, including their fellow citizens, to a military conflict.

The post-9/11 landscape of violence in politics has shaped the practice of contemporary Custerology, but it may be equally significant that the language of the nineteenth-century Indian Wars continues to surface in discussions about the employment of U.S. military force across the globe. Sometimes these references to Custer and the Little Bighorn illustrate how firmly embedded in our shared consciousness the image of the Last Stand remains: "We were like Custer," Sergeant James J. Riley told newspaper reporters to describe how badly outnumbered his company was when it surrendered to Iraqi troops in Nasiriyah. "We were surrounded. We had no working weapons. We couldn't even make a bayonet charge—we would have been mowed down."[5] Riley, who was speaking on a plane as he was being evacuated immediately after his rescue by U.S. marines, may have had little time to think through the implications of the analogy he was drawing—a fact that makes his choice of comparisons all the more significant. Custer and the Little Bighorn still function as meaningful symbols when the United States goes to war, especially against peoples considered darker in both hue and civilization.

Indeed, U.S. soldiers in Iraq and Afghanistan, following the lead of their predecessors in Vietnam, continue to refer to zones of unrest and danger as "Indian Country." Arguing that "the American military is back to the days of fighting the Indians," the *Atlantic Monthly* writer Robert D. Kaplan has offered a highly influential explanation of the analogy between the U.S.-Indian military conflicts of the nineteenth century and the twenty-first-century deployment of U.S. troops to combat terrorism across the globe. "The red Indian metaphor is one with which a liberal policy nomenklatura may be uncomfortable," Kaplan wrote on the editorial page of the *Wall Street Journal* in 2004, "but Army and Marine field officers have embraced it because it captures perfectly the combat challenge of the early 21st century." As in the Indian Wars of the nineteenth century, he explained, the United States military must deploy small tactical units in hostile territory. Its engagements will be low-intensity skirmishes, involving small numbers of combatants and spilling over frequently into civilian populations, more often than full-scale battles against other professional soldiers. Like the frontier army of the nineteenth century, the U.S. military of the twenty-first will regularly incur the wrath of media and humanitarians "demanding the application of abstract principles of universal justice that, sadly, are often neither practical nor necessarily synonymous with American national self-interest."[6]

Kaplan's article—in which he insists that his comparison is not a "slight against the Native North Americans"—later became the introduction to *Imperial Grunts: The American Military on the Ground,* a book-length account of his experiences among U.S. troops deployed around the world in the "war on terror." According to Kaplan, "Indian Country" (or "Injun Country" as he sometimes calls it) is everywhere: Colombia, Mongolia, east Africa, the Philippines, Afghanistan, and, of course, Iraq. The Wild West has gone global: "The War on Terrorism was really about taming the frontier," he writes.[7] In *Imperial Grunts*—a book that the White House announced was one of two being read by President Bush during his 2005 holiday vacation—the comparison between the U.S. army of the frontier Plains and the global forces of the twenty-first century does more than present an argument for a decentralized, flexible military prepared to intervene in a range of conflicts at a moment's notice.[8] The analogy is also crucial to Kaplan's full-throated cry for Americans to continue their work of civilizing the globe. The "white man's burden" advocated by imperialists like Rudyard Kipling at the turn of the twentieth century, he explains, "meant only the righteous responsibility to advance the boundaries of free society and good government into zones of sheer chaos."[9] And the heroes of this work are the practical, plain-spoken soldiers who, as Custer claimed, understand the indigenous populations better than their intellectual Washington counterparts because of their willingness, in the words of one soldier deployed in Afghanistan, to "go a little native."[10] Kaplan writes, "As I traveled from continent to continent, . . . my most recurring image would be one that [Frederick] Remington"—the painter and sculptor of the American West—"himself might have painted: singular individuals fronting dangerous and stupendous landscapes."[11]

Kaplan is not the only one to have taken up this comparison between the nineteenth-century Indian Wars and America's most recent interventions abroad; for instance, John Brown, a former State Department official who resigned during the buildup to the Iraq War, employed the same analogy for the opposite purpose, to criticize the Bush administration's decisions to deploy the military so aggressively. In " 'Our Indian Wars Are Not Over Yet: Ten Ways to Interpret the War on Terror as a Frontier Conflict," Brown argues that the new American imperialism, like its nineteenth-century counterpart, is driven by a mistaken belief in the superiority of American "civilization" over "primitive" societies, and that it will create in Afghanistan and Iraq situations that resemble the Indian reservations of the nineteenth century, in which the indigenous populations have no independent political structure and rely on their occupiers for the administration of crucial resources.[12]

In response to Kaplan, Brown, and others, the newspaper *Indian Country Today* published an editorial in 2006 bemoaning the fact that "bad analogies from American Indian history are becoming the fad among pundits on the Middle East" and asking that they "cut it out," regardless of whether they are arguing to support the U.S. involvement abroad or to criticize it.[13] The key distinction between the nineteenth-century Indian Wars and the current military engagements of U.S. troops, according to the editors, are the treaties that both preceded and concluded the conflicts between the United States and the American Indian tribes—treaties that have no analogue in the current U.S. fight against al Qaeda, the regime of Saddam Hussein, or the Iraq insurgency that followed the demise of that regime. The newspaper's argument, which seeks to reaffirm the unique relationship between American Indian tribes and the United States, is persuasive; historical analogies of this kind, after all, only go so far. But even more instructive may be the drawing by Oglala Lakota cartoonist Marty Two Bulls Sr. that accompanied the editorial. In the cartoon, a braided Indian, drinking from a coffee mug bearing the U.S. flag, sits at a counter alongside a bearded Iraqi. "Hey, buddy," the Indian says, "you know, when they start referring to the war in Iraq using 'Old West' terms like 'cavalry,' 'Indian country' or 'treaties,' what they're really saying is . . . they want to keep your lands."[14]

Two Bulls' cartoon makes clear the significance of the analogy between the American imperialism of the nineteenth century and the new American empire of the twenty-first. Regardless of the objections of his newspaper's editors, the echoes of the earlier age of expansion will continue to be heard by Indians and non-Indians alike as Americans debate the scope and ultimate goal of U.S. military deployment. This historical connection between nineteenth-century Manifest Destiny and the exercise of U.S. power abroad has been made before, not only by historians but also in the realm of popular culture. Arthur Penn's film version of *Little Big Man,* to name one example, pointedly recasts the fighting at Washita and the Little Big Horn as an earlier version of what was taking place in another "Indian Country," Vietnam. What may be different about the twenty-first century, if books like Kaplan's are any indication, is that now the historical analogy is being drawn by proponents, and not just critics, of U.S. military intervention overseas.

The Indian Wars, in other words, have become valuable again as a historical resource for thinking about the actions of the United States on the global stage, and Custerology will serve as a medium that transforms the ungainly chaos of that history into a usable past—and usable for more than one purpose. Contemporary Custerology has been shaped by the demands of multiculturalism—tolerance, recognition, pluralism—but it is equally well suited to our age of small-scale conflicts, morally difficult questions of imperial power, and violence that cuts across the divide between the military and civilians. This suitability, in fact, may be what separates Custerology from the forms of devotion that Americans pay to its other violent conflicts: the scores of books written about the American Revolution, the films that replicate the battles of World War II, and, of course, the famous reenactors of the U.S. Civil War. Unlike those other arenas of public history, Custerology offers Americans a chance to consciously reflect on its colonial and imperial legacy and how that legacy is literally contained within its borders. Custerology now invites us to consider how the "Indian Country" abroad might be linked to the Indian Country of the North American Plains—and what those ties might mean for both the tribal populations of the United States and the reach of American power across the globe.

Recall the sentence painted on the wall of the Fire Lightning visitor center at Wounded Knee: "The Indian Wars Are Not Over." That phrase now has a double set of meanings, neither of which should be separated from the other. Just how difficult it would be to disentangle those histories might be best illustrated by another element of the 130th anniversary of the Battle of the Little Bighorn: the participation of the U.S. 10th Army Special Forces Group. The unit, which had returned to its Colorado base between tours of duty in Iraq, sent representatives to conduct parachute drops, first at a ceremony held by the Crow tribe to honor veterans and then the commemorative ceremonies held at the battlefield on the day of the anniversary. The soldiers even saluted General Custer before one of the performances of the Real Bird reenactment. On all of these occasions, Lieutenant Colonel Richard Steiner told the audiences that the Special Forces—colloquially known as the Green Berets—traced its heritage as a unit, in part, to the Indian scouts who served with the frontier army in the nineteenth century.

It seemed fitting, then, that the Crow tribe, which contributed scouts to the U.S. army at the Little Bighorn and elsewhere, would hold a ceremony in which the Special Forces soldiers were smudged with smoke to protect them in combat. This took place at the Veterans Commemorative Park constructed and dedicated by the Crows during the time that

I was researching this book; the park sits prominently by the interstate just a few miles from both the Little Bighorn Battlefield National Monument and the family ranch where the Real Birds hold their annual reenactment. Among those attending this special ceremony to honor all veterans were the relatives of Private First Class Lori Piestewa, the Hopi Indian who was the first Indian servicewoman to die in combat. Piestewa's family had been honored guests three years previously at the dedication of the Little Bighorn Indian Memorial; this time, they were joined by families of other soldiers, both Indian and non-Indian, who had been killed in Iraq and Afghanistan. Cecilia Fire Thunder, then president of the Oglala Lakota Tribe and a descendant of the Lakotas who fought both Custer's cavalry and the Crows at the Little Bighorn, praised both the resistance of her own ancestors 130 years previously and the much more recent sacrifice of the Piestewa family.[15] As in so many commemorations held on the anniversary of the Battle of the Little Bighorn, it was possible to honor both those who fought against the United States and those who fought for it. The difference this time was that the commemoration was held by a tribal nation that Custer and his contemporaries had surely believed would quickly and quietly disappear into the corporate mass of the United States in the decades after they aided America's campaign against the Lakota Sioux.

Before the course of the ceremony, Carl Venne, the chairman of the Crow tribe and a Vietnam veteran himself, presented the flag of the Crow Nation to Steiner as a kind of talisman. "You take it there in safety," he told the soldiers, referring to their redeployment to Iraq, "and while you're there, go through the turmoil without being touched, and return home with the flag unsmudged, untattered, clean. Return, and we will greet you in good health and safety."[16] It was a flag from one Indian Country to be carried into another, from the site of one century's violence to the battlefield of the new one. The gift of that flag to Steiner and his men may signal the allegiance of Venne and his tribe to the United States, but it is a flag that also represents their independence as a tribal people who claim a special status within that same nation. The Crow flag is one product of a long, continuing struggle for governance over the land of the North American Plains, and it will be carried by soldiers whose very presence in the Middle East signals their involvement in another such struggle. As it travels across the earth, that flag and its symbolic journey may say more about the significance of Custerology to the twenty-first century than anything else that I have described here. I hope that it returns intact.

ACKNOWLEDGMENTS

My research for this book has been possible only because of the gener osity of others in their willingness to speak to me about their interest in the nineteenth-century Indian Wars. Many of these people are quoted in the book, but just as many are not. Among those particularly deserving of thanks are Steve and Sandy Alexander, Tony and Joy Austin, Steven Black, Vincent A. Heier, Lawrence H. Hart, Wendy Lauritzen, Neil Magnum, Alden Miller, Chuck Merkel, Henry Real Bird, Richard Sobek, and Donovin Sprague. The staffs of both the Little Bighorn Battlefield National Monument and the Washita Battlefield National Historic Site have been enormously helpful, and I have been impressed with how thoughtfully they approach the difficulty of presenting these violent histories to the public. I received modest grants for my research from the Charles Redd Center of Brigham Young University and the Beinecke Library of Yale University. George Miles of the Beinecke deserves particular praise, as does Carl Katafiasz of the Monroe County Library; Mary Jane Warde of the Oklahoma Historical Society provided me with crucial assistance for chapter 3. Orin Starn and Frances Smith donated Custerology documents to me that had belonged to the late Warren Smith, and I am grateful to them as well. Andrew Beck Grace and Bartley Powers provided fellowship, good humor, and access to their own documentary efforts during two summers of fieldwork, and in doing so made important contributions to chapters 1 and 6.

Ashley Rye spent a year with a microfilm machine as my research assistant, and I am equally thankful for the crack team of interlibrary loan librarians at the Woodruff Library of Emory University for helping to locate and borrow that microfilm. Sarah Schiff helped me finish the book by handling all manner of research requests with skill and speed; one could not ask for an assistant with greater diligence or a better sense of humor. Sarah Peterson came to my aid to help with the proofs and index. As I drafted this book, I was fortunate enough to have friends and colleagues who read and responded to individual chapters: Renée Bergland, Kate Brown, Mark Gardner, Arnold Krupat, Joshua Miller, David Morgen, Claudia Stokes. Louise Barnett read the entire manuscript with scrupulous attention to every detail and made several key suggestions based on her own vast knowledge of Custerology. My two readers for the University of Chicago Press, Carlo Rotella and Richard Slotkin, offered indispensable commentary as well. My editor at the University of Chicago Press, Douglas Mitchell, showed faith in the book long before there was good reason to have any, and the value of his support cannot be calculated. His assistant, Tim McGovern, has also been invaluable in guiding the book through the publication process. Finally, Ruth Goring has been both diligent and good-humored in her office as manuscript editor.

No one has sacrificed more to see this book into print than Jennifer Mathews, who has been repeatedly abandoned in the summer months—and then forced to endure countless anecdotes about the world of Custerology. The time that I spent composing this book roughly coincides with the young life of our son, Gabriel. As I have been completing the manuscript, I have been intrigued by the thought that he may read it some day and inspired by the possibility that he could find reflected in its pages, somewhere, a small measure of the beauty and grace that he has brought into our lives.

NOTES

INTRODUCTION

1. *The Royal Tenenbaums*, DVD, directed by Wes Anderson, 2001 (Burbank, CA: Touchstone Pictures, 2002).

2. *Smoke Signals*, DVD, directed by Chris Eyre, 1998 (Burbank, CA: Miramax Pictures, 1999). See also the original screenplay version of the scene in Sherman Alexie, *Smoke Signals* (New York: Hyperion, 1998), 17–18.

3. David A. Hollinger, *Cosmopolitanism and Solidarity: Studies in Ethnoracial, Religious, and Professional Affiliation in the United States* (Madison: University of Wisconsin Press, 2006), 180–84.

4. Edward Tabor Linenthal, *Sacred Ground: Americans and Their Battlefields* (Urbana: University of Illinois Press, 1991), 63.

5. Richard Slotkin, *The Fatal Environment: The Myth of the Frontier in the Age of Industrialization* (New York: Atheneum, 1985), esp. 433–76 and the discussion of Vietnam at 16–17. Custer and the Last Stand also figure in Slotkin's subsequent volume, *Gunfighter Nation: The Myth of the Frontier in Twentieth-Century America* (New York: Atheneum, 1992).

6. Evan S. Connell, *Son of the Morning Star* (San Francisco: North Point, 1984); Robert M. Utley, *Cavalier in Buckskin: George Armstrong Custer and the Western Military Frontier* (Norman: University of Oklahoma Press, 1988); Louise Barnett, *Touched by Fire: The Life, Death, and Mythic Afterlife of George Armstrong Custer* (New York: Henry Holt, 1996); Jeffry D. Wert, *Custer: The Controversial Life of George Armstrong Custer* (New York: Simon and Schuster, 1996).

7. *Dances with Wolves*, video, directed by Kevin Costner, 1993 (New York: Orion Pictures, 1990).

8. Michael Blake, *Marching to Valhalla: A Novel of Custer's Last Days* (New York: Villard, 1996).

9. Richard Nixon, "Special Message to the Congress on Indian Affairs," July 8, 1970, in *Public Papers of the Presidents of the United States: Richard Nixon, 1970* (Washington, DC: Government Printing Office, 1974), 564.

10. David E. Wilkins and K. Tsianina Lomawaima, *Uneven Ground: American Indian Sovereignty and Federal Law* (Norman: University of Oklahoma Press, 2001), 250. In addition to this volume, useful resources on tribal sovereignty include David E. Wilkins,

American Indian Sovereignty and the U.S. Supreme Court: The Masking of Justice (Austin: University of Texas Press, 1997), and Vine Deloria Jr. and Clifford M. Lytle, *The Nations Within: The Past and Future of American Indian Sovereignty* (New York: Pantheon, 1984). For a brief bibliography on the topic, see Charles F. Wilkinson and Anna Nikole Ulrich, "Annotated Bibliography of the Basic Literature Needed for an Understanding of Tribal Governance," *Wicazo Sa Review* 17, no. 1 (Spring 2002): 7–12.

11. Vine Deloria Jr., "Intellectual Self-Determination and Sovereignty: Looking at the Windmills in Our Minds," *Wicazo Sa Review* 13, no. 1 (Spring 1998): 26–27. Interestingly, Deloria asserts here that sovereignty has been too widely deployed in recent years, "having lost its political moorings and now . . . adrift on the currents of individual fancy."

12. Charles Wilkinson, *Blood Struggle: The Rise of Modern Indian Nations* (New York: W. W. Norton, 2005), 207. Wilkinson's book also gives a brief but quite useful overview of what Indian gaming has meant for Indian Country as a whole (rather than focusing, as most accounts do, on the wealth generated by the top Indian casinos). See 329–51.

13. Deloria and Lytle make this point in *Nations Within*, 237. They contrast the "ethnic" Indian basis of this late-1960s activism with the emphasis on tribal affiliation that emerged in the early 1970s; they name the 1972 March on Washington as the turning point.

14. Kerwin Lee Klein, "On the Emergence of *Memory* in Historical Discourse," *Representations* 69 (2000): 127.

15. Barry Schwartz, *Abraham Lincoln and the Forge of National Memory* (Chicago: University of Chicago Press, 2000), 10.

16. Maurice Halbwachs, *On Collective Memory*, edited and translated by Lewis A. Coser (Chicago: University of Chicago Press, 1992), esp. 53.

17. Klein discusses the way that "memory" has been opposed to "history" at much greater length in "On the Emergence of *Memory*," 127–50.

18. Jacques Le Goff, *History and Memory*, translated by Steven Rendall and Elizabeth Claman (New York: Columbia University Press, 1992), 19, 95.

19. Nora writes, in a sentence that I will quote again in chapter 6: "Unlike historical objects, *lieux de mémoire* have no referents in reality; or, rather, they are their own referents—pure signs. "General Introduction: Between Memory and History," in Pierre Nora, gen. ed., *Realms of Memory: Rethinking the French Past*, vol. 1, *Conflicts and Divisions*, English-language edition edited by Lawrence D. Kritzman, translated by Arthur Goldhammer (New York: Columbia University Press, 1996), 17, 19.

20. Linenthal, *Sacred Ground*, and *The Unfinished Bombing: Oklahoma City in American Memory* (New York: Oxford University Press, 2001); Richard Handler and Eric Gable, *The New History in an Old Museum: Creating the Past at Colonial Williamsburg* (Durham, NC: Duke University Press, 1997).

CHAPTER ONE

1. Sherman Alexie, "Ghost Dance," in *McSweeney's Mammoth Treasury of Thrilling Tales*, edited by Michael Chabon (New York: Vintage, 2003), 342–43.

2. Unless otherwise noted, information about the dedication of the Indian Memorial comes from my observations and interviews conducted on June 25, 2003. I have also used the following newspaper accounts to corroborate mine: Lorna Thackeray, "Completing the Circle," *Billings Gazette*, June 26, 2003, 1A, 12A; Gwen Florio, "Balance at Little Bighorn," *Denver Post*, June 26, 2003, 1A, 10A; Andrew Metz, "A Struggle for History," *Newsday* (New York), June 26, 2003, A7; James B. Meadow, "Honor to All the Fallen Warriors," *Rocky Mountain News* (Denver), June 26, 2003, 22A; Brian Maffly, "Healing Wounds," *Salt Lake City Tribune*, June 26, 2003, A1, A5.

3. Russell Means interview with Andrew Grace and Bartley Powers, June 25, 2003. Quoted courtesy of Amalgamation Films.

4. For a chronology of the Battle of the Little Bighorn, I have relied on Gregory S. Michno, *Lakota Noon: The Indian Narrative of Custer's Defeat* (Missoula, MT: Mountain, 1997), and John S. Gray, *Centennial Campaign: The Sioux War of 1876* (1976; rpt. Norman: University of Oklahoma Press, 1988), esp. 298–307.

5. This point proves confusing for most modern readers: Custer was promoted during this Civil War within the volunteer army and then also received an honorary rank, or "brevet rank," of major general within the *regular* army. However, after the Civil War, he reverted to his rank of captain in the regular army.

6. Gray, *Centennial Campaign,* 151.

7. Quoted in John G. Niehardt, *Black Elk Speaks* (1932; rpt. Lincoln: University of Nebraska Press, 1988), 123.

8. Michno discusses these estimates in *Lakota Noon,* 6–12.

9. Fred H. Cate, Dennis H. Long, and David C. Williams, eds., *The Court-Martial of George Armstrong Custer* (Bloomington: Indiana University School of Law at Bloomington, 2001), 89. The "court" later announced a sentence that dismissed Custer from the United States army (101).

10. *Wooden Leg: A Warrior Who Fought Custer,* interpreted by Thomas B. Marquis (1931; rpt. Lincoln: University of Nebraska Press, 1957), 237–38 (on rumors of mass suicide); Orin G. Libby, ed., *The Arikara Narrative of Custer's Campaign and the Battle of the Little Bighorn* (Norman: University of Oklahoma Press, 1998), 58, 62 (on Custer's rumored political ambitions); Mark Gardner, foreword to Charles J. Brill, *Custer, Black Kettle, and the Fight on the Washita* (1938; rpt. Norman: University of Oklahoma Press, 2001), 9, and Brill's text, 38, and Mari Sandoz, *Cheyenne Autumn* (New York: McGraw-Hill, 1953), 21, 273 (on Custer's possible Cheyenne son).

11. Elizabeth B. Custer, *"Boots and Saddles," or Life in Dakota with General Custer* (1885; rpt. Norman: University of Oklahoma Press, 1961), 178.

12. Henry Wadsworth Longfellow, *Poems and Other Writings,* edited by J. D. McClatchy (New York: Library of America, 2000), 649.

13. "President Grant: A Free Talk on Questions of the Day," *New York Herald,* September 2, 1876, 2.

14. "Custer's Massacre," *New York Herald,* July 8, 1876, 6.

15. Louis S. Warren, *Buffalo Bill's America: William Cody and the Wild West Show* (New York: Alfred A. Knopf, 2005), 264.

16. The classic study of this dichotomy is Roy Harvey Pearce, *Savagism and Civilization: A Study of the Indian and the American Mind* (1953; rpt. Berkeley: University of California Press, 1988). More recent works on this topic include Susan Scheckel, *The Insistence of the Indian: Race and Nationalism in Nineteenth-Century American Culture* (Princeton, NJ: Princeton University Press, 1998), and Shari M. Huhndorf, *Going Native: Indians in the American Cultural Imagination* (Ithaca, NY: Cornell University Press, 2001).

17. George Armstrong Custer, *My Life on the Plains, or Personal Experiences with Indians* (1874; rpt. Norman: University of Oklahoma Press, 1962), 22.

18. Paul Andrew Hutton, "From Little Bighorn to Little Big Man: The Changing Image of a Western Hero in Popular Culture," in *The Custer Reader,* edited by Paul Andrew Hutton (Lincoln: University of Nebraska Press, 1992), 400.

19. Walt Whitman, *Poetry and Prose,* edited by Justin Kaplan (New York: Library of America, 1982), 593. (Whitman later changed the title of the poem to "From Far Dakota's Cañons.")

20. Ibid., 910.

21. Thodore W. Goldin, "The Benteen-Goldin Letters," in *The Custer Myth,* edited by W. A. Graham (1953; rpt. Mechanicsburg, PA: Stackpole, 2000), 189–211. A more complete record of Benteen's correspondence about Custer is in John M. Carroll, ed., *The Benteen-Goldin Letters on Custer and His Last Battle* (1974; rpt. Lincoln: University of Nebraska Press, 1991).

22. Theodore W. Goldin to Albert W. Johnson, July 28, 1928, in *Benteen-Goldin Letters,* ed. Carroll, 14.

23. I refer to Walter Camp, E. A. Brininstool, John S. Gray, and Lawrence A. Frost.

24. Brian W. Dippie, *Custer's Last Stand: The Anatomy of an American Myth* (1976; rpt. Lincoln: University of Nebraska Press, 1994), has been a crucial source to me in following the history of Custerology during its first century.

25. Robert Taft, "The Pictorial Record of the Old West: Custer's Last Stand—John Mulvany, Cassily Adams, and Otto Becker," in *Custer Reader,* ed. Hutton, 439−42.

26. L. G. Moses, *Wild West Shows and the Images of American Indians, 1883−1933* (Albuquerque: University of New Mexico Press, 1996), 35; Warren, *Buffalo Bill's America,* 268, 270. Warren contends, persuasively, that historians have overstated the importance of "Custer's Last Rally" to the Wild West show. Not only was the scene featured in the show only sporadically after it was introduced in 1887, but it was not always situated as the climax.

27. Frederick F. Van de Water, *Glory-Hunter: A Life of General Custer* (Indianapolis: Bobbs-Merrill, 1934).

28. For much more complete discussions of Custer in film and television, see Paul Andrew Hutton, "'Correct in Every Detail': General Custer in Hollywood," in *Legacy: New Perspectives on the Battle of the Little Bighorn,* edited by Charles E. Rankin (Helena, MT: Montana Historical Society Press, 1996), 231−70; Dippie, *Custer's Last Stand,* 96−124; and John Philip Langellier, *Custer: The Man, the Myth, the Movies* (Mechanicsburg, PA: Stackpole, 2000).

29. Robert M. Utley, *Cavalier in Buckskin: George Armstrong Custer and the Western Military Frontier* (Norman: University of Oklahoma Press, 1988).

30. Sherman Alexie, "Custer Speaks," in *Old Shirts and New Skins* (Los Angeles: American Indian Studies Center, University of California−Los Angeles, 1996), 38.

31. Harold G. Moore and Joseph L. Galloway, We *Were Soldiers Once . . . and Young: Ia Drang, the Battle That Changed the War in Vietnam* (New York: Random House, 1992), 24−25.

32. *We Were Soldiers,* DVD, directed by Randall Wallace, 2002 (Hollywood: Paramount Pictures, 2002).

33. The sole exception was Lt. John Crittenden, whose remains were left at the battlefield at the request of his father. Dutch [Richard G.] Hardoff, "Burials, Exhumations, and Reinterments: A View of Custer Hill," in *Custer and His Times,* bk. 2 (Ft. Worth, TX: Little Big Horn Associates, 1984), 41−83.

34. Don Rickey Jr., *History of Custer Battlefield* (Billings, MT: Custer Battlefield Historical and Museum Association, 1967), 29, 51, 88, 90.

35. Douglas McChristian provides an overview of the anniversary celebrations in "Burying the Hatchet: The Semicentennial of the Little Bighorn," *Montana: The Magazine of Western History* 46, no. 2 (Summer 1996): 50−65. Another excellent resource on the anniversaries, which became available only as I was completing this manuscript, is Richard Upton, *The Battle of the Little Big Horn and Custer's Last Fight: Remembered by Participants at the Tenth Anniversary, June 25, 1886, and the Fiftieth Anniversary, June 25, 1926* (El Segundo, CA: Upton and Sons, 2006), a collection of newspaper articles, photographs, and other documents relating to these two anniversary commemorations.

36. See the newspaper articles and the account by Edward S. Godfrey in *Custer Myth,* ed. Graham, 87−96.

37. While other sources discuss the 1916 commemorative ceremonies, the only reference I have found for the "Peace and Reconciliation" theme is the pamphlet produced by the National Park Service for the 2003 Indian Memorial Dedication: *"Peace through Unity": Indian Memorial Dedication* (Crow Agency, MT: Little Bighorn National Monument, 2003), 8. On the 1913 celebration at Gettysburg, see Cecilia Elizabeth O'Leary, "Blood Brotherhood: The Racialization of Patriotism, 1865−1918," in *Bonds of Affection:*

Americans Define Their Patriotism, edited by John Bodnar (Princeton, NJ: Princeton University Press, 1996), 77–78.

38. Edward Tabor Linenthal, *Sacred Ground: Americans and Their Battlefields* (Urbana: University of Illinois Press, 1991), 136.

39. M. E. Hawkins, "The Burial of the Hatchet," in *The Custer Semi-centennial Ceremonies* (Casper, WY: Casper Printing and Stationery, 1926), 42.

40. Ibid., 45, 43.

41. Ibid., 43, 44.

42. Edward Lazarus, *Black Hills/White Justice: The Sioux Nation versus the United States, 1775 to the Present* (New York: HarperCollins, 1991), 138–49.

43. Mario Gonzalez and Elizabeth Cook-Lynn, *The Politics of Hallowed Ground: Wounded Knee and the Struggle for Indian Sovereignty* (Urbana: University of Illinois Press, 1999), 3–7; see also Elizabeth Cook-Lynn's review of *Black Hills/White Justice* by Edward Lazarus, *Wicazo Sa Review* 8, no. 1 (Spring 1992): 102, 101.

44. Vine Deloria Jr., *Custer Died for Your Sins* (1969; rpt. Norman: University of Oklahoma Press, 1988), 148.

45. Michael J. Koury, introduction to *Custer Centennial Observance,* edited by Koury (Fort Collins, CO: Old Army Press, 1978), 7–25; Linenthal, *Sacred Ground,* 143–46; Utley, *Cavalier in Buckskin,* 11.

46. An invaluable resource on these conflicts is the *Little Big Horn Associates Newsletter.* See, for instance, John M. Carroll's letter in vol. 11, no. 5 (May 1977), 4 (on the Black Elk quotation), and the "special report" and letters in vol. 19, no. 4 (April 1985), on the visitor center bookstore.

47. James Hagengruber, "Built out of Protest," *Billings Gazette,* June 25, 2003, 12A.

48. Linenthal, *Sacred Ground,* 159.

49. Frank Del Olmo, "Activists' Plaque at Little Bighorn Honors 'Patriots' Who Beat Custer," *Los Angeles Times,* July 4, 1988, 24; also quoted in Linenthal, *Sacred Ground.*

50. *Congressional Record,* 101nd Cong., 2nd sess., 1990, 136, no. 114, H7675.

51. *Congressional Record,* 102nd Cong., 1st sess., 1991, 137, no. 26, E494.

52. "Conflict Emerges over Custer Park," *New York Times,* October 11, 1991, 37.

53. Senate Committee on Energy and Natural Resources, *Little Bighorn Battlefield National Monument,* 102nd Cong., 1st sess., 1991, 102 S. Rpt. 173, accessed at Lexis Nexis, September 23, 2005.

54. *Congressional Record,* 102nd Cong., 1st sess., 1991, 137, no. 98, H4895–96.

55. "Conflict Emerges," 37; and see the letters in the *Little Big Horn Associates Newsletter* 25, no. 5 (September 1991): esp. 7–8.

56. Brice C. Custer, *The Sacrificial Lion, George Armstrong Custer: From American Hero to Media Villain* (El Segundo, CA: Upton and Sons, 1999), 11.

57. Don Schwarck, "Sundance Closes Battlefield Roadway," *Little Big Horn Associates Newsletter* 26, no. 6 (August 1992): 2.

58. Wayne M. Sarf and William P. Wells, "End the Racist Regime: A Call for the Dismissal of Gerard Baker," *Custer/Little Bighorn Battlefield Advocate* 3, no. 2 (Summer 1996): 1–2.

59. Bill Wells, "Little Bighorn Diary," *Little Big Horn Associates Newsletter* 25, no. 4 (May 1991): 4.

60. Maffly, "Healing Wounds," A5, and my interviews. Another of the controversial features of Cutschall's sculpture is the inclusion of a woman aiding the warriors, which some Indian men believe to be an inaccurate representation of the battlefield. Cutschall's own statement on this feature can be found at www.sisterwolf.com/sculpture/lastrider .html (accessed March 26, 2004).

61. Sandy Barnard, *Digging into Custer's Last Stand,* 3rd ed. (Terre Haute, IN: AST Press, 2004), 179–80. Barnard's book includes his own thorough account of the Indian Memorial dedication.

62. Thackeray, "Completing the Circle," A1.

63. See, for instance, Russel Lawrence Barsh, "War and the Reconfiguring of American Indian Society," *Journal of American Studies* 35 (2001): 371–410; Alison R. Bernstein, *American Indians and World War II* (Norman: University of Oklahoma, 1991).

64. The Crow man was Richard Real Bird, who was speaking at the reenactment of the Battle of the Little Bighorn that his family sponsors each year.

65. See, generally, Frederick E. Hoxie, *A Final Promise: The Campaign to Assimilate the Indians, 1880–1920* (Lincoln: University of Nebraska Press, 1984).

66. Kenneth E. Foote, *Shadowed Ground: America's Landscapes of Violence and Tragedy*, rev. ed. (Austin: University of Texas Press, 2003), 322.

67. On the commemoration of Vietnam, an excellent starting point is Marita Sturken, *Tangled Memories: The Vietnam War, the AIDS Epidemic, and the Politics of Remembering* (Berkeley: University of California Press, 1997), 44–144.

68. The Omnibus Parks and Public Lands Management Act of 1996 directs the National Park Service to "provide opportunities for American Indian groups including the Cheyenne-Arapaho Tribe to be involved in the formulation of plans and educational programs for the national historic site" (Public Law 104-333, 104th Congress, sec. 607). The Sand Creek Massacre National Historic Site Establishment Act of 2000 is even more explicit in instructing the Park Service to accommodate the needs of descendants from tribes that suffered in the massacre (Public Law 106-465, 106th Congress).

69. Richard R. Flores, *Remembering the Alamo: Memory, Modernity, and the Master Symbol* (Austin: University of Texas, 2002), 1–12.

70. *The Alamo*, directed by John Lee Hancock (Burbank, CA: Touchstone Pictures, 2004).

71. Wolfgang Schivelbusch, *The Culture of Defeat: On National Trauma, Mourning, and Recovery*, translated by Jefferson Chase (New York: Henry Holt, 2003), 31.

72. Ibid., 100.

73. Hawkins, "Burial of the Hatchet," 42.

74. The speaker was Leland Spotted Bird of the Fort Peck Reservation in Montana.

75. Robert M. Utley, *The Lance and the Shield: The Life and Times of Sitting Bull* (New York: Henry Holt, 1993), 248–80.

76. Perhaps just as telling is George W. Bush's response to a question about tribal sovereignty at a convention for journalists of color in August 2004: "Tribal sovereignty," Bush said, "means just that; it's sovereign. You're a—you've been given sovereignty, and you're viewed as a sovereign entity. And, therefore, the relationship between the federal government and tribes is one between sovereign entities." Critics seized on Bush's stumbling delivery (a video clip even circulated on the Internet) and, more substantively, his misunderstanding of tribal sovereignty, which tribal advocates consider to be recognized rather than "given" by the United States. I find it equally telling, however, that Bush understood that he should valorize the concept of tribal sovereignty, even though he evidenced little understanding of its legal and political dimensions (Lewis Kamb, "Bush's Comment on Tribal Sovereignty Creates a Buzz," *Seattle Post-Intelligencer*, August 13, 2004; available at http://seattlepi.nwsource.com/national/186171_bushtribes13.html [accessed August 30, 2004]).

77. Ernest LaPointe, Little Bighorn Battlefield National Monument, June 25, 2005.

78. Catherine A. Corman, "9/11 and Acoma Pueblo," *Common-Place* 5, no. 1 (October 2004), www.common-place.org/pastimes/200408.shtml (accessed January 15, 2005).

CHAPTER TWO

1. Richard Slotkin, *The Fatal Environment: The Myth of the Frontier in the Age of Industrialization, 1800–1890* (New York: Atheneum, 1985); see also Bruce A. Rosenberg, *Custer and the Epic of Defeat* (University Park: Pennsylvania State University Press, 1974),

as well as Philip J. Deloria's comments about the importance of the defensive stand to U.S.-Indian relations in *Indians in Unexpected Places* (Lawrence: University Press of Kansas, 2004), 20.

2. W. S. Penn, *Feathering Custer* (Lincoln: University of Nebraska Press, 2001).

3. In this chapter, I rely heavily on three biographies of Custer: Louise Barnett, *Touched by Fire: The Life, Death, and Mythic Afterlife of George Armstrong Custer* (New York: Henry Holt, 1996); Jeffry D. Wert, *Custer: The Controversial Life of George Armstrong Custer* (New York: Simon and Schuster, 1996); and Robert M. Utley, *Cavalier in Buckskin* (Norman: University of Oklahoma Press, 1988). In addition, I am deeply indebted to Gregory J. W. Urwin's history of Custer's Civil War career, *Custer Victorious* (East Brunswick, NJ: Associated University Presses, 1983).

4. *They Died with Their Boots On*, videocassette, directed by Raoul Walsh, 1941 (Culver City, CA: MGM/UA Home Video, 1990).

5. Gregory J. W. Urwin, preface to Frederick Whittaker, *A Complete Life of General George A. Custer*, 2 vols. (1876; rpt. Lincoln: University of Nebraska Press, 1993), 1:xiv-xx.

6. The entire proceedings of the Reno Court of Inquiry are available in Ron Nichols, comp., *Reno Court of Inquiry: Proceedings of a Court of Inquiry in the Case of Major Marcus A. Reno*, 2nd ed. (Hardin, MT: Custer Battlefield and Historical Museum Association, 1996). For a much briefer account, see Barnett, *Touched by Fire*, 310–18.

7. Whittaker, *Complete Life*, 1:5.

8. Ibid., 1:17.

9. Ibid., 1:9–10.

10. Ibid., 1:33.

11. Ibid., 1:106.

12. Ibid., 1:169.

13. "The Massacre," *New York Herald*, July 7, 1865, 5.

14. Slotkin, *Fatal Environment*, 454–55. I am also indebted to Susan Lee Johnson's attention to Slotkin on this point in "'A Memory Sweet to Soldiers': The Significance of Gender in the History of the 'American West,'" *Western Historical Quarterly* 24 (1993): 507–8. As Johnson observes, *masculinity* and *femininity* were fluid terms during this period, and a person like Custer could rely on a kind of manliness that would no longer be possible in the twentieth century.

15. On the terms *manhood* and *masculine* in the late-nineteenth-century United States, see Gail Bederman, *Manliness and Civilization: A Cultural History of Gender and Race in the United States, 1880–1917* (Chicago: University of Chicago Press, 1995), 17–20.

16. Kenneth Kidd, *Making American Boys: Boyology and the Feral Tale* (Minneapolis: University of Minnesota Press, 2004), 60.

17. Johnson, "Memory Sweet to Soldiers," 498; for a broader discussion of ways that masculinity developed into less fluid configurations at the turn of the twentieth century, see Bederman, *Manliness and Civilization*, esp. 1–44, as well as E. Anthony Rotundo, *American Manhood: Transformations in Masculinity from the Revolution to the Modern Era* (New York: Basic Books, 1993), generally.

18. Bederman, *Manliness and Civilization*, 178–96.

19. Whittaker, *Complete Life*, 1:38. The quotation also appears in George Armstrong Custer, *Custer in the Civil War: His Unfinished Memoirs*, compiled and edited by John M. Carroll (San Rafael, CA: Presidio, 1977), 83. Carroll's volume collects the reports that Custer wrote during the Civil War and the series of articles he wrote to compose a memoir that remained unfinished at the time of his death.

20. Elizabeth B. Custer, *"Boots and Saddles," or Life in Dakota with General Custer* (1885; rpt. Norman: University of Oklahoma Press, 1961), 72.

21. Utley, *Cavalier in Buckskin*, 6.

22. For instance, Jenny Thompson's study of twentieth-century war reenactors, *War*

Games: Inside the World of Twentieth-Century War Reenactors (Washington, DC: Smithsonian Books, 2004), notes that few who participate in that hobby express an interest in discussing the larger political forces that generated the wars they portray. Tony Horwitz's more anecdotal *Confederates in the Attic: Dispatches from the Unfinished Civil War* (New York: Pantheon, 1998) suggests something similar about Civil War reenactors.

23. Margaret Merington, ed., *The Custer Story: The Life and Letters of General George A. Custer and His Wife Elizabeth* (1950; rpt. New York: Barnes and Noble Books, 1994), 66.

24. Ibid., 57.

25. William J. McCulloch, "G. A. Custer Not the Youngest General," *Little Big Horn Associates Newsletter* 2, no. 7 (July 1968): 3–4. For instance, Charles Cleveland Dodge, born September 16, 1841, was promoted to the general's rank on November 29, 1862, at twenty-one years of age. Later, in 1865, Galusha Pennypacker would be promoted to general at the age of twenty.

26. Urwin, *Custer Victorious*, 68.

27. J. H. Kidd, *Riding with Custer: Recollections of a Cavalryman in the Civil War* (1908; rpt. Lincoln: University of Nebraska Press, 1997), 129.

28. Whittaker, *Complete Life*, 1:169.

29. Frederic F. Van DeWater, *Glory-Hunter: A Life of General Custer* (Indianapolis: Bobbs-Merrill, 1934), 57.

30. Wert, *Custer*, 83.

31. Theodore Lyman, *Meade's Headquarters, 1863–1865*, selected and edited by George R. Agassiz (Boston: Atlantic Monthly, 1922), 17.

32. George B. Sanford, *Fighting Rebels and Redskins: Experiences in Army Life of Colonel George B. Sanford, 1861–1892*, edited by E. R. Hagemann (Norman: University of Oklahoma Press, 1969); quoted in Urwin, *Custer Victorious*, 58.

33. References to Michiganders as "wolverines" date at least to the 1830s. Willis F. Dunbar, *Michigan: A History of the Wolverine State*, revised by George S. May (Grand Rapids, MI: Eerdmans, 1980), 256, 752n3.

34. Whittaker reproduces this report verbatim in his *Complete Life*, 1:177–78.

35. The artist was James E. Taylor of *Frank Leslie's Illustrated Newspaper*; quoted in Urwin, *Custer Victorious*, 51.

36. James Harvey Kidd, letter, June 3, 1864, in *One of Custer's Wolverines: The Civil War Letters of Brevet Brigadier General James H. Kidd, Sixth Michigan Cavalry*, edited by Eric J. Wittenberg (Kent, OH: Kent State University Press, 2000), 88.

37. *Harper's Weekly*, March 19, 1864, 1; "Sheridan's Victory," *New York Times*, October 27, 1864, p. 2.

38. Merington, *Custer Story*, 91; letter from Elizabeth to Mr. and Mrs. Bacon, April 1864.

39. Urwin, *Custer Victorious*, 276.

40. Wittenberg, ed., *One of Custer's Wolverines*, 189.

41. Quoted in "The Heroes of the Custer Tie," in *Bards of the Little Bighorn*, edited by Brian W. Dippie and John M. Carroll (Bryan, TX: Guidon, 1978), 287.

42. Albert Barnitz, "With Custer at Appomattox," *By Valor and Arms* 2, no. 1 (Fall 1975): 38.

43. Ibid., 39.

44. Wert, *Custer*, 223.

45. Merington, *Custer Story*, 158–59.

46. Lawrence A. Frost, *General Custer's Libbie* (Seattle: Superior, 1976), 131.

47. "From the Shenandoah Valley," *New York Daily Tribune*, August 22, 1864, 6; quoted in Urwin, *Custer Victorious*, 36.

48. Nina Silber uses the phrase for her book title: *The Romance of Reunion: Northerners*

and the South, 1865–1900 (Chapel Hill: North Carolina University Press, 1993); for a more complete treatment of postbellum reconciliation, see David Blight, *Race and Reunion: The Civil War in American Memory* (Cambridge, MA: Harvard University Press, 2001).

49. Quoted in Elizabeth Bacon Custer, *The Civil War Memories of Elizabeth Bacon Custer: Reconstructed from Her Diaries and Notes,* edited by Arlene Reynolds (Austin: University of Texas Press, 1994), 161.

50. Ibid., 160–62; Lawrence A. Frost, *Custer Legends* (Bowling Green, OH: Bowling Green University Popular Press, 1981), 123–25; Whittaker, *Complete Life,* 1:314.

51. Van de Water, *Glory-Hunter,* 126.

52. Talcott E. Wing, *History of Monroe County, Michigan* (New York: Munsell, 1890), 86–87.

53. Frost's chapter "Custer Slept Here" (in *Custer Legends,* 7–35) gives an overview of George Custer's relationship to the city.

54. Shirley A. Leckie, *Elizabeth Bacon Custer and the Making of a Myth* (Norman: University of Oklahoma Press, 1993), 226–27. The two quotations come from Leckie as well; the first is from the *Detroit Free Press,* the second from Elizabeth Bacon Custer to Vinnie Ream (Hoxie), March 15, 1880.

55. Leckie, *Elizabeth Bacon Custer,* 233–35.

56. Frost, *Custer Legends,* 32–33; Leckie, *Elizabeth Bacon Custer,* 294–95; Barnett, *Touched by Fire,* 386–387.

57. Tom O'Neil, *Dr. Lawrence A. Frost: A Fond Remembrance* (Brooklyn, NY: Arrow and Trooper, 1991), 2–5; Elisa Tomaszewki, "Custer Authority Frost Dies," *Monroe Evening News,* August 15, 1990, 1A, 12A; "Biographical Sketch of Lawrence A. Frost," n.d., genealogy files, Monroe County Library, Monroe, MI.

58. O'Neil, *Dr. Lawrence A. Frost,* 43. See O'Neil's volume for other testimonies to Frost's influence.

59. Frost, *Custer Legends,* 34.

60. Dick and Jeannie Micka, two Monroe residents who have been deeply active in the preservation of local history, were extraordinarily generous with their time when I first visited Monroe in April 2003; Dick told me the story about the pranks played on the statue.

61. Statistics such as this one are available at http://factfinder.census.gov. It is worth pointing out that because the current census allows individuals to identify their own affiliation, it does not state how many of these people are enrolled members of tribes or whether those tribes were once based in present-day Michigan.

62. Charles E. Cleland, *Rites of Conquest: The History and Culture of Michigan's Native Americans* (Ann Arbor: University of Michigan Press, 1992), 172–73.

63. Kevin Merrill, "Bone Find: It's a Woman . . . and a Man," *Monroe Evening News,* July 2, 1990, 3A; Kevin Merrill, "Burial Ceremony Planned for Sept. 13 for Lotus Fountain Bones," *Monroe Evening News,* August 10, 1990, 3A.

64. Author telephone interview with Matthew Switlick, May 6, 2003; Switlick was the director of the museum and the Monroe County Historical Society at that time.

65. Frost, *Custer Legends,* 8.

66. Utley, *Custer in Buckskin,* 18; Wert, *Custer,* 46, 65.

67. Interview with Switlick.

68. George Armstrong Custer, *My Life on the Plains, or Personal Experiences with Indians* (Norman: University of Oklahoma Press, 1962), 22.

69. Custer, *My Life on the Plains,* 22–23.

70. Sherry L. Smith points out that other officers shared Custer's stated preference for those tribes who engaged in active warfare rather than lived on reservations: *The View from Officers' Row: Army Perceptions of Western Indians* (Tucson: University of Arizona, 1990), 37.

71. Custer, *My Life on the Plains,* 21.

72. Philip J. Deloria, *Playing Indian* (New Haven, CT: Yale University Press, 1998), 186, 184.

73. Deloria discusses the rise of boy camps, particularly the role of Ernest Thompson Seton in founding the Woodcraft Indians and the Boy Scouts; see *Playing Indian,* especially 95–127.

74. Ralf Henricksen, *Romance of Monroe,* oil on canvas, 1938.

75. Reprinted in Ernest Lisle Reedstrom, *Bugles, Banners, and War Bonnets* (Caldwell, ID: Caxton, 1977), 311.

76. Author interview with Steve and Sandy Alexander, April 26, 2003, Monroe, MI. Subsequent quotations come from this interview, though I have also relied on follow-up conversations that I have had with the Alexanders.

77. I witnessed Steve Alexander perform this monologue for the annual meeting of the Little Big Horn Associates, Lawrence, KS, July 24, 2003.

78. Marita Sturken makes the point that Vietnam War films of the 1980s and 1990s "have a recurring theme of Americans fighting not the North Vietnamese Army or the Vietcong but themselves." Therefore, these films work to absolve Americans for their treatment of Vietnam veterans but have little to say about the violence enacted against the Vietnamese. *Tangled Memories: The Vietnam War, the AIDS Epidemic, and the Politics of Remembering* (Berkeley: University of California Press, 1997), 104, cf. 121.

79. "Presidential Inaugural Parade 2005," *Little Big Horn Associates Newsletter* 39, no. 2 (March 2005): 8; "Hoven Announces North Dakota Float for Presidential Inaugural Parade," press release, January 19, 2005, www.governor.state.nd.us/media/news -releases/2005/01/050119.html, accessed March 29, 2005; James MacPherson, "His Horse Is Thunder Is Elected," *Bismarck Tribune,* September 30, 2005, www.bismarcktribune .com/articles/2005/09/30/news/state/102979.txt, accessed December 2, 2005. The other figures portrayed on the float were Sekakawea (or Sacajawea), Meriwether Lewis, William Clark, and Theodore Roosevelt.

CHAPTER THREE

1. Jeffry D. Wert, *Custer: The Controversial Life of George Armstrong Custer* (New York: Simon and Schuster, 1996), 241–3.

2. Louise Barnett, *Touched by Fire: The Life, Death, and Mythic Afterlife of George Armstrong Custer* (New York: Henry Holt, 1996), 126.

3. Ibid., 127–44; Minnie Dobbs Millbrook, "The West Breaks in General Custer," in *The Custer Reader,* edited by Paul A. Hutton (Lincoln: University of Nebraska Press, 1992), 116–58.

4. I have largely followed the account of the fighting (and the campaign preceding it) set out in Jerome A. Greene, *Washita: The U.S. Army and the Southern Cheyennes, 1867–1869* (Norman: University of Oklahoma Press, 2004). In addition, I have consulted Stan Hoig, *The Battle of the Washita* (1976; rpt. Lincoln: University of Nebraska Press, 1979), and Charles J. Brill, *Custer, Black Kettle, and the Fight on the Washita* (originally published as *Conquest of the Southern Plains,* 1938), foreword by Mark L. Gardner (Norman: University of Oklahoma Press, 2002).

A book that appeared just as I was completing this one will be indispensable to future writers on Washita: Richard G. Hardorff, comp. and ed., *Washita Memories: Eyewitness Views of Custer's Attack on Black Kettle's Village* (Norman: University of Oklahoma Press, 2006). Many of the accounts that I quote in this chapter and attribute to other sources are included in Hardorff's volumes, including the accounts of Edward S. Godfrey, John Ryan, Moving Behind Woman, and Ben Clark.

5. Greene, *Washita,* 136.

6. Edward S. Godfrey, "Some Reminiscences, Including the Washita Battle, November 27, 1868," in *Custer Reader,* ed. Hutton, 173.

7. "Indian Relics," *New York Times,* June 13, 1869, 3.

8. John Ryan describes taking a scalp in his memoir, *Ten Years with Custer: A Seventh Cavalryman's Memoir,* edited by Sandy Barnard (Terre Haute, IN: AST Press, 2001), 77–78; the scout Ben Clark says the mutilations of Cheyenne bodies were by the Osages in "Custer's Washita Fight," *New York Sun,* May 14, 1899, 3.

9. Greene, *Washita,* 124; see also "The Indian War," *New York Times,* December 20, 1868, p. 1.

10. "Custer's Washita Fight."

11. George Armstrong Custer, *My Life on the Plains, or Personal Experiences with Indians* (Norman: University of Oklahoma Press, 1962), 250.

12. "Custer's Washita Fight."

13. Theodore A. Ediger and Vinnie Hoffman, "Some Reminiscences of the Battle of the Washita," *Chronicles of Oklahoma* 33 (1955): 139.

14. Hugh Lenox Scott, *Some Memories of a Soldier* (New York: Century, 1928), 153. See also Greene, *Washita,* 195–196.

15. Greene, *Washita,* 196.

16. Howard F. Van Zandt, "The Battle of the Washita, Revisited," *Chronicles of Oklahoma* 62 (1984): 65.

17. Among the sources that I have consulted regarding the history of the Cheyennes in the nineteenth century are Donald J. Berthrong, *The Southern Cheyennes* (Norman: University of Oklahoma Press, 1963), and *The Cheyenne and Arapaho Ordeal* (Norman: University of Oklahoma Press, 1976); George Hyde, *Life of George Bent Written from His Letters,* edited by Savoie Lottinville (Norman: University of Oklahoma Press, 1968); Peter J. Powell, *People of the Sacred Mountain: A History of the Northern Cheyenne Chiefs and Warrior Societies, 1830–1878, with an Epilogue, 1969–1974,* 2 vols. (San Francisco: Harper and Row, 1981); and on the postallotment history of the Southern Cheyennes, Loretta Fowler, *Tribal Sovereignty and the Historical Imagination: Cheyenne-Arapaho Politics* (Lincoln: University of Nebraska Press, 2002).

18. On the origin of the Cheyenne-Arapaho alliance, see John H. Moore, *The Cheyenne* (Cambridge, MA: Blackwell, 1996), 90–93.

19. Robert M. Utley, *The Indian Frontier of the American West, 1846–1890* (Albuquerque: University of New Mexico Press, 1984), 65–98.

20. Stan Hoig, *The Sand Creek Massacre* (Norman: University of Oklahoma Press, 1961), 58–62; Greene, *Washita,* 15–16.

21. Hoig, *Sand Creek Massacre,* 110–21; Greene, *Washita,* 17–18. Gregory F. Michno has published a dissenting account of this conference, in which he contends that Evans and Chivington took pains to make themselves clear to the Cheyennes and that the Cheyenne chiefs understood that they were not at peace: *Battle at Sand Creek: The Military Perspective* (El Segundo, CA: Upton and Sons, 2004), 166–67. Michno's provocative book attempts to revise the standard history of Sand Creek by suggesting that Chivington has been unfairly portrayed by his detractors and that the fighting there was more two-sided than has been represented. These questions are obviously germane to the representation of the Washita fight, but I have not sifted the evidence in regard to Sand Creek. I include in this chapter the standard account of Sand Creek because, as Michno himself admits, the characterization of the Coloradoans' actions as duplicitous and cruel mattered significantly in the years that followed.

22. Hoig, *Sand Creek Massacre,* 163–73; Greene, *Washita,* 22–23. The adjectives are from "Massacre of Cheyenne Indians," in the Report of the Joint Committee on the Conduct of the War, 1865, Senate Report 142, 38-2, serial 1214, iii–iv.

23. Francis Paul Prucha, *The Great Father: The United States Government and the American Indians,* 2 vols. (Lincoln: University of Nebraska Press, 1984), 1:461. Even Michno, who hopes to revise this judgment, states that "the portrayal of Sand Creek has remained remarkably static" (*Battle at Sand Creek,* 2).

24. Custer, *My Life on the Plains,* 25.

25. Prucha, *Great Father*, 527–33.

26. A justly influential study of this topic is Brian W. Dippie's *The Vanishing American: White Attitudes and U.S. Indian Policy* (Middletown, CT: Wesleyan University Press, 1982).

27. Randolph De Barthe Keim, *Sheridan's Troopers on the Borders: A Winter Campaign on the Plains* (1870; rpt. Williamstown, MA: Corner House, 1973), 3.

28. The Friends of the Indian would fully come into their own in the 1880s, but the germination of the movement began in the immediate aftermath of the Civil War. See Francis Paul Prucha, *American Indian Policy in Crisis, 1865–1900* (Norman: University of Oklahoma Press, 1976).

29. United States Commissioner of Indian Affairs, *Report of the Commissioner of Indian Affairs, 1865* (Washington: GPO, 1866), 525–26.

30. United States Department of War, *Annual Report of the Secretary of War, 1878*, 2 vols. (Washington: GPO, 1879), 1:36–37; quoted in Paul Andrew Hutton, *Phil Sheridan and His Army* (Lincoln: University of Nebraska Press, 1985), 182–83.

31. Robert M. Utley, ed., *Life in Custer's Cavalry: Diaries and Letters of Albert and Jennie Barnitz, 1867–1868* (New Haven, CT: Yale University Press, 1977), 115.

32. Hutton, *Phil Sheridan and His Army*, 38; Jeff Broome has also written an extensive account of these raids, focusing on the perspective of the Kansas settlers, in *Dog Soldier Justice: The Ordeal of Susanna Alderdice in the Kansas Indian War* (Lincoln, KS: Lincoln County Historical Society, 2003), 7–33, 45–55.

33. Greene, *Washita*, 70–71; Hoig, *Battle of the Washita*, 46–53.

34. The speeches of Black Kettle and Hazen are reprinted in Hoig, *Battle of the Washita*, 89–92.

35. Greene, *Washita*, 102–3.

36. Ibid., 104; article 11 of Treaty with Cheyenne and Arapaho, in *Indian Affairs: Laws and Treaties*, compiled and edited by Charles J. Kappler (Washington: GPO, 1904), 2:988.

37. Ediger and Hoffman, "Some Reminiscences of the Battle," 138.

38. Michno has reproduced different versions of the speech Chivington gave before his attack at Sand Creek in *Battle at Sand Creek*, 206.

39. Godfrey, "Some Reminiscences," 177.

40. Custer, *My Life on the Plains*, 269.

41. Hutton, *Phil Sheridan and His Army*, 54.

42. Perry D. Jamieson, *Crossing the Deadly Ground: United States Army Tactics, 1865–1899* (Tuscaloosa: University of Alabama Press, 1994), 37–45. To go further, the larger 1868–69 campaign conducted by Sheridan actually included three converging columns, a tactic that Jamieson says was widely endorsed during the period.

43. Greene, *Washita*, 59.

44. Phil Sheridan to William T. Sherman, March 18, 1870, quoted in Hutton, *Phil Sheridan and His Army*, 185.

45. House of Representatives Executive Document 240, 41st Congress, 2nd Session, reprinted in *General Custer and the Battle of the Washita: The Federal View*, edited by John M. Carroll (Bryan, TX: Guidon, 1978), 80.

46. Ibid., 81. Wynkoop's letter of resignation was also printed in "Col. Wyncoop's [sic] Letter Resigning His Agency," *New York Times*, December 19, 1868, 3.

47. "The United States Indian Commission," *New York Herald*, December 24, 1868, 5.

48. Senate Executive Document 18, 40th Congress, 3rd Session, reprinted in *General Custer and the Battle of the Washita*, ed. Carroll, 36.

49. House of Representatives Executive Document 240, reprinted in *General Custer and the Battle of the Washita*, 253.

50. "The Indian Troubles," *New York Times*, December 27, 1868, 1. The *Times* ar-

ticle is in fact a reprint of an article that had appeared three days previously in the *St. Louis Republican.*

51. *Army and Navy Journal,* January 2, 1869; quoted in Greene, *Washita,* 165.

52. Custer, *My Life on the Plains,* 270. Note that Custer does not actually use the phrase "Indian Ring" in this particular instance.

53. Ibid., 19, 14, 22.

54. One exception is a slender work of popular fiction, Clay Fisher's *Yellow Hair* (1954; rpt. New York: Pocket Books, 1961).

55. Paul Andrew Hutton writes that a scene in which Wayne's Ethan Edwards confronts "an arrogant Custer about the massacre" was deleted from the final release print. "'Correct in Every Detail': General Custer in Hollywood," in *Legacy: New Perspectives on the Battle of the Little Bighorn,* edited by Charles E. Rankin (Helena, MT: Montana Historical Society Press, 1996), 252.

56. *Little Big Man,* DVD, directed by Arthur Penn, 1970 (Hollywood: Paramount, 2003).

57. John H. Moore, *The Cheyenne Nation: A Social and Demographic History* (Lincoln: University of Nebraska Press, 1987), 211–13.

58. "Crowd of 5000 Witness Ceremonial at Cheyenne," *Cheyenne Star* (OK), December 4, 1930, 1.

59. "Unknown Indian Grave Unmarked," *Cheyenne Star* (OK), April 14, 1932, n.p.

60. See the "Project Summary" and interviews in Mary Jane Warde, *Conduct Oral History Research for Washita Historical Site,* Final Report on Cooperative Agreement 1443CA125098002, Modification 1, September 30, 1999, Oklahoma Historical Society, Oklahoma City.

61. Mrs. L. L. Males, "Almost Too Real," letter to the editor, *Daily Oklahoman,* December 8, 1968, A28.

62. "Thousands Attend Battle of Washita Centennial," *Cheyenne Star* (OK), December 5, 1968, 1–2. This is the only account I have come across that mentions the reading of Magpie's speech.

63. Males, "Almost Too Real."

64. Francis Thetford, "Battle of the Washita Centennial, 1968," *Chronicles of Oklahoma* 46 (Winter 1968–69): 360. In a note to this article, Thetford is described as a well-known columnist for the *Daily Oklahoman.*

65. Interview with Lawrence H. Hart by Mary Jane Warde and Rodger Harris, January 14, 1999, Oklahoma City, transcribed by Vicky Gardner. Transcript included in Warde, *Conduct Oral History Research.*

66. Lawrence H. Hart, "Legacies of the Massacre and Battle of the Washita," *Oklahoma Today* 50, no. 3 (May/June 1999): 62. Hart revised this article as "A Cheyenne Legacy at the Washita River," in *Gathering at the Hearth: Stories That Mennonites Tell,* edited by John E. Sharp (Scottdale, PA: Herald, 2001), 21–25. See also Hart's account in his interview with Warde and Harris in Warde, *Conduct Oral History Research.* In that report, Warde also interviews Lucille Youngbull, the Cheyenne woman who draped the blanket over the coffin, who tells Warde that she was not pleased that it was given to a cavalry reenactor.

67. Hart's testimony of July 25, 1996 is quoted by Edward Linenthal in the published proceedings *Washita Symposium: Past, Present, and Future, November 12–14, 1998, Cheyenne, Oklahoma* (Cheyenne, OK: National Park Service, 2001), 64. See also Hart, "Legacies of the Massacre," 62–63, where he explains how the Oklahoma City bombing enabled him to articulate the significance of Washita in terms that members of Congress would understand.

68. Sigmund Freud, "The Uncanny," translated by David McLintock, in *The Uncanny* (New York: Penguin, 2003), 123–62.

69. Edward T. Linenthal's *The Unfinished Bombing: Oklahoma City in American*

Memory (New York: Oxford University Press, 2001), esp. 133–35, has guided my discussion of the Washita fight in this context. See also Kenneth E. Foote, *Shadowed Ground: America's Landscapes of Violence and Tragedy*, rev. ed. (Austin: University of Texas Press, 2003), esp. 166, 291–92.

70. Bob Blackburn in *Washita Symposium*, 84–86.

71. The report is mentioned in "To Be or Not to Be, Part 2," *Cheyenne Star* (OK), January 18, 1996, 1. It worth pointing out that I have not been able to locate this actual report, but the figures I name (100,000 visitors, $12 million) were mentioned several times in newspaper articles during the period that the National Historic Site was being debated.

72. Blackburn in *Washita Symposium*, 87.

73. H.R. 3099, 104th Congress, 2d Sess., incorporated into Public Law 104-333, 104th Congress, sec. 607.

74. S. 2950, 106th Congress, 2d Sess., incorporated into Public Law 106-465, 106th Congress.

75. M. E. Sprengelmeyer, "Sand Creek Nears Final Hurdle to Become Protected Historic Site," *Rocky Mountain News* (Denver), online edition, August 2, 2005; accessed September 20, 2005.

76. Blackburn, *Washita Symposium*, 88.

77. Jill Cowely, *Cultural Landscape Inventory, Level Two, Washita Battlefield National Historic Site*, Santa Fe (NM) Support Office, November 1999, 67, 106.

78. The rationale for placing the visitor center in its off-site location, as well as other alternatives, is discussed in U.S. National Park Service, *Final General Management Plan / Environmental Impact Statement: Washita Battlefield National Historic Site* (Denver: National Park Service, 2001).

79. H.R. 3099, 104th Congress, 2d Sess., incorporated into Public Law 104-333, 104th Congress, sec. 607.

80. Custer, *My Life on the Plains*, 14.

81. Brill, *Custer, Black Kettle, and the Fight*, 14, 151–80.

82. Elmo Scott Watson and Don Russell, "The Battle of the Washita, or Custer's Massacre?" in *"Such Signal Success"? Confrontations along the Washita*, edited by Kevin E. Galvin (London: Westerners, 2003), 29–40. See Francis B. Taunton's foreword to this volume (p. iv) on the publication history of the debate.

83. Hoig, *Battle of the Washita*, 1.

84. "Battle or Massacre?" in *Washita Symposium*, 42–47.

85. Greene, *Washita*, 188–91.

86. Hart, "Legacies of the Massacre," 63.

87. Interview with Wendy Lauritzen and Alden Miller, Cheyenne, OK, May 8, 2006. Miller has since moved to another unit of the Park Service.

88. Blackburn in *Washita Symposium*, 84; Lauritzen also addressed this history during my May 8, 2006, interview with her.

89. I quote in this paragraph from transcripts of interviews contained in Warde, *Conduct Oral History Research:* Melvin Whitebird (Cheyenne-Arapaho), interviewed by Mary Jane Warde, Oklahoma Historical Society, Oklahoma City, August 11, 1999, 7; Larry Roman Nose, interviewed by Warde, El Reno, OK, May 12, 1999, 11; Frances Beard, interviewed by Warde and Jim Anquoe, El Reno, July 15, 1999, 10.

90. U.S. National Park Service, "Interpretation and Education," chap. 7 in *2001 NPS Management Policies*, http://nps.gov/policy/mp/chapter7.htm (accessed May 10, 2006).

91. U.S. National Park Service, *Final General Management Plan*, 9.

92. Robert M. Utley, *A Clash of Cultures: Fort Bowie and the Chiricahua Apaches* (Washington, DC: National Park Service, 1977).

93. This biographical information comes from an obituary that fails to mention Lawrence's interest in the Little Bighorn: "Elizabeth Lawrence, 74, Scholar of Animal-

Human Relations," *Boston Globe,* November 18, 2003, online edition, www.boston.com/news/globe/obituaries/articles/2003/11/18/elizabeth_lawrence_74_scholar_of_human_animal_relations (accessed January 30, 2006). Lawrence's book on Comanche is *Comanche: His Very Silence Speaks* (Detroit: Wayne State University Press, 1989).

94. Elizabeth Lawrence, "A Clash of Cultures — The Issues behind the Battle of the Little Big Horn," in *Custer and His Times,* edited by Paul A. Hutton, vol. 1 (El Paso, TX: Little Big Horn Associates, 1981). Hutton mentions the date and place of Lawrence's original paper in his introduction (p. 5).

95. Timothy Braatz attempts to unravel the history of this phrase in "'Clash of Cultures' as Euphemism: Avoiding History at the Little Bighorn," *American Indian Culture and Research Journal* 28, no. 4 (2004): 110–11, 123n26. Braatz's article is a well-argued, trenchant critique of the "clash of cultures" model that appeared after I had reached similar, albeit less critical, conclusions.

96. United States National Park Service, "Little Bighorn Battlefield," brochure 491-282/40176, GPO, 2002.

97. Interview with Lauritzen and Miller.

98. Braatz, *"Clash of Cultures* as Euphemism," 109.

99. Loretta Fowler, *Ethnographic Overview (Phase II) for Washita Battlefield National Historic Site,* Final Report on Cooperative Agreement 1443CA125098002, Modification 3, National Park Service, June 26, 2001, 84.

100. John H. Moore, Margot Liberty, and A. Terry Strauss, "Cheyenne," in *Plains,* edited by Raymond J. DeMallie, vol. 13 of *Handbook of North American Indians,* edited by William C. Sturtevant (Washington, DC: Smithsonian Institution, 2001), 876–80.

101. Lawrence H. Hart in *Washita Symposium,* 6.

102. United States National Park Service, "Washita Battlefield," brochure 310-394/00270, GPO, 2005.

103. John M. Carroll, ed., *The Benteen-Goldin Letters on Custer and His Last Battle* (1974; rpt. Lincoln: University of Nebraska Press, 1991), 271.

104. James R. Foley, "Walter Camp and Ben Clark," *Research Review: The Journal of the Little Big Horn Associates* 10, no. 1 (January 1996): 24.

105. Custer, *My Life on the Plains,* 282–83.

106. Elizabeth B. Custer, *Following the Guidon* (1890; rpt. Norman: University of Oklahoma Press, 1966), 95.

107. Barnett, *Touched by Fire,* 196.

108. Robert M. Utley, *Cavalier in Buckskin: George Armstrong Custer and the Western Military Frontier* (Norman: University of Oklahoma Press, 1988), 107; Greene, *Washita,* 196.

109. As I discuss later in this chapter, it is also known that Monahseetah married another white man later in her life, something that could have detracted further from her reputation among the Cheyennes.

110. Charlotte DeClue, "To the Spirit of Monahsetah," in *A Gathering of Spirit: A Collection by North American Indian Women,* edited by Beth Brant (Ithaca, NY: Firebrand, 1984), 52–54; Maurice Kenny, "Monahsetah . . . A Cheyenne Girl," in *On Second Thought: A Compilation* (Norman: University of Oklahoma Press, 1995), 119–20.

111. Brill, *Custer, Black Kettle, and the Fight,* 46; Mari Sandoz, *Cheyenne Autumn* (New York: McGraw-Hill, 1953), 21, 273n1. Mark Gardner's introduction to the reprint of Brill's volume discusses correspondence between Brill and Sandoz on this point (8–10).

112. Gregory F. Michno, *Lakota Noon: The Indian Narrative of Custer's Defeat* (Missoula, MT: Mountain, 1997), 31.

113. The information attributed to Gail Kelly-Custer about her family history comes from two telephone interviews by the author, September 5, 2005, and October 10, 2005. I have not made an attempt to verify Kelly-Custer's genealogical evidence.

114. Peter Harrison, e-mail correspondence to author, October 26, 2006.

115. Powell, *People of the Sacred Mountain*, 2:707–11; Hyde, *Life of George Bent Written from His Letters*, 325; Brill, *Custer, Black Kettle, and the Fight*, 227–28; John Stands in Timber and Margot Liberty, *Cheyenne Memories* (New Haven, CT: Yale University Press, 1967), 82–83; Richard G. Hardorff, comp. and ed., *Cheyenne Memories of the Custer Fight* (Lincoln: University of Nebraska Press, 1998), 141–42.

116. Kate Bighead, as told to Thomas Marquis, "She Watched Custer's Last Battle," in *Custer Reader*, ed. Hutton, 376.

CHAPTER FOUR

1. Several accounts of the Ghost Dance and the Wounded Knee Massacre are available. One contemporary volume that is particularly useful is James Mooney's *The Ghost-Dance Region and the Sioux Outbreak of 1890* (1896; rpt. Lincoln: University of Nebraska Press, 1991). A more recent useful resource is William S. E. Coleman, ed., *Voices from Wounded Knee* (Lincoln: University of Nebraska Press, 2000).

2. Lawrence A. Frost, "The Beginning of the LBHA," *Little Big Horn Associates Newsletter* 20, no. 1 (January 1987): 3-4.

3. Robert J. Ege, untitled editor's note, *Little Big Horn Associates Newsletter* 1, no. 1 (January 1967): 1.

4. For the early history of the Little Big Horn Associates, the collection of LBHA newsletters available at the Dorsch Memorial Library, Monroe, MI, has been invaluable.

5. A complete list of LBHA conferences is available at www.lbha.org/Conferences .htm, accessed June 7, 2005.

6. Author interview with Vincent A. Heier, University City, MO, March 19, 2004.

7. Richard Handler and Eric Gable, *The New History in an Old Museum: Creating the Past at Colonial Williamsburg* (Durham, NC: Duke University Press, 1997), 82. Handler and Gable also quote a Colonial Williamsburg administrator comparing the past to a puzzle "that can never be completed" (73–74).

8. This may be the place for me to say a word about my research methodology in writing about the Little Big Horn Associates. I joined the LBHA in 2002 and attended the 2003, 2004, and 2005 conventions. While the chapter that follows focuses on the 2005 conference in Rapid City, I have tried to characterize it by drawing on my experiences at other conferences.

In the course of attending the conferences, I have naturally had dozens of informal conversations with participants about their interest in Custer, their background, and their responses to the conference program. However, I have not quoted from those conversations unless I informed the interlocutor that I was taking notes for the purposes of this book. I would like to emphasize that the members of the LBHA have been extremely generous with their time, and this chapter does not adequately reflect the efforts they have made to speak with me.

After the 2005 conference in Rapid City, I also conducted a survey with those participants who registered an e-mail address with the permission of Bill Blake, the chairman of the LBHA board of directors at the time. In the end, I received approximately 40 responses, and those survey results also inform this chapter. I cite to these survey results here as "LBHA Survey."

9. Francis Prucha, *The Great Father: The United States Government and the American Indians* (Lincoln: University of Nebraska Press, 1984), 1:492–94; the treaty councils reproduced in Vine Deloria Jr. and Raymond De Mallie, eds., *Proceedings of the Great Peace Commission* (Washington, DC: Institute for the Development of Indian Law, 1975), from April and May 1868 are also instructive, because they suggest that the Lakota leaders understood that the war they had been fighting was a defense of their territory and that cessation of the conflict signaled Lakota control over that territory. For instance, Swift Bear, a Brulé or Sicangu Lakota, stated, "It pleases me that you are making peace. Whoever has got anything likes to keep it. You [the United States] occupy a large space of country

and you can protect each other. You do not like anybody to pass through your country and you get mad. I know how you all live. There is a value with everything you have. We have the same" (109). In other words, just as the United States had a legitimate reason to defend itself against invasion, so too did the Lakota Sioux.

10. The Fort Laramie Treaty of 1868 is printed in Charles J. Kappler, *Indian Affairs: Laws and Treaties* (Washington, DC: GPO, 1904), 2:998–1007.

11. Quoted in Donald Jackson, *Custer's Gold: The United States Cavalry Expedition of 1874* (New Haven, CT: Yale University Press, 1966), 14.

12. "Bishop Hare's Protest" [July 13, 1874], reprinted in *Prelude to Glory: A Newspaper Accounting of Custer's 1874 Expedition to the Black Hills* , edited by Herbert Krause and Gary D. Olson (Sioux Falls, SD: Brevet, 1974), 153–54; Jackson, *Custer's Gold*, 23–24.

13. "The Black Hills: A Valley of Flowers" [August 17, 1874], reprinted in *Prelude to Glory*, ed. Krause and Olson, 210.

14. "Custer's Field Report No. 1" [July 30, 1874], reprinted in *Prelude to Glory*, ed. Krause and Olson, 243.

15. Theodore Ewart, *Theodore Ewart's Diary of the Black Hills Expedition of 1874*, edited by John M. Carroll and Lawrence A. Frost (Piscataway, NJ: CRI Books, 1976), 22.

16. James Calhoun, *With Custer in '74: James Calhoun's Diary of the Black Hills Expedition*, edited by Lawrence A. Frost (Provo, UT: Brigham Young University Press, 1979), 40.

17. "Black Hills," 210.

18. I have summarized geological information from Sven G. Froiland, *Natural History of the Black Hills and Badlands* (Sioux Falls, SD: Center for Western Studies, 1999), 11–39.

19. Badger Clark, "The Mountain That Had Its Face Lifted," in *The Black Hills*, edited by Roderick Peattie (New York: Vanguard, 1952), 222–23; Robert J. Casey, *The Black Hills and Their Incredible Characters* (Indianapolis: Bobbs-Merrill, 1949), 106–7.

20. Paul Horsted explains this process in Ernest Grafe and Paul Horsted, *Exploring with Custer: The 1874 Black Hills Expedition* (Custer, SD: Golden Valley, 2002), 163.

21. Louis Jacobson, "Following Custer's Photographer Into the Black Hills," *New York Times*, August 15, 2002, E3.

22. Author interview with Paul Horsted, June 9, 2005.

23. Grafe and Horsted, *Exploring with Custer*, xi.

24. Ewart, *Theodore Ewart's Diary*, 43.

25. "The Black Hills" (August 16, 1874), reprinted in *Prelude to Glory*, ed. Krause and Olson, 90.

26. "The Black Hills" (August 18, 1874), reprinted in *Prelude to Glory*, ed. Krause and Olson, 121. Other accounts state that a nephew, rather than a son, of Bloody Knife had been killed in the Lakota attack on the Arikara village.

27. Ewart, *Theodore Ewart's Diary*, 67.

28. Jackson, *Custer's Gold*, 77–81, 93; Grafe and Horsted, *Exploring with Custer*, 49–55, 94.

29. Author interview with Don Schwarck, June 17, 2005. Don Schwarck, "W. H. Illingworth: A Biography," in Grafe and Horsted, *Exploring with Custer*, 271–75.

30. E-mail communication to author, July 14, 2005.

31. Jean Baudrillard, "The System of Collecting," translated by Roger Cardinal, in *The Cultures of Collecting*, edited by John Elsner and Roger Cardinal (Cambridge, MA: Harvard University Press, 1994), 13.

32. Kevin Melchionne, "Collecting as an Art," *Philosophy and Literature* 23, no. 1 (1999): 148–56. I am particularly interested in Melchionne's debt to Michael Thompson's *Rubbish Theory: The Creation and Destruction of Value* (New York: Oxford University Press, 1979); Thompson posits, says Melchionne, that scavenging is "an act of freedom, innovation, even dissent, which the challenges of reigning taste" (154). See also the edi-

tors' introduction to *The Cultures of Collecting,* edited by John Elsner and Roger Cardinal (Cambridge, MA: Harvard University Press, 1994), 1–6, on collecting as a form of self-fashioning.

33. Ewart, *Theodore Ewart's Diary,* 25.

34. "A Promising Surface Yield" [August 28, 1874], reprinted in *Prelude to Glory,* ed. Krause and Olson, 218, 126.

35. All these sources are reprinted in *Prelude to Glory,* ed. Krause and Olson: "The New Gold Country" [August 29, 1874], 222; "The New Eldorado" [September 9, 1874], 144; "Gold!" [August 27, 1874], 126.

36. Quoted in Jackson, *Custer's Gold,* 87; for a newspaper article reprinting the report, see "Custer's Field Report No. 1," reprinted in *Prelude to Glory,* ed. Krause and Olson, 242–45.

37. "Gold!" 128.

38. Ibid., 127.

39. Watson Parker, *Gold in the Black Hills* (Norman: University of Oklahoma Press, 1966), 54, 66–68; see also Richard Irving Dodge's account of Crook's meetings with the prospectors in *The Black Hills* (1876; rpt. Minneapolis: Ross and Haines, 1965), 112–14.

40. It is worth mentioning that Chris Kortlander, the director of the privately owned Custer Battlefield Museum, has recently displayed a photograph that he believes to depict Crazy Horse. That claim, however, remains disputed. See, for instance, James Hagengruber, "Man Without a Face: Mystery Continues in the Hunt for Chief Crazy Horse," *Billings Gazette,* November 16, 2003, online edition, www.billingsgazette.net/articles/2003/11/16/magazine/export131457.txt, accessed January 13, 2004.

41. Author interview with Donovin Sprague, June 27, 2005.

One Native intellectual who has voiced her criticism of the Crazy Horse Memorial is Elizabeth Cook-Lynn (Crow Creek Sioux). See the essay "Is the Crazy Horse Monument Art? or Politics?" in her book *Anti-Indianism in Modern America: A Voice from Tatekeya's Earth* (Urbana: University of Illinois Press, 2001), 24–33.

42. Kappler, *Indian Affairs,* 2:1002.

43. Edward Lazarus, *Black Hills/White Justice: The Sioux Nation versus the United States, 1775 to Present* (New York: HarperCollins, 1991), 81.

44. See the "Report of the Commission Appointed to Treat with the Sioux Indians for the Relinquishment of the Black Hills," in *Annual Report of the Commissioner of Indian Affairs to the Secretary of the Interior for the Year 1875* (Washington, DC: GPO, 1875), 184–201; the quotations above appear on pages 188, 189, 190–91.

45. "Report of the Commission Appointed to Obtain Certain Concessions from the Sioux," in *Annual Report of the Commissioner of Indian Affairs to the Secretary of the Interior for the Year 1876* (Washington, DC: GPO, 1876), 330–57; Lazarus, *Black Hills/White Justice,* 85–93.

46. This was an anonymous response to the LBHA survey.

47. The LBHA distributes a roster of registered participants before each convention; however, it is an imperfect set of data because it does not include last-minute registrants—nor do all registrants list spouses or partners who might be accompanying them. With that caveat, of the 175 participants listed on the roster for the 2005 convention, 76 men registered as unaccompanied by a spouse or companion, 15 women registered as unaccompanied by a spouse or companion, and 42 couples made up of a man and woman registered. According to these (incomplete) figures, the total attendance at the convention was about two-thirds male and one-third female, with unaccompanied females totaling between 8 and 9 percent of all participants.

48. E-mail communication to author, July 7, 2005.

49. LBHA survey.

50. LBHA survey.

51. Robert M. Utley, *Custer and Me: A Historian's Memoir* (Norman: University of Oklahoma Press, 2004), 202.

52. Ibid., 186.

53. Author interview with Ron Nichols, June 5, 2005.

54. Author interview with Chuck Merkel, July 24, 2005.

55. Richard Slotkin, *The Fatal Environment: The Myth of the Frontier in the Age of Industrialization, 1800–1890* (New York: Atheneum, 1985), esp. 442–52.

56. Income figures are from the U.S. Census Bureau, available at http://factfinder .census.gov, accessed July 19, 2005. For a typical news story listing Buffalo and Shannon Counties as the poorest in the United States, see the Associate Press wire story "Gap Grows between Rich and Poor in South Dakota," July 1, 2002, accessed via Factiva database, July 19, 2005.

57. David Melmer, "Senate Committee Addresses Suicide," *Indian Country Today,* May 5, 2005, online edition, www.indiancountry.com, accessed May 15, 2005.

58. United States v. Sioux Nation of Indians et al., 448 U.S. 371 (1980), at 388.

59. Ibid., at 435.

60. Lazarus, *Black Hills / White Justice,* 428.

61. Elizabeth Cook-Lynn, review of *Black Hills / White Justice: The Sioux Nation versus the United States, 1775 to the Present,* by Edward Lazarus, *Wicazo Sa Review* 8, no. 1 (Spring 1992): 102, 101.

62. Charles Wilkinson, *Blood Struggle: The Rise of Modern Indian Nations* (New York: W. W. Norton, 2005), 231.

63. Mario Gonzalez and Elizabeth Cook-Lynn, *The Politics of Hallowed Ground: Wounded Knee and the Struggle for Indian Sovereignty* (Urbana: University of Illinois Press, 1999), 6–7.

64. For an overview of the Taos Pueblo recovery of Blue Lake, see Wilkinson, *Blood Struggle,* 206 220.

65. Author interview with Donovin Sprague, November 17, 2006.

66. Ibid.

67. Author interview with Donovin Sprague, June 27, 2005.

68. For a succinct overview of tribal efforts to assert stewardship of the land in recent decades, see Wilkinson, *Blood Struggle,* 304 28.

69. The list, compiled by Sacred Sites International, is available online at www .sacred-sites.org/preservation/endangered_most.html (accessed May 25, 2005). The Web site of the Defenders of the Black Hills provides information about the group's activities, as well as its mission statement: www.defendblackhills.org.

70. Jomay Steen, "Montana Tribe Buys Bear Butte Acreage," *Rapid City Journal,* March 22, 2006, online edition, http://rapidcityjournal.com/articles/2006/03/22/news/ top/news02.txt, accessed March 29, 2006.

71. Author interview with Charmaine White Face, June 14, 2005.

72. In fact, I have given an academic paper on the same topic. My talk was titled "President Custer," and I delivered it at the annual convention of the American Studies Association in Hartford, CT, November 2003. For what it is worth, Heier's list of examples was much more comprehensive than mine.

73. For an enthusiastic response by one longtime LBHA member, see Kevin Connelly's review of *Little Bighorn Mysteries* and *More Little Bighorn Mysteries* in the *LBHA Newsletter* 39, no. 6 (July 2005): 6.

74. Roger Darling, *Custer's Seventh Cavalry Comes to Dakota: New Discoveries Reveal Custer's Tribulations en Route to the Yellowstone Expedition* (El Segundo, CA: Upton and Sons, 1989).

75. Utley, *Custer and Me,* 202–3.

76. Gonzalez and Cook-Lynn, *Politics of Hallowed Ground,* 109.

77. See Carroll's letter in the *Little Big Horn Associates Newsletter* 11, no. 5 (May 1977): 4.

78. For those who read contemporary American Indian literature, this phrasing recalls a well-known epigram printed on the flyleaf of Leslie Marmon Silko's *Almanac of the Dead:* "The Indian Wars have never ended in the Americas. Native Americans . . . seek nothing less than the return of all tribal lands" ([New York: Simon and Schuster, 1991], n.p.).

CHAPTER FIVE

1. Joseph Mills Hanson, *The Conquest of the Missouri* (1909; rpt., New York: Murray Hill, 1946), 273–75; Walter Mason Camp, *Custer in '76: Walter Camp's Notes on the Custer Fight,* edited by Kenneth Hammer (1976; rpt. Norman: University of Oklahoma Press, 1990), 165, 169.

2. Hanson, *Conquest of the Missouri,* 275.

3. Camp, *Custer in '76,* 168–69.

4. Jerome A. Greene provides a brief introduction to the difficulties of using this testimony to reconstruct the action of the Battle of the Little Bighorn in "The Uses of Indian Testimony in the Writing of Indian Wars History," *Journal of the Order of the Indian Wars* 2, no. 1 (Winter 1981): 1–7, and his introduction to his edited collection *Lakota and Cheyenne: Indian Views of the Great Sioux War, 1876–1877* (Norman: University of Oklahoma Press, 1994), xiii–xxvi.

5. Edward S. Godfrey, "General Godfrey's Comment on Gall's Story," in *The Custer Myth,* edited by W. A. Graham (1953; rpt. Mechanicsburg, PA: Stackpole, 2000), 93; Edward S. Godfrey, "Custer's Last Battle," in *The Custer Reader,* edited by Paul Andrew Hutton (Lincoln: University of Nebraska Press, 1992), 300–301. Robert M. Utley notes the curious symmetry of Gall's account and Godfrey's in *Custer and the Great Controversy: The Origin and Development of a Legend* (1962; rpt. Lincoln: University of Nebraska Press, 1998), 109–10.

6. Alan Trachtenberg, *Shades of Hiawatha: Staging Indians, Making Americans, 1880–1930* (New York: Hill and Wang, 2004), 248–56.

7. "Which Indian Killed Custer?" in Thomas B. Marquis, *Custer on the Little Bighorn,* 2nd ed. (Algonac, MI: Reference Publications, 1986), 57. David Humphreys Miller discusses the council in *Custer's Fall: The Indian Side of the Story* (New York: Duell, Sloan, and Pearce, 1957), 211–14. For a more recent analysis of this story, see Raymond J. De-Mallie, "'These Have No Ears': Narrative and Ethnohistorical Method," *Ethnohistory* 40 (1993): 517–18, and Arnold Krupat, *Red Matters: Native American Studies* (Philadelphia: University of Pennsylvania Press, 2002), 55–56. DeMallie's and Krupat's approaches to recorded American Indian speech and their considerations of what "history" means in Indian traditions have informed this chapter substantially beyond what this single footnote reflects.

8. Utley, *Custer and the Great Controversy,* 86.

9. Orin G. Libby, ed., *The Arikara Narrative of Custer's Campaign and the Battle of the Little Bighorn* (Norman: University of Oklahoma Press, 1998), 58, 62 (on Custer's rumored political ambitions); Wooden Leg, *Wooden Leg: A Warrior Who Fought Custer,* interpreted by Thomas B. Marquis (1931; rpt. Lincoln: University of Nebraska Press, 1957), 237–38 (on rumors of mass suicide).

10. Richard G. Hardorff, comp. and ed., *Cheyenne Memories of the Custer Fight: New Sources of Indian-Military History* (Lincoln: University of Nebraska Press, 1998), 93–134; Hardorff, comp. and ed., *Lakota Recollections of the Custer Fight* (Lincoln: University of Nebraska Press, 1997), 129–40; Hardorff, comp. and ed., *Indian Views of the Custer Fight* (Spokane, WA: Arthur H. Clark, 2004), 107–15.

11. Miller, *Custer's Fall,* ix–x.

12. Camp to E. B. Custer, October 31, 1917, in *On the Little Bighorn with Walter*

Camp: A Collection of Walter Mason Camp's Letters; Notes and Opinions on Custer's Last Fight, edited by Richard G. Hardorff (El Segundo, CA: Upton and Sons, 2002), 138. For biographical information on Camp, see Kenneth Hammer's biographical sketch in Camp, *Custer in '76,* 1–3.

13. In *Custer and Company: Walter Camp's Notes on the Custer Fight,* edited by Bruce R. Liddic and Paul Harbaugh (originally published as *Camp on Custer: Transcribing the Custer Myth* (Spokane, Wash.: Arthur H. Clark, 1995; rpt. Lincoln: University of Nebraska Press, 1998), 17.

14. Most of the books I refer to here appear elsewhere in the notes to this chapter. The Camp volumes are Camp, *Custer in '76; On the Little Bighorn with Walter Camp;* and *Custer and Company.* Other edited volumes include Hardorff, comp. and ed., *Cheyenne Memories of the Custer Fight, Lakota Recollections of the Custer Fight,* and *Indian Views of the Custer Fight.* In addition, Greene's edited volume *Lakota and Cheyenne* includes accounts of the Battle of the Little Bighorn. The trade volume to which I refer is Herman J. Viola, *Little Bighorn Remembered: The Untold Indian Story of Custer's Last Stand* (New York: Crown, 1999).

15. Sandra L. Brizée-Bowen, *For All to See: The Little Bighorn in Plains Indian Art* (Spokane, WA: Arthur L. Clark, 2003).

16. Thomas Jefferson, *Writings,* edited by Merrill D. Peterson (New York: Library of America, 1984), 189.

17. Roy Harvey Pearce, Savagism *and Civilization: A Study of the Indian and the American Mind* (1953; rpt. Berkeley: University of California Press, 1988), 79.

18. David Murray, *Forked Tongues: Speech, Writing and Representation in North American Indian Texts* (Bloomington: Indiana University Press, 1991), 34–41, 70.

19. Jerome A. Greene, *Nez Perce Summer, 1877: The U.S. Army and the Nee-Me-Poo Crisis* (Helena: Montana Historical Society Press, 2000), 309; see also Greene's note (484–85n106) on the recording of the speech. As Greene explains, Haruo Aoki has found that Chief Joseph's "speech" was in fact largely a message delivered via writing, rather than oratory coincident with his raising his gun over his head, as was reported. Aoki's article also describes the dissemination of this famous speech: "Chief Joseph's Words," *Idaho Yesterdays* 33 (Fall 1989): 16–21.

20. Biographical details in this paragraph come from Robert M. Utley, *The Lance and the Shield: The Life and Times of Sitting Bull* (New York: Henry Holt, 1993), 14–15, 26–37, 75–89. Utley quotes Four Horns on page 83 from an account provided by One Bull to Walter Campbell (better known as Stanley Vestal). Furthermore, Utley notes, "scarcely any event in Sitting Bull's life has bred more confusion in the sources than his designation as supreme chief. The year, the place, the dynamics of the selection, and its meaning are all muddled in the surviving evidence" (350n10).

21. "The Indian War," *New York Herald,* June 19, 1876, 2.

22. "A Bloody Battle," *New York Herald,* July 7, 1876, 5; "An Indian Victory," *New York Times,* July 7, 1876, 4; *New-York Tribune,* July 7, 1876, 1; *New York Herald,* July 7, 1876, 4.

23. John M. Coward, *The Newspaper Indian: Native American Identity in the Press, 1820–90* (Urbana: University of Illinois Press, 1999), 164. Coward's chapter on the press coverage of Sitting Bull (159–95) has informed my own discussion.

24. Captain Fred[erick] Whittaker, *Seth Slocum, Railroad Surveyor, or The Secret of Sitting Bull: A Tale of the Great Northern Pacific Road-Building* (1883; rpt. New York: M. J. Ivers, 1903).

25. For reports of Sitting Bull's death, see *New York Tribune,* July 15 and 21, 1876, and "The Indian War," *New York Times,* July 21, 1876, 1.

26. "Sitting Bull's Autobiography," *New York Herald,* July 9, 1876, 3.

27. M. W. Stirling, *Three Pictographic Autobiographies of Sitting Bull,* Smithsonian Miscellaneous Collections 97, no. 5 (Washington, DC: Smithsonian Institution, 1938), 3.

28. "Sitting Bull," *New York Herald,* July 12, 1876, 3.

29. Stirling, *Three Pictographic Autobiographies,* 14.

30. Porte Crayon, ed., "Sitting Bull: Autobiography of the Famous Sioux Chief," *Harper's Weekly,* July 29, 1876, 627.

31. "Sitting Bull," *New York Herald;* see Stirling, *Three Pictographic Autobiographies,* 10, for the original description that the reporter would have read: "Lances a Crow Indian."

32. "Sitting Bull," *Harper's Weekly,* 625–26.

33. "Sitting Bull's Autobiography," *New York Herald.*

34. Two extensive interviews with Kill Eagle are reprinted in *Custer Myth,* ed. Graham, 46–56.

35. These stories are quoted in Coward, *Newspaper Indian,* 172–73.

36. "Sitting Bull Talks," *New York Herald,* November 16, 1877, pp. 3–4; "The Sioux's Savior," *Chicago Times,* November 14, 1877, 5. The *Herald* interview is reprinted in *Custer Myth,* ed. Graham, 65–73, and both interviews are reprinted in *The Army and Navy Journal on the Battle of the Little Bighorn and Related Matters, 1876–1881,* edited by James S. Hutchins (El Segundo, CA: Upton and Sons, 2003), 219–33.

37. "Sitting Bull Talks," in *Custer Myth,* ed. Graham, 69.

38. "The Sioux's Savior," in *Army and Navy Journal on the Battle,* ed. Hutchins, 233.

39. "A Savage Talking Sense," *New York World,* November 18, 1877, 1; reprinted in *Army and Navy Journal on the Battle,* ed. Hutchins, 234–35.

40. "A Savage Talking Sense," in *Army and Navy Journal on the Battle,* ed. Hutchins, 236.

41. *Army and Navy Journal,* November 24, 1877, 249, reprinted in *Army and Navy Journal on the Battle,* ed. Hutchins, 169. It is worth pointing out that this doubt cast by the editor of the *Army and Navy Journal,* William Conant Church, actually focused on the date of the supposed *World* interview; Church reasoned that it could not have reached a New York newspaper so quickly and therefore might be a fake. Church continued, "There are also certain dramatic and peculiarly French touches about the [*World*] interview that give it a doubtful air."

42. Utley suggests that Major James M. Walsh of the North-West Mounted Police, who commanded the fort near Sitting Bull's camp and facilitated the other interviews, may have provided other dispatches to the *New York World.* Utley does not comment on this particular article, however (*The Lance and the Shield,* 372n16).

43. The two pamphlets, bound together, can be found in the Beinecke Library, Yale University: [R. D. Clarke], *The Works of Sitting Bull, Including Part II* (Chicago: Knight and Leonard, 1878). This copy includes a second title page, presumably used for the first pamphlet—*The Works of Sitting Bull in the Original French and Latin, with Translations Diligently Compared*—with a copyright page attributing authorship to R. D. Clarke, U.S. Army, in 1877. A comment in the first pamphlet about Sitting Bull's refusal to return to the United States suggests that it was printed not long after the interviews by Diehl and Stillson were published.

44. *Works of Sitting Bull, Including Part II,* 2:8.

45. Paul Reddin, *Wild West Shows* (Urbana: University of Illinois Press, 1999), 80; Louis S. Warren, *Buffalo Bill's America: William Cody and the Wild West Show* (New York: Alfred A. Knopf, 2005), 254.

46. Stanley Vestal, *Sitting Bull: Champion of the Sioux* (Boston: Houghton Mifflin, 1932), 168.

47. Luther Standing Bear, *My People, the Sioux* (1928; rpt. Lincoln: University of Nebraska Press, 1975), 185–86. Interestingly, in his acknowledgments Standing Bear thanks his "friend" E. A. Brininstool, who is listed on the title page as the editor of the volume; Brininstool was a well-known amateur historian of the Battle of the Little Bighorn.

48. "The 'Standard' Curley Story," in *Custer Myth,* ed. Graham, 10–12; "War with the Sioux," *Army and Navy Journal,* August 5, 1876, 837.

49. "Several Indian Tribes Uneasy," *New York Times,* July 9, 1876, 1.

50. Frederick Whittaker, *A Complete Life of General George A. Custer* (1876; rpt. Lincoln: University of Nebraska Press, 1993), 2:599.

51. Camp, *Custer in '76,* 165; this 1909 interview with Curly was translated by Russell White Bear and recorded by Camp.

52. Usher Burdick, *David F. Barry's Notes on "The Custer Battle,"* enl. ed. (Baltimore: Wirth Brothers, 1949), 23.

53. Cyrus Townsend Brady, *Indian Fights and Fighters* (1904; rpt. Lincoln: University of Nebraska Press, 1971), 256.

54. Camp, *Custer in '76,* ix; see also Michael J. Koury, introduction to *Custer Centennial Observance* (Fort Collins, CO: Old Army Press, 1978), 13–14, for discussion of the publication of this volume.

55. Trachtenberg, *Shades of Hiawatha,* 248–49.

56. Joseph K. Dixon, *The Vanishing Race,* concept by Rodman Wanamaker (Garden City, NY: Doubleday, Page, 1913), xv, 25, 212.

57. Ibid., 151–52.

58. Ibid., 158, 163.

59. Ibid, 141.

60. W. A. Graham, The *Story of the Little Big Horn* (1926; rpt. Mechanicsburg, PA: Stackpole, 1994), 141.

61. Fred Dustin, *The Custer Tragedy* (1939; rpt. El Segundo, CA: Upton and Sons, 1987), xv; see also Dustin's chapter "The Crow Scouts," 163–66.

62. Charles Kuhlman, *Legend into History* (1951; rpt. Fort Collins, CO: Old Army Press, 1977), 165–66, 236–39; biographical information comes from an unpaginated account by Fay Kuhlman included in this edition.

63. Utley, *Custer and the Great Controversy,* 137–38.

64. John S. Gray, *Centennial Campaign: The Sioux War of 1876* (Fort Collins, CO: Old Army Press, 1976), n.p.

65. Ibid., 346–57.

66. John S. Gray, *Custer's Last Campaign: Mitch Boyer and the Little Bighorn Reconstructed* (Lincoln: University of Nebraska Press, 1991), 373, 382.

67. Ibid., 357–72.

68. Ibid., 373.

69. Ibid., 382.

70. For a quick overview of the archaeological methodology, see Douglas D. Scott, et al., *Archaeological Perspectives on the Battle of the Little Bighorn* (Norman: University of Oklahoma Press, 1989), 24–35.

71. Douglas D. Scott, P. Willey, and Melissa A. Connor, *They Died with Custer: Soldier Bones from the Battle of the Little Bighorn* (Norman: University of Oklahoma Press, 1998).

72. Richard Allan Fox Jr., *Archaeology, History, and Custer's Last Battle* (Norman: University of Oklahoma Press, 1993), 173–94.

73. Ibid., 15; see also 201, 216, 330.

74. For instance, Michael Koury likens Fox's argument about the Seventh Cavalry's failure to mount an effective battle to other debunking attempts by the "PC police." In fact, says Koury, Fox's claim constitutes the "cruelest blow of all," because it extends beyond "heroes" to the "rank and file." Mike [Michael] Koury, "Digging Fox Holes: An Examination of Richard Fox's Book *Archaeology, History and Custer's Last Battle,*" in *10th Annual Symposium Custer Battlefield Historical and Museum Association, Hardin, Montana, June 21, 1996,* 47. See also Koury's debate with Fox: "Debate—Nature of Fighting at the

Little Big Horn," in *12th Annual Symposium Custer Battlefield Historical and Museum Association, Hardin, Montana, June 26, 1998*, 61–83.

75. Fox, *Archaeology, History*, 342 n17.

76. Ibid., 18; see also 278.

77. Wooden Leg, *Wooden Leg*; Thomas B. Marquis, *Memoirs of a White Crow Indian* (New York: Century, 1928).

78. Thomas B. Marquis, *Keep the Last Bullet for Yourself*, 2nd ed. (Algonac, MI: Reference Publications, 1985), 15.

79. Ibid.; this chapter (155–71) provides the arguments summarized here.

80. See esp. Fox, *Archaeology, History*, 147–51, 199–200.

81. Ibid., 136.

82. It is worth pointing out that Koury's highly critical review of Fox's book also notes this same passage. For Koury, calling the suicide testimony of Cheyenne oral history "nonsense" epitomizes a selective use of Indian testimony that he finds problematic. "Digging Fox Holes," 47–48.

83. Louise Barnett points out that another competing theory is that in the aftermath of the battle, the Cheyenne and Lakota warriors believed they would be punished by the United States for the deaths of Custer and their men, and for that reason they told non-Indians that the soldiers had committed suicide (personal communication).

84. James Welch, with Paul Stekler, *Killing Custer* (New York: W. W. Norton, 1994), 20.

85. Ibid., 44.

86. Ibid., 46.

87. Wayne M. Sarf, *The Little Bighorn Campaign: March–September 1876*, rev. ed. (Conshohocken, PA: Combined Publishing, 2000), 10.

88. Sherry L. Smith describes the neglect of military matters by the New Western History in "Lost Soldiers: Re-searching the Army in the American West," *Western Historical Quarterly* 29 (Summer 1998): 149–63.

89. See also Walter M. Camp's interview with He Dog in Camp, *Custer in '76*, 205–8.

90. Hardorff, comp. and ed., *Lakota Recollections of the Custer Fight*, 77–78.

91. Ibid., 78–79.

CHAPTER SIX

1. Montana Department of Labor and Industry, "Montana Annual Civilian Labor Force Statistics: 2004," July 2004, http//ceic.mt.gov/Data_maps.html; accessed November 9, 2005.

2. Montana Department of Labor and Industry, "Montana Reservations Labor Force, 2000–2003," www.ourfactsyourfuture.org/article.asp?PAGEID=&SUBID=&ARTICLEID=108&SEGMENTID=1; and Bureau of Indian Affairs Calculation of Unemployment Rates for Montana Reservations, http://dli.mt.gov/resources/indianlabor market.asp. Both accessed November 9, 2005. Thanks to Brad Eldredge of the Research and Analysis Bureau of the Montana Department of Labor and Industry for explaining the difference in methodology that generates such disparate unemployment figures.

3. Richard Handler and Eric Gable emphasize the significance of an "internal audience" to living history in their ethnography of Colonial Williamsburg, *The New History in an Old Museum: Creating the Past at Colonial Williamsburg* (Durham, NC: Duke University Press, 1997), 11.

4. Harry Roach, "Reenacting: A Retrospective," http://wesclark.com/jw/roach.html, accessed September 28, 2004; this article originally appeared in the *Camp Chase Gazette* in 1986.

5. Lisa A. Bacon, "Refighting the Civil War, with Government Help," *New York Times*, September 27, 2004, A12.

6. Jenny Thompson, *War Games: Inside the World of Twentieth-Century War Reenactors* (Washington, DC: Smithsonian Institution Press, 2004).

7. See, for instance, Richard Handler and William Saxton, "Dyssimulation: Reflexivity, Narrative, and the Quest for Authenticity in 'Living History,'" *Cultural Anthropology* 3 (1988): 242–60; Dennis Hall, "Civil War Reenactors and the Postmodern Sense of History," *Journal of American Culture* 17, no. 3 (Fall 1994): 7–11; and Randal Allred, "Catharsis, Revision, and Re-enactment: Negotiating the Meaning of the American Civil War," *Journal of American Culture* 19, no. 4 (Winter 1996): 1–14.

8. Pierre Nora, "General Introduction: Between Memory and History," in Nora, gen. ed., *Realms of Memory: Rethinking the French Past*, vol. 1, *Conflicts and Divisions*, English language edition edited by Lawrence D. Kritzman, translated by Arthur Goldhammer (New York: Columbia University Press, 1996), 12.

9. Hall, "Civil War Reenactors," 11.

10. Thompson, *War Games*, 52.

11. Bob Lampe, who returns annually to portray a Seventh Cavalry sergeant at the Real Bird reenactment, put it this way: "When my friends ask me why I do this, I tell them they have to come out with me [as a participant] to understand." Author interview, June 24, 2005.

12. Nora, "General Introduction," 17, 19.

13. Joy S. Kasson, *Buffalo Bill's Wild West: Celebrity, Memory, and Popular History* (New York: Hill and Wang, 2000), 35–37. See also Paul Reddin, *Wild West Shows* (Urbana: University of Illinois Press, 1999), 58. Interestingly, Louis S. Warren's voluminous biography of Cody downplays Cody's connection to Custer and emphasizes that most people who saw Buffalo Bill's Wild West Show did not see versions that featured Custer's Last Stand (*Buffalo Bill's America: William Cody and the Wild West Show* [New York: Alfred A. Knopf, 2005], 270).

14. Kasson, *Buffalo Bill's Wild West*, 113. See also Reddin, *Wild West Shows*, 80–84; and L. G. Moses, *Wild West Shows and the Images of American Indians, 1883–1933* (Albuquerque: University of New Mexico Press, 1996), 35–37, 147–148.

15. Brick Pomeroy, "Buffalo Bill's Realism," *Pomeroy Democrat*, July 3, 1886; quoted in Kasson, *Buffalo Bill's Wild West*, 61.

16. David Glassberg, *American Historical Pageantry: The Uses of Tradition in the Early Twentieth Century* (Chapel Hill: University of North Carolina Press, 1990).

17. Ibid., 122–23.

18. Author interview with Joseph Medicine Crow, June 23, 2004, at the Custer Battlefield Museum, Garryowen, Montana.

19. Ibid.

20. Among the many articles in the *Billings Gazette* and *Hardin Herald-Tribune*, see especially "Guard Chief Takes Role of Custer in Re-enactment," *Billings Gazette*, June 18, 1964, 14; Kathryn Wright, "Tourists Overflow in Hardin as Indians Take Custer Twice," *Billings Gazette*, June 28, 1964, 10.

21. "As the Crow Fights," *Newsweek*, July 13, 1964, 56.

22. Anne Chamberlin, "Bad Day Ahead for the Army's Greatest Loser," *Saturday Evening Post*, August 27, 1966, 71.

23. "Last Stand Attendance Shows Decrease," *Hardin Herald-Tribune*, July 6, 1972, n.p.

24. See the following articles in the *Billings Gazette* by Lorna Thackeray: "Developments Could Boost Hardin's Tourism" (June 11, 1990, 1A, 15A); "Town on the Rebound" (June 17, 1990, 1D); and "Merchants Revive Harding Street" (June 17, 1990, 1D).

25. Lorna Thackeray, "Big June for Battlefield Visitors," *Billings Gazette*, July 9, 1991, p. 1B.

26. Carl Rieckmann, "Family Plans Reenactments on 'Sacred' Little Bighorn Ground," *Big Horn County News* 97, no. 25 (June 24, 2004): A1–A2.

27. J. C. Furnas, *Goodbye to Uncle Tom* (New York: William Sloane Associates, 1956), 279–80.

28. Interview with Joseph Medicine Crow.

29. I attended performances of the Hardin "Custer's Last Stand" and Real Bird "Battle of the Little Bighorn" from 2002 to 2006. When possible, I attended multiple performances of each show. While some details of the performances vary from year to year, I have tried to limit my commentary to elements that remain constant, as well as to identify only those reenactors who participated in multiple years.

30. Interview with Joseph Medicine Crow.

31. Frederick Hoxie discusses the roots of this nineteenth-century antagonism in *Parading through History: The Making of the Crow Nation in America, 1805–1935* (New York: Cambridge University Press, 1995).

32. Over the course of three years, I spoke with approximately fifty different patrons of the Hardin reenactments and approximately thirty patrons of the Real Bird reenactments. As I suggest, these were brief, informal interviews, sometimes lasting only a minute or so, occasionally lasting five or six minutes. Because they were not conducted with any kind of methodological rigor, I can rely on only the most general findings, such as those discussed in this paragraph.

33. Glassberg, *American Historical Pageantry*, 92, 145.

34. I do not wish to suggest that all of the white and Indian participants in the reenactment have deep, abiding friendships. However, it is clear that the core group of reenactors and stagehands who return to the show annually share a genuine camaraderie that crosses racial boundaries.

35. Gregory F. Michno discusses several competing arguments about Medicine Tail Coulee Ford in *Lakota Noon: The Indian Narrative of Custer's Defeat* (Missoula, MT: Mountain, 1997), 108–9; and Richard Allan Fox Jr. also provides a good summary of accounts of this episode (as well as his own) in *Archaeology, History, and Custer's Last Battle* (Norman: University of Oklahoma Press, 1993), 275–81, 312–18.

36. Author interview with Paul Kicking Bear, June 23, 2003.

37. Rieckmann, "Family Plans Reenactments."

38. The 2004 performances of the Real Bird reenactment were the first in which I saw this prologue dramatizing the scene of oral transmission.

39. Richard Real Bird, "In Search of Peace and Prosperity: The Crow Tribal Struggle for Economic Sovereignty," address to the Malcolm Weiner Center for Social Policy, Harvard University, Cambridge, Massachusetts, April 1988, 16–17. Document available at http://www.ksg.harvard.edu/hpaied/pubs/pub_148.htm, accessed August 25, 2004.

40. For a sympathetic account of Richard Real Bird's administration and his incarceration, see Lloyd G. Mickey Old Coyote and Helene Smith, *Apsaalooka: The Crow Nation Then and Now*, rev. ed. (Greensburg, PA: MacDonald Sward, 1993), 180–92.

41. Author interview with Henry Real, June 26, 2004, Garryowen, MT.

42. Author interview with Bill Rini, August 9, 2004. Rini later posted another version of this story on an Internet bulletin board for reenactors who participate in the Real Bird reenactment (http://groups.msn.com/custerclan). In fact, Rini's fifteen-part history of the Real Bird reenactment, posted as a series of e-mails to the bulletin board from July to October 2005, gives a detailed, albeit partisan, account of the often tense relationships between at least some of the reenactors and the Real Bird family, as well as among the reenactors themselves.

43. Interview with Henry Real Bird.

44. Ibid.

45. "Love and Dreams" and "Rivers of Horses" both appear in Henry Real Bird, *The Best of Hank Real Bird* (n.p., 1995), 22, 26–27; they are quoted here with permission of the author.

46. Joseph Medicine Crow, *From the Heart of Crow Country: The Crow Indians' Own Stories* (Lincoln: University of Nebraska Press, 1992), 106–7.

47. Elizabeth Lawrence was also the name of a veterinarian, discussed briefly in chapter 3, who wrote a book about Comanche, the Seventh Cavalry horse who was found alive on the Little Bighorn battlefield. I have not been able to discover a connection between the actual Elizabeth Lawrence and this character, however.

48. Kathy Clark, *Cody's Last Stand*, American Romance 442 (New York: Harlequin, 1992), 240.

49. Ibid., 240.

50. Dean Cousino, "Parade Enthralls," *Monroe Evening News*, November 20, 2000, 1A, 11A.

51. In Montana v. Crow Tribe 523 U.S. 696 (1998), the Crow Tribe argued that it should have received taxes paid to the state of Montana by companies mining land to which the Crows claimed mineral rights. The Supreme Court denied the claim.

52. Hoxie, *Parading through History*, 106–8; George E. Hyde, *Life of George Bent Written from His Letters*, edited by Savoie Lottinville (Norman: University of Oklahoma Press, 1968), 27–30. See also Colin G. Calloway, "'The Only Way Open to Us': The Crow Struggle for Survival in the Nineteenth Century," *North Dakota History* 53 (Summer 1986): 25–34.

53. John S. Gray, *Centennial Campaign: The Sioux War of 1876* (1976; rpt. Norman: University of Oklahoma Press, 1988), 117.

54. Leo Killsback, "People Need to Get Little Bighorn Story Straight," letter to the *Billings Gazette*, July 1, 2004, accessed via www.billingsgazette.com/index, July 1, 2004.

55. This group of twenty to twenty-five Northern Cheyennes is led by Leroy Whiteman, who discussed his involvement with the reenactment with me in a June 2002 interview. I am also grateful to Andrew Beck and Bartley Powers of Amalgamation Films for providing me with raw footage of their video interview with Whiteman from that same month.

56. Leo Killsback, speech at the Indian Memorial, Little Bighorn National Monument, June 25, 2004.

57. Philip J. Deloria's essay "Representations" in *Indians in Unexpected Places* (Lawrence: University of Kansas Press, 2004), 52–108, and Nicholas G. Rosenthal, "Representing Indians: Native American Actors on Hollywood's Frontier," *Western Historical Quarterly*, Autumn 2005, 329–52, both provide accounts of how Indian actors and producers of mass culture in the early twentieth century shaped their performances and media for their own purposes. Deloria's *Playing Indian* (New Haven, CT: Yale University Press, 1998) has also influenced my thinking on these matters.

58. Eli S. Ricker, *Voices of the American West*, vol. 1, *The Indian Interviews of Eli S. Ricker, 1903–1919*, edited by Richard E. Jensen (Lincoln: University of Nebraska Press, 2005), 55. Jeffrey Ostler also mentions the fight in *The Plains Sioux and U.S. Colonialism from Lewis and Clark to Wounded Knee* (New York: Cambridge University Press, 2004), 89.

59. Hazel Hertzberg's *The Search for an American Indian Identity: Modern Pan-Indian Movements* (Syracuse, NY: Syracuse University Press, 1971), a book on pan-Indianism in the early twentieth century. remains valuable; more recently, Joane Nagel discussed the role of pan-Indianism in political movements in the second half of the twentieth century in *American Indian Ethnic Renewal: Red Power and the Resurgence of Identity and Culture* (New York: Oxford University Press, 1996).

60. U.S. Congress, House Subcommittee on National Parks and Public Lands, Custer Battlefield National Monument Indian Memorial: Hearing before the Subcommittee on National Parks and Public Lands, 101st Cong., 2d sess., September 4, 1990, 19.

61. Interview with Paul Kicking Bear.

EPILOGUE

1. John A. Doerner, chief historian of the Little Bighorn Battlefield National Monument, explained the history of the change in wording on the warrior markers to me in an e-mail communication, October 23, 2006.

2. Gregory F. Michno, *Battle at Sand Creek: The Military Perspective* (El Segundo, CA: Upton and Sons, 2004), 276.

3. James Welch with Paul Stekler, *Killing Custer: The Battle of the Little Bighorn and the Fate of the Plains Indians* (New York: W. W. Norton, 1994), 12.

4. Author interview with Steve Alexander, Monroe, MI, April 23, 2003.

5. Peter Baker, "Wrong Turn in Nasiriyah Led to Soldiers' Capture," *Washington Post*, online edition, April 13, 2003; www.washingtonpost.com/wp-dyn/articles/A19192 -2003Apr13.html, accessed April 13, 2003.

6. Robert D. Kaplan, "Indian Country," *Wall Street Journal*, September 21, 2004, A22.

7. Robert D. Kaplan, *Imperial Grunts: The American Military on the Ground* (New York: Random House, 1995), 4.

8. In the "press gaggle" of December 27, 2005, the White House announced that President Bush brought Kaplan's book to Texas with him to read during his vacation: www.whitehouse.gov/news/releases/2005/12/20051227-1.html, accessed August 15, 2006.

9. Kaplan, *Imperial Grunts*, 10.

10. Ibid., 12.

11. Ibid., 11.

12. John Brown, "'Our Indian Wars Are Not Over Yet': Ten Ways to Interpret the War on Terror as a Frontier Conflict," TomsDispatch.com, January 19, 2006, www .tomdispatch.com/index.mhtml?pid=50043, accessed August 15, 2006.

13. "National Pundits Sadly Ignore American Indian History," unsigned editorial, *Indian Country Today*, online edition, February 2, 2006, http://indiancountry.com/ content.cfm?id=1096412384, accessed February 8, 2006.

14. Marty Two Bulls Sr., "War in Iraq," editorial cartoon, *Indian Country Today*, online edition, February 2, 2006, http://indiancountry.com/content.cfm?id=1096412390, accessed February 8, 2006.

15. David Melmer, "Veterans Take Center Stage," *Indian Country Today*, online edition, July 17, 2006, http://indiancountry.com/content.cfm?id=1096413323, accessed July 23, 2006. Fire Thunder, I should note, was under suspension as president of the Oglala Lakota Tribe and would be impeached during the week that followed this ceremony.

16. Becky Shay, "Paratroopers Help Crow Tribe Honor Veterans," *Billings Gazette*, online edition, June 24, 2006, www.billingsgazette.net/articles/2006/06/24/news/ state/20-honors.txt, accessed June 27, 2006.

WORKS CITED

The Alamo. DVD. Directed by John Lee Hancock. 2004; Burbank, CA: Buena Vista Home Entertainment, 2004.

Alexie, Sherman. "Custer Speaks." In *Old Shirts and New Skins,* 36–38. Los Angeles: American Indian Studies Center, University of California–Los Angeles, 1996.

———. "Ghost Dance." In *McSweeney's Mammoth Treasury of Thrilling Tales,* edited by Michael Chabon, 341–53. New York: Vintage, 2003.

———. *Smoke Signals.* New York: Hyperion, 1998.

Allred, Randal. "Catharsis, Revision, and Re-enactment: Negotiating the Meaning of the American Civil War." *Journal of American Culture* 19, no. 4 (Winter 1996). 1–14.

Aoki, Haruo. "Chief Joseph's Words." *Idaho Yesterdays* 33 (Fall 1989); 16–21.

"As the Crow Fights." *Newsweek,* July 13, 1964, 56.

Bacon, Lisa A. "Refighting the Civil War, with Government Help." *New York Times,* September 27, 2004, A12.

Baker, Peter. "Wrong Turn in Nasiriyah Led to Soldiers' Capture." *Washington Post,* April 13, 2003.

Barnard, Sandy. *Digging into Custer's Last Stand.* 3rd ed. Terre Haute, IN: AST Press, 2004.

Barnett, Louise. *Touched By Fire: The Life, Death, and Mythic Afterlife of George Armstrong Custer.* New York: Henry Holt, 1996.

Barnitz, Albert. "With Custer at Appomattox." *Valor and Arms* 2, no.1 (Fall 1975): 37–42.

Barsh, Russel Lawrence. "War and the Reconfiguring of American Indian Society." *Journal of American Studies* 35 (2001): 371–410.

Baudrillard, Jean. "The System of Collecting." Translated by Roger Cardinal. In *The Cultures of Collecting,* edited by John Elsner and Roger Cardinal. Cambridge, MA: Harvard University Press, 1994. 7–24.

Bederman, Gail. *Manliness and Civilization: A Cultural History of Gender and Race in the United States, 1880–1917.* Chicago: University of Chicago Press, 1995.

Bernstein, Alison R. *American Indians and World War II.* Norman: University of Oklahoma, 1991.

Berthrong, Donald J. *The Cheyenne and Arapaho Ordeal.* Norman: University of Oklahoma Press, 1976.

———. *The Southern Cheyennes*. Norman: University of Oklahoma Press, 1963.

Bighead, Kate, as told to Thomas Marquis. "She Watched Custer's Last Battle." In *The Custer Reader*, edited by Paul Andrew Hutton, 363–77. Lincoln: University of Nebraska Press, 1992.

"Biographical Sketch of Lawrence A. Frost." Genealogy files, Monroe County Library, Monroe, MI, n.d.

Blake, Michael. *Marching to Valhalla: A Novel of Custer's Last Days*. New York: Villard, 1996.

Blight, David. *Race and Reunion: The Civil War in American Memory*. Cambridge, MA: Harvard University Press, 2001.

"A Bloody Battle." *New York Herald,* July 7, 1876, 5.

Braatz, Timothy. "Clash of Cultures as Euphemism: Avoiding History at the Little Bighorn." *American Indian Culture and Research Journal* 28, no. 4 (2004): 107–30.

Brady, Cyrus Townsend. *Indian Fights and Fighters*. 1904; rpt. Lincoln: University of Nebraska Press, 1971.

Brill, Charles J. *Custer, Black Kettle, and the Fight on the Washita*. Foreword by Mark L. Gardner. (Originally published as *Conquest of the Southern Plains*, 1938.) Norman: University of Oklahoma Press, 2002.

Brizée-Bowen, Sandra L. *For All to See: The Little Bighorn in Plains Indian Art*. Spokane, WA: Arthur L. Clark, 2003.

Broome, Jeff. *Dog Soldier Justice: The Ordeal of Susanna Alderdice in the Kansas Indian War*. Lincoln, KS: Lincoln County Historical Society, 2003.

Brown, John. "'Our Indian Wars Are Not Over Yet': Ten Ways to Interpret the War on Terror as a Frontier Conflict." TomDispatch.com, January 19, 2006. www.tom dispatch.com/index.mhtml?pid=50043; accessed August 15, 2006.

Burdick, Usher. *David F. Barry's Notes on "The Custer Battle."* Enlarged ed. Baltimore: Wirth Brothers, 1949.

Bureau of Indian Affairs. "Calculation of Unemployment Rates for Montana Reservations." http://dli.mt.gov/resources/indianlabormarket.asp; accessed November 9, 2005.

Calhoun, James. *With Custer in '74: James Calhoun's Diary of the Black Hills Expedition*. Edited by Lawrence A. Frost. Provo, UT: Brigham Young University Press, 1979.

Calloway, Colin G. "'The Only Way Open to Us': The Crow Struggle for Survival in the Nineteenth Century." *North Dakota History* 53 (Summer 1986): 25–34.

Camp, Walter Mason. *Custer and Company: Walter Camp's Notes on the Custer Fight*. Edited by Bruce R. Liddic and Paul Harbaugh. (Originally published as *Custer on Camp: Transcribing the Custer Myth* [Spokane, WA: Arthur H. Clark, 1995].) Lincoln: University of Nebraska Press, 1998.

———. *Custer in '76: Walter Camp's Notes on the Custer Fight*. Edited by Kenneth Hammer. 1976; rpt. Norman: University of Oklahoma Press, 1990.

———. *On the Little Bighorn with Walter Camp: A Collection of Walter Mason Camp's Letters, Notes and Opinions on Custer's Last Fight*. Compiled and edited by Richard G. Hardorff. El Segundo, CA: Upton and Sons, 2002.

Carroll, John M., ed. *The Benteen-Goldin Letters on Custer and His Last Battle*. 1974; rpt. Lincoln: University of Nebraska Press, 1991.

———, comp. and ed. *Custer in the Civil War: His Unfinished Memoirs*. San Rafael, CA: Presidio, 1977.

———, ed. *General Custer and the Battle of the Washita: The Federal View*. Bryan, TX: Guidon, 1978.

———. Letter. *Little Big Horn Associates Newsletter* 11, no. 5 (May 1977): 4.

Casey, Robert J. *The Black Hills and Their Incredible Characters*. Indianapolis: Bobbs-Merrill, 1949.

Cate, Fred H., Dennis H. Long, and David C. Williams, eds. *The Court-Martial of George Armstrong Custer*. Bloomington: Indiana University School of Law, 2001.

Chamberlin, Anne. "Bad Day Ahead for the Army's Greatest Loser." *Saturday Evening Post*, August 27, 1966, 70–75.

Church, William Conant. "Custer's Last Fight: Sitting Bull's Description of the Battle." *Army and Navy Journal*, November 24, 1877, 245–46.

Clark, Badger. "The Mountain That Had Its Face Lifted." In *The Black Hills*, edited by Roderick Peattie, 221–43. New York: Vanguard, 1952.

Clark, Kathy. *Cody's Last Stand*. American Romance 442. New York: Harlequin, 1992.

[Clarke, R. D.]. *The Works of Sitting Bull, Including Part II*. Chicago: Knight and Leonard, 1878.

Cleland, Charles E. *Rites of Conquest: The History and Culture of Michigan's Native Americans*. Ann Arbor: University of Michigan Press, 1992.

Coleman, William S. E., ed. *Voices from Wounded Knee*. Lincoln: University of Nebraska Press, 2000.

"Col. Wyncoop's Letter Resigning His Agency." *New York Times*, December 19, 1868, 3.

"Conflict Emerges over Custer Park." *New York Times*, October 11, 1991, 37.

Connell, Evan S. *Son of the Morning Star*. San Francisco: North Point, 1984.

Connelly, Kevin. Review of *Little Bighorn Mysteries and More Little Bighorn Mysteries*, by Vern Smalley. *Little Big Horn Associates Newsletter* 39, no. 6 (July 2005): 6.

Cook-Lynn, Elizabeth. *Anti-Indianism in Modern America: A Voice from Tatekeya's Earth*. Urbana: University of Illinois Press, 2001.

———. Review of *Black Hills/White Justice: The Sioux Nation versus the United States, 1775 to the Present*, by Edward Lazarus. Wicazo Sa Review 8, no. 1 (Spring 1992): 100–102.

Corman, Catherine A. "9/11 and Acoma Pueblo." *Common-Place* 5, no. 1 (October 2004). www.common-place.org/pastimes/200408.shtml.

Cousino, Dean. "Parade Enthralls." *Monroe Evening News* (MI), November 20, 2000, 1A, 11A.

Coward, John M. *The Newspaper Indian: Native American Identity in the Press, 1820–90*. Urbana: University of Illinois Press, 1999.

Cowely, Jill. *Cultural Landscape Inventory, Level Two, Washita Battlefield National Historic Site*. Santa Fe, NM: Intermountain Region, Santa Fe Support Office, November 1999.

Crayon, Porte, ed. "Sitting Bull: Autobiography of the Famous Sioux Chief." *Harper's Weekly*, July 29, 1876, 625–28.

"Crowd of 5000 Witness Ceremonial at Cheyenne." *Cheyenne Star* (OK), December 4, 1930, 1.

Custer, Brice C. *The Sacrificial Lion, George Armstrong Custer: From American Hero to Media Villain*. El Segundo, CA: Upton and Sons, 1999.

Custer, Elizabeth B. *"Boots and Saddles," or Life in Dakota with General Custer*. 1885; rpt. Norman: University of Oklahoma Press, 1961.

———. *The Civil War Memories of Elizabeth Bacon Custer: Reconstructed from Her Diaries and Notes*. Edited by Arlene Reynolds. Austin: University of Texas Press, 1994.

———. *Following the Guidon*. 1890; rpt. Norman: University of Oklahoma Press, 1966.

Custer, George Armstrong. *My Life on the Plains, or Personal Experiences with Indians*. 1874; rpt. Norman: University of Oklahoma Press, 1962.

"Custer's Massacre." *New York Herald*. 8 July 1876: 6.

"Custer's Washita Fight." *New York Sun*, May 14, 1899, 3.

Dances with Wolves. Videocassette. Directed by Kevin Costner. 1990; New York: Orion, 1993.

Darling, Roger. *Custer's Seventh Cavalry Comes to Dakota: New Discoveries Reveal Custer's Tribulations en Route to the Yellowstone Expedition.* El Segundo, CA: Upton and Sons, 1989.

DeClue, Charlotte. "To the Spirit of Monahsetah." In *A Gathering of Spirit: A Collection by North American Indian Women,* edited by Beth Brant, 52–54. Ithaca, NY: Firebrand, 1984.

Del Olmo, Frank. "Activists' Plaque at Little Bighorn Honors 'Patriots' Who Beat Custer." *Los Angeles Times,* July 4, 1988, 24.

Deloria, Philip J. *Indians in Unexpected Places.* Lawrence: University Press of Kansas, 2004.

———. *Playing Indian.* New Haven, CT: Yale University Press, 1998.

Deloria, Vine, Jr. *Custer Died for Your Sins.* 1969; rpt. Norman: University of Oklahoma Press, 1988.

———. "Intellectual Self-Determination and Sovereignty: Looking at the Windmills in Our Minds." *Wicazo Sa Review* 13, no. 1 (Spring 1998): 25–31.

Deloria, Vine, Jr., and Raymond DeMallie, eds. *Proceedings of the Great Peace Commission.* Washington, DC: Institute for the Development of Indian Law, 1975.

Deloria, Vine, Jr., and Clifford M. Lytle. *The Nations Within: The Past and Future of American Indian Sovereignty.* New York: Pantheon, 1984.

DeMallie, Raymond J. "'These Have No Ears': Narrative and Ethnohistorical Method." *Ethnohistory* 40 (1993): 515–38.

Dippie, Brian W. *Custer's Last Stand: The Anatomy of an American Myth.* 1976; rpt. Lincoln: University of Nebraska Press, 1994.

———. *The Vanishing Indian: White Attitudes and U.S. Indian Policy.* Middletown, CT: Wesleyan University Press, 1982.

Dixon, Joseph K. *The Vanishing Race.* Concept by Rodman Wanamaker. Garden City, NJ: Doubleday, Page, 1913.

Dodge, Richard Irving. *The Black Hills.* 1876; rpt. Minneapolis: Ross and Haines, 1965.

Dunbar, Willis F. *Michigan: A History of the Wolverine State.* Rev. ed. by George S. May. Grand Rapids, MI: Eerdmans, 1980.

Dustin, Fred. *The Custer Tragedy.* 1939; rpt. El Segundo, CA: Upton and Sons, 1987.

Ediger, Theodore A., and Vinnie Hoffman. "Some Reminiscences of the Battle of the Washita." *Chronicles of Oklahoma* 33 (1955): 137–41.

Ege, Robert J. Untitled editor's note. *Little Bighorn Associates Newsletter* 1, no. 1 (January 1967): 1.

"Elizabeth Lawrence, 74, Scholar of Animal-Human Relations." *Boston Globe,* November 18, 2003. Online edition: www.boston.com/news/globe/obituaries/articles/2003/11/18/elizabeth_lawrence_74_scholar_of_human_animal_relations; accessed January 30, 2006.

Elsner, John, and Roger Cardinal. Introduction to *The Cultures of Collecting,* 1–6. Cambridge, MA: Harvard University Press, 1994.

Ewart, Theodore. *Theodore Ewart's Diary of the Black Hills Expedition of 1874.* Edited by John M. Carroll and Lawrence A. Frost. Piscataway, NJ: CRI Books, 1976.

Fisher, Clay. *Yellow Hair.* 1954; rpt. New York: Pocket, 1961.

Flores, Richard R. *Remembering the Alamo: Memory, Modernity, and the Master Symbol.* Austin: University of Texas, 2002.

Florio, Gwen. "Balance at Little Bighorn." *Denver Post,* June 26, 2003, 1A, 10A.

Foley, James R. "Walter Camp and Ben Clark." *Research Review: The Journal of the Little Big Horn Associates* 10, no. 1 (January 1996): 17–27.

Foote, Kenneth E. *Shadowed Ground: America's Landscapes of Violence and Tragedy.* Rev. ed. Austin: University of Texas Press, 2003.

Fowler, Loretta. *Ethnographic Overview (Phase II) for Washita Battlefield National Historic*

Site, Final Report on Cooperative Agreement. 1443CA125098002, Modification 3, prepared for the National Park Service, June 26, 2001.

———. *Tribal Sovereignty and the Historical Imagination: Cheyenne-Arapaho Politics.* Lincoln: University of Nebraska Press, 2002.

Fox, Richard Allan, Jr. *Archaeology, History, and Custer's Last Battle.* Norman: University of Oklahoma Press, 1993.

Freud, Sigmund. "The Uncanny." In *The Uncanny,* translated by David McLintock, 123–62. New York: Penguin, 2003.

"From the Shenandoah Valley." *New York Daily Tribune,* August 22, 1864, 6.

Froiland, Sven G. *Natural History of the Black Hills and Badlands.* Sioux Falls, SD: Center for Western Studies, 1999.

Frost, Lawrence A. "The Beginning of the LBHA." *Little Bighorn Associates Newsletter* 20, no. 1 (1987): 3–4.

———. *Custer Legends.* Bowling Green, OH: Bowling Green University Popular Press, 1981.

———. *General Custer's Libbie.* Seattle: Superior, 1976.

Furnas, J. C. *Goodbye to Uncle Tom.* New York: William Sloane Associates, 1956.

Gardner, Mark. Foreword to *Custer, Black Kettle, and the Fight on the Washita,* by Charles J. Brill, 3–12. Norman: University of Oklahoma Press, 2002.

Glassberg, David. *American Historical Pageantry: The Uses of Tradition in the Early Twentieth Century.* Chapel Hill: University of North Carolina Press, 1990.

Godfrey, Edward S. "Custer's Last Battle." In *The Custer Reader,* edited by Paul Andrew Hutton, 257–318. Lincoln: University of Nebraska Press, 1992.

———. "General Godfrey's Comment on Gall's Story." In *The Custer Myth,* edited by W. A. Graham, 93–96. Mechanicsburg, PA: Stackpole, 2000.

———. "Some Reminiscences, Including the Washita Battle, November 27, 1868." In *The Custer Reader,* edited by Paul Andrew Hutton, 159–79. Lincoln: University of Nebraska Press, 1992.

Gonzalez, Mario, and Elizabeth Cook-Lynn. *The Politics of Hallowed Ground: Wounded Knee and the Struggle for Indian Sovereignty.* Urbana: University of Illinois Press, 1999.

Grafe, Ernest, and Paul Horsted. *Exploring with Custer: The 1874 Black Hills Expedition.* Custer, SD: Golden Valley, 2002.

Graham, W. A., ed. *The Custer Myth.* 1953; rpt. Mechanicsburg, PA: Stackpole, 2000.

———. *The Story of the Little Big Horn.* 1926; rpt. Mechanicsburg, PA: Stackpole, 1994.

Gray, John S. *Centennial Campaign: The Sioux War of 1876.* 1976; rpt. Norman: University of Oklahoma Press, 1988.

———. *Custer's Last Campaign: Mitch Boyer and the Little Bighorn Reconstructed.* Lincoln: University of Nebraska Press, 1991.

Greene, Jerome A. Introduction to *Lakota and Cheyenne: Indian Views of the Great Sioux War, 1876–1877.* Norman: University of Oklahoma Press, 1994.

———. *Nez Perce Summer, 1877: The U.S. Army and the Nee-Me-Poo Crisis.* Helena: Montana Historical Society Press, 2000.

———. "The Uses of Indian Testimony in the Writing of Indian Wars History." *Journal of the Order of the Indian Wars* 2, no. 1 (Winter 1981): 1–7.

———. *Washita: The U.S. Army and the Southern Cheyennes, 1867–1869.* Norman: University of Oklahoma Press, 2004.

"Guard Chief Takes Role of Custer in Re-enactment." *Billings Gazette* (MT), June 18, 1964, 14.

Hagengruber, James. "Built out of Protest." *Billings Gazette* (MT), June 25, 2003, 12A.

———. "Man Without a Face: Mystery Continues in the Hunt for Chief Crazy Horse." *Billings Gazette* (MT), November 16, 2003. Online edition: www.billingsgazette.net/articles/2003/11/16/magazine/export131457.txt.

Halbwachs, Maurice. *On Collective Memory.* Edited and translated by Lewis A. Coser. Chicago: University of Chicago Press, 1992.

Hall, Dennis. "Civil War Reenactors and the Postmodern Sense of History." *Journal of American Culture* 17, no. 3 (Fall 1994): 7–11.

Hammer, Kenneth. Biographical Sketch. In Walter M. Camp, *Custer in '76: Walter Camp's Notes on the Custer Fight.* Edited by Hammer. 1976; rpt. Norman: University of Oklahoma Press, 1990.

Handler, Richard, and Eric Gable. *The New History in an Old Museum: Creating the Past at Colonial Williamsburg.* Durham, NC: Duke University Press, 1997.

Handler, Richard, and William Saxton. "Dyssimulation: Reflexivity, Narrative, and the Quest for Authenticity in 'Living History.'" *Cultural Anthropology* 3 (1988): 242–60.

Hanson, Joseph Mills. *The Conquest of the Missouri.* 1909; rpt. New York: Murray Hill, 1946.

Hardoff, Dutch [Richard G.]. "Burials, Exhumations, and Reinterments: A View of Custer Hill." In *Custer and His Times,* bk. 2. Fort Worth, TX: Little Bighorn Associates, 1984.

Hardorff, Richard G., comp. and ed. *Cheyenne Memories of the Custer Fight: New Sources of Indian-Military History.* Lincoln: University of Nebraska Press, 1998.

———, comp. and ed. *Indian Views of the Custer Fight.* Spokane, WA: Arthur H. Clark, 2004.

———, comp. and ed. Lakota *Recollections of the Custer Fight.* Lincoln: University of Nebraska Press, 1997.

———, comp. and ed. *Washita Memories: Eyewitness Views of Custer's Attack on Black Kettle's Village.* Norman: University of Oklahoma Press, 2006.

Hart, Lawrence H. "A Cheyenne Legacy at the Washita River." In *Gathering at the Hearth: Stories That Mennonites Tell,* edited by John E. Sharp, 21–25. Scottdale, PA: Herald, 2001.

———. "Legacies of the Massacre and Battle at the Washita." *Oklahoma Today* 50, no. 3 (May/June 1999): 58–63.

Hawkins, M. E. "The Burial of the Hatchet." In *The Custer Semi-Centennial Ceremonies.* Casper, WY: Casper Printing and Stationery, 1926.

"The Heroes of the Custer Tie." In *Bards of the Little Bighorn,* edited by Brian W. Dippie and John M. Carroll, 287–88. Bryan, TX: Guidon, 1978.

Hertzberg, Hazel. *The Search for an American Indian Identity: Modern Pan-Indian Movements.* Syracuse, NY: Syracuse University Press, 1971.

Hoig, Stan. *The Battle of the Washita.* 1976; rpt. Lincoln: University of Nebraska Press, 1979.

———. *The Sand Creek Massacre.* Norman: University of Oklahoma Press, 1961.

Hollinger, David A. *Cosmopolitanism and Solidarity: Studies in Ethnoracial, Religious, and Professional Affiliation in the United States.* Madison: University of Wisconsin Press, 2006,

Horwitz, Tony. *Confederates in the Attic: Dispatches from the Unfinished Civil War.* New York: Pantheon, 1998.

"Hoven Announces North Dakota Float for Presidential Inaugural Parade." Press release. State of North Dakota, January 19, 2005. www.governor.state.nd.us/media/news-releases/2005/01/050119.html.

Hoxie, Frederick E. *A Final Promise: The Campaign to Assimilate the Indians, 1880–1920.* Lincoln: University of Nebraska Press, 1984.

———. *Parading through History: The Making of the Crow Nation in America, 1805–1935.* New York: Cambridge University Press, 1995.

Huhndorf, Shari M. *Going Native: Indians in the American Cultural Imagination.* Ithaca, NY: Cornell University Press, 2001.

Hutchins, James S., ed. *The Army and Navy Journal on the Battle of the Little Bighorn and Related Matters, 1876–1881.* El Segundo, CA: Upton and Sons, 2003.

Hutton, Paul Andrew. "'Correct in Every Detail: General Custer in Hollywood." In *Legacy: New Perspectives on the Battle of the Little Bighorn,* edited by Charles E. Rankin, 231–70. Helena: Montana Historical Society Press, 1996.

———, ed. *The Custer Reader.* Lincoln: University of Nebraska Press, 1992.

———. "From Little Bighorn to Little Big Man: The Changing Image of a Western Hero in Popular Culture." In *The Custer Reader,* edited by Paul Andrew Hutton. Lincoln: University of Nebraska Press, 1992.

———. *Phil Sheridan and His Army.* Lincoln: University of Nebraska Press, 1985.

Hyde, George. *Life of George Bent Written from His Letters.* Edited by Savoie Lottinville. Norman: University of Oklahoma Press, 1968.

"Indian Relics." *New York Times,* June 13, 1869, 3.

"The Indian Troubles." *New York Times,* December 27, 1868, 1.

"An Indian Victory." *New York Times,* July 7, 1876, 4.

"The Indian War." *New York Herald,* June 19, 1876, 2.

"The Indian War." *New York Times,* December 20, 1868, 1.

"The Indian War." *New York Times,* July 21, 1876, 1.

Jackson, Donald. *Custer's Gold: The United States Cavalry Expedition of 1874.* New Haven, CT: Yale University Press, 1966.

Jacobson, Louis. "Following Custer's Photographer Into the Black Hills." *New York Times,* August 15, 2002, E3.

Jamieson, Perry D. *Crossing the Deadly Ground: United States Army Tactics, 1865–1899.* Tuscaloosa: University of Alabama Press, 1994.

Jefferson, Thomas. *Writings.* Edited by Merrill D. Peterson. New York: Library of America, 1984.

Johnson, Susan Lee. "'A Memory Sweet to Soldiers': The Significance of Gender in the History of the 'American West.'" *Western Historical Quarterly* 24 (1993): 495–517.

Kamb, Lewis. "Bush's Comment on Tribal Sovereignty Creates a Buzz." *Seattle Post-Intelligencer,* August 13, 2004. http://seattlepi.nwsource.com/national/186171_bush tribes13.html.

Kaplan, Robert D. *Imperial Grunts: The American Military on the Ground.* New York: Random House, 1995.

———. "Indian Country." *Wall Street Journal,* September 21, 2004, A22.

Kappler, Charles J. *Indian Affairs: Laws and Treaties.* Vol. 2. Washington, DC: Government Printing Office, 1904.

Kasson, Joy S. *Buffalo Bill's Wild West: Celebrity, Memory, and Popular History.* New York: Hill and Wang, 2000.

Keim, De B. Randolph. *Sheridan's Troopers on the Borders: A Winter Campaign on the Plains.* 1870; rpt. Williamstown, MA: Corner House Publishers, 1973.

Kenny, Maurice. "Monahsetah . . . A Cheyenne Girl." In *On Second Thought: A Compilation,* 119–20. Norman: University of Oklahoma Press, 1995.

Kidd, J[ames] H[arvey]. *Riding with Custer: Recollections of a Cavalryman in the Civil War.* 1908; rpt. Lincoln: University of Nebraska Press, 1997.

Kidd, James Harvey. *One of Custer's Wolverines: The Civil War Letters of Brevet Brigadier General James H. Kidd, 6th Michigan Cavalry.* Edited by Eric J. Wittenberg. Kent, OH: Kent State University Press, 2000.

Kidd, Kenneth. *Making American Boys: Boyology and the Feral Tale.* Minneapolis: University of Minnesota Press, 2004.

Killsback, Leo. "People Need to Get Little Bighorn Story Straight." Letter. *Billings Gazette* (MT), July 1, 2004. www.billingsgazette.com/index; accessed 7 July 2004.

Klein, Kerwin Lee. "On the Emergence of *Memory* in Historical Discourse." *Representations* 69 (2000): 127–50.

Koury, Mike [Michael]. "Digging Fox Holes: An Examination of Richard Fox's Book Archaeology, History and Custer's Last Battle." *10th Annual Symposium Custer Battlefield Historical and Museum Association, Hardin, MT, June 21, 1996,* 47–56.

Koury, Michael J., ed. *Custer Centennial Observance.* Fort Collins, CO: Old Army Press, 1978.

Koury, Michael, and Richard A. Fox Jr. "Debate—Nature of Fighting at the Little Big Horn." *12th Annual Symposium Custer Battlefield Historical and Museum Association, Hardin, MT, June 26, 1998,* 61–83.

Krause, Herbert, and Gary D. Olson, eds. *Prelude to Glory: A Newspaper Accounting of Custer's 1874 Expedition to the Black Hills.* Sioux Falls, SD: Brevet Press, 1974.

Krupat, Arnold. *Red Matters: Native American Studies.* Philadelphia: University of Pennsylvania Press, 2002.

Kuhlman, Charles. *Legend into History.* 1951; rpt. Fort Collins, CO: Old Army Press, 1977.

Langellier, John Philip. *Custer: The Man, the Myth, the Movies.* Mechanicsburg, PA: Stackpole, 2000.

"Last Stand Attendance Shows Decrease." *Hardin Herald-Tribune* (MT), July 6, 1972, n.p.

Lawrence, Elizabeth. "A Clash of Cultures—The Issues behind the Battle of the Little Big Horn." In *Custer and His Times,* edited by Paul A. Hutton, 1:231–42. El Paso, TX: Little Big Horn Associates, 1981.

———. *Comanche: His Very Silence Speaks.* Detroit: Wayne State University Press, 1989.

Lazarus, Edward. *Black Hills/White Justice: The Sioux Nation versus the United States, 1775 to the Present.* New York: HarperCollins, 1991.

Leckie, Shirley A. *Elizabeth Bacon Custer and the Making of a Myth.* Norman: University of Oklahoma Press, 1993.

Le Goff, Jacques. *History and Memory.* Translated by Steven Rendall and Elizabeth Claman. New York: Columbia University Press, 1992.

Libby, Orin G., ed. *The Arikara Narrative of Custer's Campaign and the Battle of the Little Bighorn.* Norman: University of Oklahoma Press, 1998.

Linenthal, Edward Tabor. *Sacred Ground: Americans and Their Battlefields.* Urbana: University of Illinois Press, 1991.

———. *The Unfinished Bombing: Oklahoma City in American Memory.* New York: Oxford University Press, 2001.

Little Big Horn Associates. *Newsletter of the Little Big Horn Associates,* 1967–present. Dorsch Memorial Library, Monroe, MI.

Little Big Man. DVD. Directed by Arthur Penn. 1970; Hollywood: Paramount, 2003.

Longfellow, Henry Wadsworth. *Poems and Other Writings.* Edited by J. D. McClatchy. New York: Library of America, 2000.

Lyman, Theodore. Meade's *Headquarters, 1863–1865.* Selected and edited by George R. Agassiz. Boston: Atlantic Monthly, 1922.

MacPherson, James. "His Horse Is Thunder Is Elected." *Bismarck Tribune,* September 30, 2005. Online edition: www.bismarcktribune.com/articles/2005/09/30/news/state/102979.txt.

Maffly, Brian. "Healing Wounds." *Salt Lake City Tribune,* June 26, 2003, A1, A5.

Males, Mrs. L. L. "Almost Too Real." Letter to the editor. *Daily Oklahoman,* December 8, 1968, A28.

Marquis, Thomas B. *Custer on the Little Bighorn.* 2nd ed. Algonac, MI: Reference Publications, 1986.

———. *Keep the Last Bullet for Yourself.* 2nd ed. Algonac, MI: Reference Publications, 1985.

———. *Memoirs of a White Crow Indian.* New York: Century, 1928.

"The Massacre." *New York Herald,* July 7, 1865, 5.

McChristian, Douglas. "Burying the Hatchet: The Semicentennial of the Little Big-horn." *Montana: The Magazine of Western History* 46, no. 2 (Summer 1996): 50–65.

McCulloch, William J. "G. A. Custer Not the Youngest General." *Little Big Horn Associates Newsletter* 2, no. 7 (July 1968): 3–4.

Meadow, James B. "Honor to All the Fallen Warriors." *Denver Rocky Mountain News*, June 26, 2003, 22A.

Means, Russell. Unedited interview by Andrew Grace and Bartley Powers. Videocassette. Taped at Crow Agency, MT, June 25, 2003.

Medicine Crow, Joseph. *From the Heart of Crow Country: The Crow Indians' Own Stories.* Lincoln: University of Nebraska Press, 1992.

Melchionne, Kevin. "Collecting as an Art." *Philosophy and Literature* 23, no. 1 (1999): 148–56.

Melmer, David. "Historic Partnership." *Indian Country Today,* February 27, 2005. Online edition: www.indiancountry.com.

———. "Senate Committee Addresses Suicide." *Indian Country Today,* May 5, 2005. Online edition: www.indiancountry.com.

———. "Veterans Take Center Stage." *Indian Country Today,* July 17, 2006. Online edition: http://indiancountry.com/content.cfm?id=1096413323; accessed July 23, 2006.

Merington, Margaret, ed. *The Custer Story: The Life and Letters of General George A. Custer and His Wife Elizabeth.* 1950; rpt. New York: Barnes and Noble Books, 1994.

Merrill, Kevin. "Bone Find: It's a Woman . . . and a Man." *Monroe Evening News* (MI), July 2, 1990, 3A.

———. "Burial Ceremony Planned for Sept. 13 for Lotus Fountain Bones." *Monroe Evening News* (MI), August 10, 1990, 3A.

Metz, Andrew. "A Struggle for History." *New York Newsday,* June 26, 2003, A7.

Michno, Gregory S. *Battle at Sand Creek: The Military Perspective.* El Segundo, CA: Upton and Sons, 2004.

———. *Lakota Noon: The Indian Narrative of Custer's Defeat.* Missoula, MT: Mountain, 1997.

Millbrook, Minnie Dobbs. "The West Breaks in General Custer." In *The Custer Reader,* edited by Paul Andrew Hutton, 116–58. Lincoln: University of Nebraska Press, 1992.

Miller, David Humphreys. *Custer's Fall: The Indian Side of the Story.* New York: Duell, Sloan, and Pearce, 1957.

Montana Department of Labor and Industry. "Montana Annual Civilian Labor Force Statistics: 2004." July 2004. http//ceic.mt.gov/Data_maps.html.

———. "Montana Reservations Labor Force, 2000–2003." www.ourfactsyourfuture.org/article.asp?PAGEID=andSUBID=andARTICLEID=108andSEGMENTID=1.

Mooncy, James. *The Ghost-Dance Region and the Sioux Outbreak of 1890.* 1896; rpt. Lincoln: University of Nebraska Press, 1991.

Moore, John H. *The Cheyenne.* Cambridge, MA: Blackwell, 1996.

———. *The Cheyenne Nation: A Social and Demographic History.* Lincoln: University of Nebraska Press, 1987.

Moore, John H., Margot Liberty, and A. Terry Strauss. "Cheyenne." In *Plains,* edited by Raymond J. DeMallie, vol. 13 of *Handbook of North American Indians,* edited by William C. Sturtevant, 863–85. Washington, DC: Smithsonian Institution, 2001.

Moore, Harold G., and Joseph L. Galloway. *We Were Soldiers Once . . . and Young: Ia Drang, the Battle That Changed the War in Vietnam.* New York: Random House, 1992.

Moses, L. G. *Wild West Shows and the Images of American Indians, 1883–1933.* Albuquerque: University of New Mexico Press, 1996.

Murray, David. *Forked Tongues: Speech, Writing and Representation in North American Indian Texts.* Bloomington: Indiana University Press, 1991.

Nagel, Joane. *American Indian Ethnic Renewal: Red Power and the Resurgence of Identity and Culture.* New York: Oxford University Press, 1996.

"National Pundits Sadly Ignore American Indian History." Unsigned editorial. *Indian Country Today,* February 2, 2006. Online edition: http://indiancountry.com/content .cfm?id=1096412384, accessed February 8, 2006.

Nichols, Ron, comp. *Reno Court of Inquiry: Proceedings of a Court of Inquiry in the Case of Major Marcus A. Reno.* 2nd ed. Hardin, MT: Custer Battlefield and Historical Museum Association, 1996.

Niehardt, John G. *Black Elk Speaks.* 1932; rpt. Lincoln: University of Nebraska Press, 1988.

Nixon, Richard. "Special Message to the Congress on Indian Affairs," July 8, 1970. In *Public Papers of the Presidents of the United States: Richard Nixon, 1970,* 564–76. Washington, DC: Government Printing Office, 1974.

Nora, Pierre, gen. ed. *Realms of Memory: Rethinking the French Past.* Volume 1, *Conflicts and Divisions.* English language ed. Edited by Lawrence D. Kritzman; translated by Arthur Goldhammer. New York: Columbia University Press, 1996.

Old Coyote, Lloyd G. Mickey, and Helene Smith. *Apsaalooka: The Crow Nation Then and Now.* Rev. ed. Greensburg, PA: MacDonald Sward, 1993.

O'Leary, Cecilia Elizabeth. "Blood Brotherhood: The Racialization of Patriotism, 1865– 1918." In *Bonds of Affection: Americans Define Their Patriotism,* edited by J. Bodnar, 53–81. Princeton, NJ: Princeton University Press, 1996.

O'Neil, Tom. *Dr. Lawrence A. Frost: A Fond Remembrance.* Brooklyn, NY: Arrow and Trooper, 1991.

Ostler, Jeffrey. *The Plains Sioux and U.S. Colonialism from Lewis and Clark to Wounded Knee.* New York: Cambridge University Press, 2004.

Parker, Watson. *Gold in the Black Hills.* Norman: University of Oklahoma Press, 1966.

Pearce, Roy Harvey. *Savagism and Civilization: A Study of the Indian and the American Mind.* 1953; rpt. Berkeley: University of California Press, 1988.

Penn, W. S. *Feathering Custer.* Lincoln: University of Nebraska Press, 2001.

Powell, Peter J. *People of the Sacred Mountain: A History of the Northern Cheyenne Chiefs and Warrior Societies, 1830–1878, with an Epilogue, 1969–1974.* 2 vols. San Francisco: Harper and Row, 1981.

"President Grant: A Free Talk on Questions of the Day." *New York Herald,* September 2, 1876, 2.

"Presidential Inaugural Parade 2005." *Newsletter of the Little Big Horn Associates* 39, no. 2 (March 2005): 8.

Prucha, Francis Paul. *American Indian Policy in Crisis, 1865–1900.* Norman: University of Oklahoma Press, 1976.

———. *The Great Father: The United States Government and the American Indians.* 2 vols. Lincoln: University of Nebraska Press, 1984.

Real Bird, Henry. *The Best of Hank Real Bird.* N.p., 1995.

Real Bird, Richard. "In Search of Peace and Prosperity: The Crow Tribal Struggle for Economic Sovereignty." Address to the Malcolm Weiner Center for Social Policy, Harvard University, Cambridge, MA, April 1988. www.ksg.harvard.edu/hpaied/ pubs/pub_148.htm.

Reddin, Paul. *Wild West Shows.* Urbana: University of Illinois Press, 1999.

Reedstrom, Ernest Lisle. *Bugles, Banners, and War Bonnets.* Caldwell, ID: Caxton, 1977.

Ricker, Eli S. *Voices of the American West,* vol. 1, *The Indian Interviews of Eli S. Ricker, 1903–1919.* Edited by Richard E. Jensen. Lincoln: University of Nebraska Press, 2005.

Rickey, Don, Jr. *History of Custer Battlefield.* Billings, MT: Custer Battlefield Historical and Museum Association, 1967.

Rieckmann, Carl. "Family Plans Reenactments on 'Sacred' Little Bighorn Ground." *Bighorn County News* (MT) 97, no. 25 (June 24, 2004): A1, A2.

Roach, Harry. "Reenacting: A Retrospective." http://wesclark.com/jw/roach.html; accessed 28 September 2004.

Rosenberg, Bruce A. *Custer and the Epic of Defeat.* University Park: Pennsylvania State University Press, 1974.

Rosenthal, Nicholas G. "Representing Indians: Native American Actors on Hollywood's Frontier." *Western Historical Quarterly,* Autumn 2005, 329–52.

Rotundo, E. Anthony. *American Manhood: Transformations in Masculinity from the Revolution to the Modern Era.* New York: Basic Books, 1993.

The Royal Tenenbaums. DVD. Directed by Wes Anderson. 2001; Burbank, CA: Touchstone, 2002.

Ryan, John. *Ten Years with Custer: A Seventh Cavalryman's Memoir.* Edited by Sandy Barnard. Terre Haute, IN: AST Press, 2001.

Sacred Sites International. *The 2005 Most Endangered Sacred Sites List.* www.sacred-sites .org/preservation/endangered_most.html; accessed May 25, 2005.

Sandoz, Mari. *Cheyenne Autumn.* New York: McGraw-Hill, 1953.

Sanford, George B. *Fighting Rebels and Redskins: Experiences in Army Life of Colonel George B. Sanford, 1861–1892.* Edited by E. R. Hagemann. Norman: University of Oklahoma Press, 1969.

Sarf, Wayne M. *The Little Bighorn Campaign: March–September 1876.* Rev. ed. Conshohocken, PA: Combined Publishing, 2000.

Sarf, Wayne M., and William P. Wells. "End the Racist Regime: A Call for the Dismissal of Gerard Baker." *Custer/Little Bighorn Battlefield Advocate* 3, no. 2 (Summer 1996): 1 2.

"A Savage Talking Sense." *New York World,* November 18, 1877, 1.

Scheckel, Susan. *The Insistence of the Indian: Race and Nationalism in Nineteenth-Century American Culture.* Princeton, NJ: Princeton University Press, 1998.

Schivelbusch, Wolfgang. *The Culture of Defeat: On National Trauma, Mourning, and Recovery.* Translated by Jefferson Chase. New York: Henry Holt, 2003.

Schwarck, Don. "Sundance Closes Battlefield Roadway." *Little Big Horn Associates Newsletter* 26, no. 6 (August 1992): 2.

———. "W. H. Illingworth: A Biography." In Ernest Grafe and Paul Horsted, *Exploring with Custer: The 1874 Black Hills Expedition,* 271–75. Custer, SD: Golden Valley, 2002.

Schwartz, Barry. *Abraham Lincoln and the Forge of National Memory.* Chicago: University of Chicago Press, 2000.

Scott, Douglas D., et al. *Archaeological Perspectives on the Battle of the Little Bighorn.* Norman: University of Oklahoma Press, 1989.

Scott, Douglas D., P. Willey, and Melissa A. Connor. *They Died with Custer: Soldier Bones from the Battle of the Little Bighorn.* Norman: University of Oklahoma Press, 1998.

Scott, Hugh Lenox. *Some Memories of a Soldier.* New York. Century, 1928.

"Several Indian Tribes Uneasy." *New York Times,* July 9, 1876, 1.

Shay, Becky. "Paratroopers Help Crow Tribe Honor Veterans." Billings Gazette (MT), June 24, 2006. Online edition: www.billingsgazette.net/articles/2006/06/24/news/ state/20-honors.txt; accessed June 27, 2006.

"Sheridan's Victory." *New York Times,* October 27, 1864, 2.

Silber, Nina. *The Romance of Reunion: Northerners and the South, 1865–1900.* Chapel Hill, NC: North Carolina University Press, 1993.

Silko, Leslie Marmon. *Almanac of the Dead.* New York: Simon and Schuster, 1991.

"The Sioux's Savior." *Chicago Times,* November 14, 1877, 5.

"Sitting Bull." *New York Herald,* July 12, 1876, 3.

"Sitting Bull Talks." *New York Herald*, November 16, 1877, 3–4.

"Sitting Bull's Autobiography." *New York Herald*, July 9, 1876, 3.

Slotkin, Richard. *The Fatal Environment: The Myth of the Frontier in the Age of Industrialization, 1800–1890.* New York: Atheneum, 1985.

———. *Gunfighter Nation: The Myth of the Frontier in Twentieth-Century America.* New York: Atheneum, 1992.

Smith, Sherry L. "Lost Soldiers: Re-searching the Army in the American West." *Western Historical Quarterly* 29 (Summer 1998): 149–63.

———. *The View from Officers' Row: Army Perceptions of Western Indians.* Tucson: University of Arizona, 1990.

Smoke Signals. DVD. Directed by Chris Eyre. 1998. Burbank, CA: Buena Vista Home Entertainment, 1999.

Sprengelmeyer, M. E. "Sand Creek Nears Final Hurdle to Become Protected Historic Site." *Rocky Mountain News,* August 2, 2005. Online edition, accessed September 20, 2005.

Standing Bear, Luther. *My People, the Sioux.* 1928; rpt. Lincoln: University of Nebraska Press, 1975.

Stands in Timber, John, and Margot Liberty. *Cheyenne Memories.* New Haven, CT: Yale University Press, 1967.

Steen, Jomay. "Montana Tribe Buys Bear Butte Acreage." *Rapid City Journal,* March 22, 2006. Online edition: http://rapidcityjournal.com/articles/2006/03/22/news/top/news02.txt.

Stirling, M. W. *Three Pictographic Autobiographies of Sitting Bull.* Smithsonian Miscellaneous Collections 97, no. 5. Washington, DC: Smithsonian Institution, 1938.

Sturken, Marita. *Tangled Memories: The Vietnam War, the AIDS Epidemic, and the Politics of Remembering.* Berkeley: University of California Press, 1997.

Taft, Robert. "The Pictorial Record of the Old West: Custer's Last Stand—John Mulvany, Cassily Adams, and Otto Becker." In *The Custer Reader,* edited by Paul Andrew Hutton, 424–62. Lincoln: University of Nebraska Press, 1992.

Taunton, Francis B. Foreword to *"Such Signal Success"? Confrontations along the Washita,* edited by Kevin E. Galvin. London: Westerners, 2003.

Thackeray, Lorna. "Big June for Battlefield Visitors." *Billings Gazette,* July 9, 1991, 1B.

———. "Completing the Circle." *Billings Gazette,* June 26, 2003, 1A, 12A.

———. "Developments Could Boost Hardin's Tourism." *Billings Gazette,* June 11, 1990, 1A, 15A.

———. "Merchants Revive Harding Street." *Billings Gazette,* 17 June 1990, 1D.

———. "Town on the Rebound." *Billings Gazette,* 17 June 1990, 1D.

Thetford, Francis. "Battle of the Washita Centennial, 1968." *Chronicles of Oklahoma* 46 (Winter 1968–69): 358–61.

They Died with Their Boots On. Videocassette. Directed by Raoul Walsh. 1941; Culver City, CA: MGM, 1994.

Thompson, Jenny. *War Games: Inside the World of Twentieth-Century War Reenactors.* Washington, DC: Smithsonian Books, 2004.

Thompson, Michael. *Rubbish Theory: The Creation and Destruction of Value.* New York: Oxford University Press, 1979.

"Thousands Attend Battle of Washita Centennial." *Cheyenne Star* (OK), December 5, 1968, 1–2.

"To Be or Not to Be, Part 2." *Cheyenne Star* (OK), January 18, 1996, 1.

Tomaszewki, Elisa. "Custer Authority Frost Dies." *Monroe Evening News* (MI), August 15, 1990, 1A, 12A.

Trachtenberg, Alan. *Shades of Hiawatha: Staging Indians, Making Americans, 1880–1930.* New York: Hill and Wang, 2004.

Two Bulls, Marty, Sr. "War in Iraq." Editorial cartoon. *Indian Country Today*, February 2, 2006. Online edition: http://indiancountry.com/content.cfm?id=1096412390; accessed February 8, 2006.

United States Census Bureau. American FactFinder. http://factfinder.census.gov.

United States Commissioner of Indian Affairs. *Annual Report of the Commissioner of Indian Affairs to the Secretary of the Interior for the Year 1875*. Washington, DC: Government Printing Office, 1875.

————. *Annual Report of the Commissioner of Indian Affairs to the Secretary of the Interior for the Year 1876*. Washington, DC: Government Printing Office, 1876.

————. *Report of the Commissioner of Indian Affairs, 1865*. Washington, DC: Government Printing Office, 1866.

United States Congress. *Congressional Record*. 101st Cong., 2nd sess., 1990. 136, no. 114.

————. *Congressional Record*. 102nd Cong., 1st sess., 1991. 137, no. 26.

————. *Congressional Record*. 102nd Cong., 1st sess., 1991. 137, no. 98.

United States Congress, House Subcommittee on National Parks and Public Lands. Custer Battlefield National Monument Indian Memorial: Hearing before the Subcommittee on National Parks and Public Lands. 101st Cong., 2d sess., September 4, 1990.

United States Congress, Joint Committee on the Conduct of the War. *Report of the Joint Committee on the Conduct of the War, Massacre of the Cheyenne Indians*. 38th Cong., 2d sess., 1865. 38 S. Rpt. 142.

United States Congress, Senate Committee on Energy and Natural Resources. Little Bighorn Battlefield National Monument. 102nd Cong., 1st sess., 1991. 102 S. Rpt. 173.

United States Department of War. *Annual Report of the Secretary of War, 1878*. 2 vols. Washington, DC: Government Printing Office, 1879.

"The United States Indian Commission." *New York Herald*, December 24, 1868, 5.

United States National Park Service. *Final General Management Plan/White Environmental Impact Statement: Washita Battlefield National Historic Site*. Denver: National Park Service, 2001.

————. "Interpretation and Education." Chapter 7 in 2001 NPS Management Policies. http://nps.gov/policy/mp/chapter7.htm.

————. "Little Bighorn Battlefield." Brochure 491-282/40176. Government Printing Office, 2002.

————. *"Peace through Unity": Indian Memorial Dedication*. Crow Agency, MT: Little Bighorn National Monument, 2003.

————. "Washita Battlefield." Brochure 310-394/00270. Government Printing Office, 2005.

"Unknown Indian Grave Unmarked." *Cheyenne Star* (OK), April 14, 1932, n.p.

Upton, Richard. *The Battle of the Little Big Horn and Custer's Last Fight: Remembered by Participants ant the Tenth Anniversary, June 25, 1886, and the Fiftieth Anniversary, June 25, 1926*. El Segundo, CA: Upton and Sons, 2006.

Urwin, Gregory J. W. *Custer Victorious*. East Brunswick, NJ: Associated University Presses, 1983.

————. Preface to *A Complete Life of General George A. Custer*, by Frederick Whittaker. 2 vols. Lincoln: University of Nebraska Press, 1993.

Utley, Robert M. *Cavalier in Buckskin: George Armstrong Custer and the Western Military Frontier*. Norman: University of Oklahoma Press, 1988.

————. A *Clash of Cultures: Fort Bowie and the Chiricahua Apaches*. Washington, DC: National Park Service, 1977.

————. *Custer and Me: A Historian's Memoir*. Norman: University of Oklahoma Press, 2004.

————. *Custer and the Great Controversy: The Origin and Development of a Legend.* 1962; rpt. Lincoln: University of Nebraska Press, 1998.

————. *The Indian Frontier of the American West, 1846–1890.* Albuquerque: University of New Mexico Press, 1984.

————. *The Lance and the Shield: The Life and Times of Sitting Bull.* New York: Henry Holt, 1993.

————, ed. *Life in Custer's Cavalry: Diaries and Letters of Albert and Jennie Barnitz, 1867–1868.* New Haven, CT: Yale University Press, 1977.

Van de Water, Frederick F. *Glory-Hunter: A Life of General Custer.* Indianapolis: Bobbs-Merrill, 1934.

Van Zandt, Howard F. "The Battle of the Washita, Revisited." *Chronicles of Oklahoma* 62 (1984): 56–59.

Vestal, Stanley. *Sitting Bull: Champion of the Sioux.* Boston: Houghton Mifflin, 1932.

Viola, Herman J. *Little Bighorn Remembered: The Untold Indian Story of Custer's Last Stand.* New York: Crown, 1999.

"War with the Sioux." *Army and Navy Journal,* August 5, 1876, 837.

Warde, Mary Jane. *Conduct Oral History Research for Washita Historical Site, Final Report on Cooperative Agreement 1443CA125098002, Modification 1. September 30, 1999.* Report for the National Park Service. Oklahoma City: Oklahoma Historical Society.

Warren, Louis S. *Buffalo Bill's America: William Cody and the Wild West Show.* New York: Alfred A. Knopf, 2005.

Washita Symposium: Past, Present, and Future; Proceedings of a Symposium Held November 12–14, 1998, Cheyenne, Okla. Cheyenne, OK: National Park Service, 2001.

Watson, Elmo Scott, and Don Russell. "The Battle of the Washita, or Custer's Massacre?" In *"Such Signal Success"? Confrontations along the Washita,* edited by Kevin E. Galvin, 29–40. London: Westerners, 2003.

We Were Soldiers. DVD. Directed by Randall Wallace. 2002; Hollywood: Paramount Pictures, 2002.

Welch, James, with Paul Stekler. *Killing Custer.* New York: W. W. Norton, 1994.

Wells, Bill. "Little Bighorn Diary." Little *Big Horn Associates Newsletter* 25, no. 4 (May 1991): 4.

Wert, Jeffrey D. *Custer: The Controversial Life of George Armstrong Custer.* New York: Simon and Schuster, 1996.

Whitman, Walt. *Poetry and Prose.* Edited by Justin Kaplan. New York: Library of America, 1982.

Whittaker, Captain Fred[erick]. *Seth Slocum, Railroad Surveyor, or The Secret of Sitting Bull: A Tale of the Great Northern Pacific Road-Building.* 1883; rpt. New York: M. J. Ivers, 1903.

Whittaker, Frederick. *A Complete Life of General George A. Custer.* 2 vols. 1876; rpt. Lincoln: University of Nebraska Press, 1993.

Wilkins, David E. *American Indian Sovereignty and the U.S. Supreme Court: The Masking of Justice.* Austin: University of Texas Press, 1997.

Wilkins, David E., and K. Tsianina Lomawaima. *Uneven Ground: American Indian Sovereignty and Federal Law.* Norman: University of Oklahoma, 2001.

Wilkinson, Charles. *Blood Struggle: The Rise of Modern Indian Nations.* New York: W. W. Norton, 2005.

Wilkinson, Charles F., and Anna Nikole Ulrich. "Annotated Bibliography of the Basic Literature Needed for an Understanding of Tribal Governance." *Wicazo Sa Review* 17, no. 1 (Spring 2002): 7–12.

Wing, Talcott E. *History of Monroe County, Michigan.* New York: Munsell, 1890.

Wittenberg, Eric J., ed. *One of Custer's Wolverines: The Civil War Letters of Brevet Brigadier General James H. Kidd, 6th Michigan Cavalry.* Kent, OH: Kent State University Press, 2000.

Wooden Leg. *Wooden Leg: A Warrior Who Fought Custer.* Interpreted by Thomas B. Marquis. (Originally printed as *A Warrior Who Fought Custer.*) 1931; rpt. Lincoln: University of Nebraska Press, 1957.

Wright, Kathryn. "Tourists Overflow in Hardin as Indians Take Custer Twice." *Billings Gazette,* June 28, 1964, 10.

INDEX